The Guide to Practical Property Management

John Philip Bachner
Property Management Association
Silver Spring, Maryland

McGraw-Hill, Inc.
New York   St. Louis   San Francisco   Auckland   Bogotá
Caracas   Lisbon   London   Madrid   Mexico   Milan
Montreal   New Delhi   Paris   San Juan   São Paulo
Singapore   Sydney   Tokyo   Toronto

For Libbey and Milt

Library of Congress Cataloging-in-Publication Data

Bachner, John Philip.
   The guide to practical property management / John Philip
Bachner.
    p.   cm.
   ISBN 0-07-002843-5
   1. Real estate management. I. Property Management Association.
II. Title.
HD1394.B33 1991
333.33'8'068—dc20   91-20521
                                                  CIP

1 2 3 4 5 6 7 8 9 0 DOC/DOC 9 7 6 5 4 3 2 1

ISBN 0-07-002843-5

*The sponsoring editor for this book was Joel Stein, the editing
supervisor was Ingeborg M. Stochmal, and the production supervisor
was Pamela A. Pelton. This book was set in Century Schoolbook. It
was composed by McGraw-Hill's Professional Book Group composition
unit.*

Printed and bound by R. R. Donnelley & Sons Company.

Contents

Preface

The Property Management Association (PMA) was established in the Washington, D.C., area in the early 1950s. It consisted of little more than a group of property managers who had tremendous responsibilities, but whose roles were not fully defined. Truly, in PMA's case, necessity was the mother of invention. The property managers who formed the group were eager to share the information needed to cope with the increasing demands of their clients and employers.

Much has changed over the intervening years. While the level of education and training has increased dramatically, so, too, have the complexities of managing. The physical plants involved have become far more challenging in terms of size, equipment installed, and the sheer variety of different materials that may have to be confronted in any given building. Consider, too, the myriad federal, state, and local laws and regulations that must be followed. As remarked by some of those who still recall the original meetings of PMA, it is almost like taking ten steps forward, then ten steps back. As much as is learned, one quickly realizes that there is still much more knowledge to be acquired. This explains the continuing growth and popularity of PMA, an organization that still holds as its principal mission service as a source for practical education through its meetings, seminars, and mini-seminars, its annual Property Management Exposition, and a variety of other activities, including the development of its much-heralded contract guides on which this work is based.

Each of PMA's contract guides has been subject to in-depth research using practical experience, rather than written theory, as the principal source of information. In a typical research session, a group of specialty contractors and a group of property managers would meet to identify the most important issues and what was to be discussed about each. While there almost always was wrangling over what was most important, or what approach worked best, there always—ultimately—was agreement, fostered by the desire to be of genuine service by providing the best advice available.

No effort was made, nor is there an effort now being made, to relate everything there is to know about a subject. The volumes written on roofing alone are enough to fill a library. Likewise, there are tomes available about asphalt maintenance, swimming-pool care, and the many other subjects covered. The goal was and is to provide a synopsis of each concern and to relate to property managers those vital elements that, once absorbed, become practical guidance.

No property manager will be able to perform the work described based solely on what is said here. However, a property manager should be able to discern whether or not the work should be done by in-house crews, through reliance on specialty contractors, or by some combination of the two. The property manager should also learn something about contracting issues, especially with respect to selecting contractors and others who have to be relied on in order to make a property work and to maintain its value over time.

The guidance given with respect to contracts is not meant as a substitute for counsel, which can come only from a qualified attorney. But by the same token, property managers need to know how to deal with attorneys in order to derive optimal results. Too often, people will allow their attorneys to think for them, and that's not right. The situations involved relate to property management, and attorneys should help the property manager achieve intended results. Contracts that are written in "legalese" benefit no one except the lawyers, because the people most affected by them can find them unintelligible. The contractor and the property manager should sit down together to develop the scope of work and to discuss the terms and conditions. These terms and conditions should be fair. When either party hopes to benefit at the other's expense, the real goal—preserving an owner's property—can become lost, leading to delays, claims, disputes, and other problems that could have been avoided. Likewise, when a party tries to shift risks to someone else, typically through indemnifications, problems can ensue. All too often the party that gets "stuck" with an indemnification is not in a position to make good should the need arise, and the party using the indemnification as free insurance winds up with no insurance at all. Still and all, many lawyers continue to encourage such approaches. But lawyers alone are not to blame. What they do in this respect obviously appeals at least to some of their clients, especially those who fail to heed the wisdom of "there's no such thing as a free lunch."

The works on which this volume is based were developed through a series of highly successful cooperative ventures of property managers and the contractors they have come to rely on. This same attitude should be applied for the performance of any given contract. The goal should always be getting the work done well on behalf of the owner. For that to occur, the property manager needs to understand the basics in order to participate in the development of the work scope, and the property manager must know how to select that contractor who is willing to perform well for a reasonable fee, who takes pride in the quality of work produced, and who is looking to build long-term relationships by providing value to customers.

Acknowledgments

The Property Management Associaton (PMA) began its contractor guidelines series in 1981 under the leadership of its President John N. Gallagher, CPM (Shannon & Luchs Company) and the Chairperson of the Associate Membership Committee Thomas F. Warner (The Warner Corporation). Since then, the work has been supported by each succeeding PMA President and Associate Membership Committee Chairperson.

A number of firms and individuals have been supportive by providing the time and materials needed in research. Individuals have included Stephen Brock, Thomas B. Cohn, Arthur Ebersberger, John N. Gallagher, L. Peyton Harris, Jr., Ron Helming, Gene Kijowski, Nick Kovacic, John B. Murgolo, Paul Norris, James D. Palmer, Thomas Rector, Duane Robbins, Steve Sadle, Brian R. Smith, John Stickley, Joseph P. Shuffleton, Barbara Ullmann, Harvey Vermillion, Charles Wagner, and Douglas Wanko.

Firms have included Aldon Management Corporation; Aqualin Aquatics, Inc.; Blacktop, Inc.; Century Pool Management, Inc.; Charles E. Smith Management, Inc.; Community Pool Management, Inc.; Country Club Lawns, Inc.; Duron Paints and Wallcoverings; Engineering and Technical Consultants, Inc.; Natural Landscape Contractors, Inc.; NS PAVCO; Palmer Brothers Contractors, Inc.; Paramount Pest Control; Ro/Co, Inc.; Shannon & Luchs Company; The Asphalt Institute; Wagner Roofing Company; and Western Termite and Pest Control.

Special thanks are extended to Samia Abdel-Malak whose above-and-beyond efforts at finalizing the work represent professionalism at its finest.

To the author John Bachner, PMA extends its deepest and most profound gratitude. John has served as PMA's Chief Staff Officer since January 1, 1973. His role in helping shape today's PMA cannot be overstated, nor can it be praised too highly.

CHRISTOPHER LEE SHERREN, R.P.A.
President, Property Management Association

ABOUT THE AUTHOR

John Philip Bachner is executive vice president of the
Property Management Association based in Silver Spring,
Maryland. He is the author of hundreds of manuals, texts,
and guidebooks in the areas of public relations and
marketing, professional liability loss prevention,
alternative dispute resolution, contracting, energy
management, lighting, health care facility management,
and occupational safety and health. He has written dozens
of monographs for the National Electrical Contractors
Association, and has compiled research reports for such
organizations as ASFE/The Association of Engineering
Firms Practicing in the Geosciences, the Property
Management Association, the National Electrical
Manufacturers Association, and many others. Mr. Bachner
also authored *Practice Management for Design
Professionals* and *Public Relations for Nursing Homes*, and
he coauthored *Marketing and Promotion for Design
Professionals*. He has written numerous magazine articles
and film scripts. He is president of Bachner
Communications, Inc., and resides in Great Falls, Virginia.

Grounds Care

Introduction

Grounds care is an important aspect of property management. Well-kept grounds improve a project's appearance and image, help increase or, at least, maintain its value, and create a sense of pride among residents and tenants. These benefits contribute to still others, such as reduced turnover, enhanced rentability, and justification for higher rates. In short, effective grounds care yields a host of benefits, even beyond those listed, whose value can far exceed the investment required to attain them.

Working with a Grounds Maintenance Contractor

The role of a grounds maintenance contractor is determined by the property manager in light of the owner's goals and objectives; budgetary restrictions; and the availability, capability, and cost of in-house personnel and equipment. Grounds maintenance may be performed totally by contract or, at the other extreme, totally by in-house staff. Most commonly, a combination of the two is used.

Generally speaking, it is less expensive and less troublesome to rely on a contractor for most services. In this way, property managers and their on-site staffs avoid the problems and paperwork associated with seasonal employees, as well as the less than satisfactory results—and sometimes damage—that can occur when workers are not trained thoroughly. In addition, the contractor, not the owner, is the one who makes the investment in the equipment and who has to shoulder the expense of maintaining and storing it. Also, contractors earn their reputations based on the quality of the work they perform, which gives them a strong incentive for creating owner/manager satisfaction.

The need to monitor

Some property managers have noted wide differences in the bids they receive from grounds care contractors for performing the same work. In some cases this reflects varying company methods, procedures, and productivity. In others, however, it may be due to the use of materials inferior to those proposed or—worse—failure to apply materials that are specified or paid for. For this reason it is essential that the contractor be selected with care and that some type of monitoring procedure be applied to help ensure that the contractor provides the services and materials specified.

Specifying the Service

Any contract issued needs to include a work or performance specification. The more comprehensive the work specification, the better, since it leaves that much less to interpretation. This helps ensure that everything that needs to get done does get done, and that all bidders (if bidding is used) are basing their quotes on the same scope. Note that a performance specification identifies what has to get done, regardless of whether the work is performed 100 percent by in-house crews or 100 percent by contract.

This section is organized along the lines of an actual performance specification, such as would be used to obtain bids for grounds care services and serve as a contract. Note, however, that it contains more items of service than probably are needed. This has been done to demonstrate one approach to handling each of the many different concerns involved. Note, too, that the performance specification has been designed such that the contractor can fill in the blanks. Some property managers find this an excellent approach, given the way in which they are organized. As will be seen, however, other approaches are also used and, in fact, may be more common.

Be advised that none of the approaches illustrated may be wholly satisfactory for your purposes. Obtain competent professional assistance as necessary and appropriate, and as befits your responsibility.

Line-item bids

Line-item bids, which require contractors to quote a price for each function, are recommended in particular for grounds care. Although most contractors would prefer to bid debris removal, mowing, clipping removal, and trimming "as a piece," a line-item breakdown can be of advantage in those instances where some of the work may be performed most cost-effectively by in-house personnel, or where residents (typically condominium unit owners) may become involved. If the contractor prefers to bid the various elements of mowing and trimming as a unit, it nonetheless is appropriate to indicate the specific unit elements.

Naturally, some contractors will quote lower prices if the entire package of services is obtained. In such situations it is often worthwhile to examine the bids submitted and then finalize the contract on a negotiated basis with the contractor who offers the best value. Specification wording that can be used in this instance is:

You are being asked to submit line-item bids for two important reasons.

First, if we select you as our contractor for this project, and if the total price is more than we can afford, having the line-item prices permits us to identify our options for reducing the overall price.

Second, should there be a question about a task having or not having been performed properly, line-item pricing permits us to pay you promptly for the performance of those tasks about which there are no questions.

Mowing and trimming

The mowing and trimming section of the specification could be phrased as follows, beginning with specifying the service frequency (that is, the frequency of "turf cuts"). In the Washington, D.C., area, low frequency comprises 20 to 22 cuts per season, medium frequency, 23 to 25 cuts, and high frequency, 26 to 30 cuts. Determine how these frequencies would be defined in your area.

---

1. *Mowing and trimming*
    a. Prices for mowing and trimming quoted below on a **per-service basis** assume that mowing and trimming will be performed by CONTRACTOR at least [_____] times during the growing season.
    b. For purposes of this section, minor debris is defined as that amount of debris which CONTRACTOR can collect within one

person-hour. **The cost of removing minor debris per service shall be $**_____.

c. CONTRACTOR shall notify on-site management when major debris exists and is impeding schedule fulfillment. If on-site management indicates that personnel is unavailable to perform major debris removal in a timely manner, CONTRACTOR shall remove major debris and charge for such removal on an hourly basis, such time to be the total less one person-hour to account for minor debris removal. **The cost per person-hour shall be $**_____.

As will be indicated in item *d*, it is essential to identify the proper mowing height. PMA members report that typical mowing heights for various turf grasses are:

Turf grass	Mowing height, inches
Bermuda grass	½–1
Creeping red fescue	2–3
Kentucky bluegrass	2–3
Tall fescue	2½–3
Zoysia grass	¾–1

d. CONTRACTOR shall mow general turf areas to a mowing height of [_____] when the grass reaches a height of no more than one-third greater than the mowing height. The mowing height of cool season turf grasses will be increased by 25 percent in summer to reduce total turf stress. A high quality of cut shall be provided by mowers with sharp cutting edges. **The cost per service shall be $**_____.

e. CONTRACTOR shall collect clippings from turf areas after each mowing and remove them from the site. **The cost per service shall be $**_____.

f. CONTRACTOR shall collect clippings from all sidewalks, ground-floor patios, curbs, parking lot gutters, etc., after each mowing and remove them from the site. **The cost per service shall be $**_____ .

g. CONTRACTOR shall repair or replace any trees, shrubs, sprinklers, etc., damaged by mowing. In addition, CONTRACTOR shall repair or replace any grass damaged by mowing due to occurrences such as, but not limited to, "crowning" or "scalping" caused when the cutting blade of a tractor cutting deck goes over the top of a hill.

Trimming around trees and shrubs can be performed by hand, with mechanical devices, or through the use of herbicides. The application of any chemical presents potential problems with respect to applicable laws and regulations, and also in terms of potential injuries, as to children who may be present. Toddlers who fall on a treated area of ground may have some of the material on their hands, rub it into their eyes, and so on. The language indicated below may not be fully adequate in the event a herbicide is used. Learn about any local restrictions that may exist. Comply fully with all applicable laws and regulations, as well as the basic precepts of effective risk management.

h. CONTRACTOR shall trim around trees and shrubs after each mowing using [herbicides] [hand labor] [mechanical devices]. [Herbicides shall be applied under the supervision of a Certified Pesticide Applicator, in accordance with label use and approved industry practice.] **The cost per trimming shall be $**_____.

Edging

Several techniques are available for edging. Mechanical edging usually gives the best results and thus is preferred. Speak with contractors, consultants, and other property managers to learn about other techniques used and how satisfactory they may be.

2. *Edging*
   a. CONTRACTOR shall mechanically edge all accessible sidewalks, curbs, and patios once per [_____] during the growing season, and shall remove dirt and debris immediately after mechanical edging has been completed. **The cost per service shall be $**_____.

Leaf collection and removal

It usually is satisfactory to collect and remove leaves once every 30 days. A number of factors must be considered, of course, such as the climate, the number of trees, and the "look" that the owner wants to achieve during different seasons.

3. *Leaf collection and removal*
   a. CONTRACTOR shall collect leaves from the site [_____] times per year, at the following intervals:

Between [_____] and [_____]
Between [_____] and [_____]
Between [_____] and [_____]
Between [_____] and [_____]

The cost per service shall be:

For all turf areas: $_____

For all ornamental tree, shrub, and
    flower beds: $_____

For all walkways, driveways, and
    ground-floor patios: $_____

Soil analysis

The contractor should be able to handle all soil analyses. It usually is sufficient to obtain a report within 30 days after a contract commences and, thereafter, 48 hours before chemicals are applied. Of course, your specific needs may differ.

---

4. *Soil analysis*
    a. CONTRACTOR shall accomplish all soil analyses and shall furnish the report of each soil analysis to PROPERTY MANAGER. CONTRACTOR shall furnish the first such report within [thirty (30)] days of execution of this contract, and all others not less than [forty-eight (48)] hours before any chemicals are to be applied. **The cost per analysis shall be $_____.**

Fertilization

Proper fertilization is essential to the health of turf grass. What is proper for one type of grass in one area may not be proper for the same grass in another area. For example, suburban Washington, D.C., lawns containing Kentucky bluegrass, tall fescue, creeping red fescue, or perennial ryegrass require the equivalent of 3 to 5 lb of soluble nitrogen per 1000 ft^2 per year. Lawns containing Bermuda grass or zoysia grass require the equivalent of 4 to 4½ lb of soluble nitrogen per 1000 ft^2 per year.

The exact amount necessary within these ranges depends upon factors such as soil type, moisture availability, type of grass, length of growing season, and type of nitrogen fertilizer being used, among other factors. The following specification is biased toward the national capital area.

5. *Fertilization*
   a. The fertilization program will provide the equivalent of
      [_____] lb of soluble nitrogen per 1000 ft^2 per year.
      (1) Where Kentucky bluegrass, tall fescue, creeping red fescue,
          or perennial ryegrass is being maintained, approximately
          eighty (80) percent of the total nitrogen will be applied in
          appropriate split applications between the dates of [August
          15 and December 31], with the remainder to be applied from
          [May 15 to June 30] of each year.
      (2) Where Bermuda grass or zoysia grass is being maintained,
          nitrogen will be applied in appropriate split applications be-
          tween the dates of [March 1 and August 1] of each year.
      Corrective amounts of phosphorus and potassium fertilizer will
      be provided as indicated necessary by the soil test submitted
      with this specification and by subsequent soil tests.
   b. If conventional granular fertilizers will be applied, **the total
      cost of each application, on a per pound of fertilizer basis,
      shall be** $_____/lb. For purposes of management plan-
      ning, CONTRACTOR estimates that an average of [_____] lb
      of granular fertilizer will be required for each of [_____]
      applications.
   c. If liquid fertilizer will be applied, **the total cost of application,
      on a per gallon of fertilizer basis, shall be** $_____/gal.
      For purposes of management planning, CONTRACTOR estimates that
      an average of [_____] gal of fertilizer will be required for
      each of [_____] applications.

Liming

Both agricultural ground limestone and pelletized agricultural
ground limestone are acceptable liming materials. The pelletized material does not produce as much dust as the nonpelletized material.
Lime dust can be offensive in some situations.

6. *Liming*
   a. CONTRACTOR shall uniformly distribute [identify liming material]
      at [_____]-day intervals until the total amount indi-
      cated necessary by soil analysis is applied. In that a total of
      [_____] ft^2 is involved, and that the liming material
      shall be applied at the rate of [_____] lb/1000 ft^2,
      [_____] lb shall be used per [_____]-day appli-
      cation. **The cost per application shall be** $_____.

Herbicide application

As a general rule, property managers need to minimize their risk. Herbicides create risk, not only in terms of their application, but also in terms of storage and transport. If herbicides are to be used on an in-house basis, the property manager requires a thorough understanding of all applicable federal, state, and local regulations, approved industry practices, and so on. Included in the regulations are right-to-know requirements through which in-house personnel and tenants or residents may have to be apprised of the dangers involved.

Reliance on contractors helps reduce risk exposures, in large part because a contractor is, or certainly should be, aware of all appropriate dos and don'ts, and also because the contractor must assume some of the responsibility. Simply having a contractor do the work does not result in a total liability transfer, however, nor does it mean that the results of the service will be as desired. Management must make a good-faith effort to ensure that it relies on a competent and qualified contractor, and one that has the necessary insurance should the safeguards it uses not be adequate.

In the specification that follows, the contractor is notified about responsibilities. To ensure that the notice cannot be missed, it is suggested that it be indicated in all capital letters and/or in boldface type, and/or that it be highlighted. In that way, the contractor cannot miss the requirement and later claim that management attempted to "slip one by" or that the notice was not seen and the cost of abiding by it therefore was not included in the agreement.

---

7. *Herbicide application*
    a. CONTRACTOR shall apply herbicide for the control of annual grassy weed, using preemergence herbicides recommended by the Cooperative Extension Service of [state] and in accordance with label instructions. In newly overseeded areas, the preemergence herbicides used shall allow the continuing germination of turf seed. Assuming that [name of preemergence herbicide] is used, it shall be applied at the rate of [_____] per 1000 ft^2, and **the cost per application shall be** $ _____ .
    b. CONTRACTOR shall apply herbicide for the control of existing broadleaf weeds, using herbicides or herbicide mixtures recommended by the Cooperative Extension Service of [state] and in accordance with label instructions. Assuming that [name of chemical] is used, it shall be applied at the rate of [_____] per 1000 ft^2, and **the cost per application shall be** $_____ .

c. CONTRACTOR shall apply appropriate nonselective or preemergence herbicide as recommended by the Cooperative Extension Service of [state] to sidewalks, curbs, gutters, and streets to prevent growth of grass and weeds in these areas. If foliage growth appears, CONTRACTOR shall pull it up and remove it from the site. Preventive chemicals shall be applied once in [month] and thereafter as needed, in accordance with the manufacturer's specifications for each application. **The cost of each application, including foliage removal, shall be $_____ .**

d. **CONTRACTOR shall apply all herbicides under the supervision of a Certified Pesticide Applicator. CONTRACTOR accepts total responsibility for any injury or damage that may result from herbicide applications.**

Fungicide and insecticide application

Many of the warnings applicable to herbicides are applicable to insecticides and fungicides as well. These are also discussed in Chap. 6. Specifically with reference to fungicides and insecticides, however, applications can be either *preventive* or *curative*. Preventive implies an extensive spray program, which could be necessary as frequently as every 7 to 10 days with fungicides, or every 25 to 30 days with insecticides. Curative implies spraying only when the disease or insect is active and threatening to damage the turf grass seriously.

8. *Fungicide and insecticide application*
   a. CONTRACTOR shall apply fungicide and/or insecticide on a preventive basis to prevent common turf-grass diseases and/or insects from causing serious damage. Disease and/or insect control will be achieved using materials and rates recommended by the Cooperative Extension Service of [state] and in accordance with label instructions. **The cost per application for the prevention of the various types of disease shall be as follows:**

	Material	Amount per application	
Dollar spot	_____	_____	$_____
Fusarium blight	_____	_____	$_____
Helmintho-sporium leaf spot	_____	_____	$_____

	Material	Amount per application	
Rhizoctonia brown patch	_____	_____	$_____
Snow mold	_____	_____	$_____
[_____]	_____	_____	$_____

The cost per application for the control of the various types of insects shall be as follows:

	Material	Amount per application	
White grub	_____	_____	$_____
Chinch bug	_____	_____	$_____
Cutworm, armyworm, or sod webworm	_____	_____	$_____
Billbug	_____	_____	$_____
[_____]	_____	_____	$_____

b. Whether or not fungicide and/or insecticide is applied by contractors or any other entity in whole or in part, CONTRACTOR shall inspect all turf areas during each visit to the site and shall in a postvisit report inform PROPERTY MANAGER of any turf disease or insect problems found, methods suggested for eliminating or alleviating each such problem (materials required and application schedule, indicating when certain amounts of identified materials should be applied), and the cost involved. **The cost of this inspection/ planning service on a seasonal basis shall be $_____.**

Aeration

In the mid-Atlantic area of the nation, aeration is generally most beneficial on cool-season grasses when provided between August 15 and November 15 in association with overseeding and fall fertilization. On warm-season grasses, such as Bermuda grass and zoysia grass, aeration is generally most beneficial during the summer months (June 15 to August 15). In situations where traffic is excessive, additional aeration treatments may be prescribed.

In most instances it is desirable not to collect aeration cores. They tend to reinoculate the thatch layers and thus promote thatch decomposition.

9. *Aeration*

   a. CONTRACTOR shall accomplish aeration using a roller, drum, or piston-type aerator with coring or open-spoon tines of ½- to ¾-diameter. Tines will penetrate the soil to a minimum of 1½ inches. The final aeration pattern shall provide a minimum of four aeration holes per square foot of surface area. Aeration shall be provided:

   Between [_____] and [_____]
   Between [_____] and [_____]

   The cost per aeration shall be $_____.

Dethatching

Thatch control is best accomplished with a preventive program through which dethatching is performed periodically to avoid excessive buildup. In the event that thatch has accumulated to an undesirable thickness, repeated dethatching at a light or moderate rate will avoid excessive damage to the turf. Dethatching should be limited to the seasons in which grass is growing rapidly, and it should be performed in such a manner that turf will recover in 2 weeks. The appropriate time period for cool-season grasses is between April 1 and June 1 or between August 15 and October 15, depending upon geographic location. In cooler regions, May or August is appropriate; in hotter regions, April and September are appropriate. Bermuda grass and zoysia grass should be verticut early in the summer, after they have greened completely and are growing vigorously.

10. *Dethatching*

    a. CONTRACTOR shall accomplish dethatching as needed to maintain thatch levels less than ½ inch thick. Dethatching blades will be adjusted so as not to cause damage to the turf, which will detract from the quality of the turf for 2 weeks after dethatching. CONTRACTOR shall remove from the site debris brought to the surface in the dethatching process. Dethatching shall be performed:

    Between [_____] and [_____]
    Between [_____] and [_____]

    The cost per dethatching shall be $_____.

Overseeding

In paragraph 11, the term "management-designated...areas" is used. Note the subsequent sentence, which references a plan. Preparing a plan to indicate precisely which areas are involved can be somewhat of a chore, but—in reality—it only involves a small investment of time that can save major headaches later on. By being precise, it is far more likely that the desired results will be achieved. Imprecision leads to different perceptions of what is needed, such that someone's expectations are not met. Failed expectations are among the most common triggers to claims and disputes.

---

11. *Overseeding*
    a. CONTRACTOR shall overseed management-designated cool-season turf areas during [August 15 to September 15] or [February 15 to March 30]. These cool-season turf areas are marked CSTA on the attached plan. CONTRACTOR shall use a device or system that places the seed in direct contact with the soil. Blends of mixtures used shall be those recommended by the Cooperative Extension Service of [state]. [All Kentucky bluegrass and tall fescue mixtures shall contain [state] recommended label.] Rates for overseeding existing turf areas shall be as follows:

	Rate (lb/1000 ft^2)	
Seed being planted	Area has greater than 50% turf cover	Area has less than 50% turf cover
Kentucky bluegrass	1	2
Tall fescue	3	6

The cost per 1000 ft^2 shall be:

Kentucky bluegrass $_____

Tall fescue $_____

    b. Overseeding of areas shall be preceded by dethatching as noted in Section 10 when thatch buildup exceeds ½-inch thickness.

Ornamental tree, shrub, and flower bed maintenance

Owners can make significant investments in ornamental trees and shrubs. It is essential to ensure that those selected to maintain the investment know exactly what they are doing. A firm that is fully capable of providing top-quality lawn care service may not be as astute when it comes to the ornamentals. Deal only with a firm that has successful experience.

12. *Ornamental tree, shrub, and flower bed maintenance*
    a. By [date], CONTRACTOR shall apply a preemergence herbicide to all ornamental tree, shrub, and flower beds. **The cost of this service shall be $_____.**
    b. By [date], CONTRACTOR shall apply for ornamental trees and shrubs a fertilizer with equal parts N-P-K at the rate of 1 lb of actual nitrogen per 1000 ft^2. **The cost of this service shall be $_____.**
    c. By [date], CONTRACTOR shall conduct a soil analysis of ornamental tree, shrub, and flower beds, and it is estimated that [_____] analyses shall be required for this purpose. If analysis reveals that special fertilizers are required to correct nutrient deficiencies, CONTRACTOR shall so inform PROPERTY MANAGER. Special fertilizers typically used for this purpose include the following:

    _____ $_____/1000 ft^2
    _____ $_____/1000 ft^2
    _____ $_____/1000 ft^2

    It is recognized that fertilizers other than those listed above may be required. If so, CONTRACTOR shall inform PROPERTY MANAGER of requirements and costs involved.
    d. By [date], CONTRACTOR shall edge all ornamental tree, shrub, and flower beds for definition, weed all beds, turn existing mulch (if any), and apply new mulch so that all beds are neat and attractive and contain no more than 3 inches of total mulch. CONTRACTOR shall ensure that the water basins around plants are large enough to accommodate the amount of water required to establish moisture through the major root zones. **The cost of this service shall be $_____.**
    e. CONTRACTOR shall prune all shrubs and ornamental trees in order to maintain neat appearance in accordance with the following schedule:

Between [_____] and [_____]
Between [_____] and [_____]

Trees shall be pruned to select and develop permanent scaffold branches that are smaller in diameter than the trunk or branch to which they are attached, and which have vertical spacing of 18 to 48 inches and radial orientation so as not to overlay one another; to eliminate diseased or damaged growth; to eliminate narrow V-shaped branch forks that lack strength; to reduce toppling and wind damage by thinning out crowns; to maintain a natural appearance; and to balance the crown with roots.

Under no circumstances shall any stripping of lower branches ("raising up") of young trees be permitted. Lower branches shall be retained in a tipped back or pinched condition with as much foliage as possible to promote caliper trunk growth (tapered trunk). Lower branches can be cut flush with the trunk only after the tree is able to stand erect with staking or other support.

All pruning cuts shall be made to lateral branches, or buds, or flush with the trunk. Stubbing shall not be permitted.

"Tree seal" shall be used as appropriate.

The objective of shrub pruning is the same as for ornamental trees. Shrubs shall not be clipped into balled or boxed forms unless such is required by the design. **The cost of each such pruning shall be $_____. The cost of each additional pruning specified by PROPERTY MANAGER shall be $_____.**

   f. CONTRACTOR shall develop for review by PROPERTY MANAGER a preventive insect and disease control plan for all ornamental trees, shrubs, and flowers. Such plan shall be segregated by season or month, as follows:

   Dormant season
   [February to early April]
   April
   May
   June
   July
   August
   September to October

For each season or month, the plan shall identify the types of insects and/or diseases to which the various ornamental trees, shrubs, and flowers may be susceptible, the materials required to help prevent insect and disease problems, the quantity of materials involved per application, and the cost of each such application. **Whether or not** CONTRACTOR **is engaged to implement such a plan, in whole or in part, the cost of developing the plan shall be $**_____.

g. Whether or not a preventive insect and disease control plan is implemented, in whole or in part, by CONTRACTOR or any other entity, CONTRACTOR shall inspect all ornamental trees, shrubs, and flowers during each visit to the site and shall in a postvisit report inform PROPERTY MANAGER of any insect or disease problems found, methods suggested for eliminating or alleviating each such problem (materials required and application schedule, indicating when certain amounts of identified materials should be applied), and the cost involved. **The cost of this inspection/planning service on a seasonal basis shall be** $_____.

Sod installation or replacement

Property managers should be aware of differences in sod. *Certified turf-grass sod* is superior sod grown from "certified" seed. It is inspected and certified by the state certifying agency to assure genetic purity, overall high quality, and freedom from noxious weeds as well as excessive amounts of other crop and weed plants at the time of harvest. It may be composed of a mixture of two or more varieties or species. The sod must meet published state standards and bear an official state "certified sod" label on the delivery receipt. The purchaser should require labels when sod is delivered.

Approved turf-grass sod is inspected and approved by the state certifying agency to assure overall high quality and freedom from noxious weeds and excessive amounts of other crops and weed plants at the time of harvest. It may be composed of a mixture of two or more varieties or species. The sod must meet published state standards and bear an official state "approved sod" label on the delivery receipt. The purchaser should require such labels when sod is delivered.

A detailed quality specification should be provided for all sod other than state "certified" or "approved" classes. Such specifications should include species and/or varieties and the following quality standards: weed content, other crop contaminants, thatch, diseases, insects, mowing height, uniformity, and overall quality. The quality standards are automatically covered in the state "certified" and "approved" classes. If assistance is needed in developing quality standards for sod, contact the county extension agent in the county where the work is to be performed.

13. *Sod installation or replacement*

    a. CONTRACTOR shall, upon approval by PROPERTY MANAGER, install sod as needed or directed. CONTRACTOR shall use [certified] [approved] [other than certified or approved] sod for this purpose. **The cost of this sod and its proper installation shall be, on a per-square-foot basis, $_____/ft^2.**

    b. CONTRACTOR shall develop a watering plan for all sod CONTRACTOR installs, indicating the extent and frequency of watering required and the cost of such watering when performed by CONTRACTOR. **Whether or not such watering is performed by CONTRACTOR, the cost of developing the watering plan shall be $_____.**

Maintenance management plan

The plan referred to below can be used as a checklist to help ensure that all work, including that done by in-house personnel, has been performed properly.

14. *Maintenance management plan*

    a. CONTRACTOR agrees to develop a comprehensive grounds maintenance management plan which indicates all tasks necessary for comprehensive grounds care, including those tasks to which this agreement applies and those for which PROPERTY MANAGER shall secure other labor. The grounds maintenance plan will specify who is responsible for which tasks, the frequency thereof, and such other pertinent information as PROPERTY MANAGER may request. **The cost of developing this plan shall be $_____.**

As part of this work it may be appropriate to have the contractor develop a visitation report that will be signed by the contractor's representative. Most contractors already have such forms. Note, however, that a generally applicable form may not be as valuable as one that is more specific and can include wording developed by the property manager to meet the property manager's specific needs. As an example, see Fig. 1.1.

Name of Property_____
Address_____
Date_____ Arrival Time_____ Departure Time_____

LAWN PROGRAM

Turfgrass   _____   (Cut No._____)
Edging   _____   (Edge No._____)
Liming   _____
Fertilization   _____   (Rate:_____)
Weed Control   _____   (Analysis:_____)
Insect Control   _____
Other

_____ _____
_____ _____
_____ _____

ORNAMENTAL PLANT CARE

	Trees	Shrubs
Pruning	_____	_____
Fertilization	_____	_____
Bed Edging	_____	_____
Watering	_____	_____
Bed Weed Control	_____	_____
Mulch Application	_____	_____
Irrigation Check	_____	_____
Other		

_____ _____ _____
_____ _____ _____
_____ _____ _____

Authorized by_____

By signature affixed below, I hereby certify that all services indicated above as having been performed have been performed in fact, and according to the contractual agreement of (*date*) between (*name of contractor*) and (*name of property or its owner or manager, as appropriate*). It is recognized by all parties that wilfull failure to perform in accordance with the specifications identified in the contractual agreement, or duly obtained exceptions thereto, may subject (*name of contractor*) and/or crew leader or other representatives of (*name of contractor*) to legal prosecution.

Signature of Crew Chief_____

Printed Name of Crew Chief_____

FORWARD A COPY OF THIS REPORT TO _____

Figure 1.1   Plant and turf care visitation report.

2

Asphalt Pavement Maintenance and Repair

Introduction

Asphalt is a mixture of rock and sand held together by a liquid, petroleum-based cement. Typically it is laid on a base of stabilized, crushed rock and then compacted. In some cases a prior layer (lift) of coarse, stronger asphalt is applied before the final lift.

Asphalt is installed to create a surface for areas where it would be inappropriate or impossible to rely on earthen or other existing materials. Multifamily residential and commercial facilities use asphalt principally for parking lots and access roads, as well as for walkways, recreational areas (for example, tennis and basketball courts), and certain specialized purposes such as holding ponds or rooftop parking areas.

No matter where asphalt is placed, or for what purpose, it begins to deteriorate soon after installation. The nature, rate, and extent of deterioration depend on a number of factors, including the conditions imposed by usage and the ability of the asphalt and other installation elements to resist this deterioration.

Preventive maintenance and effective repair are the best defense against asphalt deterioration and the problems it can cause. The most significant of these problems often is the cost of correcting the extensive damage that can result from relatively minor, easy-to-correct deficiencies. For example, just a few small cracks can allow water to penetrate to the subbase, causing it to weaken. Vehicle loads transferred to the weakened subbase cause the asphalt to sink and crack, letting in more water and causing further weakening. Later the water can freeze, with the resulting expansion leading to more cracking, potholes, and disintegration. In relatively short order, then, a small problem, which could have been corrected in 2 or 3 hours for less than $100, can lead to a major repair that causes traffic disruption for several days or longer, and an unanticipated expense in excess of $10,000.

At one time the repair was not nearly as expensive as it is today. Binder-quality crude, the material left over after other operations to refine petroleum, at the time, was both plentiful and inexpensive. Today's high petroleum prices have encouraged refiners to install better equipment, so there are far fewer leftovers. The relative scarcity of the product has resulted in increased prices and lower quality. Whereas a properly designed and constructed parking lot surface installed in 1970 was expected to last 15 to 18 years with only minor maintenance, the one installed in 1992 might not last through 1996 unless it is well cared for.

The high cost of replacing an asphalt surface or effecting major repairs is not the only problem that can result from inadequate maintenance. Another significant consideration is the legal liability to which a property owner may be exposed when a crack or pothole leads to a tripping accident or damage to a vehicle. Such conditions can also result in vehicle-vehicle, vehicle-pedestrian, or vehicle-cyclist accidents. While insurance may (or may not) cover such problems, avoiding them through effective maintenance and repair makes far more sense. Insurance cannot repay an owner for the time and aggravation associated with a claim or lawsuit, nor can it compensate for the impact of negative publicity. One also must consider how poorly maintained asphalt can affect a property's image and "curb appeal," especially since the asphaltic access road and parking lot are usually the first things seen when a person enters a property and the last things seen when leaving. Would you want your home or office associated with an eyesore or hazard of any type? Would you want to shop where the parking lot is in such a state of disrepair that you might trip or crack your car's axle?

In short, well-maintained asphalt surfaces are an asset to any property, and those which are "let go" are a liability. It is a property manager's responsibility to preserve the value of an owner's asset. The work necessary to do so can be performed totally by in-house personnel, totally by contractors, or—as is most common—through a combination of the two. The approach that is best for any given property depends on a value analysis. While it may seem to be less expensive to do the work on an in-house basis, genuine savings are realized only when the results are of professional quality. If not, the in-house repair will last only a short while, and the cost of repeated repair will quickly exceed the premium paid for having the work done properly by a contractor.

In some cases an in-house repair will only cure a symptom, thereby masking the real problem which, left unattended, will lead to the need for a major repair. In other words, if a property manager can muster the equipment, the materials, and the expertise required to produce professional-quality results, in-house repair is acceptable, provided its cost is significantly less than what a contractor would charge. If the cost difference is not significant, it generally is wiser to spend the additional funds for contractor performance. The additional amount thus spent is merely the small premium required for having someone else accept the risks and liabilities involved.

In all cases, careful contractor selection is an absolute necessity. Special knowledge and experience are required to diagnose a problem correctly and to specify the "fix" that is most appropriate for the conditions at hand, including the owner's short-term versus long-term cost preferences. The contractor must also demonstrate trustworthiness and a willingness to abide by the agreed-to specifications scrupulously.

When major repairs are needed, or when a large amount of asphalt-surfaced area is involved, it may be best to rely on a pavement consultant who can evaluate existing problems, develop precise specifications, prequalify contractors, evaluate their bids, and monitor their adherence to specifications in the field.

Asphalt Basics

The following discussion is limited to conventional techniques and materials. The asphalt price hikes of the recent past have spurred the development of new techniques and materials for use in conjunction with or instead of asphalt. Typical of the materials used with asphalt are the many geotextiles designed for use in developing a strong base, often at less cost than conventional methods yielding equivalent utility. Innovative asphalt substitutes include those that their distributors claim are less costly than asphalt when installed on a structurally sound base, are impervious to the physical and chemical agents that destroy asphalt and concrete, and maintain a dark appearance throughout their life. Some come with a 4-year guarantee.

Given the conventional repair and maintenance options that exist, as well as the new materials that can be applied, it often is best to rely on a qualified consultant for guidance. Using a "cookbook approach" to design can have a negative outcome. Effective pavement structure design, that is, the selection of the types and thicknesses of materials to be used, requires a thorough knowledge of the engineering properties of all materials involved, from the subgrade up. If a long-lasting pavement is to result, those in charge must also consider a number of factors unique to the specific application. Some of these factors include:

The physical characteristics of the subgrade, such as permeability, compressibility, and susceptibility to volume change

The physical properties of available materials

The anticipated volume, weight, and speed of traffic using the pavement

Basic materials

Asphalt is a petroleum product refined from crude oil, with a solid or semisolid consistency at temperatures below 100°F. For maintenance operations it is made liquid or semiliquid by heating (cement), by dissolving it in a petroleum solvent (cutback), or by combining it with water (emulsion). Each of the three types of asphaltic materials used in maintenance—cements, cutbacks, and emulsions—is rated and graded based on standardized tests. Several materials with different ratings and gradings often are applicable for a given purpose, provided each is applied properly to a surface that has been prepared correctly.

Asphalt cement. The basic material of the asphalt family, asphalt cement is a semisolid used to make hot mixes, penetration surface treatments, and certain types of crack fillers. Its consistency is rated using standardized tests. The oldest of these, developed early in the twentieth century, involves a penetration test. Results are indicated by five gradings: 40–50, 60–70, 85–100, 120–150, and 200–300. The higher the grading, the softer (less viscous) the material.

Two tests are used to grade the viscosity of asphalt cement. Ratings established using the original test, developed in the 1950s, are prefixed by AC (AC-40, AC-20, AC-10, AC-5, and AC-2.5). A second viscosity grading system was developed in the 1970s. Ratings based on this test are prefixed by AR (AR-16,000, AR-8000, AR-4000, AR-2000, and AR-1000). The higher the AC or AR number, the harder (more viscous) the material.

Cutbacks. Cutbacks are asphalts that are liquefied by means of a petroleum solvent. Once they are spread on a pavement, the solvent evaporates, leaving the asphalt cement behind. Cutbacks are rated according to their curing time: RC (rapid curing), MC (medium curing), or SC (slow curing). RC cutbacks generally use a naphthalike solvent, while MC cutbacks use a solvent similar to kerosene. An SC grade actually is not a cutback. Sometimes referred to as road oil, its solvent, somewhat akin to a heavy fuel oil, is left in during the refining process, rather than being added.

Each of the three types of cutbacks is available in four grades: 70, 250, 800, and 3000; the lower the number, the more solvent the material contains. A special MC-30 grade has been developed principally for prime coating and dust laying.

Emulsions. Asphalt emulsions are liquid mixtures of minute globules of asphalt cement suspended in water and an emulsifying agent. Two types are available, anionic and cationic. The asphalt globules in an anionic emulsion have a negative electrical charge, while those in a cationic emulsion are positively charged. An emulsion's coating and bonding properties are greatly enhanced when its electrical charge is the opposite of the aggregate's.

Both anionic and cationic emulsions are rated by the time required for them to "break" (come out of suspension). Three ratings are used: RS (rapid setting), MS (medium setting), and SS (slow setting), with each of the three being prefixed by a C (CRS, CMS, and CSS) when applied to a cationic emulsion. Most of the ratings are graded as either 1 or 2, with the lower number indicating more fluidity. The designation h indicates a harder grade of base asphalt (such as CMS-2h); HF indicates a high-float emulsion (such as HFMS-2), a material developed for application during periods of temperature extremes. (A float test is applied to ascertain an emulsion's capabilities in this regard, thus leading to the designation "high float" for emulsions having the desired characteristics.)

Mixtures

Mixture are combinations of asphalt and aggregate. A variety of mixtures is available for different purposes, with the aggregate serving to add strength and antiskid characteristics. Typical mineral aggregates are crushed stone, crushed or uncrushed gravel, slag, sand, stone screenings, mineral dust, or a combination of these. They are rated by weight, size (percentage that flows through a standard-size screen or sieve), and abrasion characteristics.

Mixtures can be broadly categorized as plant mixes or road mixes. A plant mix is produced in an asphalt mixing plant and is any mixture of mineral aggregate uniformly coated with asphalt. The "top-of-the-line" plant mix is asphalt concrete. This is a thoroughly controlled mixture of well-graded, high-quality aggregate and asphalt cement. It is mixed at high temperature and should be laid and compacted before its temperature falls below 185°F.

Road mix is mixed at the site, using cutbacks or emulsions and (typically) local aggregates.

The design of an asphaltic mixture, that is, the specification of its composition, is based on many factors. These include the anticipated traffic volume, the intended pavement thickness, the exact physical properties of the asphalt to be used, and the size (gradation) of the available mineral aggregates, among others. For the most part, reputable plants furnish standard mixes designed to meet the requirements of local public works or highway departments. The design and selection of mixtures should be left to the contractor who will perform the work or a pavement consultant.

Coatings

Three types of coatings are commonly used in maintenance operations: prime coats, tack coats, and seal coats.

Prime coats. The terms prime coat and priming both refer to a cutback or emulsion that is sprayed onto the surface of a nonasphalt base course to waterproof it, plug capillary voids, coat and bond loose mineral particles, stabilize the base and harden its surface, and promote adhesion between the base course and the surface treatment. MC cutbacks are generally the preferred materials used in priming, with the viscosity selected being determined by the composition of the base. Several types of emulsified asphalts (emulsions) can be used if the preferred MC cutback is not available.

Tack coats. A tack coat is applied to create a bond between an existing pavement and a course to be placed over it. The material most commonly used is an emulsion (SS-1, SS-1h, CSS-1, or CSS-1h) that is diluted with an equal amount of clean water.

Seal coats. Regular application of a seal coat is the best defense against asphalt deterioration. Generally speaking, maximum value is obtained by using only those seal coats that can hold aggregate or sand (antiskids); two coats are recommended. (Light coatings are used principally for cosmetic purposes, last only for a year or less, and can create a slipping hazard.)

As in other applications, proper surface treatment prior to coating is essential. Cleaning is performed by sweeping with a stiff-bristled broom, followed by compressed air. Cracks should be filled using any acceptable filler. In parking areas it is prudent to evaluate the existing layout before applying the seal coat. A new parking pattern may be beneficial and can be accommodated easily after seal coating, through striping.

Seal coat technology is being improved continually, with the seal coats in most common use relying on a coal tar cement as the protective component. (Coal tar is a distillate of coal rather than oil.) Some seals also use additives such as latex or thermoplastic resins to modify their performance characteristics. When dealing with contractors, it is advisable to have them submit detailed information on the seal coats they can use, indicating the materials comprised by each and relative quantities, rate of application, amount of aggregate (such as sand) used, and so on. In this way you can ensure that the seal coat you select is best for the application, and that the proposals of the contractors are evaluated on an "apples-to-apples" basis. Note that reliance on a well-known, reputable contractor is particularly appropriate when it comes to seal coating, because it is so easy to dilute the material and thereby enhance profit by cheating on the quantity and quality installed.

Crack fillers

Small cracks (other than hairline cracks) can be filled with any asphalt material that can be made liquid enough to flow into the openings. Slurry seals and emulsions generally are preferred; hot paving-grade asphalt tends to bridge a crack rather than flow into it. For larger cracks, slurry seals and emulsions generally are mixed with fine aggregate and broomed into the openings.

Patching materials

Asphalt concrete is the preferred patching material, given its strength and long life. A great deal of equipment usually must be mobilized to deliver and apply it, however, so the minimum charged for its use may be prohibitive when just one or two small patches are required. The most common alternative is a plant mix using cutback or emulsion that is laid cold (cold patch). The effectiveness of a cold patch will depend on the quality of the mix used and the care employed in the installation. The next alternative is a road mix using a medium- or slow-curing cutback and local aggregate.

Asphalt structures

Many terms are used to connote different asphalt structures and their various elements. Some of the more common terms include the following.

Asphalt pavement.   A pavement whose surface consists of mineral aggregate coated and cemented together with asphalt cement. Substrata may consist of asphalt, crushed stone, gravel or slag, or portland cement concrete, brick, or block.

Surface course.   Also known as the wearing course, this is the top layer of an asphalt pavement, typically using a mix designed to provide skid resistance and smoothness.

Base course.   The bottom layer of an asphalt pavement, usually comprising an asphalt mix designed to provide high strength and stability.

Base.   A layer of material, usually gravel, between the subbase and the asphalt pavement.

Subbase.   A layer of material between base and subgrade. Inexpensive granular fill is commonly used.

Subgrade.   Naturally occurring soil or imported fill prepared to support an asphalt pavement structure or system. The subgrade material's relative strength and stability are major factors in pavement design, affecting the thickness of the base and the subbase in particular. A weaker subbase requires a more substantial pavement profile (thickness of material above the subgrade level).

Asphalt pavement structure.   A pavement structure placed above the subgrade or improved subgrade, whose courses consist of asphalt-aggregate mixtures.

Thick-lift asphalt pavement.   An asphalt pavement structure whose asphalt base course is placed in one or more lifts, each having a compacted thickness of 4 inches or more.

Full-depth asphalt pavement.   An asphalt pavement structure laid directly on the subgrade or improved subgrade, using asphalt mixtures for all courses.

Deep-strength asphalt pavement.   A term registered with the U.S. Patent Office by The Asphalt Institute to connote an asphalt pavement structure constructed of asphalt on an asphalt base in accordance with design concepts established by the Institute.

Asphalt leveling course.   A course of variable thickness applied to eliminate irregularities in the contour of an existing surface before additional treatment or construction.

Asphalt overlay.   One or more courses applied to an existing pavement, usually consisting of a leveling course and one or more additional courses to provide the necessary thickness.

Asphalt surface treatment.   An asphalt coating to any type of pavement surface, with or without a cover of mineral aggregate, which produces a thickness increase of less than 1 inch.

Inspections

As soon as asphalt is placed, it begins to deteriorate. This deterioration is caused by the sun (oxidation), temperature changes (expansion and contraction), weather conditions, changing subsurface conditions, inability of the drainage system to handle the flow (due to improper design, faulty installation, or failure), improper pavement design or construction, excess wheel loading, and oil or chemical spills, among many other factors, including ordinary wear and tear. Nothing can be done to eliminate deterioration altogether, but the life of an asphalt surface can be extended for many years if the symptoms of deterioration are detected soon after they appear and prompt remedial action is taken.

The single most important aspect of asphalt maintenance is frequent inspection of the surfaces involved and areas adjacent to them, with particular emphasis on whatever drainage structures may exist, to help ensure that water is being handled properly. In fact, water is perhaps the worst enemy of an asphalt surface, because, as it penetrates or otherwise seeps beneath a surface, it weakens the subgrade. This weakness causes the surface to flex, which leads to cracking and the entry of still more water. As this occurs, the surface begins to deteriorate seriously. Over the winter the water can freeze and expand, causing the surface to give out altogether through the development of large potholes, major deflections, and other problems.

It is suggested that inspections be performed at least twice a year, once prior to winter and once after. It also is wise to conduct a quick inspection several hours after a rainfall, to determine the adequacy of the drainage system and to see whether any ponding exists. Ponding indicates a deflection in the paved surface. Left unattended, it will lead to water seeping through cracks and—ultimately—a condition that could destroy a large section of pavement.

Persons assigned to perform inspections must be properly trained for the task. They should be able to recognize and identify the different types of problems they may encounter.

Proper inspection reporting is also important. The most comprehensive approach involves the creation of a form which includes a single-line diagram of each paved area and the various structures within or adjacent to that area. When possible, traffic flow patterns as well as surface drainage patterns should also be indicated. Problems that occur in these two areas often are more significant than those which arise in others. Likewise, proper repair procedures may have to be more exacting or more extensive if even more substantial problems are to be avoided.

Figure 2.1 illustrates a model form, which includes a diagram. A copy of this form would be used for each inspection. When a problem is encountered, its location and nature should be indicated. It may also be appropriate to use an instant-developing camera to supplement the form. By keeping inspection reports on file, it will be possible to record the history of each area and quickly identify those locations

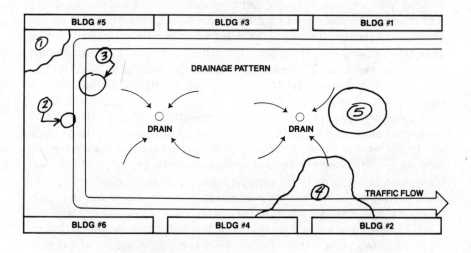

Date of Inspection _August 7, '92_ Time _2:15 PM_
Date and Time of Last Rainfall _August 7, 11 AM_
Inspector's Name _John Doe, Res. Mgr._

Remarks

1	severe alligatoring
2	large pothole (2½' di)
3	" " (4' di)
4	light alligatoring – large area
5	ponding / depression

Figure 2.1   Standard pavement inspection form, shown completed after inspection.

which are subject to persistent problems. In some instances, problems persist because the repair work is not compatible with the pavement profile, such as the thickness of the asphalt, the thickness of the stone base, or the type of subgrade soil. If information about the soil profile is not on hand, it can (and should) be developed by having core samples taken. Do not assume that the pavement profile is uniform throughout an area. For example, heavily used traffic lanes or areas near loading docks may have much thicker profiles than others.

Records of actions taken also should be maintained, and these, along with the inspection reports, should be kept in the historical files of a building. They can be invaluable in the event of disputes of any kind and for purposes of sale.

All inspections should be performed in good light and on foot. The close inspection permitted by that method helps in the detection of minor defects, which can be symptoms of something severe in the offing—something that often can be corrected at little cost before it develops into a major problem.

Typical Problems

The discussion that follows addresses some of the more common problems one encounters on an asphalt surface, with emphasis on roadways, driveways, and parking lots. Much of the information applies to recreational courts (other than tennis courts) and walkways as well.

Whoever performs inspections should be familiar with all the various types of problems that may occur. (This instruction can be given easily by a consultant or contractor who can also provide information on repairs.) Once a problem is detected, it should be attended to promptly. Failure to do so can result in the problem becoming worse, greatly expanding the complexity and cost of repair, while creating other problems in the interim, such as unsightliness, automotive damage, and slipping or tripping hazards, especially at night.

The repairs suggested in this section are fairly typical. They are not necessarily the best for your needs, nor do they reflect any of the innovative materials that can be used.

In making a repair, treat the cause, not the effect. Treating the effect does nothing to correct the real problem, so whatever is done may quickly come undone, thus wasting time, effort, and money. And despite the information given in this guide, entrust your evaluations only to an expert. Acting on a misdiagnosis can in some cases be worse than doing nothing at all.

It is sometimes appropriate to effect a temporary repair, so that all permanent repairs needed can be performed at the same time, perhaps in conjunction with a regular repair schedule. *Do not permit temporary repairs to serve as permanent repairs.* They will merely permit more damage to occur until—ultimately—only replacement will do.

Pavement surface

Several types of surface phenomena indicate pavement distress: cracking, distortion, disintegration, slipperiness, loss of cover aggregate, and streaking. Each has a cause, and it is the cause that should be corrected. Note that causes other than those discussed may exist, and that repairs other than those identified may be completely acceptable and, in some cases, more effective.

In reviewing the causes, you may be surprised to see how many relate to improper design or inadequate construction. While nothing can eliminate the gradual deterioration of an asphalt surface totally, effective design and construction can certainly extend the usable life and thereby decrease both life-cycle costs and life-cycle headaches. Conversely, there is a desire to achieve first-cost savings that will lead to the least expensive alternative, the one that almost invariably will prove most expensive in the long run. Be it for new construction, replacement, or repair, always obtain the best: the best guidance, the best materials, and the best construction practices. This approach almost always is the most cost-effective and beneficial.

Cracking.   Cracking is the most common symptom of problems, but the specific nature of the crack must be assessed. Common types include alligator cracks, shrinkage cracks, slippage cracks, edge cracks, reflection cracks, and widening cracks. In some cases, crack filling alone is enough to solve the problem. In other cases, it may be necessary to remove the affected area completely and replace it with a new section of asphalt paving. When any patching is performed, it is vitally important to remove all deteriorated soft material until a firm, stable subgrade is reached. Simply replacing distressed asphalt is not sufficient.

Alligator cracks.   These are interconnected small cracks whose lines resemble those of chicken wire, thus creating surfaces that look like an alligator's skin (Fig. 2.2). The cause typically is excessive deflection of the surface, brought about by saturation of the subgrade or granular base, which makes the subgrade or lower pavement courses unstable. In most instances only small areas are affected, and seal coating usually is sufficient for temporary repair. Permanent repair generally requires removal of the distressed area and rebuilding of the pavement structure (deep patching). Full-depth asphalt is commonly

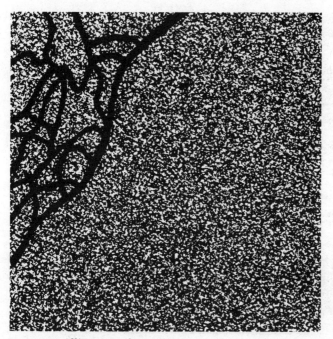

Figure 2.2   Alligator cracks.

used for the permanent repair, because only one material is required and it is applied in one operation.

Large-area cracking of a roadway, driveway, or parking lot is caused by excessive wheel loads. It generally is repaired by installing a properly designed overlay. Installation of new drainage may also be advisable.

Shrinkage cracks.   These are somewhat similar to alligator cracks, except that the area inside the crack outline is far larger, and the crack outline itself usually is characterized by sharp corners or angles (Fig. 2.3). Shrinkage cracks usually are caused by a volume change in the fine aggregate mixes that contain relatively large amounts of low-penetration asphalt. Repair requires the use of a stiff-bristled broom and compressed air to remove all loose matter from the cracks and the pavement. The pavement and crack faces are then uniformly dampened with water, followed by the application of a tack coat. An asphalt-derived seal coat such as slurry seal is then poured into the cracks and hand-leveled with a squeegee. (If large areas are involved, all is sealed.) Once the seal has cured, the entire surface is sealed again or otherwise surface-treated.

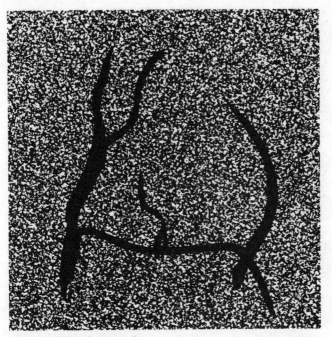

Figure 2.3   Shrinkage cracks.

Slippage cracks. These usually are crescent-shaped cracks (Fig. 2.4) which, due to wheel thrust, point in the direction of traffic. (Sometimes they point away from traffic flow, typically on downhill slopes, as a result of vehicle braking.) The presence of slippage cracks usually indicates a lack of effective bonding between the surface course of a roadway and the course beneath it. Improper bonding can be the result of failure to apply a tack coat; too high a sand content in the surface course or the one beneath; improper compaction, which has caused an otherwise effective bond to fail; or the entry, during construction, of dust, oil, rubber, dirt, or some other nonadhesive material between the surface course and the one beneath it. The only effective repair is removal of the asphalt to the depth where an effective bond is found, and then application of a plant-mixed asphalt patch.

Edge cracks. These cracks run parallel to and about 1 foot away from the edge of the pavement, and sometimes are accompanied by transverse cracks (Fig. 2.5). They develop when lateral (shoulder) support is lost due to settlement or yielding of material beneath the crack. This condition can result from the drying out of the surrounding earth, poor drainage, or frost heaves. Cracks wider than ⅛ inch are repaired temporarily by cleaning them out with a stiff-bristled broom and compressed air, and

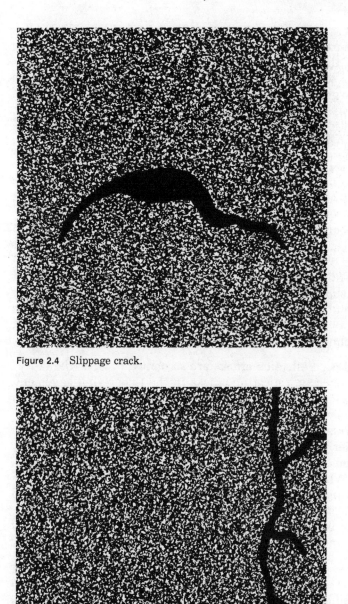

Figure 2.4 Slippage crack.

Figure 2.5 Edge cracks.

then filling them with a slurry or an emulsion mixed with sand. After the filler has cured, the crack should be sealed with an emulsion. This technique may also do for a permanent repair, depending on the cause of the problem. In some cases it may be necessary to bring the edge of the pavement up to grade using a plant-mix patching material, or to improve existing drainage, as through installation of underdrains. Trees, shrubs, or other vegetation next to the pavement edge may cause the earth there to dry out and lead to cracks. They should be removed.

Edge joint cracks. An edge joint crack is actually a seam that opens between the pavement and the shoulder. The line formed by the crack generally is straighter than that associated with an edge crack, and there seldom are transverse cracks branching to the pavement's edge. The seam typically is caused by alternate wetting and drying beneath the shoulder because of poor drainage. Typical reasons for the poor drainage are a shoulder that is higher than the pavement, a ridge of grass or joint-filling material, or depressions between the pavement edge and the shoulder. Any of these trap water and cause it to seep through the joint, which results in separation. When poor drainage is the problem, its cause must be eliminated before the crack is filled. The filling technique is that used for edge cracks.

Reflection cracks. Reflection cracks are so named because they occur in an asphalt overlay, reflecting cracks in the underlying pavement. They are more common in asphalt overlays installed on top of nonasphaltic material, such as portland cement concrete. In such instances the cause often is temperature or moisture changes which cause the underlying pavement to move. Other causes include traffic or earth movement, or the loss of moisture in subgrade with a high clay content. When reflection cracks appear in an overlay placed on top of an existing asphalt surface, improper repair of cracks in the old surface is indicated. The same type of repair method as used for edge cracks usually is effective. In some areas these cracks are filled by pressure-injecting asphalt from below.

Widening cracks. These essentially are reflection cracks which occur between an old section of pavement and a new section that has been added as a result of widening. They are treated like reflection cracks.

Lane joint cracks. These are almost the same as widening cracks, that is, separation along the seam between two paving lanes. They are repaired like reflection cracks.

Distortion. Pavement distortion takes the form of grooves or ruts, shoving, corrugations, depressions, and upheavals that may or may not be accompanied by cracking. Its cause usually is movement of the subgrade soil or compaction of the subgrade soil or base.

Grade depressions. Depressions are caused by the settlement of lower pavement layers, excessive load, or poor construction. They are most easily detected after a rainfall because they are the cause of ponding. Left unattended, depressions will lead to serious problems. When filled with water they can also be the source of a skid hazard and, in winter, a pedestrian slipping hazard as well. Depressions are repaired by filling them with asphalt.

Channels (ruts). Channels or ruts are depressions in the surface which form wheel tracks (Fig. 2.6). They are caused by the consolidation or lateral movement of one or more underlying courses, usually brought about by insufficient compaction during construction or by plastic movement in a mix which has insufficient stability to support the traffic flow. Repair is effected by filling the channels with a hot plant-mix asphalt until they are level with the pavement. A thin plant-mix asphalt overlay then is applied.

Figure 2.6   Ruts (frontal cross section).

Corrugations and shoving. Corrugations or "washboarding" are a form of plastic movement typified by ripples across a surface (Fig. 2.7). Shoving is similar, except that it results in a localized bulge (Fig. 2.8). Both effects are commonly found around sharp corners and areas where vehicles stop and start, bounce, or brake on a downgrade. Their cause is an asphalt layer that lacks stability, often because the mix used is too rich in asphalt, contains too high a proportion of fine aggregate, or contains aggregate that is too round or too smooth. The lack of stability can also be due to excessive moisture, oil spills, or inadequate aeration during the placement of a mix using an emulsion or cutback.

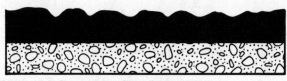

Figure 2.7   Corrugation (lateral cross section).

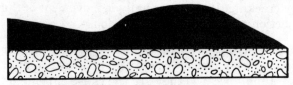

Figure 2.8 Shoving (lateral cross section).

Shoved areas are repaired by excising the affected area and installing a deep patch. The proper repair of corrugations depends on the pavement design. When the pavement has more than 2 inches of asphalt surface and base, the corrugations can be removed with a planer, followed by the application of a seal coat or plant-mix surface. When the pavement has an aggregate base and a thin surface treatment, the surface can be scarified, mixed with the base, and recompacted before a new surface is installed.

Utility cut depressions. These depressions follow a cut made for the installation or repair of a utility line. The cause generally is inadequate compaction of the backfill placed over the line after repair or installation is completed. They are repaired like other depressions.

Upheaval. This is a localized upward displacement of the pavement, often accompanied by alligatoring or disintegration. The most typical cause is moisture in the subgrade or a lower course, which expands upon freezing. It may also be caused by the swelling of expansive soils, which is also caused by moisture. Deep patching is generally used for repair.

Disintegration. Potholes and raveling are the two most common forms of disintegration, a condition marked by pavement breaking into small loose fragments. Unless its cause is eliminated, disintegration will worsen until the entire pavement must be rebuilt.

Potholes. Upheavals that weaken the surface, followed by continuous traffic, are just one cause of potholes. Others include weakness in the surface due to too little asphalt or too thin a surface, failure of the base, or poor drainage. Potholes are repaired temporarily by installing a premixed patching compound. A deep patch is used for permanent repair.

Raveling. This is the progressive separation of aggregate from the asphalt, starting from the surface downward or from the edges toward the center. Its causes typically are inadequate compaction during construction; installation of a thin pavement lift during cold weather; too little asphalt in the mix; overheating of the mix; or the use of dirty or disintegrating aggregate in the mix. Seal coating usually is an effective temporary repair. It also is the first step of a permanent repair, followed by the application of a surface treatment or hot-mix overlay.

Slipperiness. Slipperiness can lead to accidents for vehicles and pedestrians alike. Two common conditions leading to slipperiness include bleeding asphalt and polished aggregate.

Bleeding asphalt. Bleeding, or flushing, takes place when asphalt moves upward through a pavement structure to create an asphalt film on the surface. This usually occurs in hot weather as a result of too rich a mix, too heavy a prime or tack coat, or an improper seal coat. Repeated application of hot sand, hot slag screenings, or hot rock screenings often will be sufficient to blot up excess asphalt. When only light bleeding is involved, a seal coat of absorptive aggregate may be sufficient to correct the problem. When particularly heavy bleeding exists, it may be necessary to apply a low-asphalt-content plant-mix leveling course, followed by a new surface course to prevent raveling. In particularly severe cases, planing or even replacement of the surface may be required.

Polished aggregate. Some types of aggregates, particularly limestone aggregates, quickly become polished by traffic; some types of gravel are naturally polished. In either case the polished aggregate presents a skidding or slipping hazard under dry conditions, and an even worse hazard under wet conditions. The only effective repair is the installation of a new antiskid surface, such as a plant-mix overlay or a sand or aggregate seal coat using hard, angular, and nonpolishing aggregate.

Other pavement surface problems. A variety of other problems may be noted, including those which indicate ineffective prior repairs. Some of the most common of these are loss of cover aggregate, streaking, and transverse streaking.

Loss of cover aggregate. The loss of cover aggregate from surface-treated pavement leaves the asphalt exposed. One cause is the passage of too much time between placing the asphalt on the surface and placing the aggregate on top of the asphalt. (Usually aggregate should be placed no more than 1 minute after the asphalt has been installed to prevent the asphalt from cooling too much to hold the aggregate in place.) Other causes of loss of cover aggregate include the use of aggregate that is too wet or too dirty and failure to roll the aggregate immediately after placement.

Streaking. This condition consists of alternating lean and heavy lines of asphalt running parallel to the centerline of a roadway. Its cause often can be traced to construction faults, such as an improperly adjusted spray bar on the asphalt distributor, improper asphalt pump speed or pressure, or the use of asphalt that is not hot enough. The only satisfactory solution usually is planing the existing surface and applying a new surface treatment.

Transverse streaking. This consists of alternating lean and heavy lines running across a road surface, often resulting in corrugations. Its cause usually is improper asphalt pump speed, or a pump problem such as worn or loose parts. Planing and application of a new surface treatment are required for repair.

Vegetation

Vegetation will sometimes grow through an asphalt surface or, more commonly, between an abutment (such as a curb or gutter) and the paved surface. Vegetation is more than an unsightly nuisance. In pushing its way through an opening, it pushes up the base and the asphalt, creating a water problem. The cause of vegetation often is organic matter in the fill (soil below the pavement). For this reason, inorganic fill should be specified, and the fill should be tested for organic matter prior to placement.

If large areas of growth are occurring, chances are the only effective remedy will be removing the affected area entirely and replacing it with a proper structure. In the case of vegetation growing between an abutment and the asphalt surface, the most effective repair usually is removing manually all vegetation, including roots and leaves, and then applying a defoliant. (Defoliants should be applied twice a year thereafter.)

Contractors advise that usually it is a waste of money to create an asphalt seal between an abutment and a paved surface, because of the different coefficients of expansion between the abutment material and that of the paved surface. However, some available new materials supposedly can create an effective seal when applied properly.

Drainage system

The drainage system also should be inspected carefully, because water is the single most common source of problems. All ditches, culverts, pipes, and so on must be kept free of vegetation and debris. Inspection should be made after a rainfall to determine how well the system works and where, in particular, corrective action is called for.

Gaining Tenant Cooperation

When the area being repaired is subject to discretionary use, such as a recreational court or a sidewalk, it generally is sufficient to post a no-

---

OUR BASKETBALL/TENNIS/VOLLEYBALL COURT IS BEING REPAVED!

The time has come to repave our recreational court so that we can once again have a nice smooth surface to play on. Work is scheduled to start on Monday, November 8, and the court should be ready for play again by the weekend. If we are hampered by rain or other conditions, however, it may take a little longer. As ever, we will do our best.

Please note that the contractor will be leaving some equipment on the grounds overnight while work is being performed. Please do not let your children play near or on the equipment, and please keep them away from the recreational court. They may injure themselves playing with the equipment, or they may come into the building and into your apartment and onto your carpeting with tar on their shoes, etc. *And by all means,* do *not* let them play near the recreational court while work is ongoing. An ounce of prevention is worth a pound of cure.

Thanks for your understanding and assistance.

XYZ Gardens

Jane Doe, Resident Manager

Notice 2.1

tice advising that repairs will begin on a certain date, and that the area will once again be ready for use by a given time if everything goes as planned. Such a notice can be posted in several conspicuous areas, or it can be typed for delivery to each resident, or both. (Both are preferred.) Notice 2.1 gives typical wording.

A parking lot generally does not involve discretionary use; people have to put their cars somewhere. It generally is important to identify alternative parking areas for tenants and guests, and to provide guidance. This can be done with a notice which could include a map. It is suggested, however, that one or more tenant meetings be held to help ensure that everyone understands the instructions. Consider Notice 2.2, and consider also the effort management obviously is making to help assure tenant safety and satisfaction.

Why all that trouble? On the one hand, it helps ensure good tenant relations; management has made it obvious that it is genuinely concerned about tenant safety and security. If tenants follow instructions, no problems should occur for anyone. On the other hand, problem avoidance is extremely important. Were a tenant to be assaulted, it could be alleged—perhaps successfully—that the assault never would have occurred had the tenant been warned not to use the poorly illuminated shortcut. And in any event, whenever a lawsuit is filed, the only clear winners are those who work at resolving others' disputes. By taking pains to avoid problems, you avoid disputes. By avoiding disputes, you avoid the high cost of resolving them, even if you are found to be perfectly innocent.

Memorandum

TO: ALL TENANTS
FROM: XYZ GARDENS
            Jane Doe, Resident Manager
RE: PARKING LOT REPAVING

Work will begin next week on repaving our parking lot. Barring inclement weather, unanticipated conditions, and so forth, we expect to have all the work completed in 5 days.

The progress of the work has been designed in such a way that about half of all the spaces will be available each night. However, if you choose to park in a recently paved area, recognize that you may get some road tar on your car. PARK IN SUCH AREAS SOLELY AT YOUR OWN RISK. Do note that the location of our handicapped spaces will be clearly marked with temporary signs, and that we will be using plywood boards to help ensure that wheelchairs can exit the cars with ease and without getting tar on the wheels. UNAUTHORIZED PARKING IN A HANDICAPPED SPACE WILL BE DEALT WITH SWIFTLY and without sympathy.

If you are unable to park in the lot and have groceries or packages to unload, you may unload them at the main entrance by parking there for a few moments. We will have someone standing by to assist. When the main entrance area is being repaved, please use the loading dock in the rear of the building. At that time we will have two people on duty (until 11 P.M. each night). One will take your packages to the front desk for you.

We have arranged with the Doe Grocery Chain to permit you to park overnight in their lot across the street. There is ample room in their lot for almost all the cars that normally park at XYZ. And for once an XYZ sticker on your car's rear bumper will mean you can park overnight in their lot! During this period we have arranged for extra security to patrol the Doe store lot in order to help assure the safety of your vehicle.

As you know, there is a shortcut between the Doe lot and the entrance to XYZ. There is also a long way. (See the map on the back of this notice.) We urge you as strongly as possible, DO NOT TAKE THE SHORTCUT. It is not well illuminated and therefore constitutes a security risk. Take the route marked.

If for some reason you should get splatter on your car, remove it with a commercial road tar remover, which you can buy at any hardware store. Our contractor recommends either TARGO or TARBEGONE, but others are available. In all cases follow the manufacturer's instructions. DO NOT remove particularly troublesome spots with a sharp object. You will only scratch your paint. Use an automotive paste wax and some elbow grease.

Watch your kids, please. Do not let them play near the equipment while construction is ongoing or at night, when the equipment is parked. There is always a risk of injury. And be sure to tell them about watching where they walk, too.

We will be having a meeting to discuss this issue on Tuesday, September 7, at 8 P.M. in the party room. Please bring your questions. If you cannot make it to the meeting, call me (555-1212) or Mary Smith (555-2121).

Notice 2.2

Role of the Consultant

When any type of significant repair is involved, reliance on a qualified paving consultant is a wise idea. Who is a paving consultant? Some asphalt contractors employ individuals they call consultants but, for the most part, their primary job is selling and recommending which of their employer's products and services are the best. In fact, some are employed on a commissionable basis, creating a built-in incentive for the "consultant" to recommend the most expensive method. This definitely does not mean that a consultant or sales person employed by a contractor is not to be trusted. Some are extremely knowledgeable and pursue their work with complete integrity, whether or not a commission is involved. Nonetheless, none is a consultant in the true sense of the word because, in fact, they are not working for you. Particularly when major work may be needed, a property manager should rely on an individual who is independent, experienced, and regarded by others as competent and trustworthy.

The role of an effective consultant can vary, from performing an inspection or training others to do so, through specification of mix design and observation of construction. You need someone you can trust to "tell it like it is," to help ensure the wisest possible expenditure of funds.

The search for a top-quality consultant begins by assembling names of prospective consultants. Include those whom you have heard about (but have not dealt with); those who are listed in the directories of groups such as the Property Management Association (PMA); and those who have been retained by or are known to fellow property managers. Also consider contacting ASFE/The Association of Engineering Firms Practicing in the Geosciences for recommendations. ASFE members include consulting geotechnical engineering firms throughout the United States. The vast majority of these firms can provide extensive asphalt paving consultive services, such as review, testing, and evaluation of existing pavements, design and specification of remedial measures, and monitoring performance of these measures.

Specific techniques for identifying consultants and working with them are covered in Chapter 12.

Work Specification

Many property managers rely on a consultant to develop an effective work specification for them. The work specification can take one of two forms: performance or prescriptive. A performance specification identifies the work in terms of what is wanted as the final result. To a very real extent, it is up to the contractors to determine how they will achieve the final result. This approach is not recommended, because it vests too much control with the contractor. Even if the work is guaranteed, a great deal of time, effort, and frustration is involved when it has to be redone.

A design professional, such as a professional engineer, may be in the best position to create a prescriptive work specification that identifies all steps associated with achieving the end product sought. This helps ensure that each contractor is bidding on exactly the same scope of work, because nothing is left to assumption. The work specification should detail the following items, among others.

1. *Area.*   The exact area should be identified on a site layout. If necessary, the area should be surveyed to ensure that there are no discrepancies.

2. *Time.*   The time of repair is an important concern. In some cases it may be necessary to perform the work at night or on weekends to minimize traffic problems.

3. *Barricades.*   The type of barricades to be used and their location can be specified on a layout. If flagholders are needed, they can be specified as well.

4. *Repair techniques.*   The method to be used to remove the existing asphalt, the depth of cuts, and the specific nature of the replacement materials all can be specified with precision, along with the compaction requirements. All appropriate standards should be referenced. The predominant standard setters are the American Association of State Highway and Transportation Officials (AASHTO) and the American Society for Testing and Materials (ASTM).

5. *Materials verification.*   Indicate which tests are to be performed to assure that the mixtures specified are those that the contractor uses. Note that contractors generally cannot be 100 percent certain that what they specify from the asphalt supplier will be received.

6. *Performance verification.*   Identify tests to assure that compaction has been performed properly.

7. *Curing.*   The time required for an asphalt product to cure, or the conditions that must be achieved to indicate a cure, can be indicated specifically.

8. *Striping.*   If the contractor is to provide new striping, this, too, can be specified. When a complete resurfacing is involved, a new parking layout might be considered.

9. *Cleanup.*   The disposal of debris and other cleanup activities should be specified.

Although the foregoing list is not all-inclusive, it is instructive in several ways. First, it indicates that a great number of factors are involved. All should be thought through thoroughly by the property manager, preferably in consultation with a professional. By considering all the details beforehand, that much less is left to chance, and the more likely it is that all bids received will be for exactly the same work.

Second, there is a great deal to consider. By leaving nothing to chance, the likelihood of receiving exactly what you want is greatly enhanced. As the review of typical asphalt pavement problems should indicate, a great many stem from improper workmanship, improper materials, and similar causes.

Third, specifications presuppose that what is anticipated beneath the surface will actually exist there. Sometimes it works out that way and sometimes it doesn't. Because the latter outcome always is a possibility, the value of effective professional monitoring is underscored. Whoever is monitoring the work must be knowledgeable, or at least knowledgeable enough to spot an irregularity and call for guidance from an appropriate individual. By having monitoring performed by a consultant, unanticipated problems can be handled "on the spot." Contractors can be asked to bid eventualities, too, such as installing new drainage.

Sources of Additional Information

A variety of organizations can provide more information about asphalt paving and its maintenance and repair. Key among these is The Asphalt Institute, which has developed a number of publications ranging from do-it-yourself guides to exhaustive technical treatises. The Institute is headquartered at The Asphalt Institute Building, College Park, Md. 20740. It has engineering offices throughout the United States.

For in-depth information about the various standards that apply to asphalt, organizations that can be contacted in addition to The Asphalt Institute include the American Association of State Highway and Transportation Officials (AASHTO, 444 North Capitol Street, N.W., Suite 225, Washington, D.C. 20001) and the American Society for Testing and Materials (ASTM, 1916 Race Street, Philadelphia, Pa. 19103).

For referrals to consulting geotechnical engineering firms that specialize in asphalt evaluation, design, and specification, contact ASFE/The Association of Engineering Firms Practicing in the Geosciences (ASFE, 8811 Colesville Road, Suite G106, Silver Spring, Md. 20910).

Referrals to asphalt paving contractors can be obtained from the National Asphalt Pavement Association (NAPA, 5100 Forbes Boulevard, Lanham, Md. 20706).

3

Roofing

Introduction

Roofing is one of the most complex issues that a property manager encounters. Many types of roofs exist, and each type comprises a number
of variants. Property managers are not expected to know the infinite
details of roofing inspection, maintenance, repair, and replacement.
They are not, nor can they be expected to act as roofing consultants or
contractors. However, property managers are expected to know exactly how to deal with roofing: how to obtain, monitor, and evaluate
design, preventive maintenance, repair, and replacement services.

The importance of dealing properly with roofing concerns cannot be
overemphasized. The roof is one of the most expensive components of a
building; it is subject to more abuse from weather conditions and temperature extremes than any other part. Furthermore, even minor roofing problems can become major ones very quickly, resulting in far
more serious difficulties: disruption of tenant activities; damage of
tenant facilities, equipment, and furnishings; loss of roof insulative
value and resulting energy waste and occupant discomfort; and, of
course, roofing repairs that will become far more expensive than they
otherwise would have to be.

This chapter provides general guidance, thus enabling the property
manager to take proper action in maintaining the building owner's investment. It is far from a be-all and end-all. Additional reference
sources are given.

Covering Selection

When the time comes to replace a roof covering, the obvious question
is, "What type of roof covering should I use?" This is not a simple question. Roofing technology is advancing at such a rate that staying
abreast of the latest developments is almost a full-time job.

A property manager's best sources of information are independent roofing engineers/consultants or reputable roofing contractors. They are constantly exposed to the most current technology and can provide knowledgeable recommendations for roof replacement systems and workable alternatives.

Selection factors

In deciding which roof covering is best suited for a particular project, the following factors, among others, should be considered.

1. Building age, use, construction, and condition
2. Existing roof slope, deck condition, and drainage patterns
3. Climate; special wind, rain, or snow conditions; and any nearby contaminant sources (such as factories, airports, or refineries) whose output might affect the roof membrane
4. Amount of equipment or mechanical units on the roof and any special roof use (such as sun deck)
5. Building energy use requirements affecting the amount or type of insulation that may be used

Sloped roofs. A few roof coverings are used exclusively for highly sloped roofs (those having a pitch of at least 2 or 3 inches per foot). These include asphalt or wood shingles, slate, wood shakes, and clay tile. Each of these has advantages and disadvantages; some require special structural support systems. Even though they may be fairly common materials, final selection should be made only by knowledgeable, experienced personnel.

Roof coverings such as metal, single-ply sheet, and built-up systems can be applied for a wide range of roof slopes, from less than 1 to well over 4 inches per foot. The characteristics and requirements of each type and manufacturer vary so greatly that advice is needed from a qualified contractor or engineer/consultant.

Flat roofs. Replacing a flat roof is the most common roofing problem a property manager must confront. Various built-up or single-ply membranes ordinarily are used.

Built-up membranes. A built-up membrane is a continuous, semi-flexible material that consists of two or more alternate plies of felt (normally fiberglass), fabric, or mat. These are assembled in place and adhered to each other with layers of bituminous products (asphalt or coal-tar pitch), then covered with a heavy layer of bitumen (asphalt or pitch) into which aggregate surfacing is embedded. Alternately, the membrane may be coated or covered with other materials, or it may be left exposed to the elements. The coating, covering, or surfacing is placed to protect the membrane. It is not a waterproofing component.

Single-ply membranes. Today's single-ply membranes can be grouped into three classifications, based upon their basic composition.

1. *Elastomeric* membranes are commonly referred to as "rubber" systems. EPDM (ethylene, propylene, diene monomer) is the most popular material. Others are neoprene, CSPE (chlorosulfonated polyethylene, often called Hypalon), PIB (polyisobutylene), and NBP (nitrile butadiene). Each has unique characteristics.

2. *Thermoplastic* membranes are typified by PVC (polyvinyl chloride), which is the most widely used. Others are available. Almost all can be manufactured using several different processes, and some are reinforced with glass fibers or polyester fabric. Each manufacturer's membrane has its own peculiar properties and characteristics.

3. Membranes of *modified bitumens* comprise composite sheets of bitumen, modifiers, and reinforcement. The polymer modifiers generally used are styrene butadiene and atactic polypropylene. The reinforcing materials used usually are plastic film, polyester mat, glass fibers, felt, or fabric. These may be embedded within or laminated to the surface of the membrane.

System selection

The proper selection of a roof system can be a complicated process. The following factors need to be considered.

1. Tensile strength and elasticity of the membrane
2. Water absorption and vapor transmission rate of the membrane
3. Strength properties of membrane seams and flashings
4. Membrane resistance to temperature extremes, exposure to sunlight, and aging
5. Compatibility with commonly used or in-place materials (Note that some membranes are not compatible with roof cement or other frequently used roof repair materials.)
6. The manufacturer's reputation, warranty/guarantee provisions, and reliability in providing competent (and swift) leak repairs during the term of the warranty/guarantee (normally 10 or more years)

Design considerations

To complicate matters further, the roof system (including insulation, surfacing, and other elements) must be designed carefully with respect to several important factors.

1. The completed roof system must be rated properly to meet insurance and building-code requirements for resistance to fire and wind uplift (blow-off).

2. The roof system must drain water properly. Lack of proper drainage is one of the leading causes of premature roof failure. Roof drainage can be improved by various means, such as using tapered (sloped) insulation under the membrane, correcting roof deck defects, and adding drains and other water conductors (such as gutters).

3. The weakest parts of a roof system are the flashings, such as metal counterflashings, copings, and pitch pockets. They must be detailed and designed properly to prevent leakage and promote ease of maintenance. Be cautious about reusing old metal flashings, installing pitch pockets, or supporting mechanical units on the membrane instead of the roof deck. Such procedures can cause problems by increasing roof leakage and maintenance needs.

4. The installation and the membrane must be dimensionally stable and able to resist normal loads such as wind and foot traffic. The insulation used (if any) must be compatible with the membrane. (Some are not.) Improper selection of the type or amount of insulation can lead to rapid deterioration of the roof system.

The typical types of roof insulation used today are listed below. Each has its own properties, characteristics, and insulating values, which must be considered carefully.

1. *Expanded polystyrene (EPS)* board is formed from a plastic (polystyrene) polymer, which is supplied by several companies to regional converters. The material is molded into blocks, processed into sheets, and, in some cases, applied as facer material. EPS is flammable; it is incompatible with products such as coal-tar pitch. EPS will deteriorate if exposed to sunlight for extended periods.

2. *Extruded polystyrene* board is formed from a polystyrene polymer. Closed cells are integrally formed within the insulation materials during the expansion process. The continuous extrusion produces a tight and complete skin (free of open cells) which forms on each side of the insulation board. Boards are expanded to a specific thickness during the manufacturing process.

3. *Glass-fiber* roof board insulation is a rigid insulating material composed of fine glass fibers. The glass-fiber-reinforced asphalt and kraft paper top surface of the insulation boards provides a tough, impact-resistant mopping surface upon which the membrane may be applied. Glass-fiber roof insulation vents moisture vapor through the insulation boards. In the event of damage to the membrane, moisture vapor can be vented and free water can drain out of the roof system. Once the roof insulation has dried, the original thermal value is restored.

4. *Cellular glass* roof insulation is a rigid insulating material composed of heat-fused, closed-glass cells. It is available in standard insulation board of block form, and in special tapered blocks that help provide drainage.

5. *Phenolic foam* insulation board is a closed-cell, rigid thermosetting phenolic foam core material manufactured in various thicknesses. Currently the most popular product is a phenolic foam core of approximately 3.0 pounds per cubic foot density, which is laminated to a corrugated kraft foil laminate on the top surface and a felt bottom surface.

6. *Fiberboard* insulation is a preformed rigid fibrous-felted, homogeneous panel, composed principally of wood or cane fibers treated with waterproofing binders.

7. *Perlite* roof board insulation is a rigid insulating material manufactured from expanded volcanic materials combined with organic fibers and waterproofing binders. The top surface of perlite roof insulation is generally treated to minimize absorption and to provide an intimate bond with roofing materials.

8. *Polyurethane* foam board insulation is produced from a urethane chemical base and is manufactured in the form of rigid boards. The polyurethane material is often sandwiched between asphalt-saturated organic or inorganic felt facer sheets.

9. *Polyisocyanurate* foam board insulation is produced from a polyisocyanurate-based chemical. The polyisocyanurate material is usually sandwiched between asphalt-saturated organic or inorganic felt facer sheets. Glass-fiber reinforcement used in some foam cores provides additional fire resistance and greater dimensional stability.

While this information may be useful, it is far from a complete course on roof selection and design. When the time comes that you must face roof replacement, obtain expert help.

Inspections and Related Concerns

Property managers customarily retain and update an historical maintenance record of each building they manage. This record is essential to the owner for a variety of reasons, not the least of which are those associated with the potential sale of a building.

Roofing always is a subject of major concern, and this merits special consideration in historical maintenance records. Information that should be kept on file includes the following items.

1. An as-built drawing of the roof, updated to indicate present status, including rooftop equipment.

2. A layout of the roof used for inspection purposes. Typically, areas of the roof are sectioned off and lettered, so that inspection reports can be correlated with lettered areas, such as "Loose tiles found in area A, April 1, 1991." (See Fig. 3.1.)

3. Inspection reports and details of corrective actions taken (nature of actions, when taken, by whom, etc.). (See Fig. 3.2.)

4. Guarantees, warranties, bonds, and so on.

In-house personnel often perform routine roof inspection and maintenance and make minor repairs. This approach has led to some serious problems.

In-house personnel should be relied upon to perform routine inspections and maintenance only if they have been fully trained to do so. Minor roofing problems that go unnoticed, or that are handled improperly, can soon grow to major proportions, particularly when a small irregularity is actually a surface symptom of a serious breakdown below the surface. Misinterpreting these surface symptoms can permit serious conditions to become even more serious, especially so when the

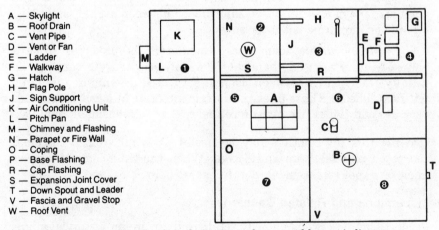

A — Skylight
B — Roof Drain
C — Vent Pipe
D — Vent or Fan
E — Ladder
F — Walkway
G — Hatch
H — Flag Pole
J — Sign Support
K — Air Conditioning Unit
L — Pitch Pan
M — Chimney and Flashing
N — Parapet or Fire Wall
O — Coping
P — Base Flashing
R — Cap Flashing
S — Expansion Joint Cover
T — Down Spout and Leader
V — Fascia and Gravel Stop
W — Roof Vent

Figure 3.1 Rooftop layout. Numbers designate roof areas and letters indicate specific roof features listed in key.

SEMI-ANNUAL MAINTENANCE INSPECTION CHECK LIST

Building _____ Date _____

Location _____ Inspected by _____

		Problem			Repairs			
	OK	Minor	Major	Comment	Performed By	Date	Inspected By	Date
I. SUPPORTING STRUCTURE								
A. **Exterior and Interior Walls**								
Moisture Stains								
Expansion/Contraction								
Settlement Cracks								
Deterioration								
Physical Damage								
Other								
B. **Exterior and Interior Roof Deck**								
Water Stains								
Attachment of Felts/Insulation								
Securement to Supports								
Expansion/Contraction								
Structural Deterioration								
Physical Damage								
New Equipment/Alterations								
Other								
II. ROOF CONDITION								
A. **General Appearance**								
General Condition								
Debris								
Drainage								
Physical Damage								
New Equipment/Alterations								
Other								
B. **Surface**								
Alligatoring/Cracking								
Bare Spots in Gravel								
Slippage								
Other								
C. **Membrane**								
Ridging								
Blistering								
Fishmouthing								
Splitting								
Loose Felt								
Punctures								
Fasteners								
Securement to Substrate								
Slippage								
Other								

Figure 3.2 Typical roof inspection form for built-up flat roof.

"early warning" value of these "minor problems" is concealed through in-house repair. In other words, an unnecessary risk is created by relying on persons who are not thoroughly equipped to do what is being asked of them. Given the potentially high cost of improper action, it is worthwhile to spend the additional sums required to help ensure the longest possible roof life with a minimal amount of difficulties.

As a general rule, in-house personnel should be used to supplement professional inspections only if they are fully trained to do so. Their

		Problem			Repairs			
	OK	Minor	Major	Comment	Performed By	Date	Inspected By	Date
III. FLASHING CONDITION								
A. Base Flashing								
Ridging or Wrinkling								
Blistering								
Open Laps								
Punctures								
Deterioration								
Attachment								
Other								
B. Counter Flashing								
Caulking								
Open Laps								
Punctures								
Fasteners								
Rusting								
Attachment								
Other								
C. Coping								
Caulking								
Punctures								
Open Fractures								
Fasteners								
Rusting								
Attachment								
Drainage								
Other								
D. Wall								
Movement Cracks								
Spalling								
Mortar Joints								
Other								
IV. ROOF EDGING/FASCIA								
Splitting								
Felt Deterioration								
Punctures								
Rusting								
Fasteners								
Securement								
Other								
V. EXPANSION JOINT COVERS								
Punctures/Splits								
Open Joints								
Rusting								
Fasteners								
Securement								
Other								
VI. ROOF PENETRATIONS								
A. Equipment Base Flashing								
Open Laps								
Punctures								
Attachment								
Other								

Figure 3.2 (*Continued*) Typical roof inspection form for built-up flat roof.

repair work usually should be limited to emergency repairs of a temporary nature, unless they have appropriate guidance. What is "appropriate guidance?" Consider the following list, which describes the contents of a roofing manual that can be prepared for in-house use.

1. It describes the existing roofing system and how it works, supplementing the narrative description with an as-built drawing.

	OK	Problem			Repairs			
		Minor	Major	Comment	Performed By	Date	Inspected By	Date
B. Equipment Housing								
Caulking								
Counter Flashing								
Open Seams								
Drainage								
Physical Damage								
Other								
C. Equipment Operation								
Excessive Traffic Wear								
Discharge of Contaminants								
Other								
D. Roof Jacks/Vents								
Vents Operable								
Physical Damage								
Attachment								
Other								
VII. PITCH PANS								
Fill Material Shrinkage								
Attachment								
Other								

Figure 3.2   (*Continued*) Typical roof inspection form for built-up flat roof.

2. Using lay language, it describes exactly what existing guarantees and warranties do and do not cover, how to obtain assistance, and how to protect your rights and coverage.

3. It develops a detailed inspection checklist for the specific roof involved.

4. It identifies the tools and roof-compatible materials and other supplies needed for routine roofing maintenance, also identifying sources for them.

5. It details the procedures associated with preventive maintenance of flashing, caulking, painting, and other components; quick-fix repairs, and more permanent repairs.

Such manuals use photographs to illustrate key points, and training programs customarily are developed to introduce in-house personnel to the guidance literature.

A roof should be subject to a comprehensive formal inspection at least once each year, usually in the spring. However, most experts stress the need for two formal inspections per year: one in the fall (before winter) and one in the spring (after winter). Winter weather conditions usually impose the most severe stress on a roof.

Formal inspections should be made in conjunction with a checklist prepared specifically for a given roof. A typical checklist for a built-up flat roof is shown in Fig. 3.2, for use in conjunction with a rooftop diagram or layout such as the one shown in Fig. 3.1. (Note that the checklist and the rooftop diagram are for illustrative purposes only.

They should not be used for any other purpose. Each roof requires a unique checklist and diagram.)

Warranties and Guarantees

For many years it was common practice for manufacturers to bond roofs installed by a manufacturer-approved contractor using manufacturer-approved design, materials, and procedures. The bond was backed by a surety who would assume the manufacturer's liability in the event of roof failure. Bonds were relatively limited, however, and typically would be nullified if water was permitted to pond, if repair work was performed without the manufacturer's supervision or approval, or if the roof was damaged by a natural disaster (windstorm, hurricane, tornado, hail, lightning, or earthquake). Bonds also tended to be somewhat expensive, and the maximum financial recovery they afforded usually represented but a fraction of the actual repair costs.

Guarantees and warranties backed by the manufacturer rather than a surety have for the most part replaced the bonds. Although their coverage periods are shorter (typically 5 to 10 years, rather than the 20-year maxima offered by some bonds), their liability limits generally are far higher (in some cases they are unlimited). This gives an owner far better protection, particularly because most problems show up within the first 5 years.

The guarantees of single-ply manufacturers are generally about the same as those offered by manufacturers of conventional built-up roof materials. Both exclude damage caused by natural disasters, vandalism, abuse, negligent maintenance, and, in some cases, repairs not performed by authorized manufacturer representatives. They also exclude coverage of consequential damages (damage to building contents, business interruptions, etc.). In addition, most guarantees do not cover membrane damage caused by ponded water. There are some exceptions to this industry standard, however; for the most part these occur in some single-ply manufacturers' guarantees.

The major differences between guarantees tend to center on their cost and duration. Some provide protection without cost for the first 5 years and then are renewable on a premium basis. Some offer unlimited liability for the first 5 years and limited liability thereafter. In some instances 20-year guarantees are available from manufacturers, but only for special systems and, understandably, at a somewhat higher price. In all cases, manufacturers' guarantees should be read very cautiously, especially so because a salesperson's claims may not always agree with the "fine print" of what you are being offered in writing.

Note that a roofing contractor also provides a guarantee in most cases. This guarantee typically supplants the manufacturer's for the first 1 or 2 years. Thus when a 2-year contractor's guarantee is involved, the manufacturer will inspect the roof after 18 months and require the contractor to repair any defects before the manufacturer assumes responsibility. (This does not relieve the manufacturer of its liability to the owner. If the contractor does not perform, the manufacturer must.)

A typical roofing contractor's guarantee covers defects in materials or workmanship, and excludes damages caused by natural disaster, foundation settlement, roof deck cracking or failure, vapor condensation beneath the membrane, faulty construction of related elements such as parapets, copings, and chimney, and clogged drains. It also excludes consequential damages. In many cases roofing contractors will be willing to expand the items covered by their guarantee and to extend its duration.

In all cases it is important to require the manufacturer and the installer to specify exactly who is responsible for what, and the procedures used and criteria applied to determine whether or not a warranty or guarantee covers a given problem. Also, determine how things are prorated, if they are. For example, if a guarantee-covered problem occurs in the fifth year of a 10-year guarantee, does it mean that 50% of the total cost will be borne by the manufacturer? 50% of the material cost alone?

If you have a consultant preparing a bid specification for you, you can write your own warranty or guarantee in plain English, and bidders would be responsible for meeting its terms and conditions. While some contractors may accept such language, manufacturers may not. Note also that manufacturers may decline to warrant their systems or materials unless they review and approve the roofing design. A typical guarantee is shown in Fig. 3.3.

Roofing Consultants

Roofing consulting is highly risk-prone work. Property managers generally advise that one should deal only with an individual or firm that has a proven track record, and who is independent. Independence is the key, since a property manager cannot rely on biased recommendations, that is, recommendations that are skewed toward a particular type of system or brand of product, because the "consultant" is somehow beholden. In other words, manufacturers' representatives and contractors' employees are not generally in a position to provide effective consultation. Those with limited experience may be essentially in the same boat. As such, property managers need to consult experienced individuals who are knowledgeable about virtually all types of roofs and who are thus in the best position to make solid recommendations.

The ABC Company warrants that ABC Roofing Systems, when installed by a roofing contractor approved by ABC, will be free of defects in materials and workmanship and will provide satisfactory service life without need of maintenance or repair for a period of _____ years from the date installation is completed. Should the roofing system require repair within this warranty, ABC will make the necessary repairs at no charge.

This warranty covers only the roofing system as defined in ABC's product literature. It does not cover other materials or preparatory or finishing labor which entails the use of such materials. It does not cover structural damage on the roofing system physically inflicted by accidents, man or man-made causes, acts of God, acts of nature and the like, or wear through misue or abuse.

This express warranty is in lieu of all other warranties. ABC's responsibility shall not extend beyond the warranty period. ABC shall not be liable for damages of any nature for failure of the roofing system and in no event shall ABC's liability under this warranty or otherwise exceed the initial cost of installing the ABC Roofing System. The owner's sole and exclusive right and remedy and ABC's sole obligation for any failure of the roofing system shall be as provided under this warranty.

This warranty will extend to the owner identified below for the building specified upon the owner's acceptance of its terms. It shall not be assignable but shall reissue to subsequent owners during the warranty period upon their acceptance of its terms by written signature on a duplicate form and its submittal to ABC.

Claims under this warranty should be directed to:

The ABC Company
Roofing Systems
Anywhere, U.S.A. 12345

Building Owner

Address of Building

Date Installation Complete   **Date Final Inspection and Approved**

AGREED   **THE ABC Company**

BY _____   By _____
    Building Owner

Figure 3.3   Typical roofing warranty.

For the most part, one usually is best served by relying on a professional engineer or architect, as opposed to an unregistered roofing consultant, especially when plans and specifications must be prepared or when expert witness services are required. More details about selecting and dealing with consultants are given in Chapter 12.

References

The publications identified here have been particularly helpful to a number of property managers. Others are available and should be consulted.

Architectural Sheet Metal Manual, Sheet Metal and Air Conditioning Contractors National Assoc. (SMACNA), Vienna, Va. 22180.

Copper and Common Sense, 7th ed., Revere Copper Products, Inc., Rome, N.Y. 13440.

Handbook of Accepted Roofing Knowledge, National Roofing Contractors Assoc., Chicago, Ill. 60631.

Manual of Built-Up Roof Systems, McGraw-Hill, New York, 10020.

Manual of Roof Maintenance and Roof Repair, National Roofing Contractors Assoc., Chicago, Ill. 60631.

The NRCA Roofing and Waterproofing Manual, National Roofing Contractors Assoc., Chicago, Ill. 60631.

The 1982 NRCA Rooftop Equipment Program, National Roofing Contractors Assoc., Chicago, Ill. 60631.

Roofing: Estimating, Applying, Repairing, Shelter Publications, Chicago, Ill. 60624.

Roofing Materials Guide, National Roofing Contractors Assoc., Chicago, Ill. 60631.

Slate Roofs, Vermont Structural Slate Co., Fair Haven, Vt. 05743.

Painting

Introduction

Painting is far from simple, and those who approach the subject simplistically are likely to suffer dire consequences. As an example, one of the trickiest aspects of painting is identifying the exact nature of whatever type of paint now exists. If the new paint is not compatible, intercoat adhesion problems will occur. The likely consequence: the new coat of paint will soon begin to peel. In some cases it is necessary to perform laboratory tests to determine the nature of the existing paint and, at times, even laboratory tests will not yield the necessary information. It takes knowledge and experience to identify the best means for analyzing the existing paint, and to determine which coatings will and will not be compatible. Unless in-house personnel truly are expert in this area, some type of competent, reliable, trustworthy outside assistance should be obtained.

In obtaining outside assistance, or in the development of a work plan of any type, it is essential to determine the owner's goals at the outset. Two alternatives, or combinations of the two, may be involved. The first is to minimize initial costs, that is, to get the work performed as inexpensively as possible. The second is to minimize long-term or life-cycle costs. Generally speaking, the former emphasizes cost while the latter emphasizes quality.

Most of today's owners emphasize a quality-oriented approach, realizing that cheap work generally is the most expensive over even a relatively short period of time, such as 3 to 5 years. In this regard, the cost impact of labor versus materials should be recognized.

In fact, labor can comprise as much as 75 percent (or more) of the total contract price. As such, it will in many cases be worthwhile to specify the best products, because the relatively small premium paid can greatly enhance the longevity of the work involved. However,

even the best materials cannot make up for incompetent work specification or execution. As such, especially when relatively large-scale,
complex, or somewhat dangerous work is involved, only those with
successful experience and a reputation for good work should be retained to do it. While naturally no one wants to spend more than is
reasonably necessary to get the work done, undue emphasis on minimizing initial costs can result in far greater cost later on.

Indoor Painting

Indoor painting can be discussed in terms of general concerns, and
those related to specific areas or types of areas, as indicated below.

General concerns

Some of the general indoor painting concerns include the following.

1. *Cost savings.*   Most painting contractors will charge less to perform indoor painting during the winter months, at least in those areas
that experience winter.

2. *Ventilation.*   Particularly when stairwell and hallway painting
is involved, adequate ventilation is extremely important. However,
adequate ventilation is always important, no matter where painting is
going on indoors. All necessary precautions should be taken, both by
the building owner or manager, and by the painting contractor or in-
house personnel. If ventilation requirements are not spelled out in the
specifications, they should be requested and detailed by the contractor.

3. *Reflectivity.*   Particularly in office areas, a good coat of high-
reflectivity paint can be an extraordinarily effective energy saver, because it can significantly reduce the amount of electric illumination
otherwise necessary to attain a given lighting level. It can also contribute to certain problems, such as glare on video display terminal
(VDT) screens. The paint's impact on lighting should be discussed
with a lighting consultant. Lighting consultants can be located
through a local section of the Illuminating Engineering Society of
North America (IES/NA), headquartered in New York City. Many
electrical contractors can provide pertinent information, too, as can
many electrical distributors and lighting manufacturers' representatives. Also contact the local electric utility.

4. *Application method.*   Primer and paint can be applied with a
brush, roller, or spray. The nature of the surface and the paint must

be considered thoroughly to determine which method is best for a given area. Generally speaking, the glossier a surface is, the more likely it is to show substratum defects. This problem is offset principally through spray application.

5. *Asbestos ceiling.* It may be discovered that a certain space or room is fitted with an asbestos ceiling. Be aware that *asbestos is a carcinogen and must be treated with utmost care.* Guidance should be sought from appropriate consultants and public agencies. *Under no circumstances should an asbestos ceiling be painted* without first consulting proper governmental authorities.

Stairwells and hallways

Tenant preparation is a key concern whenever indoor painting is involved, but especially so when it comes to residential building stairwells and hallways. Although the paints commonly used do not give off seriously toxic fumes, they do give off odors.

Older people in particular find these objectionable, and physical problems can be inflicted on anyone with a severe allergic condition or who is pregnant.

One way to solve the odor problem is to use a low-odor paint, such as latex. Latex paints are far less durable than the alkyds usually employed, however, which will result in more painting (and greater expense) in the long term.

Assuming that an alkyd or other odorous paint is selected, *it is essential to provide ample warning to all residents who may be affected.* Note that more than those close to the area being painted may be affected, because of natural and forced (ventilation) convective currents in the building. A warning could be in the form of a sign in the lobby, hallway, stairwell, or elevator. It could also take the form of a notice put into message boxes or slipped under doors. For purposes of liability loss prevention, it generally is best *to post notices conspicuously in several areas, and to issue notices to all affected tenants.* Notice 4.1 gives a possible wording.

Obviously, such a warning should be posted one to two weeks before the painting occurs, to help ensure that residents have sufficient time to make alternative arrangements.

In all cases it should be possible to minimize the spread of odors and fumes through the use of large portable air movers. The painters should understand how convection currents in the building move to help ensure that air movers are properly located and directed. If the building has a smoke control system (a ventilation control system that can pressurize all areas except those where painting is occurring), it

---

WARNING

All hallways and stairwells are being painted over the July 4 weekend. Odors may be offensive to some, and fumes could be harmful to those who suffer from severe allergies or are pregnant. We will do our very best to minimize odors and fumes. However, if you believe the odors or fumes may be harmful to you, please stay out of your unit from 6 P.M. on July 3 to 12 noon on July 5. We regret any inconvenience and look forward to your cooperation.

Notice 4.1

can be used to supplement or perhaps even substitute for portable air movers.

In all cases, work specifications should indicate specifically how paint odor and fume control will be effected in terms of the equipment to be used, how it will be used, and who will supply it.

Work scheduling also is an important concern for fume and odor control as well as for other purposes. In the sample warning, for example, it is indicated that painting will occur over a holiday weekend. This type of approach is recommended particularly for office buildings or in those residential buildings where many residents typically go on trips during holiday periods. This reduces the number of people who are inconvenienced. It also means less traffic into and out of a building, thus creating less interference with the painters. Less traffic also occurs during evening hours.

In most cases, not all stairwells and hallways will be painted at the same time. Rather, the work will be staggered over a several-day period. For this reason it is important to know the typical traffic patterns in a building to help minimize inconvenience to both occupants and painters.

Stairwells. For stairwell ceilings and walls, a flat latex paint is usually applied if it is compatible with the existing paint. Some prefer to create a 4-foot (or so) dado (defined lower portion of a wall), using a better-quality alkyd semigloss washable paint (usually in a contrasting color) that can withstand the higher level of abuse the lower wall area suffers.

An alkyd gloss or semigloss usually is applied to risers, rails, and the carriage, when compatible with the existing paint. Treads and landings usually are treated in the same manner as boiler room floors (see below), and antiskid is often included in the paint.

A bright red paint is usually applied around fire extinguishers; standpipes and other piping are painted in accordance with a standard color code.

If the contractor will be required to perform stenciling to indicate floor numbers, the location of fire extinguishers or standpipes, exits, and so on, the specific wording and its location should be spelled out clearly in the work specifications.

Hallways. Hallways generally require a paint of better quality than that used in stairwells. An alkyd gloss or semigloss usually is applied. Note that a color change, even from white to off-white, will probably require a second coat.

Lobby

The approach to lobby painting is essentially similar to that used for hallways. The problem of odors and fumes generally is not as severe. Nonetheless, people should be warned about the painting, and steps should be taken to help prevent migration of the odors and fumes throughout the entire building.

Boiler room

Most boiler rooms have poured concrete walls and ceilings and slab floors. Many owners now are painting their boiler rooms as well as the pipes and equipment inside. The reasons include the following.

1. *Enhanced safety.*   The use of standard Occupational Safety and Health Administration (OSHA) safety colors as well as standard piping colors calls more attention to those items that can be hazardous. It can help prevent people from burning their hands on a hot-water pipe or cutting into a gas line. Note that pathways can be painted on the floor to indicate a safe passage around exposed moving equipment. Different parts of the moving equipment also can be painted, so the motion is more obvious. Color-coding information can be obtained from paint manufacturers, painting contractors, coating consultants, and OSHA. Some manufacturers produce a line of paints pigmented specifically to meet OSHA requirements.

2. *Prolonged equipment life.*   A good coat of paint prevents or at least inhibits corrosion and rust. The savings involved can more than pay back the cost of painting.

3. *Better appearance and image.*   Particularly when a conversion is involved or when a building is being offered for sale, a well-painted boiler room conveys the impression that the owner, manager, and staff pay close attention to detail and sweep nothing under the rug. Likewise, in new buildings or those recently converted, this same type of impression can be conveyed to prospective unit purchasers. Some— perhaps many—will also like the "high tech" appearance of a painted boiler room.

4. *Prompter maintenance.*   Painted surfaces reveal drips and leaks far faster than unpainted ones. As such, problems can be detected far sooner, before they have a chance to grow into major, expensive difficulties.

5. *Improved employee morale.*   Very often a boiler room also serves as a building engineer's office. The better appearance of the room can boost engineers' morale, and help them feel better about themselves and their work. It can also result in extra efforts to maintain the good appearance of the space.

It must be understood that painting boiler rooms, piping, and equipment is almost an art form, requiring a high degree of knowledge. Simply "slapping on" some paint will result in a total waste of money, and will have the opposite of the effect desired when the paint starts to discolor and peel not too long after it is applied. If boiler room painting is to be done at all, it should be done right. Work with a qualified individual to determine how much it will cost and evaluate cost in light of the benefits to be obtained. Note that a shabby appearance could in part be due to inadequate lighting. Better illumination could possibly reduce the need for painting, but in any event should be installed (if needed) after painting is complete.

Unpainted ceilings and walls.   Surface preparation of concrete or masonry walls is an important concern. Most unpainted ceilings and walls will be covered with dirt, grease, grime, and efflorescence (calcium carbonate leaching to the surface). For the paint to last, walls should therefore be cleaned by high-pressure (greater than 2000 lb/in^2) water blasting.

Primer and paint selection should be made with extreme care, considering numerous factors. If the room is well-ventilated, has a low relative humidity, is not subject to temperature extremes, and is generally kept clean, an inexpensive flat latex paint applied without primer may be adequate for the ceiling and that portion of the walls subject to the least abuse (usually from the 5-foot level to the ceiling). Better, longer-lasting results will be obtained through application of a primer, typically a reduced (diluted) top coat, or through two coats of paint. It generally is recommended that an adhesion promoter be added (at a relatively low cost) to the paint or the primer to promote better bonding of the paint to the concrete surface.

The dado—the portion of the walls between the floor and the 4- or 5-foot mark—requires better paint to help offset the greater wear and tear it experiences. Recommended is a maintenance performance paint whose good cleaning properties resist moisture, scrubbing, and abrasion. Alkyd-base gloss, urethane, and epoxy paints are used for this purpose. Chlorinated rubber paint is also used when resistance to chemical spills is important.

Future recoatability should be considered when selecting the paint to be applied to a raw surface. As an example, only epoxy paint can be used to paint over an epoxy-painted surface. To use another type of paint, the existing epoxy surface would have to be removed.

Walls (and most other poured concrete surfaces) can be painted using a sprayer or a roller; brushes should be used for tight spaces. A roller is generally recommended for raw masonry surfaces.

Note: In some cases the moisture content of an interior concrete or masonry wall should be checked before paint is applied. New concrete walls should not be painted until they have been thoroughly cured. Both these issues are discussed in the section on outdoor painting.

Unpainted floor. If an owner is unwilling to spend the amount required for proper floor preparation, it is senseless to paint the floor at all. Proper preparation is critical. Water leaks and condensate will otherwise ruin appearances.

Preparation begins with high-pressure water-blast cleaning. The next step is acid etching, a process of applying a 10 percent muriatic acid solution with a mop. This cleans the floor, breaks the surface to permit better penetration of the paint, and reduces alkalinity of the concrete to permit better paint adhesion. Once acid etching is complete, the floor must be washed (or water-blasted) to neutralize the acid. Paint is then applied, and several basic alternatives are available.

The least expensive approach is to apply two coats of alkyd enamel paint formulated specifically for use on decks. The first coat is a primer, which consists of a reduced top coat. In areas where there are leaks, or which otherwise are subject to frequent wet conditions, an antiskid (such as sand) can be added to the top coat.

As so often is the case, the least expensive method is far from the best. The one most recommended involves the same process, but relies on a primer coat of reduced water-reducible epoxy and a top coat of the same paint full strength. This type of paint withstands normal wear and tear better and is more resistant to moisture, abrasion, and chemicals. Antiskid can also be added if needed.

Aliphatic urethane enamel is even more durable than water-reducible epoxy, but extraordinary care is required during application. The paint gives off highly toxic fumes; its low flash point creates an explosion hazard.

Previously painted concrete surfaces. Generally speaking, the procedure is to high-pressure water blast the surfaces involved and then apply a new surface of compatible paint. Speak with a knowledgeable source to determine your options among compatible paints.

Metal surfaces. When it comes to painting metal surfaces in a boiler room, the importance of relying on an experienced, knowledgeable, insured contractor cannot be overstressed, as the following discussion points out.

Surface preparation. Most metal surfaces will already be painted. If the paint is not "too far gone," the surface (other than pipes) can be cleaned by high-pressure water blasting, followed by handwork (sandpaper, wire brush, and so on). Pipes also should be water-blasted. Then, to obtain best results, they should be heated with a torch, wire-brushed (to remove the condensate), and primed while still warm. The pipe sweating, which results from heating, can create problems unless experienced workers are used.

Note that the use of a torch may require a permit. *All local codes and ordinances must be obeyed.* Torching obviously creates a safety hazard. Should an accident occur, its consequences will be magnified greatly if it is found that codes or ordinances have been disregarded.

If the existing paint is in particularly poor condition, it may be necessary to high-pressure water blast, then perform chemical cleaning and heat cleaning, followed by handwork and sandblasting (using sand, walnut shells, or other abrasives). Individual permits are likely to be needed for chemical cleaning, heat cleaning, and sandblasting. Sandblasting should be performed only if there is sufficient space.

To the extent possible, it is generally recommended to rely on something other than chemical cleaning. The chemicals must be neutralized before painting, and this usually is done with high-pressure water blasting, a process that causes metal surfaces to start rusting immediately.

Paint selection. Different paints are available for different types of metal surfaces; compatibility is important. Generally speaking, a primer and a top coat should be used. Typically, rust-inhibitive primer coats are selected. Note, however, that these are available in different grades, for different temperature extremes. *Be sure the primer selected is appropriate for both the types of metal and the temperature extremes involved.* It is usually acceptable to paint (top coat only) pipe insulation.

Garage

Garage ceilings and walls usually should be high-pressure water blasted before painting. An inexpensive latex paint often is sufficient.

A 4- to 5-foot dado may be desirable, using an alkyd gloss or semi-gloss.

The garage deck usually is not painted, but it may be appropriate to apply a sealer to help prevent cracking and damage from salt buildup. The deck should be sand- or water-blasted first, and cracks should be routed. Any exposed structural steel (reinforcing bars, I-beams, or expansion joints) should be wire-brushed or sandblasted clean. Then the deck can be acid-etched (if necessary), cracks should be filled with a high-performance urethane-based sealant, and exposed steel should be primed and painted with a rust-inhibitive paint. Specify traffic paint for parking space striping and stenciling. (Note that the location and wording of all stenciling, including that on deck, walls, and doors, should be identified completely in the work specification.) As the final step, the deck is coated with a sealer designed for the purpose. Note that all striping and stenciling should be completed before the sealer is applied.

Pipes in the garage can be handled much as those in a boiler room. Special types of paints are available for making subgrade garage walls more moisture-resistant. According to reputable contractors and engineering consultants, however, this provides a temporary "fix" at best and 90 percent of the time is near useless. If it is decided to use this approach, proper surface preparation is essential. A clean, solid surface is required, and handwork (using a wire brush) generally is the best way to obtain it.

Laundry room

The approach to laundry-room painting is essentially the same as that for boiler rooms, except that high-pressure water blasting usually is not required.

Individual units

Individual residential unit painting requirements often are met by "turnover specialists." More often than not these are "contractors" who operate inexpensively from the back of a pickup truck. Why would a property manager select such an individual over a more established painting contractor? Low price.

As a point of practical fact, property managers must recognize that there is a substantial risk in using "fly-by-night," often uninsured operators for turnover work. Selection is based almost exclusively on price; little if anything is done to investigate the character or reputation of the individuals involved. Commonly, the work is performed without a signed written contract.

Recent court decisions make it abundantly clear that judges and juries are imposing ever stricter standards on owners and property managers when it comes to resident/occupant safety and security. When an individual is injured, physically, emotionally, or monetarily, and the person who causes that suffering is unable to pay restitution, the goal of contemporary justice prompts a search for "deep pockets." If it can be shown that those with deep pockets somehow acted irresponsibly, as by not taking readily available prudent steps, chances are they will have their deep pockets picked. This makes it incumbent upon every property manager and owner to ask, "What if?" How do you think a jury would decide in a suit brought against you by a tenant who had been raped by someone you hired without a signed contract or any background checks? Are the savings associated with the use of turnover specialists retained in an unprofessional manner sufficient to justify the tremendous risk exposure that results? In the author's opinion: *No.*

It is recommended that turnover work be obtained strictly on a contract basis, through selection procedures similar to those used for any other type of painting contractor, as discussed below. In this case, however, an open-ended contract can be signed by each of several contractors. Such a contract would spell out unit rates only, and would not specify how many units, if any, will be painted over the contract's term (typically 1 year).

An open-ended contract can be bid on or negotiated, but can and should include in all cases each element of the sample specification presented later in this guide. It is only by approaching the matter of turnover work in such a responsible manner that an owner or property manager can have an adequate defense should something go wrong. And, of course, by acting in such a responsible manner, the likelihood of something going wrong is reduced significantly.

Work specification.   A typical work specification for turnover work can take many forms. It can be on a per-type-of-unit basis (efficiency, one-bedroom, one-bedroom-plus-den, two-bedroom, and so on), or it can be on a subunit basis, that is, cost per kitchen, den, bedroom, bathroom, and so on. In either case, prices should be obtained both for standard and for nonstandard extra work.

Typical *standard work* includes:

All walls and ceilings in all areas except kitchen, bathroom(s), and powder room(s): apply one coat of flat latex paint in the existing approved color.

All doors (except bifolds); door and window frames; baseboards, kitchen cabinets, walls, and ceilings; and bathroom and powder room walls and ceiling: apply one coat of alkyd semigloss paint in existing approved color.

Prices quoted assume that a reasonable amount of minor surface preparation is required.

Nonstandard work usually is performed as an extra, by the piece or on a time-and-materials (T&M) basis. Typical extras, and methods used to price them, include:

Remove wallpaper, contact paper, or mirrors: time and materials.

Paint bifold doors: time and materials, or per closet.

Caulk door frames, windows, baseboards, outlets, switches: time and materials.

Repair large holes in wall: time and materials.

Varnish kitchen cabinets or other surfaces: time and materials, or per cabinet or kitchen.

Apply second coat: time and materials, or by room.

Paint occupied unit: time and materials, or flat fee.

If you deal with a painting contractor who you feel is particularly trustworthy, you may prefer to simply have that contractor do whatever is required and send a bill. Generally speaking, however, even such a contractor will prefer to have the resident or building manager preview the unit to specify whatever extras may be required, and inspect it after work has been completed, to ensure that everything needed was well done.

Outdoor Painting

Why does a building's exterior require new paint? In some cases it's due to simple aging, brought about principally by ultraviolet (UV) radiation from the sun. However, in other cases the principal cause may be far different. Failure to identify the cause precisely can result in serious waste—an expensive paint job that all too quickly deteriorates.

Comprehensive inspection

Comprehensive inspection is essential before specifying outdoor painting and related requirements. Consider the following typical problems.

1. *Ultraviolet (UV) radiation.*   It causes paint to change its state, from a solid to a gas. This is normal aging. Nothing can be done to prevent the sun from shining, but special precautions can be taken on those portions of the building surface (south-facing) exposed to the most sunlight.

2. *Paint fatigue.*   This results from having so many layers of paint that differential expansion occurs between them and the sub-strata. To add yet another layer of paint to a surface already exhibiting signs of paint fatigue ("alligatoring" or cracking, for example) is foolish. The old paint should be removed before a new coat is applied.

3. *Expansion and contraction.*   These are normal reactions to changes in temperature extremes, as well as wetting and drying. Some types of wetting can be prevented.

4. *Moisture.*   Rain, like sun, cannot be prevented. However, caulking can be applied to prevent moisture from seeping in where it's not wanted. Gutters and downspouts can also be used for this purpose and should be kept in good condition and free from debris at all times. (Most painting contractors also offer a gutter-cleaning service. Some can repair gutters and downspouts as well.)

5. *Airborne chemicals.*   Airborne chemicals, caused by acid rain and other forms of air pollution, can be a problem. Little can be done to prevent airborne chemicals, but proper paint selection can help minimize the damage they do.

6. *Fungus.*   This usually is an indication of a moisture problem of some type.

7. *Poor paint selection.*   The last coat of paint applied may not have been proper for the surface involved, or for other concerns, such as maximum exposure to sunlight or type of metal. If a problem cannot be prevented (such as UV radiation), proper paint selection and other steps can help ensure that the problem's impact is minimized.

8. *Poor workmanship.*   Failure to apply paint well, failure to install the proper type of caulk in a correct manner, and similar problems all can lead to premature paint failure. It is essential to select a painting contractor with care. There is far more to good painting than applying a coat of paint!

A thorough inspection also includes the roof, guttering, and down-spouts. Adequate control of run-off water is absolutely essential to help minimize its impact on a painted surface among other damage it can cause.

Environmental considerations

Most manufacturers specify the temperature and humidity restrictions associated with the use of their products. For the most part, the range is 45 to 100°F at 0 to 85 percent relative humidity. However, in Washington, D.C., for example, strictly adhering to manufacturers' recommendations would yield less than 60 days per year for outdoor painting. Guidance from a qualified coatings consultant or painting contractor is required.

Note: If a painting contractor advises that work should not commence until proper conditions are attained, or that an alternative material should be used to deal with existing conditions, owners or property managers may be solely liable for any problems that occur if they insist on the use of products not suited for existing conditions.

Recent rainfall also is an important environmental consideration, in that it can affect the moisture content of the substrata. If a contractor is retained to perform exterior painting, specifications should require the contractor to use a moisture meter before priming and painting a surface. As a general rule, *primer or paint should not be applied when the moisture content of the material to be painted is 15 percent or more.* High moisture content can be particularly troublesome when oil-based paint is used. Latex paints generally are less affected because they permit moisture to "breathe" through to the atmosphere. Other considerations are involved, however, as discussed later.

Caulking

Caulking is a particularly important concern. It generally is least expensive to have the painting contractor apply caulk during the exterior painting process, while all equipment and personnel are in place.

Caulking's role in energy conservation is already well known and requires little elaboration. However, it is worthwhile to point out that effective caulking can pay for itself quickly because of its ability to reduce unwanted air infiltration and exfiltration. Thus the amount of energy expended to heat infiltrated air in winter and to remove heat from air induced by exfiltration in summer is also reduced. Of course, effective caulking also saves considerable sums by preventing the wood rot that otherwise can occur when water gets behind a paint barrier.

A polyurethane-based sealant is strongly recommended for general outdoor usage. Cured by moisture, it is flexible, durable, and "breathes" somewhat, permitting trapped moisture to escape. When properly installed, it should last up to 15 years. By contrast, an inexpensive latex caulk will generally begin to break down within a year or so.

The importance of proper application cannot be stressed enough. *Three-point adhesion must be avoided* to minimize the expansion and contraction that can cause premature caulk deterioration. (Three-point adhesion occurs when, for example, caulk is applied between a brick surface and a window frame. The caulk adheres to the brick, to the window frame, and to the common backing of the two.) *For maximum caulking effectiveness and durability, rely on two-point adhesion.* This is obtained through use of a closed-cell polyethylene backer rod. This material is similar to the polyethylene "bubble pack" used in shipping, except that it comes in cylindrical lengths. The backer rod diameter selected for any given application should be slightly larger than the opening into which it is fitted. Once fitted in, caulk is installed. Thus in the example situation, the caulk will adhere only to the brick and the window frame, and not to the common backing.

Conventional wood surfaces

Proper surface preparation is essential to obtain a high-quality, long-lasting paint job. All surface preparation should be completed before caulking and paint are applied. Typical preparation work includes the following.

1. *Replace rotten wood.* Any wood that has become rotten due to moistures should be replaced. Painting contractors often can handle minor work. Otherwise a carpenter may be required.

2. *Replace all unsound glazing compound around windows.* A high-quality, long-lasting glazing compound should be applied after all unsound glazing compound is removed.

3. *Reset all exposed nails.*

4. *Remove mildew.* A 10 percent household bleach solution can be used to remove mildew. The solution either is applied manually with a sponge or is sprayed on, and then is rinsed off. The wood must be permitted to dry thoroughly before painting. In areas that have exhibited mildew, apply a paint to which a special mildew preventive has been added.

5. *Remove all deteriorated paint.* Depending on how many layers of paint are involved and the type of paint, any one of several methods of paint removal can be used. Hand scraping and power sanding are the methods used most often. Chemical removal can also be used; a permit may be required. *Extreme caution must be used with chemicals* to prevent any from falling on people, pets, or plantings. Proper on-site storage of chemicals is essential to prevent children from playing with them. Note that chemicals *must be neutralized* before new paint is applied.

In some rare cases it may be necessary to burn old paint off with torches. Only a thoroughly experienced contractor should be allowed to use this method. A permit must be obtained, the fire department must be notified, extinguishers and other fire-fighting apparatus should be on hand, and someone should remain on site for at least 1 hour after the torch work is complete for monitoring and protection purposes. Be aware that extensive sanding will be required after the paint has been burned off to remove all charring. In most instances, contractors will charge for paint removal on a time and materials basis.

6. *Spot-prime all knots.*

A top-quality oil-based primer should be applied to all bare wood surfaces. A tint close to the top coat color should be added to the primer so that it continues to look good as the top coat thins due to UV radiation and other aging phenomena.

If extensive paint removal is not required, only spot priming should be used. Applying more primer than necessary increases labor and material costs and contributes to paint fatigue. If it is decided to leave cracked or alligatored paint in place, full priming over those areas generally is a worthwhile procedure.

Paint selection.   If the wood has been painted with latex paint, without extensive priming, latex paint should be used again. It permits moisture to breathe far more than oil-based paint, thus minimizing moisture problems that could occur otherwise. However, breathing generally will occur only when a comparatively high humidity is maintained indoors, creating the pressure required to force moisture through the paint to the atmosphere. Latex paint tends to last longer and to have better color retention properties than oil-based paint. Nonetheless, regardless of the type of paint used, some colors tend to fade faster than others. Check with a supplier, manufacturer, or reputable contractor for recommendations in this regard.

Note: Do not use latex on horizontal surfaces such as window sills and decks or in high-traffic areas. Oil-based paint is preferred for these areas because of its superior water resistance and durability. If water resistance is a primary concern, oil-based paint may be superior to latex overall.

Consider applying an extra coat of paint or performing additional paint removal on south-facing exposures, as well as on north-facing exposures where, due to shadows, moisture is likely to remain far longer.

T111 siding and other wood surfaces

It may be more appropriate to stain rather than paint new T111 siding (plywood), as well as wood decks, fences, and gates. Latex and oil-based stains (both semitransparent and solid hide) are available for this purpose. The relative benefits and drawbacks of oil-based and latex stains must be examined closely. Latex is a surface application only. Some feel that oil-based stains and paints penetrate more and thus also act as wood preservatives.

If these wood surfaces have been stained, the same type of stain should be applied again to prevent potential intercoat adhesion problems. Particularly when it comes to cedar, pine, hemlock, and redwood, however, the age of the material and its condition must be considered. In some cases it may be better to resurface with paint, using latex paint if latex stain was used, oil-based paint if oil-based stain was used. Paint will not be effective if the plywood has started to check and crack.

Paint or stain should be either brushed (preferred) or rolled onto grooved siding. The grooves create air pockets that make spray application inadvisable.

Masonry and concrete surfaces

New concrete pours should be painted only after sufficient curing has occurred. This usually means a 5 to 7 percent moisture content, although more moisture may be acceptable if latex paint is used.

Prepare existing masonry and concrete surfaces by removing all deteriorated paint (typically through high-pressure water blasting) and replacing all deteriorated masonry.

Either latex or oil-based masonry paint can be applied to masonry or concrete. However, unless the masonry or concrete surface is ideally dry (7 percent moisture content or less), latex is preferable because it permits the moisture to breathe. Oil-based paint does not have this quality and thus will trap moisture, which will result in premature failure of the paint surface.

If the surface is bare, a reduced top coat primer should be used. A binding agent may be needed if mortar joints are deteriorating. (In that event, first strike the joints and point them up with a material compatible with existing mortar.) Primer or paint should not be sprayed into raw masonry. A roller or brush should be used to help ensure good penetration.

If the building has a history of above-grade water problems caused principally by wind-blown rain, and the problem persists despite effective operation of gutters and downspouts, the use of a water-repellant masonry sealer should be considered. In this regard, all surface covering must be removed. Then an acid wash should be applied to neutralize lime emanating from the mortar. The acid wash (if used) is rinsed off and, once the surface has dried, one coat of moisture-resistant or water-repellant paint is applied.

Some may recommend the use of a silicon-in-solvent solution as a water repellant. Experience indicates that this type of material has a very short life span.

Galvanized metal surfaces

In the case of galvanized metal surfaces, such as gutters, downspouts, and flashing, surface preparation must be performed by hand because high-pressure water blasting will cause damage. Once handwork has been completed, the surface should be wiped down with mineral spirits and rinsed. The surface should then be primed with galvanized metal primer, followed by the application of the same top coat as that used for the trim.

Note that galvanized metal has extremely poor paint adhesion properties. Even under the best of circumstances, it is likely that a new coat of paint properly applied will begin to peel within 1 year. Thus when it comes time to replace galvanized metal components, consider the use of factory-finished aluminum in a color close to the top coat or trim used. Vinyl components also are available, but they are more expensive than aluminum and do not last as long, according to property managers and contractors.

Other ferrous metal surfaces

Other ferrous metal surfaces are prepared by removing all rust and scale by whatever means necessary. (If chemicals are used, neutralization is essential.) Then spot-prime the bare metal with rust-inhibitive primer, and apply a top coat of rust-inhibitive oil-based paint.

Work Specification

A highly definitive prescriptive work specification is strongly recommended when it comes to painting. Each space to be painted should be defined, as on a set of plans or single-line drawings showing dimensions. For each space, specifications should establish exactly what has to be painted, something done easiest by identifying:

1. Specific surface preparation required
2. Type of primer (if any) to be applied and how it will be applied
3. Exact type of paint to be applied, how it is to be applied, how many coats are needed, and any additives to be used
4. Any stenciling needed and the type of paint to be used and
5. Safety precautions that must be exercised

As an example, consider the following specification.

Boiler room: Walls

CONTRACTOR shall:

1. Clean all walls using a high-pressure (greater than 2000-lb/in^2) water-blast method.

2. Use a wire brush to remove any other materials which could affect the appearance, durability, or adhesion of the primer and/or paint to be applied.

3. Check the moisture content of the walls before applying primer, and apply primer only if moisture content is less than 7 percent.

4. Have a duly authorized representative of on-site management inspect the cleaned surface before applying the primer coat.

5. Assemble in the boiler room, prior to applying primer and paint, all cans containing primer and paint to be used, and call for an inspection by a duly authorized representative of on-site management personnel. All such paints shall be in manufacturer provided and labeled cans.

6. Apply one primer coat of the general top coat specified below, reduced to 40 percent of intensity, and including one part XYZ brand "MNO Adhesion Promoter" per ten parts of primer. Application may be by spray, roller, or brush, at the contractor's discretion, but it is expected that CONTRACTOR shall use a brush to assure complete coverage of those corners and other areas that may not otherwise be covered.

7. From a point 5 feet from the floor, and to the ceiling, apply one coat of general top coat, XYZ brand "ABC Flat Latex" paint, "hot yellow" in color. Application may be by spray, roller, or brush, at CONTRACTOR's discretion, but it is expected that CONTRACTOR shall use a brush to assure complete coverage of those corners and other areas that may not otherwise be covered.

8. From a point 5 feet from the floor—the dado—CONTRACTOR shall apply one coat of PQR brand "Maintenance Performance" alkyd-base gloss paint, "garnet green" in color. Application may be by spray, roller, or brush, at CONTRACTOR's discretion, but it is expected that CONTRACTOR shall use a brush to assure complete coverage of those corners and other areas that may not otherwise be covered.

9. Stenciling shall be applied as indicated on drawings: BR1 (north wall), BR2 (east wall), BR3 (south wall), and BR4 (west wall), according to the following key:

A = FIRE EXTINGUISHER
B = STANDPIPE
C = REPLACE HOSE CAREFULLY

Letters shall be 1½ inches high, and painted in PQR brand "Maintenance Performance" alkyd-base gloss paint, "firetruck red" in color.

It is strongly recommended that performance-type specifications not be used in the work specification, and that "or equals" not be permitted, at least insofar as primer and paint are concerned. Although some paint labels will indicate the paint's content analysis, such a content analysis seldom is 100 percent precise. In fact, two paints with identical content analyses may differ. This makes it inappropriate to performance specify paint on a content-analysis basis, especially so because content analyses are not available for all paints. It would be even more problematical to specify something such as "top-quality paint," since many manufacturers will have four or more grades considered top-quality, and even the best of one manufacturer's "top-quality" paint may not be as good as another's medium quality.

In essence, the more detailed your specification, the more pleased you will be with and the more value you will derive from the completed work. Furthermore, and most importantly, it helps ensure that all contractors are bidding on the same work. All too often price differences between contractors' bids are due to different concepts of what the customer wants, not lower overhead, faster workers, superior methods, or smaller profit margins. By leaving no questions as to what is desired, bid prices will reflect the other most telling differences.

Note that the work specifications could indicate the contractor's guarantee, such as the following.

Guarantee
Contractor's guarantee of workmanship and materials shall extend in time for a period equivalent to the manufacturer's warranty of the materials involved.

5

Water Treatment

Introduction

Classically referred to as "the universal solvent," water is a chemical combination of two parts hydrogen and one part oxygen (H_2O or HOH). When pure, it is colorless, odorless, and tasteless. The water provided to buildings is never pure, however, because water moves in a constant cycle. As shown in Fig. 5.1, solar heat causes water to evaporate from the surface of the earth and ascend to the atmosphere. There the moisture encounters dust particles and clings to them, creating droplets. The weight of these droplets causes them to fall (rain) and, as they do, they absorb gases naturally present in the air (oxygen, nitrogen, and carbon dioxide) as well as airborne dirt, smoke, fumes, bacteria, and the spores of microscopic organisms. After it returns to earth, the water flows across and percolates through an upper layer of soil, absorbing more carbon dioxide. This increases the amount of carbonic acid in the water, enhancing its ability to dissolve minerals as it continues to filter through the earth's crust. Ultimately it reaches the sources of our water supply, categorized as surface water (reservoirs, lakes, ponds, rivers, or streams) or ground water (deep wells, shallow wells, and springs), as illustrated in Fig. 5.2.

As a result of the water cycle, both surface and ground water contain three types of impurities: gases, dissolved solids, and suspended solids, as listed in Table 5.1.

1. The *gases* consist principally of carbon dioxide and oxygen, absorbed from the air and from decaying matter water contacts as it moves across and through the earth's surface.

2. The *dissolved solids* (minerals in a dissolved state) consist mainly of calcium carbonate, calcium sulfate, magnesium sulfate, sil-

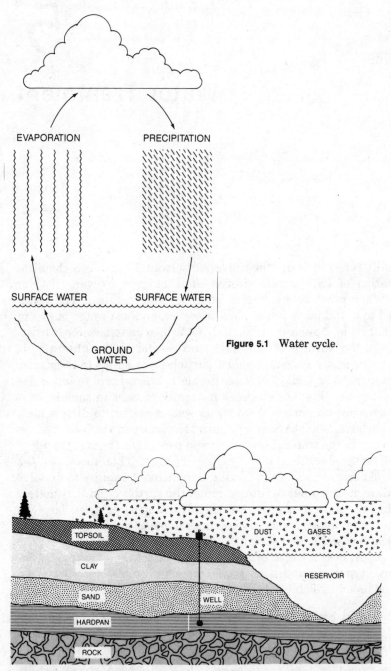

Figure 5.1 Water cycle.

Figure 5.2 Water absorbs a variety of impurities as it travels from the atmospl to our sources of supply.

TABLE 5.1 Typical Impurities of Fresh Water

Gases	Dissolved solids	Suspended solids
Carbon dioxide	Calcium	Soil
Oxygen	Magnesium	Decaying vegetable matter
Nitrogen	Silica	Precipitated minerals
	Iron	Oil
	Manganese	Trade waste
	Sodium chloride	Microorganisms
	Sulfates	Clay
	Fluorides	
	Carbonates	
	Bicarbonates	
	Aluminum	

ica (sand), sodium chloride, sodium sulfate, and small quantities of iron, manganese, fluoride, aluminum, and other substances.

3. *Suspended solids* include fine particles of minerals, microorganisms, organic matter, clay, and silt. These tend to give water a murky or turbid appearance. Water that appears to have color usually contains wastes such as oils, fats, grease, sewage, and effluents.

Before they send source water through their distribution networks, public agencies provide filtration and usually add small amounts of chlorine, sometimes in addition to other chemicals. Almost all the source water's impurities remain in it, however, and, left untreated, they can have serious and costly effects on the heating, air-conditioning, and plumbing systems of commercial, multifamily residential, and other buildings. Gases lead to corrosion and solids cause deposits. In some instances, problems can be so severe that even major systems must be overhauled or replaced altogether. At the least, improper treatment can result in unnecessarily high maintenance bills, lost efficiency, and needlessly high energy costs, as well as the lost effectiveness and frequent service interruptions that lead to occupant discomfort and complaints.

Water Analysis

Proper water treatment always begins with a comprehensive analysis to identify impurities precisely and thus to determine the counteracting additives needed to help assure effective and efficient equipment operation, uninterrupted occupant comfort, and extended system life. *Frequent analysis is essential; never assume that the composition of source water remains unchanged.* The types of impurities source water contains and the quantity of each depend on what the water contacts and for how long. Even if a water authority relies on one source only, the composition of the water will vary considerably from season to season. In fact, most public agencies rely on several sources, and it is not at all uncommon for a building to receive water from different sources over the course of a year or even a single season. Unless the water is tested frequently, the chemicals added to it may not be appropriate for the impurities it contains. Not only may this limit the effectiveness of these additives, it can actually aggravate the problems otherwise created.

A typical water analysis reporting form is shown in Fig. 5.3. As indicated, impurities are measured in parts per million (ppm), meaning one unit of impurity per million units of basic substance; for example, one gallon of impurity X in every million gallons of water. The metric equivalent of ppm is milligrams per liter (mg/l) when used specifically for liquid measure. In addition to identifying impurities, the analysis also is used to determine the acidity or alkalinity of water. This is in-

---

REPORT OF
WATER ANALYSIS

DATE: _____

SOURCE: _____

DATE ANALYZED: _____

TOTAL DISSOLVED SOLIDS	_____ ppm	CALCIUM	_____ ppm
ORGANIC MATTER	_____ ppm	MAGNESIUM	_____ ppm
SUSPENDED MATTER	_____ ppm	SODIUM AND POTASSIUM	_____ ppm
CHLOROFORM (OIL, etc.)	_____ ppm	BICARBONATE	_____ ppm
pH	_____	CARBONATE	_____ ppm
PHENOLPHTHALEIN ALK.	_____ ppm	HYDROXIDE (as OH)	_____ ppm
METHYL ORANGE ALK.	_____ ppm	CHLORIDE	_____ ppm
HYDROXIDE ALK.	_____ ppm	SULFATE	_____ ppm
HARDNESS	_____ ppm	NITRATE	_____ ppm
SPECIFIC CONDUCTANCE	_____ ppm	CARBON DIOXIDE	_____ ppm
SILICA	_____ ppm	TURBIDITY	_____ ppm
IRON	_____ ppm	OTHER _____	_____ ppm
OTHER _____	_____ ppm		

REMARKS:

Figure 5.3   Water analysis reporting form.

dicated by its pH, measured on a scale of 0.0 to 14.0. A pH of 7.0 means the water is neutral. Any pH below 7.0 indicates acidity; the lower the number, the more acidic the water. Any number above 7.0 indicates alkalinity; the higher the number, the more alkaline the water. A public water supply's pH usually is slightly alkaline, ranging from 7.4 to 7.6.

Boiler Water and Its Treatment

Gas- and oil-fired boilers are used most commonly for space heating in multifamily residential and commercial buildings, and the following discussion concentrates on these types. Nonetheless, many of the principles involved apply also to other types of space-heating systems, as well as to systems used for service water heating.

Three factors are commonly used to categorize a system: boiler design (fire-tube or water-tube), heating medium (hot water or steam), and circuit or loop design (open or closed). The systems most commonly installed are closed (all steam or hot water produced is returned to the boiler for reuse) and use a fire-tube boiler to produce steam or hot water. (All hot-water systems are closed-loop. Only certain types of steam systems rely on open-loop design.)

Fire-tube and water-tube boilers are illustrated in Figs. 5.4 and 5.5, respectively. In a fire-tube boiler a flame or hot gases (products of combustion) are passed through tubes that are surrounded by water inside the boiler shell. Heat is transferred by conduction through the tubes to the water to produce either steam or hot water, depending on the equipment's design. In a water-tube boiler the process is reversed: water is circulated through tubes that are surrounded by a flame or hot gases. Heat is transferred by conduction through the tubes to the water inside them.

In a typical *closed* system used to produce steam, water exiting the boiler as steam is trapped and condenses, causing it to return to a liquid state (condensate). The condensate is held in a condensate return tank and is automatically fed to the boiler as needed. Theoretically, no water is lost in the process, thereby minimizing the amount of utility-provided "make-up" water. In practice, however, some make-up water almost always is required due to losses associated with worn pump packings, faulty steam traps, and line leaks. (A typical 100-hp packaged fire-tube steam boiler contains 700 gallons of water; a 10 percent daily loss would amount to more than 2000 gallons lost per month. Each gallon lost means money spent needlessly on water and sewerage fees as well as on energy.)

Figure 5.4 Typical fire-tube boiler. (*Courtesy of Cleaver-Brooks.*)

The nature of closed systems suggests that they should operate with few problems if only minimal attention is given them. Never assume that a closed system can operate trouble-free without any attention whatsoever. In fact, it is precisely such assumptions that have led to serious and costly problems. Manufacturers and water treatment specialists should be called upon to recommend effective programs. In all cases, the make-up water line should be metered separately to monitor water consumption and thereby indicate any leaks that would otherwise go undetected.

In an *open* system a portion of the steam is intentionally not recovered, typically because it is used for other purposes, such as humidification. *Blowdown* is another source of open-system water loss, comprising the intentional draining of water. This is done to permit the introduction of *feed water,* that is, a combination of condensate and make-up (utility-provided) water, both entering the boiler automatically from the condensate return tank. Feed water reduces the amount of dissolved solids in the boiler system's water, thus preventing the problem-causing deposits dissolved solids can create. Although the feed water itself will have some dissolved solids in it, principally from the make-up water, the concentrations involved will be far lower than those associated with the water still in the boiler. This occurs because water leaves its solids behind when it is transformed into steam.

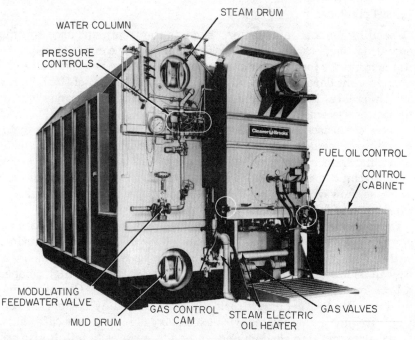

WATER COLUMN

PRESSURE CONTROLS

STEAM DRUM

Cleaver-Brooks

FUEL OIL CONTROL

CONTROL CABINET

MODULATING FEEDWATER VALVE

MUD DRUM

GAS CONTROL CAM

STEAM ELECTRIC OIL HEATER

GAS VALVES

Figure 5.5 Typical water-tube boiler. (*Courtesy of Cleaver-Brooks.*)

The constant loss of steam without a corresponding loss of solids thus causes a steady increase in the proportion of solids in the water left behind. The feed water dilutes the concentrations of dissolved solids in the system.

Cycles of concentration is the term used to express the ratio between dissolved solids in the boiler water and dissolved solids in the make-up water. For example, when the amount of dissolved solids in the boiler water is five times the amount in the make-up water, the boiler would be operating at five cycles of concentration. Most steam boilers (open or closed) operate at five to ten cycles of concentration as a maximum before requiring blowdown. Blowdown is accomplished by opening a valve on the blowdown line at the bottom of the boiler. Some larger boilers are equipped with *continuous* blowdown, also known as *skimmer* or *surface* blowdown. This comprises a small adjustable draining device that removes water automatically. It is located about 4 inches below the normal water surface inside the boiler, where dissolved solids tend to be at their highest concentration.

It is vitally important to control cycles of concentration properly, because dissolved solids may become precipitated minerals that build up inside the boiler and its attendant tubes or piping (*water-side surfaces*).

Typical problems

Depending upon several factors, such as the treatment used (if any), operating temperatures and pressures, and their composition, precipitated minerals form either sludge or scale. *Sludge* is a soft, relatively nonadherent deposit that tends to settle at the bottom of the boiler. It seldom creates problems and usually is removed by blowdown or, in hot-water systems, by flushing.

Scale comprises a crystalline, rocklike buildup that adheres firmly to waterside surfaces. It greatly reduces the efficiency of heat transfer, particularly in open or closed steam systems where just a $\frac{1}{32}$-inch buildup can cause a 5 percent efficiency loss. If the scale is allowed to increase, however, restricted heat transfer can cause boiler tubes to overheat and fail at "hot spots."

Corrosion is another serious problem that effective water treatment can control. It is most commonly caused by dissolved gases (principally oxygen) in the feed water (both make-up water and condensate) as well as low (acidic) pH. High chloride concentrations, high temperatures, or high velocities can aggravate the problem. Corrosion may produce either a "general attack" (usually caused by low pH) or "pitting" (frequently associated with excess oxygen). In either case, corrosion causes metal to weaken and waterside surfaces to fail. It also produces products that can increase boiler deposits. Corrosion tends to be at its worst when boilers are out of service and air comes into contact with wet surfaces.

Testing procedures

Titration, colorimetric testing, and conductance testing are the three methods commonly used to test boiler water.

1. *Titration* is used to determine how much of a given chemical is present in the water. A standard test solution is added slowly to a sample of water until it changes color. The amount of test solution required to effect the color change indicates how much of the chemical in question is present in the water.

2. The *colorimetric test* is similar to titration. A given amount of test solution is added to a water sample causing it to change color. The amount of a given chemical in the water or its pH is then determined by comparing the sample's color with standards that indicate concentrations.

3. The *conductance test* is used to determine the amount of total dissolved solids in water. It is performed with a conductivity meter, a device that measures the ability of water to conduct electricity. The greater a water sample's conductivity, the more dissolved solids it con-

tains. Distilled water, which contains no dissolved solids, conducts no electricity at all. (Dissolved solid testing can also be performed using a titration- or colorimetric-based chloride test. The conductivity test is generally considered more accurate.)

Table 5.2 indicates the tests applicable to determine various conditions or the presence of certain chemicals.

Treatment

Boiler water is subject to various analyses and treatments principally to prevent the buildup of scale, to prevent corrosion, and to determine proper blowdown quantities and intervals.

Scale prevention. Scale buildup is prevented by water pretreatment or by using a scale inhibitor. *Pretreatment* is performed through water softening, whereby calcium and magnesium ions (the principal causes of hard water and scale) are removed from the water before it is allowed to enter the boiler system. This is done through *ion exchange,* a process that occurs on the surface of the exchange medium, typically a synthetic resin located inside the water softener's tank. As water passes over the resin, calcium and magnesium ions are exchanged for sodium ions on the resin's surface. (Sodium ions do not under normal conditions form scale.) After several days, when no sodium ions remain on the exchange medium, it is regenerated by being dipped into a tank containing a sodium solution. This liberates the calcium and magnesium ions and replaces them with sodium ions. Some modern softening equipment can perform regeneration automatically.

When water-softening pretreatment is not used, a *scale inhibitor* should be added to the boiler water. Sodium phosphate is used when

TABLE 5.2 Typical Water Tests

	Applicable method		
Test for	Titration	Colorimetric	Conductance
Phosphate (scale inhibitor)		x	
pH (general)		x	
pH (condensate)		x	
Alkalinity (acid neutralization)	x		
Sulfite (oxygen scavenger)	x		
Nitrite (filming inhibitor)	x		
Molybdates (corrosion inhibitor)	x		
Iron (corrosion inhibitor)		x	
Cycles of concentration			
Dissolved particles			x
Chlorides	x	x	

the water contains relatively high concentrations of calcium and magnesium. When introduced to the water with an alkalinity builder (that is, a caustic), the chemical reacts with ions of the scale-forming minerals, causing them to fall to the bottom of the boiler as sludge. Dispersants such as sodium polyacrylates or polymers are the scale inhibitors used when low-hardness feed water is available. They keep ions of calcium and magnesium in suspension (sequestered) so that they do not have a chance to precipitate and form scale. They also keep sludge and mud in suspension.

In all cases the specific amount and type of scale inhibitors (or chemicals applied for any other purpose) proper for a given installation can be ascertained only through careful analysis of the make-up water composition and quantity.

Corrosion prevention. Several methods are used to prevent corrosion. One of the most common, used to prevent general corrosion, is adding an alkalinity or pH booster to feed water to maintain a pH of 10.0 to 11.0, or 400 to 600 ppm total alkalinity. Boiler-water pH or alkalinity should be tested frequently and treatment should be modified as required.

Neutralizing amines are used to neutralize acid when the pH of condensate is less than 7.5. These are volatile chemicals, which means that they are carried off with steam. Those most commonly used are morpholine, cyclohexamine, diethylethanolamine (DEEA), and aminomethylpropanol. Two or more are used customarily in combination because each travels a certain distance in the system before it reacts, causing immediate acid neutralization. They are fed into the boiler system along with other chemicals. The amount required should be sufficient to maintain condensate pH at no less than 7.5 and no more than 8.5.

Catalyzed sodium sulfite helps prevent pitting corrosion by reacting with and eliminating excess oxygen in the water. For this reason it is also known as an "oxygen scavenger." A residual amount of sodium sulfite (30 to 60 ppm generally is recommended) should remain in the boiler water at all times to help ensure that excess oxygen is eliminated. Boiler water should be subject to sulfite testing each day.

Filming or film-forming inhibitors also are used to prevent corrosion, but almost solely in hot-water systems whose operating temperatures are much lower than those of steam systems. These chemicals typically comprise a sodium nitrite/borate base with a pH builder that coats waterside surfaces to protect them from corrosion. A nitrite residual of 1000 to 2000 ppm generally is preferred. Molybdates are another type of film-forming corrosion inhibitor that is becoming a popular substitute for nitrites. Many molybdates include dispersants in the formulation to inhibit deposits, as well as buffers to raise the system pH to an alkaline level. A maintained residual level of 50 to 100 ppm sodium molybdate is recommended for proper corrosion prevention.

Note: It may also be wise to check for iron in the water, since a high level (0.5 ppm or more) may indicate that corrosion is taking place, even though pH and corrosion inhibitor levels are adequate. In such cases, the source of corrosion may be galvanic action (electrolysis) caused by dissimilar metals contacting one another.

Blowdown regulation. The amount and frequency of blowdown required to maintain the cycles of concentration within predetermined limits are established by testing the water for dissolved solids, using either a specific conductance test or a titration test for chlorides. Both boiler water and feed water should be analyzed. Cycles that are too low result in needlessly high water and chemical consumption. Cycles that are too high may cause scale formation.

Chemical feed

Chemicals can be added to a boiler system either manually or automatically. The manual method uses a bypass feeder (Fig. 5.6) to which chemicals are added. The rate at which they are fed to boiler water is controlled by adjusting a valve manually. An extensive amount of labor is involved, particularly when chemicals are used in powdered form. (In recent years, there has been a growing trend toward the use

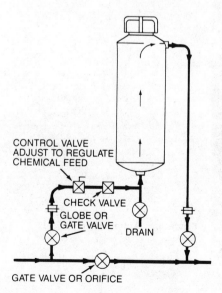

CONTROL VALVE
ADJUST TO REGULATE
CHEMICAL FEED

CHECK VALVE
GLOBE OR
GATE VALVE

DRAIN

GATE VALVE OR ORIFICE

Figure 5.6 Bypass feeder for manual chemical feed.

of liquid chemicals because they are easier to handle.) Moreover, those performing the work must take precautions to avoid any mishandling or accidents, and recent court rulings suggest that it is incumbent upon property owners or managers to provide comprehensive training and monitoring to assure that safe practices are known and maintained. Proper logging and other record-keeping requirements also must be observed, and temporary personnel must be closely supervised. Given these various requirements, and recognizing the inherent problems associated with any type of manual system, manual feed is not recommended.

An automatic or continuous chemical feed system comprises a chemical feed pump mounted on top of a chemical feed tank (Fig. 5.7). Chemicals are fed to the system on the discharge side of the circulating pump when a user-programmed time clock activates the feeder

Figure 5.7 Automatic chemical feeder.

pump, when the boiler calls for feed water, or on a continuous basis. The feed pump is adjustable to permit control of the chemical flow.

Cooling Water and Its Treatment

Mechanical cooling systems provide comfort by removing heat from the air. Although systems differ, all operate on two basic laws of nature. First, heat always is attracted from a warmer substance to a cooler one by conduction (contact), convection (air currents), or radiation. Second, increasing the pressure on a confined liquid causes its temperature to increase and, conversely, increasing its temperature causes its pressure to rise.

The vast majority of all central cooling systems used in multifamily residential, commercial, and other large buildings use the basic refrigeration cycle in a three-loop arrangement. The hydronic system illustrated in Fig. 5.8 is typical. As can be seen, cool water is circulated through conditioned spaces via the chilled water loop to attract heat, thus lowering the temperature of the room air and increasing the temperature of the water. Eventually the water arrives at the evaporator. This device is part of the refrigerant loop and comprises a coiled tube containing a flow of low-temperature, low-pressure freon. Because the water loop and refrigerant loop contact one another at this point, room heat contained in the water is transferred by conduction to the much cooler liquid refrigerant. This lowers the temperature of the water, which then continues through its loop to once again pick up heat from the spaces it serves. The refrigerant goes through a much more complicated process, however.

Because freon is much more sensitive to temperature and pressure changes than water, the heat it attracts from the water causes it to change state and become a warm, low-pressure gas. It moves through the refrigerant loop to the compressor, an electrically powered device that increases its pressure substantially, also causing its temperature to rise. Now transformed into a high-temperature, high-pressure vapor, the refrigerant travels to the condenser, a device served by the cooling tower loop. Cool water flows through the condenser's coiled tube. Because the refrigerant line contacts the cooling tower line in the condenser, heat from the refrigerant vapor is attracted to the cool water. This lowers the vapor's temperature enough to cause it to change state once more, to a warm, high-pressure liquid. This liquid then continues on through the refrigerant loop to the thermal expansion valve, a device that causes a sudden lowering of the refrigerant's pressure and temperature, so it once again becomes a low-temperature, low-pressure liquid on its way to the evaporator.

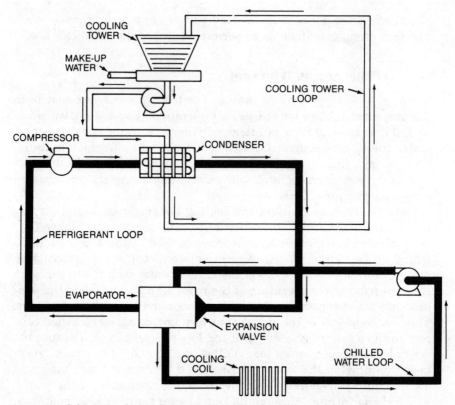

Figure 5.8 Schematic of typical three-loop mechanical cooling system.

Insofar as water treatment is concerned, the principal issue is the cooling tower loop. After water picks up the refrigerant's heat at the condenser, it is brought to the cooling tower for heat rejection. It enters at the top of the tower and is sprayed down as droplets. Large blowers (fans) create a mechanical draft by moving air across the droplets, causing some of the water to evaporate. Evaporation comprises a change of state, that is, water turns to gas or vapor. Energy is used to effect this change of state, lowering the temperature of the water that does not evaporate. As such, the water that lands on the bottom of the cooling tower may be 10°F or more cooler than the water that exits the condenser. The temperature is made still lower due to the inflow of the makeup that compensates for water lost due to evaporation, which can be considerable. The formula used to calculate evaporative loss is 4.32 gallons per day per degree of temperature drop times developed tonnage. Accordingly, the daily (24-hour) evaporative loss required to achieve a 10°F temperature drop in a 300-ton system would be

$$4.32 \text{ gal/day} \times 10°F \text{ drop} \times 300 \text{ tons} = 12,960 \text{ gal/day}$$

As the water evaporates, its suspended solids remain behind, increasing the cycles of concentration in the cooling tower water, in the same way that steam loss increases the cycles of concentration in boiler water. Just as boiler systems use blowdown to regulate the cycles of concentration, cooling towers use bleed off, a process whereby water is continuously drained from the system. (New, automated systems monitor cooling tower water and perform bleed off on a periodic, as-needed basis. See the section on chemical feed.)

Make-up water is used to replace the water lost by both bleed off and evaporation. Table 5.3 indicates the amount of bleed off recommended to maintain different cycles of concentration for different size conventional systems. In the Washington-Baltimore area, cooling tower water normally is maintained at four to six cycles of concentration. Assuming the 300-ton system mentioned is operated at full load for 24 hours, and that the goal is maintenance of five cycles of concentration, bleed-off losses would amount to

$$2.25 \text{ gal/min} \times 60 \text{ min/h} \times 24 \text{ h/day} = 3240 \text{ gal/day}$$

Adding this to the evaporative losses totals 12,960 gal/day + 3240 gal/day = 16,200 gallons per day. However, this is not the full total. Additional cooling tower water often is lost due to cooling tower sump overflow and line leaks. Some systems also experience losses when high winds blow the falling water droplets outside the tower.

In some large buildings absorption cooling equipment is used. This type of system uses steam to supplant some of the functions otherwise performed by the compressor. These systems became somewhat popular many years ago, when the oil or gas used to produce the steam was far less expensive. Some new interest has been expressed in them recently because of the significant cost of electrical demand imposed by

TABLE 5.3   Bleed Rate (gal/min) versus Tower Tonnage for Various Cycles of Concentration*

Tower tonnage	Cycles of concentration						
	2	3	4	5	6	7	8
50	1.5	0.75	0.5	0.37	0.3	0.25	0.21
100	3.0	1.5	1.0	0.75	0.6	0.5	0.425
200	6.0	3.0	2.0	1.5	1.2	1.0	0.85
250	7.5	3.75	2.5	1.87	1.5	1.25	1.06
300	9.0	4.5	3.0	2.25	1.8	1.5	1.27
400	12.0	6.0	4.0	3.0	2.4	2.0	1.7
500	15.0	7.5	5.0	3.75	3.0	2.5	2.12

*For absorption machines, multiply all data (except cycles of concentration) by 2.0.

the compressor operation of conventional systems. The amount of water consumed by absorption systems often is twice that consumed by conventional electric cooling systems, which results in higher water and chemical treatment expenses. Cool storage is another alternative to conventional cooling, whereby all or a major portion of on-peak cooling requirements are met by chilled water or ice that has been prepared during off-peak hours. Contact your local electrical utility for details.

Typical problems

The three principal problems affecting cooling tower water are scale buildup, corrosion, and airborne contaminants.

1. The amount of *scale* that builds up inside the cooling tower loop depends upon the concentration of dissolved solids in the water, as well as on the water's hardness and alkalinity. Scaling is most likely to occur in those areas of the condenser heat transfer surfaces that experience the highest temperatures. Scale buildup reduces heat transfer efficiency, resulting in lowered system capacity and higher energy consumption.

2. *Corrosion* in cooling tower systems usually is affected far more by heavy concentrations of oxygen in the water than by low (acidic) pH. Corrosion losses are monitored using corrosion racks (Fig. 5.9) installed in the system. These hold preweighted steel or copper corrosion strips (or "coupons") that are exposed to the cooling tower water for 30 to 60 days, removed, cleaned, and then reweighed. Corrosion rates

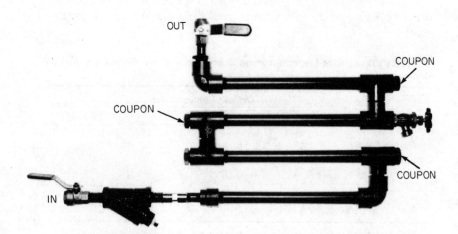

Figure 5.9   Corrosion test rack.

usually are spoken of in terms of MPY, meaning "mils (of metal loss) per year." (1 mil equals 0.001 inch.) A corrosion rate of less than 5.0 MPY for steel or 0.5 MPY for copper is considered good.

3. *Airborne contaminants* are a third source of cooling tower water problems. The nature of a cooling tower permits airborne bacteria, other microbial organisms, dirt, soot, and other contaminants to enter and become trapped in the water. The temperature of the water and its pH are usually in ranges that are optimum for nurturing the development of slime (most frequently found in condensers), algae (on cooling tower surfaces), and fungi (molds and yeasts that can thrive in virtually any part of the cooling tower system). Some of the growths involved can become particularly dense and result in fouling so severe that equipment must be taken out of service for thorough and costly cleaning. Note, too, that certain bacteria (such as anaerobic bacteria) can cause corrosion. While chemical treatment can prevent these bacteria from becoming a problem, they cannot reverse the problem once it begins. Chemical cleaning and sterilization may be the only alternatives.

Treatment

The testing methods used to analyze cooling tower water are essentially the same as those used to analyze boiler water. The treatments used for various conditions are as follows.

Scale prevention. Scale formation can be every bit as serious a problem in cooling tower systems as it is in boilers. Treatment involves the use of phosphonates and synthetic polymers. These are blended together in liquid form and fed continuously to the system to prevent scale buildup by sequestering calcium and magnesium ions, causing them to remain in suspension. The amount of chemical required usually is 100 to 200 ppm, or 1 to 2 pints per 5000 gallons of makeup.

Corrosion prevention. The principal defense against corrosion in the cooling tower loop is the use of polyphosphate or molybdate. These are usually combined with scale inhibitors in liquid form to create a thin film over metal surfaces. Continuous feeding is required to maintain a stable film. In the northeastern United States the cooling tower water pH usually should be maintained in a range of 7.5 to 8.5 at five to six cycles of concentration.

Contaminant control. System volume analyses, total bacteria counts, and visual inspection usually are used to determine the amount of multifunction nonoxidizing biocide required to inhibit cell growth.

Organosulfur compounds are commonly used, often in conjunction with polymer dispersants, to keep suspended matter in solution and free from debris deposits, thus permitting maximum circulation and effectiveness of scale and corrosion inhibitors. The specific amount of biocide needed depends on system size and operating conditions. Treatments generally are required two to three times per week in the warmest weather.

Note: Cooling towers that permit sunlight to contact the water directly are apt to experience more microorganism problems than others. Open decks should be covered.

Bleed-off regulation.   The amount of bleed off required to maintain the desired cycle of concentration is determined automatically in most systems, through conductivity analysis performed by chemical feed equipment (see below). Nonetheless, the accuracy of the automated equipment should be verified at least on a monthly basis by qualified personnel using chloride or conductivity testing.

It should be stressed that evaporation does not eliminate solids from the system. Solids are eliminated only through bleed off, leaks, or excessive winds. Make-up water dilutes solids left in the system; it also dilutes whatever chemicals have been added to it. To maintain proper chemical residuals, bleed-off rates must be selected and monitored with care; chemicals must be added each time the system is bled.

Chemical feed

The rate at which chemical concentrations are diluted and lost as a result of make-up water inflows and bleed off makes use of automatic chemical feed equipment essential for the treatment of cooling tower water. For systems sized 500 tons or less, a cooling tower conductivity control system (Fig. 5.10) often is recommended. Its wall-mounted controller continuously monitors concentrations of dissolved solids and automatically provides the bleed off necessary to maintain cycles of concentration within desired limits, based on user-programmed inputs as to the composition of make-up water. The same signal that activates bleed-off controls activates chemical feed controls as well.

For larger systems, a similar device is used, except a combination water meter/timer with a contact head is employed to monitor the precise amount of make-up water used; chemical feed is controlled by the timer. The system is more accurate than a wall-mounted conductivity controller.

No matter what type of system is used, a water meter should be used to monitor make-up water, for two reasons. First, it helps assure accurate billing by the water authority servicing the building, in that

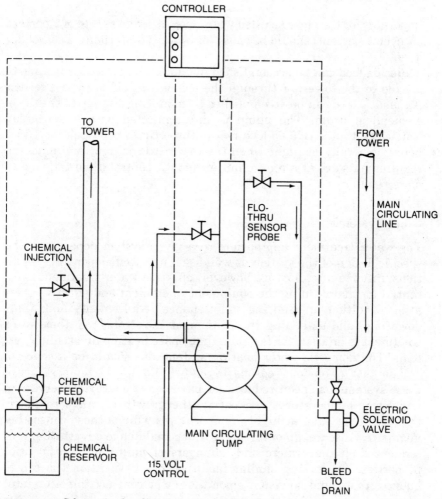

Figure 5.10 Schematic of cooling tower conductivity control system.

cooling tower water consumption may be billable at a special rate. (Most water authorities charge a sewerage fee in addition to a water fee for each gallon of water consumed, on the assumption that each gallon of water used ultimately is discharged to the sewer. Typical rates in urban areas are $1.50 to $2.50/1000 gallons for water and $2.50 to $3.00/1000 gallons for sewerage. Cooling tower make-up water can be charged at a lower rate since most of the water lost is lost to the air through evaporation rather than being discharged to the sewer system.

Second, monitoring make-up water use with a meter helps ensure that otherwise undetected leaks are noted. Metering is particularly important for the closed chilled water loop. A leakage rate of 2 percent (or even 1 percent) should be cause for concern and trigger a search for a leak.

Biocide feed can be accomplished manually, by direct application of biocide to the tower, or through the use of a modified bypass feeder. Automatic feed can be accomplished by mounting a pump to the top of a chemical drum. The pump is interconnected with a seven-day time clock that activates feed two to three times per week for 1 to 2 hours, generally at night when the tower load is light and make-up requirements are at a minimum. Automatic control almost always is more reliable.

Other Systems

The water treatment appropriate to a given system depends on the specific design of the system as well as on its specific operating conditions. In virtually all cases, however, effective water treatment is essential for maintaining the equipment in efficient and effective operating condition, minimizing maintenance requirements and, thus, downtime, and extending the equipment life. Note, too, that water treatment is an issue for far more than space heating and cooling systems. The domestic water heating system also should be a concern, and not just for obvious reasons. In many buildings the temperature of these systems has been reduced for purposes of energy conservation, and lower temperatures can permit the growth of microorganisms that could not exist at higher temperatures. One of these causes Legionnaire's disease, an outbreak of which could have devastating consequences on the owners and managers of multifamily residential properties, hotels, and similar facilities, not to mention the consequences that could be visited upon those who contract the often fatal illness.

In considering water treatment, the first question asked should be, "Where can it be beneficial?" This requires an analysis of all systems that use water to determine the potential benefits of water treatment, as well as a physical inspection of this equipment to learn specific needs based upon review and analysis of any problems that may exist.

Humidification systems comprise another area of concern and, once again, health issues are at least as important as issues affecting equipment operation and related concerns.

Other systems that use water, including the plumbing system that delivers cold water to taps, automatic lawn watering systems, fire sprinkler systems, and so on, also merit review at least from time to time. Principal issues generally focus on the constituents of the utility-provided water. Its composition could have an impact on the

taste of food, the health of lawns, and so on. Perhaps even more important, care must be taken to determine how impurities in the water
can affect system operation over time. Problems such as corrosion and
scaling can be nuisances. They can also be a cause of somewhat costly
repairs and, when for example a sprinkler system is involved, they
can even mean the difference between life and death.

Sources of Assistance

Several sources of assistance are available to property managers. One
source is the manufacturer of the water-using equipment involved.
Very often its literature will describe water treatment requirements,
and its representatives or application engineers may be able to provide updates. Note, however, that manufacturers' suggestions usually
must be general in nature, because they cannot contemplate all conditions under which their equipment will be used, nor can they be
aware of the specific constituents of your make-up water. Furthermore, the design of your equipment is static. While new models may
be available, what you have is what you have. By contrast, water
treatment technology is dynamic. A treatment that may have been appropriate 10 years ago, when your equipment was manufactured, may
be wholly obsolete by virtue of new products available.

Another source of assistance is the mechanical engineering firm
that designed or specified the water-using systems serving your building. The firm is in a position to perform a comprehensive analysis of
your system, to determine the extent of damage (if any) improper
treatment has caused. Such an analysis generally is called for before a
building is purchased or when a property manager takes on a new
building, particularly when tenants indicate that there have been
problems in the past. As a general rule, however, mechanical engineers are not water treatment experts. They can identify problems
and specify corrective measures in terms of the goals to be achieved,
but specifying the actual chemicals to be used and so on usually is a
task that should be entrusted only to a qualified water treatment specialist.

Mechanical contractors are an information source similar to mechanical engineers, and generally the same limitations exist. Some
mechanical contractors may operate or otherwise make available water treatment services, but in doing so they would be considered tantamount to water treatment contractors.

Chemical suppliers may constitute another source of assistance, although most simply sell chemicals based on customer requests. Some
may offer water analysis and related services, just as some water
treatment contractors may sell chemicals without related services. A

chemical supplier that offers water treatment services can be considered a water treatment contractor.

Other sources of assistance include public health officials, but their principal concern is microorganisms. Some may offer testing services in this regard, but, as important as proper microorganism control may be, water treatment requirements go far beyond that. Similarly, water scientists/educators affiliated with a local college or university may be able to offer assistance, but this will usually be for research purposes only. Unofficially, some may offer analytical services on a moonlighting basis, but reliance on anyone except a qualified professional with a business reputation to protect should be discouraged.

Still other sources include fire department personnel, whose range of concern would be limited to sprinkler systems, standpipes, and so on, as well as the insurer who covers the building for property damage. With these, as with many other sources, actual and potential, interest in water treatment issues tends to be parochial and their actual knowledge of specifics limited.

By far the most relied upon source is the qualified water treatment contractor. Methods of selecting one capable of meeting your needs in a professional manner are discussed in the following section.

Work Specification

Most water treatment contractors provide two levels of service: supervisory service and full service.

Supervisory service requires the water treatment contractor to visit the building or project typically on a monthly basis, or more frequently if required. During each visit the contractor should review the water treatment program in detail as follows.

Conduct chemical tests

Review operating procedures and discuss them with appropriate personnel

Issue a report that includes the test results, a description of the test results and their implications, and recommendations for modifications of any type

In-house personnel are responsible for daily chemical applications, daily testing, and adjustments.

A contractor who offers supervisory services should also provide training programs for in-house personnel, covering subjects such as the importance of water treatment, the different types of tests to be conducted and their frequency, understanding the implications of test results, techniques for adjusting applications, and safe storage and handling of chemicals. Supervisory service may also include provision of the necessary chemicals.

Full service shifts the majority of the overall responsibility to the contractor. Site visitation is conducted monthly or more frequently and includes the following.

Application of chemicals

Testing

Adjusting applications and feed equipment

Issuing reports

Automatic feed equipment is almost always used with full service and, under these circumstances, is almost always cost-effective. Most contractors can provide this equipment and install it, and some offer procurement programs that go beyond the purchase alone. Even when full service is employed, however, on-site personnel generally are required to perform frequent visual inspections of equipment and manual blowdown.

Most property managers prefer to rely on full service for two reasons. First, in-house labor, while probably less costly, has many other chores to attend to, including emergencies. Therefore, more than likely, certain in-house procedures may, from time to time, not be performed, and because in-house personnel are not specialists, may not be performed properly. The cost of correcting the resulting deficiencies can be substantial, which reinforces the second point, namely, that a specialist who performs well can generate savings by making remedial measures and their costs unnecessary.

It should be recognized, too, that full service makes the contractor responsible for conditions over which the contractor exercises control. If for any reason scale builds up, the contractor may be responsible for its elimination, assuming in-house personnel have performed their work, such as manual blowdown, properly.

In developing the work specification, note that much of what a water treatment contractor does is dynamic in nature. The contractor usually cannot agree to provide a certain amount of chemicals each month because there is no way to be certain that conditions will merit precisely that amount. As such, the work scope must give leeway to the contractor to do what is necessary, with assurance that you will pay for whatever is customarily required.

Some of the services you should consider are indicated in the following. This is not meant to be a comprehensive list. It assumes, as customary, that an annual contract is involved.

System inspections

All systems that use or are somehow affected by water use should be subject to at least annual inspection. This inspection should be confined solely to identifying any impact that impurities in the water may be having. A water treatment contractor is not a mechanical engineer and so should not be expected to report on the effectiveness or efficiency of equipment. It is unfair to expect a contractor to report on conditions beyond those in which the contractor claims competence. Moreover, it is foolhardy to evaluate the condition of important equipment based on reports of someone not expert in it. Systems inspection by a professional engineer or someone with similar qualifications and capabilities is recommended, but for purposes that go far beyond the issue of water treatment.

If a comprehensive annual inspection is to be provided, its constituents should be specified thoroughly. Identify precisely the equipment or other system elements you want inspected.

In most instances the contractor should inspect certain equipment monthly. The inspection involved is not nearly as rigorous as that associated with annual inspection. Nonetheless it should be detailed enough to help ensure that all parties have a full understanding of what is and is not required. No one should be in a position of having to make assumptions.

Assuming that the services outlined are desired, the annual agreement would have provision for one annual comprehensive inspection and eleven monthly inspections. A few factors should be noted in this regard.

There generally will be a preferred time for the annual inspection. This may be during the spring or fall months when neither heating nor air-conditioning is being used to any appreciable extent. Alternatively, it may be best to perform a comprehensive inspection of the heating system in the summer and of the cooling system in the winter. The timing of the onset of services may not coincide with the best time for an inspection. In such circumstances, the contract should be prepared specifically for needs. Then, after the contractor has put things in order, a carefully planned ideal program can possibly be implemented. Before contractors take over a project, however, they should generally want to have the full inspection performed, just as the owner or manager should. This occurs particularly when a full-service agreement is involved, because, for contractors to be responsible for the adequacy of their service, they must know "before" conditions. Furthermore, it is the knowledge of these conditions that frequently will determine near-term off-normal requirements. For example, if inspection reveals some scaling problems, a contractor would likely recommend certain chemical additives to eliminate them, and it may take 6 months to 1 year for these to become effective. Thereafter, scaling preventives would be required.

When bidding is used, it would be necessary to identify precisely what will be required during the first year, and this would presuppose an inspection has been performed and a report of findings and recommendations issued. Therefore, if bidding is to be used, consider having the inspection performed on a separate contract, and refrain from issuing the routine services bidding specification until after the inspection is complete. The alternative would be to include the inspection in the bid, but call for contractors to respond to bidding specifications on a unit price basis, an approach that can complicate budgeting.

If it is decided to rely on a separate inspection, the company that performs it should be retained on a negotiated basis. This approach helps assure that there are no incentives to cut corners during the vitally important initial inspection. Furthermore, it is difficult to bid an inspection since the full extent of the work will be unknown. It is one thing to determine visually whether or not scaling exists; it is something else to test that scale to determine its composition. Identify the contractor that you believe is best qualified and negotiate a work scope that indicates the amount of time likely to be involved, the different tests that may have to be performed as well as the unit cost of each, and the final deliverable. This should include not only a report, but also a highly specific program description that should be sufficient to ensure that conditions are improved to excellent or maintained that way. It is recognized, of course, that specific treatments and frequencies will be adjusted during the year because of factors over which no one can exercise control, such as variable make-up water sources.

In most instances a simple letter agreement should be sufficient to delineate mutual responsibilities as to the initial comprehensive inspection.

Testing

The work scope should make clear exactly what tests will be performed on a routine basis, by whom, and when. This element of the work scope can be divided into three major sections: heating season, cooling season, and year-around; alternatively, monthly listings can be used, such as April–May. Each of these major listings then could be subdivided between tests that the contractor will make and tests that in-house personnel will make. Within each of these sublistings, tests that will be performed daily, weekly, and monthly can be indicated. It is also appropriate to indicate the specific types of test that will be used, such as colorimetric tests or titration; chloride or conductivity.

Scoping out the testing routine in this manner not only ensures an effective contract by spelling out precisely who is responsible for what, it also helps ensure that all appropriate factors are taken into consideration.

Recognize that testing may reveal off-normal conditions that require more than the customary amount of testing, or tests in addition to those ordinarily performed. The contractor should be called upon to indicate the unit prices associated with each type of conventional test and each type of special test. The contractor should indicate whether unit prices are for testing only, or if they also include traveling to the facility to obtain samples. While samples can be taken by in-house personnel and brought to the contractor's laboratory, the contractor will likely—and reasonably—disavow any responsibility for the adequacy of sampling. Since trying to cut corners almost invariably results in quality breakdowns, it is advised that the contractor be given full responsibility for sampling and testing.

Recognize that, on occasion, conditions may require certain types of rarified testing the contractor does not have the capability to perform in house. For this reason the work scope should specify whether the contractor will handle all arrangements (a coordination fee normally would be required) or whether management would be responsible for having the test performed, as per the contractor's recommendations.

Provision of chemicals

You may or may not be able to save money by purchasing chemicals on your own. Contractors typically make high-volume purchases, which permits them to earn a profit and still provide materials at rates about the same as those you would obtain. Furthermore, contractors will provide most chemicals on an as-needed basis, minimizing your storage requirements. In turn, this helps reduce the risk of losses due to improper storage and the problems that can result due to handling (physical damage or personal injury). Note, too, that contractors that use the chemicals they provide are responsible for their adequacy. If problems occur and your chemicals are used, the contractor may claim—possibly with justification—that the chemicals are at fault.

The work scope should indicate the chemicals involved and the volumes likely to be needed, with the clear notation that volumes actually required may differ substantially from assumed requirements, based on conditions found. The prices that will be charged for chemicals provided by the contractor should be indicated in appropriate unit price quantities. For some this may be per gallon; pounds for others, per 100 pounds or 100 gallons.

Application of chemicals

It is economically impractical for a contractor to visit the site daily for chemical applications, and for this reason the use of automatic feed is cost-effective when full service is obtained. However, it ordinarily would be the responsibility of the contractor to put chemicals into automatic feed equipment. The same type of specification used to require this can be used insofar as chemical application is concerned, by breaking it down by seasons or months, and by the responsibilities of the contractor and of in-house personnel. If full service is obtained, and if for some reason it is necessary for a contractor to make more visits than planned, the unit price of such visits should be clarified. Note, however, that the owner should not be made responsible for additional costs involved to correct conditions that the contractor should have been able to prevent. Such factors should be considered in a separate section of the contract related to mutual responsibilities and liabilities.

Reporting

A comprehensive report on conditions is appropriate after an annual inspection. A full but not as comprehensive report is also needed when the contractor is performing supervisory service, since the owner or manager needs to know how effective the in-house program is, and whether or not in-house personnel are following instructions. When full service is obtained, however, a less extensive report usually will suffice, such as the one shown in Fig. 5.11. If off-normal conditions are encountered, they should be detailed and their probable causes identified, along with the response measures that the contractor recommends or will implement.

Training

Whether full service or supervisory service is provided, some personnel training may be required and, even when trained personnel are on hand, the contractor should want to evaluate them to assure that they are fully familiar with all requirements. A contractor who assumes an individual is trained simply because someone says so can be taking a leap of faith that puts your mechanical systems at risk. A conscientious contractor wants to ensure that in-house personnel know what they are doing relative to the contractor's perception of needs. Furthermore, a manager should always want to deal with a contractor with training capabilities, given that the trained operator the manager has on Monday may decide to relocate on Tuesday.

WATER ANALYSIS REPORT

Company: _____
Property: _____

Attention: _____

Date Samples Taken: _____
Copies To: _____

BOILER WATER		TEST RESULTS			DESIRED RANGE		CITY WATER	
Unit #	#1	#2	#3					
T D S				mm	3500 mm max.		T D S	
pH					10.0 – 11.5		pH	
P Alkalinity				ppm	600 ppm max.		CL	
Total Alkalinity				ppm	800 ppm max.			
OH Alkalinity				ppm	400 ppm max.			
Chlorides				ppm	_____ ppm			
Sulfite				ppm	40 – 60 ppm		Condensate pH: _____	
Inhibitor				ppm	___ – ___ ppm		Range: _____	
Total Hardness				ppm	___ – ___ ppm			

Comments: _____

COOLING WATER	System 1	System 2	System 3				
Chlorides				ppm	_____ ppm		
Total Hardness				ppm	900 ppm max.		
T D S				mm	_____ mm max.		Reviewed:
pH					8.8 max.		_____
Total Alkalinity				ppm	350 ppm max.		*For Initial*
Inhibitor				ppm	___ to ___ ppm ___		

Comments: _____

CLOSED SYSTEM	System 1	System 2	System 3			
						Water Meter Reading:
T D S				mm	3500 mm max.	
pH					pH: _____	_____
Inhibitor Test					___ to ___ ppm ___	

Comments: _____

Recommendations: _____

_____   _____
Customer Representative   *Service Engineer*

Figure 5.11 Concise water analysis reporting form.

If trained personnel are already on hand, the work scope should call for their evaluation, and should indicate the means involved. If they are to perform daily testing, the contractor should watch them do so, to assure that they do it properly or at least listen to an explanation of procedures.

Whether or not trained personnel are on hand, the work scope should delineate the knowledge an individual should possess given the requirements involved, the estimated hours of training, and the estimated hours of monitoring.

Provision of forms

As necessary, and depending on the specific nature of the service involved, the contractor may be called upon to develop and provide certain forms. One of these would be a checklist for in-house personnel, indicating the tests or other tasks they should perform daily, weekly, or monthly, and the specific means. Other forms may be a reporting form designed for easy review by the contractor when supervisory service is provided. Particularly when in-house personnel will be relied upon, it is essential for the contractor to help make the overall program as "goof-proof" as possible.

On-call service

In-house personnel should be at liberty to call the contractor whenever they run into a situation with which they need help. There should be no additional charge for providing guidance by telephone, assuming the calls are relatively brief and infrequent. If the contractor must visit the site at other than a scheduled time, however, an additional charge may be imposed. In developing a contract, the cost of service calls should be indicated. It may be appropriate to simply include a given number of service calls, such as up to six per year, in the contract price.

Other services

A variety of other services may be provided, including the installation and maintenance of automatic feed equipment, assistance with closing down the heating or cooling system, and so on. It is suggested strongly that the work specification/work scope also identify exactly what in-house personnel are responsible for, so that there is no confusion on the subject.

6

Pest Control

Introduction

The importance of effective pest control cannot be overemphasized. It helps preserve a property's value by preventing, or at least minimizing, the damage that pests can do. The cost of their physical damage can be extremely high, amounting to thousands of dollars in a relatively brief period of time. But the damage they cause is not all physical. Pests can cause tenants to leave a building, and the comments of those who leave can result in rumors which make it difficult to rent (or sell) vacated space. High turnover results in high turnover-related costs while also reducing the income stream, which in turn will lead to reduced building value.

We do not advocate that a property manager should in all cases rely on an outside contractor for pest control, nor do we advocate performing these services by in-house personnel. Decisions such as these should be made on a case-by-case basis. However, when a decision to rely extensively on in-house resources is made, it usually results from a financial study which shows that approach to be less costly. When such studies consider all appropriate factors, there is no reason to disregard their conclusions. But have all appropriate factors been considered?

When pest-control services are performed, toxic chemicals usually are employed, making proper application, handling, and storage essential. In fact, the risk associated with such chemicals is one of the principal reasons why most management firms use experienced contractors rather than in-house personnel.

Simply using an outside service is no guarantee that the work will be done properly, or that all applicable laws and regulations will be followed. It is management's job to obtain a reliable professional contractor, not only to ensure that the work is done properly, but also to minimize exposure to legal liability.

In fact, we live today in a litigious environment. Lawsuits have reached "epidemic" proportions. While nothing can be done to prevent someone from suing you or the company you work for, many steps can be taken to minimize causes for action. Failing to provide pest-control services could lead to problems that create a cause for action, and so can failing to assure the professionalism of whoever is retained. In either case, courts often lean toward those who have been "wronged" because, typically, those against whom claims are made tend to have "deep pockets" by virtue of their own worth or of that afforded through insurance. However, it is not appropriate to rely on insurance as an excuse for anything less than diligence. While insurance may pay a given sum to settle a claim or meet a mandated court or jury award, the fact remains that innumerable costs are not covered by insurance, such as the value of the time spent for pretrial discovery, interrogatories, and depositions; the value of the time lost and errors made due to the anxieties occasioned by a pending lawsuit; and the dollars lost due to the negative publicity that all too frequently occurs. In short, if you do contemplate pursuing pest control on your own, know what you are getting into. And even if you intend to rely totally on outside sources of assistance, know how to choose effectively.

Common Pests and Their Control

The following discussion identifies common pests encountered in multifamily residential and commercial buildings, and some of the methods generally applied to clean them out and prevent them from coming back. The pests discussed include:

Small animals

Birds

Rodents

Bats

Wood destroyers

Cockroaches

Ants and spiders

Ticks and fleas

Bees and wasps

Other indoor pests

Other outdoor pests

Note that pest control should start as early in the life of a building as possible, preferably during the design stage. In fact, a competent pest-control consultant or contractor always should be invited to review plans and specifications before construction and to recommend alterations that might help prevent potential problems from materializing. For example, soil pretreatment for the prevention of subterranean termites usually is recommended. An experienced professional may also suggest basement-window modifications to help prevent access by rodents, or trash room alterations to help eliminate potential cockroach infestations.

Most professional pest-control contractors will be pleased to review plans and specifications either at no charge or for only a nominal amount, assuming that their services will be retained (or at least solicited) after completion of the construction (in some cases during construction). Recognize that these services may be extremely valuable. The modifications needed usually require little additional expense; and the value of the savings will often pay back the premium paid many times over within just a few years.

As the following discussion points out, pests can cause damage that may take thousands of dollars to repair, and some problems can be irreparable, as when a particular infestation causes one or several occupants to relocate or creates an unfortunate reputation for a property.

In all cases the actions taken with regard to pest control should be made part of the permanent record of a property. Demonstrating that effective pest control has been performed helps ensure that the value of a property is maintained, if not enhanced.

Small animals

Small animal pests include squirrels, raccoons, skunks, and possums, among others. Typically they enter buildings through existing openings (including ventilation and exhaust ducts and chimneys) or those they make.

Small animal pests can cause a number of problems, particularly due to their chewing and gnawing behavior. These include fire hazards when electrical lines are stripped of their insulation and electronic equipment difficulties when the integrity of telephone or computer cable is breached. Energy losses and water infiltration damage can also occur when small animals chew through caulking and insulation. Chewing is not the only concern, however. The debris which small animals leave behind and their nesting materials comprise fire hazards, and their noise can lead to occupant dissatisfaction.

Another serious problem with small animals is their potential for carrying rabies, a particular concern at multifamily projects that include children among the residents.

In most areas it is illegal to poison small animals. The accepted means of eliminating them is trapping and subsequent removal from the site.

One of the most effective preventives is structural integrity. The building should be surveyed to identify areas where small animals are entering or could enter. Openings should be closed with materials small animals cannot chew through. Sanitation can be an important factor, too. Outdoor trash receptacles in particular should be sealable in a manner that prohibits entry by small animals.

Moles can be particularly annoying (and costly) pests because of the grounds damage caused by their burrowing. Moles can be poisoned (in most jurisdictions) or trapped. The best preventive is elimination of their food—grubs—which can be accomplished through effective grounds care.

Birds

Birds can be one of the worst pests confronting the owners or managers of multifamily residential and commercial properties. Some of the problems they can cause include the following.

1. *Health hazards.* Bird droppings (guano) are associated with three distinct health problems: histoplasmosis, cryptococcosis, and dermatitis. Histoplasmosis can be caused by inhaling spores of histoplasma capsulatum, a fungus organism nurtured by decaying guano-contaminated soil. (Soil does not have to show signs of heavy guano deposits to be contaminated.) In its chronic form the disease affects the respiratory system, and it can affect other organs as well. Cryptococcosis is caused by inhaling spores of cryptococcus neoformans, a fungus organism that lives in pigeon guano. The disease leads to skin eruptions or lesions (cutaneous form), or it can infect the respiratory system and the organs (generalized form). Bird feces dermatitis is a skin irritation that affects guano-sensitive people who come into direct contact with droppings or guano-contaminated products.

2. *Fire hazards.* Nesting birds in particular create fire hazards because of the flammability of the materials from which they construct their nests. They can also create fire hazards by pulling out electrical wires.

3. *Structural damage.* Birds can cause structural damage, as when their guano and carcasses collect on a canopy that ultimately collapses under the weight. Likewise, nests, carcasses, and other bird debris that collect in rain gutters can cause improper drainage, which

in turn leads to structural damage. Guano can also cause wood rot, and birds can widen holes under eaves and pull out insulation.

4. *Mechanical system problems.* Nests and carcasses in or on vents and dampers can create havoc with a building's mechanical systems, leading to occupant discomfort, costly energy waste, and even far worse problems. In addition, a buildup of feathers in a cooling tower can lead to cooling system difficulties and the need for costly remedial work.

5. *Defacement.* Guano can quickly deface a building facade. In some cases, the stains created are virtually impossible to remove.

6. *Lice and maggots.* Birds frequently enter attic areas, where they become trapped and die. Their carcasses carry lice and thus can be the cause of lice infestations. Other infestations also are possible, depending on the types of eggs on the carcasses.

As worrisome as this listing may be, it is far from complete. Typical of some of the other problems is the unsightly appearance created by birds, as well as the noise they make.

The types of birds that commonly cause problems by roosting or nesting are pigeons, starlings, grackles, house sparrows, cowbirds, crows, and red-winged blackbirds. It is essential to know exactly what type of bird is causing the problem. This determines the control approach that is best suited and, when appropriate, the type of chemicals to be used to attain the desired results from a given approach.

Knowing the type of bird involved is also essential to assure compliance with applicable federal, state, and local ordinances. These dictate the types of birds that are protected and those that are not. Furthermore, they determine the control approaches that can and cannot be used, the length of time for which they can be applied, as well as appropriate reporting requirements. In many states an individual must be certified in bird control in order to apply certain control procedures.

A number of different techniques are available to solve bird problems. All control procedures have one thing in common, however: they begin with a thorough inspection to define exactly what the problems are. Some of the solutions are listed here.

1. *Occupant assistance.* In many instances birds are attracted to buildings, in particular multifamily residential buildings, because building occupants feed them, either casually by dropping crumbs, or by having bird feeders. Leases should prohibit bird feeders. Tenants should have the problems explained to them, with emphasis on those that affect occupant health and safety as opposed to the owner's bottom line.

2. *Structural repairs or modifications.* Typically, when birds are entering attics or other interior spaces, caulking and otherwise sealing off their entrances (as with wire mesh cloth) is essential. The use of wire screens or other devices also may be in order, if not to eliminate the birds, then at least to help minimize the problems they can cause otherwise.

3. *Repellents.* Repellents can be applied to balconies, railings, window ledges, and other roosting areas after they have been cleaned of all debris, as by wire-brushing. Typically, these repellents act as irritants that stick to a bird. Repellents must be applied properly. Rain or heat can lead to structural surface staining. Repellents can also stain human skin.

4. *Avicides.* An avicide is a poison applied to perches or mixed with edible feed material such as corn. When applied to perches, an avicide enters a bird's body through its feet. Not only must the proper chemical be applied for the species involved, one must also know what perches are used. When an avicide is mixed with edible feed, birds that eat it emit a distress signal. The signal discourages other birds from using the roost. Bait stations must be located in strategic areas and must be kept filled over a period of time if a roosting problem is to be substantially diminished. Note that additives are designed for specific species and therefore must be mixed properly.

5. *Trapping.* Trapping may be preferred by those who believe it is wrong to harm other living things, no matter what damage they cause. Generally speaking, however, trapping is slow, expensive, and ineffective.

6. *Acoustic devices.* Acoustic devices also are considered humane, but according to many property managers and contractors, they seldom achieve the results desired. Any such devices should be purchased only from established organizations that guarantee the efficacy of the products they sell, and that will still be in business within a year or so to make good on the guarantee or warranty that should come with the product.

When bird control is performed on an in-house basis, it is essential for those assigned the task to take certain basic precautions. In all cases, a respirator should be worn when working in environments that contain dust from bird droppings. After working in the presence of these droppings, individuals should bathe completely and change their clothing. The hazards of working with the chemicals that may be involved also require appropriate precautions. These typically are indicated by the chemicals' manufacturers. Note that these precautions usually relate to proper storage as well as application. *In most cases, individuals who work with strong or poisonous chemicals, be it for bird control or any other pest-control purpose, must be certified by a state and/or local government agency.*

Even when a contractor is retained to eliminate a bird problem, the property manager or owner usually will have certain responsibilities. One of these is removing and properly disposing of bird carcasses, something that can be particularly important when avicides are used. Another is preparing tenants or residents for the control program. There may be opposition. Accordingly, the dimensions of the problem and its impacts (particularly those affecting people rather than dollars) must be explained through a meeting or a printed notice of some type, or both. Baiting often is conducted early in the morning, when birds are feeding, and also to minimize exposure to the public.

Rodents

Rodents can pose a number of problems. One of the worst is the damage they cause by their gnawing. In fact, gnawing is a survival tactic for them. For example, the incisor or fang teeth of a rat can grow up to 5 inches in 1 year. In order to counter this growth, rats gnaw on anything they can get their teeth into. This is how they make a hole that gives them access to a building. And this is also why, in addition to causing structural damage, they can cause a fire hazard (by gnawing electrical lines) or disrupt telephone or computer services, security systems, and fire safety systems.

Rodent damage is not limited to that caused by their gnawing. Rodents can create health hazards as a result of their droppings, and the diseases they carry can lead to serious illness should they bite someone. In addition, they usually carry insects with them, and their urine causes stains. Also, they give many people a fright. In fact, their regular appearance over a period of time in and of itself is sufficient to cause some people to move out of a building.

Rodents are somewhat difficult to control because of their dexterity. Adult rats cannot only gnaw; they can burrow, climb, and swim, reach vertically about 18 inches, and jump about 3 feet either horizontally or vertically. They can crawl through a vertical pipe with a diameter as small as 1½ inches, and can gain access to a building through an opening as small as ½ inch. (Young mice can enter through an opening as small as ¼ inch.)

There are a number of ways of controlling a rodent problem, but virtually all require continuous monitoring and action. A one-time effort will seldom be effective.

1. *Eliminate harborages.* The place to start usually is outside a building, in that rodents—rats in particular—use an outdoor harbor-

age as a base of operations. Discarded materials, rubbish, refuse, lumber, and old equipment all can serve as a harborage. All should be removed and whatever is stored outside should be kept 18 inches off the ground. Tall grass can also serve as a harborage or "runway," underscoring the need to keep grass cut properly.

Investigation may identify one or more rat burrows. These should be fumigated, but such measures must be planned carefully. Most burrows have secondary exits or escape holes, and some of these can lead into a building. Accordingly, before fumigating, it is necessary to ensure that gas will not enter the building and otherwise will pose no danger to people, animals, stored foodstuffs, and so on. After a burrow has been fumigated, it should be filled in with dirt to prevent reuse and also to simplify detection of any further activity.

It may be found that the outdoor source of rodents results from conditions on a neighboring property. In such cases the owner or manager involved should be contacted and apprised of the situation. If no action is taken to resolve the problem, it may be appropriate to contact local health officials.

2. *Mechanical means.* Mechanical means for eliminating rodents consist principally of mechanical traps and glue boards. If either is used, a program of frequent inspection is necessary to help ensure that these pests are removed quickly once immobilized. Mechanical means may be able to provide effective control within 1 to 10 days, depending on the size of the rodent population, access to the building, and food available.

3. *Rodenticides.* Several types of rodenticides are commonly used. They usually are applied as baits or tracking powder. Baits should always be placed in safe areas, which are inaccessible to people (especially toddlers) and pets. Typical locations include under stoves and refrigerators, under the false bottoms of cabinets, and in crawl spaces and attics. (It may also in some cases be prudent to install bait in outdoor burrows.) When rodenticide is applied as tracking powder, rodents pick up the poison on their feet as they travel through it. The rodenticide enters the rodents' systems orally when they lick it off their feet as part of their routine grooming process.

Problems can on some occasions result when a rodent dies in an inaccessible space, as in a wall. The odor created can be repugnant and may last for several days. Fans seldom are sufficient to eliminate the odor problem. However, there are certain odor-absorbing chemicals available, which can be injected into a wall cavity to eliminate the problem quickly. (If you are concerned about the odor problem, be sure a pest-control contractor has the ability to use odor-absorbing chemicals. The cost of this service should be identified beforehand in the contract.)

Effective sanitation and enhancing the structural integrity of a building are the most significant preventive measures. Relative to structural enhancements, it is a rule of thumb that any opening into which you can place your forefinger should be sealed. In this regard the following should be considered.

All edges into which a rodent can get its teeth should be covered with sheet metal or metal mesh cloth.

Windows that are less than 2 feet off the ground should be screened with ¼-inch hardware cloth, backed with appropriate mesh to keep out flies and other insects.

Any loose-fitting doors, windows, or screens should be made tight-fitting. (Metal flashing on doors should extend under the door and up each side by no less than 3 inches.)

Openings around pipes and conduits passing through exterior walls should be closed with brick or masonry. Alternatively, they can be fitted with a metal collar or shield (at least 24 gauge) that is fastened to the floor or wall. If concrete is used, metal mesh cloth should first be forced into the hole.

All sewers, pipes, and drains should be fitted with an iron or perforated metal cover. When a perforated cover is used, perforations should not exceed ¼ inch.

In most instances, structural enhancement methods can be used in a manner that makes the modifications relatively unnoticeable.

Bats

Bat damage is the same as damage caused by birds and rodents. They can also carry rabies. Nonetheless, their "usual" damage is frightening people.

Buildings seldom experience bat infestations; often, just one or two of the creatures create a problem. Elimination commonly is performed by mechanical means, often as basic as killing the rodent with a broom. Rodenticides in powder form can also be used in some situations.

Preventing the recurrence of a bat problem generally involves sealing the holes through which they enter. Often a caulking compound can suffice. Because bats usually leave their roosts in the evening, sealing the holes during nighttime hours can prevent the animals from returning.

Wood destroyers

The principal types of wood-destroying pests are subterranean termites, dry-wood termites, carpenter ants, carpenter bees, and bark beetles and cerambycids.

Subterranean termites. Subterranean termites require moisture to survive. For this reason they almost always live in the ground near the water table, sometimes as much as 100 feet from the surface. Survival away from the soil is accomplished by constructing mud shelter tubes. In some cases a secondary colony will establish itself away from the soil, inside a structure with a moisture problem (such as plumbing leaks, loose ceramic tiles in showers, or improper or damaged roof flashing).

Subterranean termites live on cellulose. Typically, they will enter a piece of wood (such as a beam or flooring) and eat the inside of it, leaving the outside largely intact. The damage they cause is not necessarily confined to wood. They may also eat other things containing cellulose, such as books, wallpaper, and clothing. In some cases they have been found in or beneath buildings containing no wood at all.

Subterranean termites usually swarm in the spring, and sometimes in the fall, when winged reproductives (alates) leave an established colony to start a new one. Swarming can also occur after control treatments are applied. Some people (children in particular) can become almost hysterical when they see a nearby swarm.

After subterranean termites swarm, they drop their wings, and an infestation often can be identified by the dropped wings. Other signs are the mud tubes they make for out-of-ground survival and damaged wood, especially when it contains traces of mud.

Actually seeing live or dead termites is an obvious indicator of problems, but it is essential to know the difference between a termite and a flying ant, which is illustrated in Fig. 6.1.

A relatively new approach to detection involves use of dogs that are specially trained to locate termites by scent. News reports of tests indicate that this may be the most effective detection method of all. Dogs were able to locate infestations that went undetected by trained professionals. (Reportedly, however, the trained dogs cannot differentiate between termites and ants and thus require human assistance.)

Subterranean termites cannot be eliminated altogether. However, they can be controlled, usually by treating the soil around a structure with a mixture of 1 percent chlordane. They will either avoid the chemical or, as they "commute" through it from their colony to the inside of a building, they are killed by it. Proper mixture and placement of the chemical are essential to its effectiveness. Fully trained personnel are required for the task. It is essential to ensure that the pest-control contractors you consider have adequately trained staff, and that their experience records indicate they will still be in business when needed to service the guarantee that should be part of the contract.

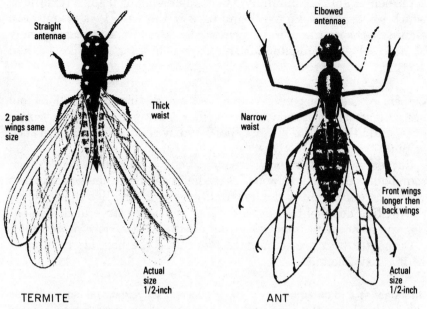

Figure 6.1 Major differences between a termite and a flying ant.

Dry-wood termites. Dry-wood termites are most commonly found in the southern portions of the United States, from California to Florida. They are sometimes found in the mid-Atlantic areas, usually because they have been imported there in an artifact of some type, or in a piece of molding or furniture that originated in an area where dry-wood termites are common.

As their name implies, dry-wood termites do not require moisture to survive, nor do they live in soil. Their "handiwork" usually can be distinguished from that of subterranean termites through examination of the tunnels they eat in wood. These tunnels will not contain mud. Instead, they will contain six-sided pellets (droppings).

A space infested by dry-wood termites must be fumigated. In the case of small objects that are infested, either heating or freezing can be effective, depending on the nature of the object involved. For heat elimination, it must be exposed to a temperature of at least 150°F for a period of 1 hour per inch of thickness. Alternatively, an object can be placed in a freezer for 72 to 96 hours.

Carpenter ants. Carpenter ants are usually black (some may have some red on their body) and large. (Workers are often ¼ inch long or longer; queens may be ⅝ inch long.) They construct their nests in wood, usually where there has been some moisture, and thus can cause structural damage.

Carpenter ants are eliminated most commonly by using a toxic dust, which workers pick up and bring back to the nest. It is essential to eliminate the nest and, in particular, the queen. In some cases it may be necessary to fumigate, but this approach is far more costly than dusting.

Carpenter bees.   Carpenter bees have three distinct body regions and are winged. They are black with yellow markings and, as carpenter ants, build their nests in wood, particularly relatively soft wood such as pine.

Carpenter bee infestations are identified by the near-perfect ½-inch round holes they drill in wood. These holes can be as much as 2 inches deep. The queen enters the hole to lay her eggs and live there. While the drilling done by the carpenter bees can cause structural weakening, the defacement it causes usually is the most serious problem.

Carpenter bees are eliminated by sealing the hole after filling it with a toxic chemical.

Bark beetles and cerambycids.   Bark beetles (scoytids) and cerambycids eat firewood, and thus can enter a dwelling on firewood brought in for utilitarian or decorative purposes. The bark beetle is a small dark stubby insect that infests green wood only. The cerambycid is a brightly colored beetlelike insect with long antennae, usually ½ to 1 inch long. It, too, infects green wood, but sometimes will emerge from new hardwoods. Both insects are attracted to windows.

Clean out is effected by removing the firewood and killing the insects with a pyrethrin aerosol. Generally no additional procedures are required because the pests do not reinfest.

Cockroaches

Cockroaches are perhaps the heartiest of all living species. They have been on earth for at least 300 million years and today exist in some 68,000 varieties. For the most part, cockroaches are more nuisances than anything else. However, some people are allergic to them and the substances they leave behind or excrete, some of which are carcinogenic (cancer-causing). Cockroaches may also carry disease organisms on their feet.

Figure 6.2 illustrates five of the more common types of cockroaches: German, American, oriental, brown-banded, and vega.

German cockroach.   German cockroaches are the most common in dwellings. Adults are colored light tan to brown and are distinguished by two stripes on their pronotum (the shields behind their

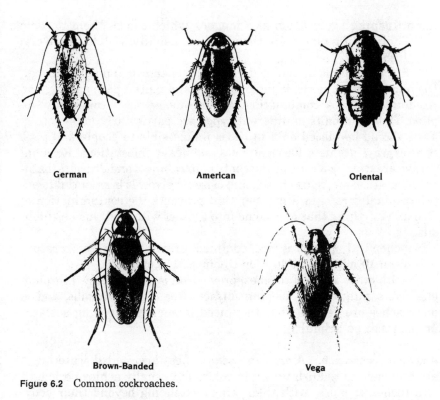

German   American   Oriental

Brown-Banded   Vega

Figure 6.2   Common cockroaches.

heads). They will usually grow to ⅛ to ½ inch in length. Perhaps the most noteworthy aspect of German roaches is their reproductive capacity. One male-female pair can produce 35,000 offspring in 1 year.

German cockroaches are far more active at night than during the day. They leave their hiding places only to find food and water, and thus are most commonly seen in kitchens and bathrooms. Their hiding places almost always are dark in the daytime, and often include cracks and crevices near dishwashing areas, dishwashers, and plumbing fixtures; under and around stoves, refrigerators, and other appliances; around garbage and laundry chutes, shelves, drawers, and false bottoms of cabinets; and inside clocks, radios, other small appliances, and electrical boxes.

If German cockroaches are found in nonfood areas, such as living rooms or bedrooms, it may be an indication of a particularly severe infestation.

Once a German cockroach problem is known to exist, the first step is to locate their hiding places. This usually is done by applying a flushing agent (such as a fogger), which causes them to come out. Their hiding places are then located, usually with the help of a flashlight.

Control mechanisms can be divided into chemical and nonchemical. Chemical control methods include dusts and baits, space sprays, and residual sprays. A combination of these measures is commonly applied. Dust and baits of different types are particularly long-lasting. They should be placed only in areas inaccessible to people and pets. Space sprays are used for clean outs and heavy infestations. Residual sprays are used as a continuing control, in cabinets and drawers, bathroom vanities, medicine chests, and closet shelves. It is essential to apply residual sprays in a manner that prevents the contamination of food and anything that may come into contact with food, such as utensils.

Nonchemical measures are confined principally to temperature extremes: 10 minutes at 40°F or 1 hour at 115 or 120°F.

As with other types of roaches, prevention is best practiced through effective sanitation. By keeping surfaces free of food, crumbs, and so on, roaches are denied what they need to survive. Keeping surfaces dry can also be helpful.

American cockroach. American cockroaches (also called waterbugs) are brownish to reddish brown in color, and usually achieve a length of 2 inches or more, with their wings extending beyond their body. (They can glide considerable distances from high spots.) They are generally similar to German cockroaches, but they seek warmer (82°F), more humid areas. For this reason they are most commonly found in ceilings, boiler rooms, crawl spaces, floor drains, chimneys, incinerators, pipe chases, and sewers. Although they sometimes live several floors up in a building, they seldom go above the ground floor and most often stay in a basement.

Because the American cockroach often favors wet areas, dusts seldom are applicable for control purposes. Depending on the amount of moisture involved, however, baits may be effective when scattered lightly throughout the infested area. Space sprays usually are highly effective, but a second treatment may be required within 30 to 60 days because the pest's eggs are highly resistant to insecticides. Residual sprays also are effective on American cockroaches, but their hiding places require thorough treatment. Treating an entire area with a residual spray often is recommended.

Nonchemical means for effecting control or supplementing other measures include the use of ventilation, dehumidifiers, or dessicants to reduce humidity, as well as ventilation or cooling to lower temperatures.

Oriental cockroach. Oriental cockroaches (also called waterbugs) are brownish blackish in color, grow up to 2 inches, and have small wing pads. Their habits are almost identical to those of American cockroaches, and often they are found in the same types of locations. However, the oriental roach is more resistant to cooler temperatures. Control methods generally are the same as those applied for American cockroaches.

Brown-banded cockroach. Brown-banded cockroaches are yellow to reddish brown in color, and are distinguished by two cross bands on their wings. They usually attain 3½ inches in length. They can fly and usually attach egg capsules to available surfaces.

Brown-banded cockroaches can be found anywhere in a building, but they commonly show a preference for high places. Unlike many other cockroach species, they usually are not found near sources of moisture and, similar to the American cockroach, prefer temperatures of 80°F or higher. The pest eats and pollutes food, and also eats wallpaper paste, bookbindings, furniture glue, and fabric; it gives off a bad odor. It is often found in and around furniture and ceiling moldings.

Control method options are essentially the same as those applicable to the German cockroach, but the method and extent of application differ. Sanitation does not play as a major a role in prevention.

Vega cockroach. Vega cockroaches are found principally in southwestern portions of the United States. They normally live in grass adjacent to the foundation of a building. Because they are sensitive to moisture changes, they usually enter a building only when it is too wet or too dry outside. They are a particular annoyance because they wander around inside a building during daylight hours. In appearance, the vega cockroach resembles a German cockroach, except that it has a black stripe between its eyes. It grows to about ½ inch.

Vega cockroaches typically are cleaned out by cutting a 4-inch swath in the grass beside a foundation wall and then dusting or spraying the area. Garbage areas, compost piles, and piles of fallen leaves are treated similarly. Indoors the treatment is essentially the same as that used for German cockroaches.

Ants and spiders

Ants and spiders usually are nuisance pests that do little damage. There are exceptions, however, and one of these is the pharaoh ant. It prefers to nest indoors, in dark warm areas accessible to moisture, such as wall voids. A colony can comprise 300,000 or more ants, and they have a habit of forming new colonies in the same building. They are trail-laying ants, that is, they move in single-file fashion, one behind another. While it is possible to follow them back to a nest, elimination of one nest may do little when a building may have many. Conventional dusts and residual chemicals have been somewhat effective for control. A growth regulator used exclusively for pharaoh ants takes longer to work, but is more effective. (The development of a chemical exclusively for this ant underscores the dimensions of the problem.)

Chemical treatments can be used for most other ants, and improved sanitation generally will be highly effective in prevention. Chemicals also work on spiders, but to a limited degree only. Generally speaking, eliminating cobwebs is about the best that can be done insofar as spiders are concerned.

Ticks and fleas

Ticks may or may not pose a health problem, depending on the type involved. The lone-star tick, American dog tick, and female wood tick carry Rocky Mountain spotted fever and tick paralysis, and they do bite humans. They occur principally in woods, fields, along paths, and in animal sleeping areas. The brown dog tick does not bite people, but it can thrive indoors in winter if a dog is present. A fully engorged female will lay eggs in cracks and crevices behind baseboards, furniture, and picture frames, among other areas.

Fleas commonly are brought indoors by dogs, cats, or rodents. Adult fleas live on blood. They customarily leave two to three small bites in a row on humans' lower legs.

Ticks and fleas are eliminated indoors by treating carpets and floors with residual spray, and by applying residual spray, dust, or aerosols in cracks and crevices around moldings, for example. Aerosol "bombs" give short-term relief only.

Before tick or flea service is provided, those with the problem should be encouraged to wash all pet bedding and throw rugs, and to vacuum floors, carpeting, and upholstered furniture (particularly beneath the cushions). Vacuum bags should be discarded in an outdoor trash receptacle. All small items on the floor (including those under beds and other furniture) should be removed, and pets should be professionally dipped.

After tick or flea service has been performed, pets and children should not be allowed on the floor until it is completely dry (usually within 2 hours or so). Floors should not be mopped or vacuumed for 2 weeks.

Bees and wasps

Bees and wasps can do some structural damage, but their major threat is the health hazard they pose to those allergic to their stings. People with even mild allergies could be severely injured—possibly fatally—by multiple stings. Those with severe allergies can be injured fatally by just a few stings. Mostly people are frightened by any type of bee or wasp, and those that build their nests in walls can create a noise nuisance.

Paper wasps and hornets generally build aerial nests that hang from eaves or trees. Bumble bees build nests in the ground, as do yellow jackets, which frequently use a wall void as well. They are a particular nuisance around garbage and food in late summer. Honey bees also build nests in wall voids, and a local beekeeper may be willing to remove them for you. Mud wasps build a mud nest that often is mistaken for a subterranean termite's mud tubing.

For the most part, there is no highly effective bee or wasp preventive, other than attempting to structurally seal those openings that some will use to gain access to a nest built in a wall void. Insofar as clean out is concerned, the physical removal of hanging nests is required, and nests in walls and the ground can be fumigated. In all cases, it is essential to use proper equipment, such as masks and gloves, to prevent being stung.

Other indoor pests

Other common indoor pests include silverfish (which eat the fiber in paper), millipedes, centipedes, sow bugs, pill bugs, bedbugs (found where people sleep), camel crickets (often found in damp basements), earwigs, and pantry pests (a large number of pests that live in food products typically stored in a pantry). Chemical methods are commonly used to eliminate most of these pests. Improved sanitation, elimination of leaks, and similar measures are the best preventives in most instances.

Other outdoor pests

Other outdoor nuisance pests include flies, gnats, mosquitoes, and numerous others. Foggers are virtually useless in eliminating them; mechanical means almost always are best. Mechanical means include "black light" devices that attract certain insects. Some use a hot electric grid to electrocute the bugs. Others use a small fan that vacuums flying insects into a bag, resulting in less noise than a "zapper." Other mechanical or nonchemical devices include those which use an aroma to attract flying insects. Note that certain outdoor pests may enter a building through cracks and crevices. For example, cluster flies enter buildings in the fall to hibernate in wall voids, window frames, and attics. Sealing points of entry is the best preventive.

Sources of Assistance

Three sources of pest control assistance are commonly relied upon by property managers: public officials and educators, pest-control consultants, and pest-control contractors.

Public officials and educators

Public officials who sometimes can be of direct assistance include those who work for a federal, state, or local government extension service. By contacting the various agencies which may be involved, you will be able to ascertain the nature and degree of assistance available. Many will at least be able to offer assistance insofar as pest identification is concerned. When small animals are involved, a public agency may be able to provide use of a trap of some type, along with instructions on how to use it. Many also can provide instructional publications and can make you aware of the various laws that apply. In some cases, the extent of regulation may be near unbelievable, as when the use of toxic chemicals involves a variety of agencies.

Educators may be part of an extension service. Usually the best starting point is a large state university. The services provided may be essentially similar to those described in the preceding paragraph. More extensive assistance may be attainable if it can be made part of a project of some type.

Either public officials or educators may be in a position to provide referrals to pest-control contractors whom they believe to be particularly well qualified.

Pest-control consultants

A pest-control consultant usually would be employed to perform a comprehensive inspection, identify the pests that already exist and their causes, as well as situations that could lead to a problem, and suggest procedures and materials to be used to eliminate existing pests.

For the most part, the services provided by pest-control consultants are also performed by many reputable contractors. The difference is that pest-control consultants are (or should be) in independent private practice. They have no incentive to recommend any particular type of product or service, or to recommend more than you need.

Pest-control contractors

Most property managers rely on pest-control contractors. The key to proper selection is a comprehensive work specification that results in each contractor submitting a bid or estimate on exactly the same work. Regrettably, specifications often are somewhat vague, forcing each contractor to make assumptions. As such, each price reflects a different concept of the work; so apples cannot be compared to apples.

Many contractors will provide an inspection as well as a work specification. Of course, they realize that the specification they develop is likely to be used in soliciting bids from themselves and from their competition. Each is therefore likely to develop the specification in a manner that tends to favor its own particular way of doing things, the products it prefers, and so on. This is natural; contractors who operate in any other way would not stay in business too long. However, this does not prevent you from asking each interested contractor to suggest alternatives and to price each one. Each such alternative should be fully explained to indicate why it is better, or at least as good as whatever is included in the specification.

Obviously, it would be a waste of time to deal with several contractors during the comprehensive inspection and specification-development stage. Select one contractor—the best, most reputable, and most experienced you know of—to provide assistance. If you do not already have a relationship with a pest-control contractor, use the procedures suggested earlier for selecting a consultant to identify the most reputable, experienced contractor you can.

Obtaining Resident/Tenant Cooperation

Mrs. Jones sees a mouse in her apartment. She becomes frightened and, in a near-panic, she trips over an ottoman and breaks her knee. She becomes incapacitated for a period of time and loses her job as a result. She contacts a lawyer to sue the owner of the building and the property manager for failure to provide adequate pest control. Absurd? Absolutely. Possible? Absolutely. But it does not mean that it's an owner's or a manager's responsibility to make sure every rodent, every cockroach, and every other pest is eliminated from a building. The task is impossible, and courts understand that (especially if the eventuality is mentioned in your lease). However, the courts would perhaps not take kindly to the owner or manager if nothing had been done to alleviate a known infestation problem, or if due diligence had not been exercised to help assure the performance of effective service. Even if an owner or manager in such a case was found not liable, costs still would be incurred.

Some may argue that litigious mania is putting society into sorry shape. Many attorneys counter that they have served to better define responsibilities, and that the fear of litigation has caused many persons (owners, property managers, doctors, design professionals—even lawyers) to "clean up their acts." And, to a very real extent, it is difficult to deny such a position.

In any event, no matter what specific pest-control strategy is used, it will work best when full tenant cooperation is obtained. Several appropriate techniques for gaining this cooperation have been described in preceding sections. In many instances, contractor or consultant assistance can be obtained to make such efforts more effective.

Consider the following suggestions. Implementing some will at least help minimize pest problems, and may even help prevent a lawsuit.

1. *Guidance at move-in.* When tenants move into a building, consider giving them some information about pest control. Something such as Notice 6.1 may serve.

2. *Precautionary advice.* Prior to the performance of regular exterminating services, each tenant should be notified of precautions to take. This is essential. Some people may become ill soon after the service is performed and will blame it on the chemicals used or their improper application. Advance warning will help ensure that no such illness in fact is caused by pest-control services. It will also document the fact that management has acted in a cautious, prudent manner. A typical warning follows (see Notice 6.2).

Welcome to XYZ Gardens. We all take pride in the appearance of the building, and we do our best to make it a desirable place to live. For this reason we take particular pains to minimize any pest problems, such as cockroaches and rodents. We have engaged a professional pest-control contractor to assist us in these areas. But the regular spreading of chemicals and use of other means is not enough. We need your help in the area of sanitation.

1. Please do not feed birds. The damage they can do is incredible (chewing electrical lines which creates fire hazards; building nests in ducts and vents; spreading disease through their droppings, and so on).

2. Keep your unit clean and dry. Tiny amounts of food and moisture are all it takes to draw cockroaches. By keeping the floor clean, not leaving dirty dishes in the sink overnight, reporting any leaks, and so on, you can help deny a cockroach what it needs to flourish. (The most common type has 35,000 offspring per year!)

3. Keep your pets clean. Ticks and fleas can be a problem, but not much of one if you regularly have your pet dipped during the warmer months. Do not leave pet food dishes on the balcony.

If you do encounter pests of any type, or evidence of them, please let us know. Note also that regular exterminating services are performed every third month. You will be notified in advance of certain precautions you should take.

Notice 6.1

On Tuesday, November 8, ABC Exterminating will be in your unit to perform chemical treatment to help eliminate all cockroaches. If you are home, you will be able to recognize the ABC technician by a blue uniform. If you are not home, a member of our staff will accompany the technician while the service is being performed.

It is essential for you to follow the instructions below to help assure health, safety, and effective treatment.

Before Treatment

- Kitchen cabinets must be treated thoroughly. **Please remove** dishes, pots, pans, and foodstuffs from **all** kitchen and pantry cabinets and drawers.

- Please clear all counter tops.

- Wipe down the sides of all kitchen cabinets.

- Empty all closets (including shelves and floors) in any room with an infestation, or where you have seen a cockroach.

- Cover fish tanks and turn off the air pump.

- Put away dog or cat food bowls.

- Remove dogs, cats, birds, or other pets from your apartment, or place them in a room which is not to be treated. Close the door to that room and put a sign on the door, for example, **"Do not enter—dog."**

During Treatment

- Remove yourself from your unit. Stay out of your unit for approximately 2 hours.

After Treatment

- Do not allow children or pets to touch any treated surface until it is completely dry. This usually takes about 2 hours (provided you've opened the windows).

- Do not wipe down treated surfaces.

- Do not leave dirty dishes, pet food bowls, and so on, in the sink overnight.

- Note that activity may increase for a few hours (or even up to 3 days) after treatment. However, if activity is still high after 2 weeks, please inform the resident manager (Mrs. Smith: 555-1212).

Thanks for your cooperation.

Notice 6.2

Speak with a pest-control consultant or contractor as to proper wording and warnings. Determine who will print and distribute the notice, how it will be delivered, and whether or not notices should be placed in other locations (such as elevator, laundry room, or community room).

3. *Pre-clean-out advice.*   If the building is about to undergo clean-out services for the first time, at least a notice such as that shown above should be issued. However, more may be appropriate, depending on the circumstances. As an example, it would be possible to hold a meeting of tenants where the contractor discusses what will be done, the nature of the chemicals to be used, precautions the contractor's personnel will use, precautions residents can take, and so on. Older people in particular tend to be concerned about matters such as these, and they often are those most susceptible to problems of one kind or another.

4. *Meetings.*   A meeting often is the most effective tool for gaining tenant cooperation when a particular problem must be eliminated, such as the presence of birds. At a meeting, the nature of the problems could be explained, emphasizing first those problems that affect tenants directly, those that create fire and other hazards, those that can lead to discomfort and energy waste, and, finally, those that can create the type of additional expense that can be recouped only through rent increases. Clean out, maintenance, and preventive measures also should be discussed, giving reasons for techniques used and not used. Perhaps a local representative of a government extension service would be able to assist at such a meeting.

5. *Seasonal guidance.*   It may be appropriate to issue certain advisories at different times of the year. In the summer, all tenants of buildings near wooded areas should be advised about ticks that can get on them. If bees and wasps are a problem from time to time, tenants should be advised to take certain precautions to avoid them.

Unquestionably, steps such as those indicated take time. But the time required can be extremely well spent. It can help minimize pest problems, as well as the legal hassles that otherwise could ensue. It also creates a very positive image for management, and thus helps improve occupancy rates, profitability, and overall building value. Note, however, that concern must be more than skin-deep. Management must also make a commitment to assuring that whomever it selects to provide pest control is qualified to do it well, has all appropriate licenses and insurances, obtains the necessary permits, abides by all regulatory requirements, and employs only honest individuals who are properly trained and supervised, among other concerns. By implementing such an attitude, property managers do far more than create the basis for a strong legal defense. They set into motion the steps required to prevent the kind of problems that can make legal defense necessary to begin with.

Work Specification

Generally speaking, the services of a pest-control contractor can be subdivided into three principal types.

1. *Comprehensive inspection.*   This service should be performed for those buildings to which pest-control services have not been applied previously, or when it is necessary to switch pest-control contractors due to the inadequacy of the one now providing the service. A comprehensive inspection usually is advisable as part of a preacquisition study, and in most cases should be performed routinely on an annual, biennial, or triennial basis.

2. *Initial services.*   Initial services, also called clean-out services, comprise those directed principally at eliminating, or at least minimizing, existing problems, as by placing bait trays and tracking powder to reduce the rodent population.

3. *Maintenance services.*   These comprise the routine ongoing services aimed at keeping the various pest problems under control (elimination where possible, or minimization) by repeated application of certain chemicals, replacement of bait trays, or other means as needed.

Two other services also are worthy of note: emergency services and "other" preventive services.

Emergency services frequently are needed after initial services have been conducted, because the application of control techniques may cause certain pests to look for new quarters. This often is a temporary condition, but one that demands attention nonetheless. In any event, if an apartment resident or office worker sees a mouse or a cockroach, chances are management will learn about it soon, and will want to have the pest-control contractor on the scene as quickly as possible, at least to demonstrate concern. A given number of emergency service calls customarily are included in a pest-control contract.

"Other" preventive services relate to certain types of structural modifications that may be desirable or necessary. These are identified through a comprehensive inspection. Pest-control contractors may or may not be able to provide some or all of these services. Even if they are, other sources of assistance almost always are available, including other types of contractors and in-house personnel. When these services are performed by someone other than the pest-control contractor, the pest-control contractor should at least be called upon to review the work in order to assure its adequacy from a pest-control viewpoint.

Comprehensive inspection

Most pest-control contractors provide inspection as a routine element of their services to identify needs and, accordingly, the services required. But this type of inspection seldom is extensive enough to meet an owner's needs. The prescriptive specification that follows is provided to indicate the type of comprehensive inspection that can be particularly valuable for a building owner. The report identifies (or should identify) virtually all the information needed to determine what needs to be done for effective pest control.

It is unrealistic to expect a pest-control contractor to perform a comprehensive inspection and provide a report free of charge. Usually best results are obtained by relying on a pest-control consultant or a reputable pest-control contractor paid on a separate fee basis. Obviously, such an inspection should be conducted before a pest-control contract is let.

CONTRACTOR shall perform a comprehensive inspection of the building's common areas and all other areas except tenant space. Based on this comprehensive inspection, CONTRACTOR shall provide a comprehensive report identifying at least the following:

1. *Evidence of past pest problems.* CONTRACTOR shall identify evidence of past pest problems, such as: staining or corrosion created by guano; wiring or insulation gnawed by rodents; and nests left by wasps or bees. CONTRACTOR shall to the best of CONTRACTOR's knowledge also identify:
   a. Remedial measures needed to repair damage caused
   b. Approximate cost of these remedial measures
   c. Methods to prevent recurrence of the problem
   d. Cost of implementing preventive measures
2. *Evidence of current pest problems.* CONTRACTOR shall identify evidence of current pest problems and, for each:
   a. The nature of the problem
   b. The specific pest(s) causing the problem
   c. The methods suggested for eliminating and subsequently controlling the pest(s) and, for each:
      (1) Specific materials to be used
      (2) Locations, methods, and frequency of application
      (3) Quantity of each material per application
      (4) Equipment required to apply the material
      (5) Special training required to apply the material safely
      (6) Approximate cost of material and its application
      (7) Federal, state, and local ordinances that must be complied

with relative to items (1) through (6) above, with identification of sources of additional information about each, including compliance measures
  (8) Feasible alternatives for items (1) through (6) above, with reasons why they are not recommended
  (9) Maintenance programs required, with specificity as suggested by items (1) through (7) above
  (10) Appropriate preventive measures beyond those identified above (structural modifications, etc.) and their estimated cost
  (11) Similar information which may be of value if the owner decides to conduct pest control partially or wholly on an in-house basis
3. *Sources of possible future problems.* CONTRACTOR shall identify all existing conditions that could lead to pest problems in the future. Such problems include, but are by no means limited to: structural defects permitting entry by rodents, birds, bats, etc.; improperly containerized trash; and grass or weeds not sufficiently cut to help prevent ticks.
4. *Other.* It is the intent of management to effect all measures necessary to eliminate all pests and prevent any further infestations. Additional information appropriate to help attaining these goals should be furnished.

It should be noted that tenant space was excluded from the survey areas identified. Full or partial (representative) inspection of tenant spaces may be desirable. An absence of tenant complaints does not necessarily mean an absence of pest problems. Likewise, a tenant complaint is not necessarily an indication of major problems.

A comprehensive survey report should be made part of the building's historical record. Reports related to corrective actions and follow-up inspections should also be part of the record.

Initial services

The initial services needed can be identified through either a performance specification or a prescriptive specification. A performance specification identifies a service in terms of the problem to be dealt with, such as, "ABC will eliminate the rodent problem now being experienced in the boiler room by applying appropriate approved chemicals." A prescriptive specification would identify exactly what chemicals (or other means) would be used, where and how they would be applied, how much would be used, and so on. If you are relying on a pest-control consultant, the consultant should be able to develop a prescriptive specification for you. Using a prescriptive specification also helps assure that all contractors are bidding on the same services, thus permitting "apples-to-apples" comparisons. Of course, when using a prescriptive specification, contractors should be encouraged to submit alternatives where they feel such alternatives should be considered. Each alternative should be explained in terms of why it should be considered instead of the procedure specified. The cost of the alternative also should be discussed.

Initial services that affect individual tenant-occupied units should be considered with care. How will the service be scheduled? Who will notify residents/occupants of the impending service? If management issues notifications, will the pest-control contractor provide instructional wording? Are contractor personnel to enter a unit accompanied or unaccompanied by management representatives? **Do not assume!** By spelling out such matters in a contract, discussion of the issues and a complete "meeting of the minds" are assured.

Maintenance services

Ongoing routine maintenance services also can be written on a performance or a prescriptive basis, and requirements usually are included in a contract for initial services. (Most contracts with pest-control companies are written on an annual basis.) Most routine services are relatively easy to identify, and can be spelled out in a prescriptive manner. However, whether using a prescriptive or a performance specification, it will be impossible to identify the services needed to deal with the unanticipated. Accordingly, it may be advisable to request a prospective contractor to indicate also the rates applicable for dealing with the unanticipated. This would include appropriate unit rates for different chemicals, with an indication of how much would be needed for certain types of pest problems, the time required to place the chemicals (if a separate trip should be needed), and such other information as will help you to know what to expect with regard to additional charges.

Emergency services

Emergency services will usually be part of an ongoing contract with a pest-control contractor. However, most contracts tend to be vague as to what emergency services actually are. Accordingly, the bid documents issued should define emergency services in the specification. Consider the following wording.

Emergency services comprise those services necessary to eliminate immediately a recurrence of a problem that the pest-control contractor (CONTRACTOR) is under contract to eliminate, and which CON-TRACTOR had endeavored to eliminate, as part of initial clean-out and/or ongoing control services. CONTRACTOR shall respond as quickly as possible to requests phoned or faxed to CONTRACTOR by an appropriate management representative, on the basis merited by the situation. For example, if a cockroach problem is identified in a unit that has been serviced to eliminate cockroaches, and only a few cockroaches are involved, follow-up service shall be provided within 48 hours after the call is received. However, if a severe infestation has been identified, much faster response (within 8 hours) shall be provided. CON-TRACTOR shall provide up to [_____] emergency service calls per month. CONTRACTOR recognizes that some of these calls may be occasioned by overreaction to a minor problem, but shall impose no additional charge in such cases, in that such situations are relatively common. If more than [_____] emergency calls are required per month, and such are not occasioned by overreaction, the efficacy of CONTRACTOR's procedures shall be reviewed before any additional fee is paid.

Obviously, if a contract relates to the control of certain specific problems, emergency services may not apply to other problems that may be noted. For example, if a contractor is retained principally to eliminate roach and rodent problems, the contractor should not be expected to provide emergency service to remove a large hornets' nest without additional charge. On the other hand, if a contractor has agreed to provide overall pest-control services, such an emergency service may be provided without additional charge, or at an additional charge that reflects certain portions of "open rates" only, such as the need for a ladder or for special equipment of some kind.

In these and other contractual matters, the mutual goal should be maintaining a property as free from pest problems as possible at a reasonable cost. This can be best attained by ensuring that all parties to a contract understand fully what can be expected.

Other services

Other services also should be spelled out. One of these may be a meeting with the board of directors of a condominium or cooperative. A pest-control contractor should also be able to provide other valuable assistance. For example, the contractor should be able to develop a small, easily readable brochure (or even a single typewritten sheet) that gives tenants guidance on what they can do to help improve sanitation and thus minimize pest problems. Likewise, the contractor could possibly lead a discussion to which all tenants are invited, explaining the service that will soon be performed, providing guidance on sanitation and safety, and answering whatever questions may arise. This latter approach, in particular, may be helpful in minimizing complaints (and possibly lawsuits) that could emanate from misunderstandings. If such additional services are desired, they should be spelled out in the specifications.

Swimming-Pool
Management

Introduction

A swimming pool is an important asset. Serving as a source of exercise, relaxation, and socialization, it helps to attract tenants or unit owners, and to reduce turnover. For these reasons, a pool can enhance the value of a property as well as its salability.

A property manager is responsible for the owner/client's real property assets and must help ensure that their value is maintained, if not increased. Swimming-pool management is particularly important in this respect. Without effective management, a pool can quickly become a liability, especially in terms of negligence claims.

Not too many years ago, a property manager's most significant swimming-pool worry was opening on time. If people weren't able to take their first swim of the year on Memorial Day, life for the property manager would not be pleasant.

Today, timely pool opening still is a concern, but many other issues also must be addressed. Almost all apply whether or not pool use is seasonal, indoors or outdoors. As examples: Are all potential safety hazards clearly marked? Are warning signs in place? Is life-saving equipment readily accessible and in good working order? Are chemicals properly stored and secured? A negative response to any of these or countless similar questions could result in someone being injured or damaged, which in turn can lead to disputes, negative publicity, and legal fees. The severity of such problems can be far greater than the difficulties associated with premature equipment failure and unnecessarily high repair bills. Nonetheless, the latter problems also involve vital concerns which, if not properly tended to, can turn an asset into a liability.

Some property managers prefer to assign all pool-related tasks to in-house personnel. Cost-effectiveness usually is the objective, but close analysis is required to determine whether cost-effectiveness really results. More risk must be assumed, not only because there is no service provider to share it with, but also because professional pool management contractors are less likely to commit errors or omissions. They have a large contingent of trained personnel to draw from, including fill-ins, who can replace absentees temporarily. In addition, field operations usually are subject to continuing quality-control inspections. In other words, contract pool management may require greater out-of-pocket expense, but often it provides more value. In some cases, the cost of contract management can actually be less.

Many multifamily residential property managers rely on pool management contractors to fulfill their needs. Typically, resident managers provide local oversight on a daily basis, with the property manager checking in once a week or more frequently.

Basic Management Functions

Basic management functions usually comprise opening, operating, and closing a pool, and performing appropriate preventive maintenance and repair. Not all pools require closing, of course, but those that do are particularly dependent on effective management. For them, effective management begins with a thorough inspection and planning for the upcoming season.

Inspection and planning

Planning for "next" season begins the day after "this" season ends. It starts with inspection. Many property managers prefer to be directly involved in the task by doing it either on their own or in conjunction with the contractor's representative. Usually it can be made an element of the winterization shutdown activities. A sample form used for this purpose is shown in Fig. 7.1.

Inspection begins with a review of the documents developed over the season just ended. These include the contractor's periodic inspection report (weekly, biweekly, or monthly), such as the one shown in Fig. 7.2, as well as notes made by the lifeguard, resident manager, or other site personnel. It may even be desirable to speak with a few residents to get their opinion of pool management. Hard facts also are required to identify any problem areas or suspected problems.

A pocket tape recorder and an instant camera or a video tape recorder can be particularly helpful when inspecting facilities. The dictating unit permits rapid notation of all relevant observations. The camera facilitates an illustrated report. This approach can be a valu-

SERVICE & EQUIPMENT ORDER

FOR _____   I.R.# _____

POOL

BUILDER _____ DATE _____

			Equip. & Materials			
	Labor Cost	Unit Cost	Total Cost	Total Labor & Parts	Authori- zation	

I. DECK EQUIPMENT & POOL FITTINGS

A. LIFEGUARD STAND(S): Make: _____ NR _____PTG. Required_____
  1. Condition: .... NR OK _____ NR Repair/Replace _____
  2. Parts Needed .... Umbrellas Reqd. _____
    a) Guard Seat .... NR OK _____ NR Repair/Replace _____
    b) Foot Board .... NR OK _____ NR Repair/Replace _____
    c) Misc. _____
B. LADDERS OR GRAB RAIL .... NR _____ NR Replace _____
  1. Parts Required:
    a) Ladder Bumpers .... NR _____
    b) Treads .... NR _____ .... Cycolac ☐ S/S ☐
    c) Tread Bolts .... NR _____ Size _____
    d) Misc. _____
  2. Repairs:
    a) Deck Anchors .... NR Reset _____ NR Replace _____ Type _____
    b) Wedges .... NR Replace _____ Type ___
    c) Misc. Repairs _____
C. HANDRAILS .... NR OK _____ NR Replace _____ Size _____
  1. Wedges .... NR Replace _____ Type _____
  2. Deck Anchors .... NR Reset _____ NR Replace _____ Type _____
  3. Misc. _____
D. DIVING STAND(S): Type _____ ☐ Low ☐ 1 Mtr ☐ 3 Mtr
  1. Condition .... NR OK _____ NR Replace _____
  2. Parts Needed .... Ptg. Required _____
    a) Tie Down Assembly Complete .... NR Replace _____ Type _____
    b) Diving Board Bolts .... NR Replace _____ Size _____
    c) Fulcrum Pad(s) .... NR Replace _____ Type _____
    d) Fulcrum Bar(s) .... NR Replace _____
    e) Misc. _____
E. DIVING BOARDS: .... NR _____ Type _____ Length(s) _____
  1. Condition .... NR Replace/Repair _____ Length _____ Type _____
  2. Resurfacing Required .... NR Boards _____ .... Type: Metal—Wood
F. FILLSPOUT: Size: _____ MIP FIP ☐ OK ☐ Replace
  Misc (I.E. Valve) _____
G. MISC. DECK EQUIPMENT _____

II. POOL FITTINGS

A. SAFETY LINE: Size: _____ Length _____ ☐ OK ☐ Replace
  1. Floats (5 × 9) 1/5' .... NR OK _____ NR Required _____
  2. Rope Hooks: .... Size _____ Type _____ NR OK _____ NR Reqd. _____
  3. Cup Anchors .... NR OK _____ NR Replace _____
B. MAIN DRAIN GRATES: .... CPB _____ Cycolac _____
  1. Main Pool ..... ☐ OK ☐ Replace .... Size _____ Type _____
  2. Wading Pool ... ☐ OK ☐ Replace .... Size _____ Type _____
C. RETURNS: .... Cover Type _____ NR Top Plate _____ Bottom _____
  1. Misc. _____
D. SKIMMERS: Type _____ NR.M.P. _____ NR.W.P. _____
  1. Wiers of Floats .... NR OK _____ NR Replace _____ Size _____
  2. Baskets: .... NR OK _____ NR Replace _____ Model _____
  3. Skimmer Lids .... NR OK _____ NR Replace _____ Size _____
  4. Throttle/Suction Plates: .... NR Needed _____ Type _____
  5. Misc. _____
E. UNDERWATER LIGHTS: Make: _____ NR _____ Volts _____
  1. Bulbs: .... Type _____ NR Needed _____ Watts _____
  2. Misc. _____
F. PRESSURE TESTING .... ☐ Skimmers ☐ Returns ☐ M.D. ☐ Vacuum
  1. Comments _____

III. POOL SHELL AND POOL AREA

A. SAFETY STENCIL PACKAGE: .... ☐ OK ☐ Redo ☐ None at Pool .....
B. DEPTH MARKINGS ON DECK: .... ☐ OK ☐ Redo
C. DEPTH TILE: .... ☐ OK ☐ Reqd. Type ....
  1. NRS Reqd.: 2's _____, 3's _____, 4's _____, 5's _____, 8's _____, 1/2's _____, Other _____
D. WATERLINE TILE: .... Type-920, 925, Other _____
  1. Main Pool .... ☐ OK ☐ Replace _____ Flat _____ Bullnose _____
  2. Wading Pool: .... ☐ OK ☐ Replace _____ Flat _____ Bullnose _____
E. COPING: .... Type- ☐ DQ ☐ DV Other _____
  1. Main Pool- ☐ OK ☐ Reset _____ ☐ Replace ST _____ RAD _____
  2. Wading Pool: ☐ OK ☐ Reset _____ ☐ Replace ST _____ RAD _____
F. CAULKING: .... ☐ OK ☐ Recommend-Length _____ W _____
G. POOL INTERIOR SURFACE: _____ ☐ OK ☐ Plaster ☐ Paint
  1. Preparation _____ ☐ Sandblast ☐ Cut Tile & Fittings
H. MISC. POOL SHELL REPAIRS
  1. _____
  2. _____

Owner's P.O. or Signature _____   Page 1 of 2

Figure 7.1 Comprehensive pool and pool area inspection form.

able addition to the building's historical record, and can also be useful in documenting needs to the party who must authorize payment.

For the most part, repairs can be made either as part of winter shutdown or as part of preopening operations. Factors typically considered in deciding this issue are the extent to which winter conditions will

POOL NAME _____   I.R.# _____

		Equip. & Materials		Total	
	Labor Cost	Unit Cost	Total Cost	Total Labor & Parts	Authori-zation

IV. FIRST AID, SAFETY & POOL MAINTENANCE EQUIPMENT
A. COT .... ☐ OK .... ☐ Replace .... ☐ None at Pool
B. BLANKETS .... ☐ OK .... ☐ Replace .... ☐ None at Pool
C. GEN'L FIRST AID KIT .... ☐ OK .... ☐ Restock .... ☐ Replace
D. RING BUOY .... ☐ OK .... ☐ Replace .... ☐ None at Pool
E. SHEPPARD HOOK .... ☐ OK .... ☐ Replace .... ☐ None at Pool
F. BACKBOARD .... ☐ OK .... ☐ Replace .... ☐ None at Pool
G. LEAF SKIMMER .... ☐ OK .... ☐ Replace .... ☐ None at Pool
H. POOL BRUSH............... ☐ OK .... ☐ Replace .... ☐ None at Pool
I. VACUUM HEAD: Make _____ .... ☐ OK   ☐ Replace
  1. Misc. _____
J. VACUUM HOSE: Length _____ DIA _____ ☐ OK   ☐ Replace
K. EQUIPMENT POLES: 4/16' Poles Required   NR OK _____ NR Replace _____
L. WATER TESTING EQUIPMENT: Type _____
  1. Chlorine/PH .... ☐ OK .... ☐ Replace .... ☐ None at Pool
  2. Alkalinity .... ☐ OK .... ☐ Replace .... ☐ None at Pool
  3. Calcium .... ☐ OK .... ☐ Replace .... ☐ None at Pool
  4. Cyanuric Acid .... ☐ OK .... ☐ Replace .... ☐ None at Pool
M. Misc. _____

V. FILTER SYSTEM EQUIPMENT
A. HAIR & LINT STRAINER: Model – M.P. _____   W.P. _____
  1. Condition: Main Pool: ....☐ OK .... ☐ Replace .... ☐ Overhaul
            Wading Pool: ....☐ OK .... ☐ Replace .... ☐ Overhaul
  2. Parts Needed:
    a. Lid .... Main Pool ☐ OK .... ☐ Replace Wading Pool ☐ OK ☐ Replace
    b. Gasket .... Main Pool ☐ OK .... ☐ Replace Wading Pool ☐ OK ☐ Replace
    c. Drain Plug .. Main Pool ☐ OK .... ☐ Replace Wading Pool ☐ OK ☐ Replace
    d. Yoke Screw Main Pool ☐ OK .... ☐ Replace Wading Pool ☐ OK ☐ Replace
    e. Yoke ...... Main Pool ☐ OK .... ☐ Replace Wading Pool ☐ OK ☐ Replace
    f. Tee Bolt(s) ....Main Pool   NR OK _____ NR Replace _____ Size _____
       ..... Wading Pool   NR OK _____ NR Replace _____ Size _____
    g. Basket(s) .... Main Pool   NR OK _____ NR Replace _____
       ..... Wading Pool   NR OK _____ NR Replace _____
B. PUMPS: Main Pool _____ H.P. _____ Wading Pool _____ H.P. _____
  1. Service/Storage Required .... ☐ Main Pool .... ☐ Wading Pool
  2. Misc. _____
C. FLOW METER(S)
  1. Main Pool: Type _____ Size _____ ☐ OK   ☐ Overhaul   ☐ Replace
  2. Wading Pool: Type _____ Size _____ ☐ OK   ☐ Overhaul   ☐ Replace
D. FILTER(S): Main Pool – Make _____   NR Tanks _____ Type _____
         Wading Pool – Type _____   NR Tanks _____ Type _____
  1. Exterior Painting Required .... ☐ Main .... ☐ Wading
  2. Recharge Sand Filter(s) .... ☐ Main .... ☐ Wading
  3. Color Code Valving......................... ☐ OK .... ☐ Provide
  4. Misc. _____

  5. Replacement of Filter Tanks................................. ☐ Main   ☐ Wading
E. CHEMICAL FEEDING EQUIPMENT:
  1. Hypochlorinator(s): Main Pool: Model _____   Serial # _____
            Wading Pool: Model _____   Serial # _____
    a. Condition: Main Pool   ☐ OK   ☐ Replace   ☐ None at Pool
            Wading Pool   ☐ OK   ☐ Replace   ☐ None at Pool
    b. Parts Needed: 1) Injection Fitting(s) .... ☐ OK ☐ Replace
             1) Strainer(s) .... ☐ OK ☐ Replace
             1) Tubing .... ☐ OK ☐ Req'd
             1) Strainer Weight .... ☐ OK ☐ Req'd
  2. Misc. _____

VI. MISCELLANEOUS REPAIRS/PARTS
A. POOL DATA CHART   ☐ OK   ☐ Provide
B. _____
C. _____
D. _____
E. _____
F. _____
G. _____

Aqualin Aquatics _____
                    Supervisor
Owner's P.O. or Signature _____

Date _____

UNIT TOTALS .... _____ _____
                         Labor   Parts
SALES TAX   _____

TOTAL DUE (Parts)........

TOTAL LABOR AND PARTS   _____

Page 2 of 2

Figure 7.1 (*Continued*) Comprehensive pool and pool area inspection form.

worsen the situation, and the cost of having the work done in the off-season, when pool contractors are anxious for work, rather than in the spring, when most contractors are busy. Contractors advise that it is most cost-effective to have major repair work, such as concrete re-

DATE _____ TIME _____
STAFF O.D. _____

POOL _____
SUPR _____
WEATHER _____

SUPERVISOR'S FIELD REPORT

POOL AREA	Exc.	Gd.	Fair	Unsat.	Item No.	Comments
1.1 First Impression	☐	☐	☐	☐	☐	_____
1.2 Gate Control	☐	☐	☐	☐		_____
1.3 Uniform	Yes ☐	No ☐				_____
1.4 Gd in Chair	Pool ☐	Deck ☐			☐	_____
1.5 Bather Load						_____
1.6 Safety Equip. (Crook, BKBD Line)	☐	On Deck				_____

CHEMICALS	Staff		Supervisor		Item No.	Comments
	MP	WP	MP	WP		
2.1 CH Level	___	___	___	___	☐	_____
2.2 PH Level	___	___	___	___		_____
2.3 Stabilizer	___	___	___	___	☐	_____
2.4 Total Alkalinity	___		___			_____

WATER	Exc.	Gd.	Fair	Unsat.	Item No.	Comments
3.1 H₂O Clarity	☐	☐	☐	☐	☐	_____
3.2 Pool Bottom	☐	☐	☐	☐		_____
3.3 Waterline Tiles	☐	☐	☐	☐	☐	_____
3.4 MD. Grate Secure	☐	☐	☐	☐		_____

4.1 Sk. Clean and Operating	☐	☐	☐	☐		Comments
4.2 Deck Equip. Secure Ladders ☐ HdRails ☐ D-Bds ☐ Guard Std ☐					☐	_____

BATHHOUSE	Men's				Ladies			
	Exc.	Gd.	Fair	Unsat.	Exc.	Gd.	Fair	Unsat.
5.1 Bathhouse Appearance	☐	☐	☐	☐	☐	☐	☐	☐
5.2 Supplies	Soap ☐	P Towels ☐	Toilet Paper ☐	Lighting ☐	Soap ☐	P Towels ☐	Toilet Paper ☐	Lighting ☐
5.3 Restroom Plumbing O.K.	MR ☐	WR ☐						

FILTER ROOM	Exc.	Gd.	Fair	Unsat.	Item No.	Comments
6.1 Filter Room Appearance	☐	☐	☐	☐	☐	_____
6.2 Flowrate	MP [ ] GPM	WP [ ] GPM				_____
6.3 Press/Diff.	MP Inf ___ Eff ___	WP Inf ___ Eff ___			☐	_____
6.4 Chlorinator Operable ☐ ☐ (Yes No) Secure ☐ ☐ (Yes No) Clean ☐ ☐ (Yes No)					☐	_____
Chemicals on Hand ☐ Sodium Gals Last Del. ___ Date/Amt. ___						_____
Test Reagent: 5 Day Supply ___ Yes ___ No						_____
6.5 Muriatic Acid Gallons On Hand						_____

GUARD ROOM	Exc.	Gd.	Fair	Unsat.	Item No.	Comments
7.1 Guard Room Appearance	☐	☐	☐	☐	☐	_____
	Yes	No				
7.2 Cert. Posted	☐ ☐	Hlth. Rcds.	Yes ☐ No ☐			_____
7.3 Payroll Rec.	☐ ☐	7.6 Placard	☐ ☐		☐	_____
7.4 Record Pkg.	☐ ☐	7.7 Employee Attitude	☐ ☐			_____
7.5 Schedule Posted	☐ ☐				☐	_____

OVERALL RATING ☐ Exc. ☐ Gd. ☐ Fair	OVERALL RATING ☐ Exc. ☐ Gd. ☐ Fair
_____	_____
_____	_____
_____	_____
Supervisor Date	Resident Manager Date

Figure 7.2 Supervisor's periodic field report form.

placement, done just after the season ends. A better price usually can be obtained and prompt repair may limit the extent of damage that failure to repair would otherwise create.

Note: Even if you decide to defer major repairs to the start of the next swim season, schedule them in the fall or winter to avoid last-minute problems.

Pump room. Inspections usually begin in a pool's pump (or filter) room. Fig. 7.3 illustrates its basic components. Key concerns in reviewing them include the following.

Turn pump and motor on and off (for a few seconds only) and listen for any abnormal sounds; check for vibration. Packings and seals should be performing well. Even tiny leaks should be noted.

Check filter equipment plant for proper operation of valves, flow meter and pressure gauge. Look for any rust or signs of leakage.

Examine strainer baskets for hair and lint. Rust or signs of any other deterioration should be noted. (It usually is wise to keep an extra basket on hand.)

Check liquid chlorine vats and chemical feeders, which are the principal chemical feed equipment, thoroughly for corrosion and leakage. In most cases, annual overhaul is needed.

Check that backwash pit drains and floor drains are clear. If there is any standing water, or if any water flows during the inspection, drains should be rechecked to prevent a potential freezing problem.

Conduct a general review to determine the overall quality of maintenance and care provided. This sometimes can yield insights as to the attitudes of the contractor's site and supervisory staff. Are there signs of chemical spills or leakage that have not been cleaned? Have gages

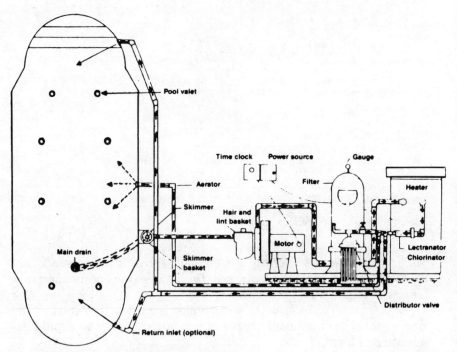

Figure 7.3   Basic pool and pump-room components.

been allowed to get dirty and scratched or have they been kept clean? In general, has someone taken obvious pride in maintaining the physical plant, or do appearances suggest an out-of-sight, out-of-mind attitude?

Pool area. The pool is the most important concern in the pool area. Check for any loose, cracked, or broken tiles or coping, as well as for concrete spalling. Also, look for any cracked or chipped plaster and peeling paint. Check skimmers, too. Inspect their throats for cracks by looking under the covers. Check the condition of O-rings.

The deck itself needs review. Openings of any type will permit the entry of water, which may result in freeze-thaw damage. Check the condition of caulking between coping and the deck, near the bathhouse, and in other areas. Look for any cracks, breaks, or other conditions that can permit water entry or create a potential slipping or tripping hazard.

Check all signs to make sure that those needed are present and in good condition. Examine the fence to determine its condition. Is there an actual or a potential loss of integrity? Are there holes or cracks that could permit animals or children to enter? What about gates?

Deck equipment. The deck equipment includes pool ladders, diving stands, hand rails, lifeguard stand, and furniture. All should be given a visual once-over. Check for structural integrity, rust, corrosion, and so on.

Bathhouse. Bathhouse equipment such as sink tops, commodes, lighting, and fans all should be checked for proper operation. Also inspect for any drips or leaks, peeling paper or paint, loose fixtures or racks, and so on. Doors should be lockable; keys should be labeled and stored.

Winterization

Although many of the inspection functions indicated can be performed as part of winterization tasks, many pool contractors advise separating the two operations. For the most part, winterization can be performed by the contractor. Inspection, however, should not be performed by the contractor alone. Even if there is absolutely no reason to doubt the contractor's integrity, or the veracity or completeness of the contractor's report, effective asset protection requires a manager's involvement. General winterization procedures are discussed in this section.

Pool area. In the pool area attention needs to be directed to the following precautions.

Drop the water level to approximately 1 foot below the tile line to prevent damage from freezing and expansion. Be sure any underwater pool lights remain submerged.

Note: To combat off-season water-level increases in an uncovered pool, either a level-actuated pump should be installed in the shallow end of the pool, or the pool should be subject to frequent visual inspection and manual draining as needed. (See discussion under Off-Season Considerations.)

Balance the water chemically and add permanent winter algaecide. This prevents the water from becoming corrosive and damaging metal pipes.

Leave baskets in skimmers with the lids on to prevent leaves or other debris from clogging skimmer lines. Remove skimmer lids if it is likely that they will be stolen.

Remove, store, and inventory deck equipment such as ladders, rails, vacuum hose, rope, and furniture.

Drain skimmer lines. If the filter system is located below the water line, skimmer lines can be cleared by opening the drain. Otherwise they can be blown out with compressed air. After that, a plug should be placed in the skimmer's throat. If there is a potential for water rising enough to enter the skimmers, there is also a potential for expansion damage. To help offset this risk, fill plastic quart bottles (such as those used for milk or algaecide) with sand and place one in each skimmer.

Open valves of water lines serving any foot baths, showers, bathhouse plumbing, and so on. Water meters and backflow preventers should be removed from these lines, inspected, inventoried, and stored. All lines then should be drained or blown out (using a hose bib connection and compressed air). Antifreeze should be put into each commode after it has been pumped out. The best type of antifreeze to use is a matter of debate. Some prefer glycol-based antifreeze because it does not evaporate. It creates a stain potential in some cases, however, and is more costly than methanol. By contrast, methanol is not as expensive and does not stain, but it may evaporate and is extremely flammable.

Equipment room. If the pump room is located indoors, certain of the winterization steps indicated here will be unnecessary. Note, however, that preventive maintenance still is essential.

Drain all lines, hair and lint strainers, filter tank, and water heater. This usually is accomplished by removing drain plugs.

Inspect the filter media after the filter tank has been drained. If sand is used, it should be loose, free, and clean. If not, it should be replaced either at this time or during preseason preparation.

If a diatomaceous earth (DE) filter is used, its elements should be removed, washed with trisodium phosphate (a degreaser), and acid-washed with a 5 percent HCL solution. (Applying the HCL solution without first using the degreaser will lock grease into the filter element.) The element should be checked for tears. If found, either the tears should be repaired or the element should be replaced.

Note: DE filters are sometimes difficult to obtain. If new ones are required, they should be ordered at the close of the season so that they will be on hand when needed.

The procedure for cleaning a paper (cartridge) filter is the same as that for a cloth filter. If tears are found, a new filter is needed. (Paper filters usually do not survive more than one or two washings.)

Next, *disconnect and remove the pump and motor.* The equipment should be stored in a cool, dry area to prevent freeze-thaw shrinkage and expansion problems as well as corrosion. All threaded fittings, plugs, and other metal parts should be greased. As an optional task, remove all rust from and scrape metal surfaces, then paint them following whatever color code may be in effect. (Many jurisdictions mandate a specific color code for safety reasons. Refer to Chapter 4.) If any operational problems have been noted, now is the time to effect repairs.

Remove all tubing from the chemical feeder, and flush the feeder and tubing with a water–white vinegar solution. Any needed repairs should be performed at this time. Otherwise store the equipment in a clean dry area.

Clean all loose equipment that will not be damaged by cold conditions and store it in the filter room. All should be inventoried, and the room locked, and the key should be in the possession of the resident manager.

Note: If for any reason it is impossible to completely drain lines that should be evacuated as part of winterization procedures, wrap them with insulation or heat tape to prevent freezing and damage.

Off-season considerations

Important off-season considerations include security, water-level inspection and pool covers, personnel requirements, jurisdictional requirements, and insurance.

Security. An out-of-sight, out-of-mind attitude in the off-season can result in serious security problems. The pool area's perimeter should be checked daily. Other facilities, such as bathhouse and pump room, should be checked at least monthly. While theft can be a costly problem, the liability exposures involved can be far more significant.

Courts of law regard pools as "attractive nuisances." Every effort must be made to prevent accidents by preventing entry. Documenting such efforts also is a wise idea.

Water-level inspection and pool covers. The water level in the pool should be checked at least monthly and after any heavy rain or snow, assuming the pool is not covered. You may wish to determine the value of a cover if you do not now use one. Depending on the type selected, you may be eligible for lower liability insurance premiums. Also, a cover will often extend the life of the white coat from its normal 7 years to 10 years.

Personnel requirements. If the pool is managed on an in-house basis, the principal off-season personnel issue will be lifeguards. Advertisements should be placed in area newspapers, college papers, and other media, such as natatorium bulletin boards, just before the Christmas break, when candidates will be at home.

The work often associated with finding and hiring lifeguards underscores the benefits of relying on a pool management contractor. Interviews must be scheduled and held; references must be checked thoroughly; stand-by assistance is needed in case of illness. In addition, any breakdown in procedures, or any undetected problems, such as drug use, can create potential safety or security breaches as well as significant liability exposure.

If a pool management contractor is to be retained, the contract should be signed by January 1. This should not be a difficult task if the existing agreement is to be extended 1 year. If there is some reluctance in this regard, issues should be addressed with the contractor promptly. All too often people will not discuss minor problems, only to have them grow to needlessly large proportions. By contacting a contractor immediately after a problem is noted, the problem usually can be resolved.

It usually is advantageous to stay with a given contractor, because the contractor and the contractor's key personnel will be familiar with the pool equipment and people involved. If the problems that occur are sporadic and reasonably unpreventable, and if rates are competitive for the level of service provided, there is not much point to changing. If a change is deemed advisable, however, be certain to be thorough in your review of prospective providers' credentials.

Jurisdictional requirements. Pools must be operated within the health and other regulatory mandates of the jurisdiction involved, state *and* local in some cases. New requirements are established somewhat frequently, and old ones are modified. All must be obeyed. Be certain to determine what they are. (Most contractors can take care of these matters for you. Many issue advisories via newsletters or memoranda.)

Insurance. Liability insurance is a major concern. The expense involved needs close scrutiny. As already noted, relying on a pool cover in winter may result in a reduced premium. Certain modifications, such as diving board removal, may also be matched with a premium reduction. But what about self-management versus management by a competent pool management contractor? Will this make a difference? It may. Furthermore, the amount of insurance carried by the contractor is a vital issue. In fact, you may be able to completely eliminate coverage for perils recognized by the contractor's policy, and the contractor may be able to obtain coverage at rates far less than those you must pay, by virtue of the contractor's volume or access to industry-sponsored group plans. In all cases, review the contractor's coverage closely to assure its extent and the legitimacy of the insurer. Check with fellow property managers to ensure that the coverage provided by a contractor is the maximum available. Be certain to resolve insurance issues by January 1 of a year.

Summerization

Summerization activities generally are the reverse of winterization. The pump and motors, chemical feed, and other equipment should be reinstalled; all lines should be opened. Next drain, clean, and acid-wash the pool, and physically inspect its interior surfaces. *It is particularly important to check the hydrostat,* a relief valve usually located in the deep end. A clogged hydrostat can cause serious problems.

The pool's return lines should be blown out with compressed air or water. Check to assure that all return covers are intact; set and adjust them as necessary. Also check the underwater lights for proper operation. (It generally is advisable to have a licensed electrician check all electrical systems, including the underwater lights.)

The pool should now be filled and, if everything seems to be operating smoothly, pumps can be started for the initial test.

Necessary supplies not yet on hand should be obtained, along with pool passes and other forms, such as those shown in Figs. 7.4 through 7.7. To the extent required, pool personnel must be trained. The pool operator must be licensed by the appropriate government agency. This individual—who usually doubles as a lifeguard—must be familiar with the proper use of pumps, filters, and chemicals, and must follow government requirements (at least) in performing other functions.

Pool Name: _____ # _____ Week: _____

DAILY CHEMICAL & MAINTENANCE REPORT

	Sunday	Monday	Tuesday	Wednesday	Thursday	Friday	Saturday
Vacuumed Pool							
Brushed Pool							
Tiles Cleaned							
Decks Cleaned							
Trash Emptied							
Bathrooms Cleaned							
Health Dept. Records Dept.							

CHEMICALS USED/ON HAND

	Sunday	Monday	Tuesday	Wednesday	Thursday	Friday	Saturday
Liquid Chlorine (Gallons)							
H.T.H. (lbs.)							
Gas Chlorine (lbs)							
Soda Ash (lbs.)							
Celite (D.E.) (lbs.)							

Test Reagant: 5 Day Supply? _____ Yes _____ No

*NOTE: Order Chemical From Office When Supply Drops Below a 5 Day Supply.

Figure 7.4   Daily/weekly maintenance and chemical use report.

Lifeguards and gate attendants also must be trained. Each should be given a handbook outlining responsibilities.

In most areas, a local government agency must inspect a pool and approve it for operation before opening. Know what the inspection requirements are (some include electrical and plumbing) and contact or have the contractor contact the agency to arrange for a preopening inspection.

(Name of Pool)	SWIMMING POOL	(Pool Telephone)
(Location)	WEEKLY OPERATING RECORD	(Management Company)

For the week beginning _____ 19 ___		SUN.	MON.	TUES.	WED.	THURS.	FRI.	SAT.
WEATHER: Sunny–S, Rainy–R, Cloudy–C								
9:00 A.M.	Chlorine							
	Cyanuric Acid PPM							
	pH							
	Rate-of-Flow Meter Reading							
	Pressure Differential							
	Maximum Number of Bathers							
	Clarity							
10:00 A.M.	Chlorine							
	Cyanuric Acid PPM							
	pH							
	Rate-of-Flow Meter Reading							
	Pressure Differential							
	Maximum Number of Bathers							
	Clarity							
11:00 A.M.	Chlorine							
	Cyanuric Acid PPM							
	pH							
	Rate-of-Flow Meter Reading							
	Pressure Differential							
	Maximum Number of Bathers							
	Clarity							
12:00 P.M.	Chlorine							
	Cyanuric Acid PPM							
	pH							
	Rate-of-Flow Meter Reading							
	Pressure Differential							
	Maximum Number of Bathers							
	Clarity							
1:00 P.M.	Chlorine							
	Cyanuric Acid PPM							
	pH							
	Rate-of-Flow Meter Reading							
	Pressure Differential							
	Maximum Number of Bathers							
	Clarity							
2:00 P.M.	Chlorine							
	Cyanuric Acid PPM							
	pH							
	Rate-of-Flow Meter Reading							
	Pressure Differential							
	Maximum Number of Bathers							
	Clarity							

Figure 7.5 Daily/weekly operating record used to report specific conditions.

Dealing with indoor pool humidity

Indoor pools frequently experience humidity problems. When air is warmed to create comfort in winter, it becomes less dense due to the molecular excitation imparted by heat energy. Moisture is attracted to the air, creating excessively humid conditions. These are physi-

For the week beginning _____ 19 ____	SUN.	MON.	TUES.	WED.	THURS.	FRI.	SAT.
3:00 P.M. Chlorine							
Cyanuric Acid PPM							
pH							
Rate-of-Flow Meter Reading							
Pressure Differential							
Maximum Number of Bathers							
Clarity							
4:00 P.M. Chlorine							
Cyanuric Acid PPM							
pH							
Rate-of-Flow Meter Reading							
Pressure Differential							
Maximum Number of Bathers							
Clarity							
5:00 P.M. Chlorine							
Cyanuric Acid PPM							
pH							
Rate-of-Flow Meter Reading							
Pressure Differential							
Maximum Number of Bathers							
Clarity							
6:00 P.M. Chlorine							
Cyanuric Acid PPM							
pH							
Rate-of-Flow Meter Reading							
Pressure Differential							
Maximum Number of Bathers							
Clarity							
7:00 P.M. Chlorine							
Cyanuric Acid PPM							
pH							
Rate-of-Flow Meter Reading							
Pressure Differential							
Maximum Number of Bathers							
Clarity							
8:00 P.M. Chlorine							
Cyanuric Acid PPM							
pH							
Rate-of-Flow Meter Reading							
Pressure Differential							
Maximum Number of Bathers							
Clarity							
9:00 P.M. Chlorine							
Cyanuric Acid PPM							
pH							
Rate-of-Flow Meter Reading							
Pressure Differential							
Maximum Number of Bathers							
Clarity							

Comments: _____

Operator's Signature: _____

Figure 7.5 (*Continued*) Daily/weekly operating record used to report specific conditions.

cally oppressing and, over time, can create structural damage, not to mention high maintenance bills for rust removal and repainting. Reducing humidity by increasing the ventilation rate can be costly, since each cubic foot of air removed must be replaced with air that must be heated. In addition, air ventilated to the outdoors carries

ACCIDENT REPORT

ACCIDENT	DATE AND TIME OF ACCIDENT		AM PM	ADDRESS OF POOL	
	LOCATION OF ACCIDENT (Deck, Bathhouse, Etc.)				
	DESCRIPTION OF ACCIDENT				

INJURED	NAME	AGE	ADDRESS	
	NAME OF PARENT IF INJURED IS MINOR			TELEPHONE

WITNESSES	NAME	ADDRESS	TELEPHONE
	NAME	ADDRESS	TELEPHONE
	NAME	ADDRESS	TELEPHONE
	NAME	ADDRESS	TELEPHONE

ADDN'L INFORMATION	STAFF ON DUTY	STAFF ON DUTY
	STAFF ON DUTY	STAFF ON DUTY
	TYPE OF FIRST AID ADMINISTERED	
	DISPOSITION OF INJURED	

Figure 7.6   Accident report.

POOL SUSPENSION REPORT

POOL _____

Name of Person	Date	Time		A.M. P.M.
Suspended By:	Age	yrs. ☐ Adult	Authorized Pool Patron ☐ Yes ☐ No	
Type of Violation: ☐ General Safety ☐ Pool Regulation ☐ Health Department Regulation ☐ Other____	Staff on Duty			
Suspension Period	Privilege Renewal Date/Time			
Comments:				
Notified: Pool Mgt. ☐ DATE_____	RENTAL OFFICE (Agent) ☐ DATE_____			

Figure 7.7   Form used when individual is suspended from pool use.

pool water and chemicals with it, elevating losses and make-up costs still more.

New heat pump–based systems now available can alleviate these problems. They are capable of reclaiming heat from exhaust air and using it for air and water heating. They can also reclaim water and chemicals through dehumidification. Although these new systems may be somewhat costly to install, the payback can often be 3 years or less due to year-round operational cost savings.

Work Specification

Basic services provided by most pool management contractors include the following.

1. Opening the pool
2. Provision of on-site management personnel (operator, lifeguard, attendants)
3. Provision of supervisory personnel (for occasional visitation)
4. Closing the pool
5. Inspection
6. Guidance as to maintenance and repair needs

Additional services commonly include ordering the necessary chemicals, collecting and accounting for user fees, and providing swimming lessons.

Some companies can also provide repair services, either through their own personnel or by subcontract. On low-cost items it generally does not pay to obtain bids. On more expensive work, bids may be advisable. In the event of particularly severe problems, reliance on a consulting engineer may be advisable.

Generally speaking, the ancillary services provided by a pool management contractor, such as concrete repair, can be obtained from a number of sources. A contractor's suitability should not be downgraded for failure to provide these services.

The following work specification assumes that a new pool management contractor is being retained, and that the contract will be signed at a time that permits any needed repairs to be made before the pool is scheduled for opening.

When a contract is being renewed, it can be assumed that the inspection report made at closing was a thorough one. Although a preopening inspection will be needed, it may not be necessary for it to be as comprehensive as that indicated here.

Bear in mind that *the following work specification is based on a number of assumptions that may not apply to your particular situation.* In all cases, prepare a work specification suited specifically to your needs. Obtain assistance if necessary.

OWNER's objective is to operate and maintain all pool and pool-area facilities in a safe, clean, hazard-free condition, in compliance with all applicable governmental requirements, and in such a manner that

residents are encouraged to enjoy use of the facilities and that all facilities and operations reflect well on OWNER and on the property. The
following work specification has been prepared to support attainment
of OWNER's objectives, but OWNER does not warrant that all appropriate
items of work and concern are enumerated below. It shall therefore be
CONTRACTOR's responsibility to review said enumeration for completeness, and to identify through an addendum to this submission any and
all additional tasks which customarily are required, and to also advise
of any additional applicable services which CONTRACTOR can make
available, along with the costs and fees associated with furnishing
each.

1. *Preopening inspection and report.* No later than 90 (ninety) calendar days prior to the scheduled opening of the pool, or no later
   than 14 (fourteen) calendar days after signing the contract,
   whichever is sooner, CONTRACTOR shall submit to OWNER a report
   of CONTRACTOR's comprehensive preopening inspection. Such report shall identify any and all items, conditions, or procedures
   which in CONTRACTOR's opinion require repair, replacement, or
   modification of any type in order to assure attainment of OWNER's
   objectives, stated above. Such inspection shall include, but not be
   limited to:
   a. The pool-area enclosure and all exits and entrances thereto
   b. The pool area itself, including the surface thereof and any pool
      appurtenances
   c. Pool surfaces and affixed equipment
   d. All interior and exterior surfaces of the bathhouse and all ap-
      purtenances therein or thereon
   e. The filter room and all permanently installed equipment
      therein
   f. Any equipment necessary for proper pool operation then in stor-
      age
   g. All furniture, furnishings, other equipment, chemicals, materi-
      als, and supplies on hand
   h. All forms, procedural guidelines, and related materials used in
      conjunction with pool operation, maintenance, and manage-
      ment
   i. The prior season's closing report, inventory, and governmental
      violation notices, if any
   If for any reason CONTRACTOR is unable to identify certain conditions
   as a result of visual inspection alone, CONTRACTOR shall use appropriate testing procedures. If for any reason such testing is not possible, or if information needed by CONTRACTOR is not made available
   to CONTRACTOR, CONTRACTOR shall so note in CONTRACTOR's report to
   ensure that such concerns are otherwise addressed.

CONTRACTOR's report shall be prepared in double-spaced typewritten format, on 8½- by 11-inch paper, or in some other format whose use has previously been approved by OWNER.

2. *Performance of necessary repairs, improvements, and so on.* For purposes of expedience, CONTRACTOR shall submit proposals for performance of any work that CONTRACTOR's report suggests is needed, and which is not covered by this agreement. OWNER shall not be required to rely on CONTRACTOR for performance of this work. Any such work shall be performed through separate agreement. However, and in any event, all such work should be completed by no later than 4 (four) weeks prior to pool opening.

3. *Pool opening.* CONTRACTOR shall prepare the pool for opening through performance of the routine services indicated below, and such additional services as may be necessary. It is understood that certain of the services indicated below may be performed during performance of the preopening inspection, or that certain inspections may be deferred to pool opening, or that pool opening and preopening inspection may be performed coincident with one another.

   a. Remove, clean, and store pool cover, using such materials and methods as are appropriate to prevent any damage as a result of cleaning, preparation for storage, or storage itself.

   b. Reinstall pump, motor, and any other equipment disconnected at the close of the prior season.

   c. Install diving board(s), ladder(s), guard chair(s), furniture, and such other items that were removed at the close of the prior season, or such replacement or additional items that OWNER may have on hand.

   d. Prepare bathhouse for use, except for any repairs or supplies that may be needed.

   e. Backwash and vacuum pool.

   f. Test pool and all related equipment and facilities for proper operation and immediately call to OWNER's attention any defects, repairs, improvements, and so on, not previously noted in the preopening inspection report.

   g. Cooperate with any contractors OWNER may engage to implement repairs, modifications, improvements, and so on.

   h. Assist OWNER in obtaining all permits routinely required, with OWNER bearing the responsibility for all fees and costs associated with said permits.

   i. Schedule and be present for any and all health department inspections required for pool opening, except as indicated below.

Certain additional requirements associated with pool opening shall be the responsibility of OWNER, and all should be fulfilled no later than 4 (four) weeks prior to pool opening. OWNER may have CONTRACTOR perform certain of these tasks through separate agreement if OWNER and CONTRACTOR mutually agree. These additional requirements include, but are not necessarily limited to:

j. Provide 4 (four) large receptacles for debris removed from pool during cleaning and have receptacles removed from pool area after cleaning is complete.

k. Inspect and assure proper operation of all electrical systems and electrically operated equipment in and around the pool area, in the bathhouse and filter room, and elsewhere in the pool area and appurtenant facilities

l. Perform any needed repairs to buildings, barriers, signs, equipment, and so on, such as required to meet OWNER's objectives.

m. Provide a start-up supply of all consumables needed for the bathhouse and pool complex, such as soap, toilet paper, and hand towels.

n. Have working telephone installed in bathhouse.

o. Arrange for and attend any health department reinspection required as a result of the pool's failure to have necessary repairs performed in a timely manner.

4. *Provision of chemicals and other materials.* CONTRACTOR shall obtain and pay for all chemicals required to open the pool, maintain the pool in conformance with appropriate requirements, and close the pool. These shall include, but not necessarily be limited to, chemicals used to clean the pool and maintain water purity. (Chemicals needed to adjust total alkalinity and calcium hardness, and to test the water [reagents] shall be priced separately, on a per-unit basis.)

OWNER shall supply at OWNER's sole expense all other consumables such as soap, toilet paper, hand towels, and light bulbs.

5. *Dates and times of operations.* The pool is scheduled to open on [day of week], [month] [day of month], [19__], and the last open day of the season shall be [day of week], [month] [day of month], [19__]. Due to holidays or for any other reason, the pool is scheduled to be closed on the following dates:

Day of week	Month	Day of month

Except as may otherwise be noted below, the pool is scheduled to be open during the hours indicated for each day of the week:

MON	_____	to	_____
TUES	_____	to	_____
WED	_____	to	_____
THU	_____	to	_____
FRI	_____	to	_____
SAT	_____	to	_____
SUN	_____	to	_____

The exceptions are as follows:

Day of week	Month	Day of month	From	To
_____	_____	_____	_____	_____
_____	_____	_____	_____	_____
_____	_____	_____	_____	_____
_____	_____	_____	_____	_____

[If the pool is staffed by only one manager/lifeguard, consider adding: On all open days, pool will close for a 1-hour dinner break at a reasonable time agreeable to the Resident Manager.]

6. *Personnel and their responsibilities.* During all pool open hours, except as otherwise indicated below, CONTRACTOR shall provide the following personnel in the following number:

Category	Number
_____	_____
_____	_____
_____	_____

[Typical personnel categories include pool manager/operator, assistant manager, lifeguard, relief guard, and gate attendant. If just one person is to be furnished, it usually would be a pool manager/operator/lifeguard. If requirements will fluctuate by day of the week or holidays, varying requirements would be stated here as follows.]

The following additional personnel shall be provided on the following dates:

Day of week	Month	Day of month	Additional personnel	Number of staff

CONTRACTOR warrants that all lifeguards provided by CONTRACTOR shall have Senior Lifesaving Certificates and that CONTRACTOR's on-site management personnel, in addition to having such certificates, shall also be Certified Pool Operators.

CONTRACTOR's on-site personnel shall:

a. Regularly clean the bathhouse, pool area, and filter room
b. Regularly vacuum the pool
c. Inform the Resident Manager of any repairs or OWNER-furnished supplies or materials needed
d. Verify each person's right to have access to the pool and pool area
e. Collect, keep secure, make an accounting of, and at the end of each day transfer to the Resident Manager all pool user fees paid by pool patrons
f. [If a portion of swimming instruction fees is to be furnished to the owner], provide swimming instruction at rates to be determined jointly by CONTRACTOR and OWNER for both private and group lessons, make an accounting of and keep secure all sums due to OWNER, and at the end of each day transfer such funds to the Resident Manager
g. Suspend from further use of the pool and pool area any individual who repeatedly fails to abide by posted rules or instruction of CONTRACTOR's on-site personnel. CONTRACTOR shall provide a form for use in the event a suspension becomes necessary, and shall furnish one copy of said form to the Resident Manager. CONTRACTOR's personnel and the Resident Manager shall together determine any length of the suspension.

CONTRACTOR shall also provide supervisory personnel who shall inspect at least once per week the operations of CONTRACTOR's on-site staff, pool, pool area, bathhouse, filter room, and other items of concern. CONTRACTOR shall furnish a form for this purpose, a completed copy of which shall be provided to the Resident Manager by CONTRACTOR's supervisor subsequent to each inspection. Supervisory personnel shall also inform Resident Manager of any repairs needed, changes of CONTRACTOR's on-site personnel, and such other information that reasonably could be assumed to be of interest or concern to OWNER.

7. *Pool closing*. CONTRACTOR shall perform all services necessary to close and winterize the pool such that the pool, pool area, bathhouse, filter room, equipment, appurtenances, and furnishings are properly stored (where practical) and otherwise protected from the effects of winter. Such services shall include, but not be limited to:

   a. Drain the appropriate amount of water from the pool and add any chemicals needed to the pool water
   b. Drain all pumps
   c. Uncover and drain the strainer
   d. Drain all recirculating and vacuum lines that require draining and whose construction permits such draining
   e. Backwash and drain filters
   f. Clean all skimmer baskets
   g. Open to 75 percent of maximum all valves required to be open
   h. Disconnect, clean, and store chlorinator, hoses, and chemical feeder
   i. Fill all bathhouse fixtures with antifreeze
   j. Drain drinking fountains
   k. Store diving board, ladders, guard chair, and all pool area furniture
   l. Disengage and store all signs except NO TRESPASSING signs
   m. Install swimming-pool cover
   n. Perform all appropriate postseason preventive maintenance, such as lubrication
   o. Prepare a complete inventory of all items being stored, indicating what has been stored and where it is located
   p. Inspect all items being moved or stored, as well as all other equipment, equipment appurtenances capable of inspection, pool, pool area, bathhouse, filter room, and other areas and facilities within the pool compound, including the fence and gates thereto, provide a report of such inspection, and inform OWNER of any repairs necessary or any modifications or additions that will help OWNER attain OWNER's objectives during the next pool season

Custodial Management

Introduction

Contract cleaning has rapidly become one of the most significant services used in the management of real property. In the mid-1960s, 85 percent of the nation's commercial and multifamily residential buildings were cleaned by in-house personnel. Today 98 percent are cleaned by independent contractors.

The growth of the contract cleaning industry is not difficult to understand. It fills a need created by federal, state, and local regulations that make the management of a large, diverse custodial work force an ever more challenging and time-consuming occupation.

Many of the management difficulties associated with a custodial work force stem from the labor pool itself, which is in many areas extraordinarily heterogeneous. The individuals involved frequently range from newly arrived immigrants with little or no mastery of the English language to college students working part-time. Recruiting, interviewing, orienting, training, managing, and motivating such a work force are substantial management challenges under the best of circumstances. But the best of circumstances seldom prevail.

Because of the relatively low wage scales of custodial workers, their loyalty to employers also is low, and turnover rates are high. This intensifies the need for ongoing orientation and training programs (sometimes in multiple languages), as well as high-level supervisory skills. Wage and hour laws, citizenship requirements, equal employment opportunity regulations, and numerous other ordinances must be followed. Regulations of the Occupational Safety and Health Administration (OSHA) also must be obeyed, particularly as they relate to the handling of various chemicals and employees' (as well as tenants' and residents') rights to know.

The paperwork associated with managing a custodial work force can be massive, especially because so much documentation usually is required in the event a claim is later made by an employee, a government agency, or both. When larger buildings or property management operations are involved, therefore, more office workers are needed to complete the necessary forms, keep the various files up to date, and provide the additional support associated with a larger work force. More office personnel create a need for more office space, more equipment, and, in general, higher overhead. Security issues also emerge, as do many others, including the need to invest in new custodial equipment, keep all powered devices in good repair, invest in spare parts, and negotiate service agreements.

For property managers, the complexities associated with effective custodial maintenance can be simplified by relying on an effective contract cleaning company. Because such companies are specialists, they can often do the work more effectively than in-house people; sometimes at less cost, all things considered. "All things" is the key. Those who find that contract cleaning is not cost-effective often have not made an all-encompassing analysis. Alternatively, they may have such a large internal custodial cleaning force that the level of expertise they bring to bear is at least as high as that of independent contractors.

The goal of this chapter is to walk through the various steps needed to get an effective "handle" on custodial management, be it completely in-house, by contract, or through a combination of the two. Effective management of cleaning issues is imperative to retain existing residents and tenants, and to attract new ones. Even in the case of owner-occupied buildings, however, effective maintenance is critical to help keep those who work in the building satisfied with their surroundings. Effective maintenance also helps minimize long-term costs by avoiding the errors that can lead to premature aging of various surfaces or coverings, and the need for early replacement.

Yet another consideration in choosing between in-house and outside sources is the ability to transfer liability for certain problems. Such transferability does not come without cost. Providers "make good" either through insurance or from their own resources. In either case, the cost is included in the overhead portion of the contractor's overall charges.

What does come "free" is the peace of mind many property managers say a top-flight custodial management contractor can provide. As one property manager summed it up, "I'm not at all convinced that relying on a custodial management contractor costs more when both long-term and short-term cost factors are considered. But even if the cost is higher, the peace of mind provided permits a level of productivity we probably wouldn't enjoy otherwise. It's reasonable to conclude that the phenomenal growth of the service indicates the need for it, the benefits it provides, and its cost-effectiveness."

Custodial Activities

Custodial activities encompass the cleaning and maintenance of virtually every surface inside a building, replenishment of exhaustible supplies, and general cleanup and removal of litter and debris. This section provides a brief review of some of the principal forms of cleaning. Since the labor, materials, and equipment associated with floor and carpet care typically comprise half or more of a custodial cleaning budget, they are emphasized. It should be noted that with floor care, as with most other maintenance operations, the proper handling of materials—chemicals in particular—is of utmost concern. Workers need to be trained with respect to all safety precautions. They also need training to help ensure that proper quantities are used and applied in the correct manner, to help prevent accidents, and to help achieve desired results without damaging surfaces.

Finished-floor care

Finished floors are those covered by materials such as asphalt tile, vinyl composition, or terrazzo. Traditional care has involved dry or wet mopping, dry buffing, finish stripping, and refinishing. Stripping and refinishing are particularly costly, because they consume so much time and require the use of expensive chemicals. Stripping can also cause premature aging of a floor, creating a shabby appearance, and accelerating the need for replacement.

Spray buffing.   Spray buffing is used to enhance the gloss of a floor finish. The process is begun by sweeping the floor, then mopping it with cold, clear water or neutral cleaner. Once cleaned, the floor is sprayed with a spray buff solution, either from a hand-held sprayer or from a spray attachment on a buffing machine. Next the floor is buffed using a high-speed machine equipped with a thick animal hair or nylon pad or a burnisher, after which the floor is mopped to remove loosened finish and soil.

Spray buffing is *not* a cleaning technique (when used on highly soiled finished floors, it usually creates an unsatisfactory appearance), nor does it eliminate the need for eventual stripping and refinishing. Mop-on buffers also are applied, with similar results.

Top scrubbing.   Top scrubbing is performed when weekly buffing does not achieve the desired results. A mixture of water and neutral cleaner (at twice normal strength) is applied to the floor, and then is scrubbed using a floor machine with the appropriate pad. In this way, the top coat of wax is removed without damaging the sealant. The floor is then damp-mopped to remove the residue, and one or two coats of floor finish are applied.

Spray buffing and recoating.   Spray buffing and recoating are performed when top scrubbing alone is insufficient. The floor is sprayed with a mixture of water and stripping solution, and then is buffed with a medium-grade synthetic pad on a 175 or 300-r/min floor machine. This removes the first few coats of wax, after which the floor is mopped with cold, clear water; then two to three coats of finish are applied.

Stripping.   Stripping should be performed as infrequently as possible, because it can cause problems due to the caustic chemicals used. When too much of the chemical is applied, the solution leaches color from ("burns") some resilient tile. In addition, when the solution is left on the floor too long, it can penetrate between cracks in a tile surface, causing the tile to loosen and curl at the edges. It also is somewhat common for the solution to evaporate, redepositing the old finish and soil on the floor surface. If this is not removed through a second application of stripper, it will be covered over by the new finish, leaving an unsightly blotch that can necessitate another round of stripping and refinishing.

Once stripping has been completed, two or three rinses usually are called for to eliminate any loose soil or detergent film, making the floor clean and ready for the new finish. Some specialists recommend the use of a neutralizer in the rinse solution to enhance the bond of the floor finish.

Baseboards should be stripped at the same time as floors. If baseboards are stripped at a different time, the chemicals used will almost certainly damage the finish of the adjacent floor. If machinery is not available to expedite the stripping of baseboards, gel strippers will prove valuable. Gel strippers also are effective for use in corners, edges, and doorways. They usually are applied before liquid strippers are used on floors.

Refinishing.   Finishing the floor—waxing it—is yet another procedure susceptible to improper performance. Too often custodial personnel apply an overly thick wax coat, believing that it protects the floor better and lasts longer. The opposite is true. Thick coats of wax create a softer finish that traps more soil, and is more apt to smear and smudge. The result is a floor that becomes dirty much faster than otherwise, and the creation of a slipping or tripping hazard. The use of a floor finish that comprises its own undercoat can reduce errors and improve productivity. Four to five thin coats, applied in opposing directions, usually are called for. The "framing method" of application generally is followed. Through this approach, the finish is applied parallel to the walls without touching the baseboard. The material is then mopped on using a figure-eight motion, staying 4 to 6 inches from the wall.

With few exceptions, a finish should be applied in thin coats only. In areas that receive heavy traffic, two to as many as ten successive coats can be put down to afford more protection. In the case of open areas, where there is little foot traffic near walls, the second or third coat would be put down about 3 to 10 inches from the baseboard.

In larger areas, a thin wax coat is usually applied with a fine-strand (string-type) cotton mop that is well wrung and pushed in a figure-eight motion. If the mop is moved back and forth, as frequently occurs, the wax begins to bubble due to the emulsifiers it contains. Later, when the wax dries, the bubbles break and so create thousands of tiny craters that collect dirt and cause the floor to lose its luster quickly.

Another common problem is failure to consider the composition of different finishes. A typical example is the use of a polymer finish on top of a carnauba wax, a process that leads to cracking or powdering of the polymer. Before large quantities of materials are purchased and time is invested in their application, small areas should be tested to help ensure problems will not result.

Mopping.   Most of the time spent on finished floor care is consumed in manual operations, principally mopping. Those who assume there is little art to mopping will learn a harsh lesson from experience. For example, when refinishing a floor, improper mopping can result in a thin, difficult-to-remove layer of wax being deposited on baseboards, furniture legs, file cabinets, doors, and jambs. In dust mopping, improper handling of an untreated mop will result in precious little dust and dirt actually being removed.

For both mops and squeegees, the handle length is an important concern. A handle should come up to the user's eye level when the mop or squeegee is standing on the floor. Handles that are too long can easily be cut to proper size.

Proper motion is also important. As a general rule, as few muscles as possible should be moved and, when movement is required, large muscles should be used before smaller ones. Applied to mopping, this means that it is better to move the body rather than the hand.

Dust mopping is performed best by holding the mop handle in one hand on or near the hip, while walking forward. In all cases, the mop head should be held on the floor as long as possible. Every time the mop head is lifted, dust falls from it to the floor surface.

Dust is held in the mop by the nature of the fibers. But impregnating materials are commonly used to enhance retention. Application of the retention-enhancing chemicals should be performed by someone trained to do so. When others do it, they tend to use too little, eliminating the "magnetic" effect, or they tend to use too much, resulting in chemicals being dropped on the floor, causing damage over time, and creating a slipping hazard. Not all retention-enhancing chemicals are alike. When in-house application is used, select a chemical that can be washed in a machine using conventional laundry powder. Alternatives to in-house application include use of disposable paper mops, and renting mops from a source that cleans them and applies chemicals.

In areas where furniture is located, a properly trained worker can move quickly by holding the mop in one hand and moving furniture with the other. In particularly congested areas, a swivel-type mop is best.

When *wet mopping,* workers should walk backward while causing the mop head to move in a figure-eight pattern. To avoid splattering the baseboards, and depositing dirty water or cleaning solution on them, a swath extending about 8 inches from a wall should be created by first moving the mop parallel to the baseboard around the room. Then, when the mopping begins, the mop head's farthest motion would penetrate the first few inches of the swath, rather than touching the baseboard itself.

One of the most common errors made in wet mopping is putting too much or too strong a detergent in the solution, from the mistaken belief that it will clean better or faster. This is not the case. Too much detergent leaves a film which, if it is not cleaned away through additional rinsing, creates a slick surface that attracts and holds more dirt. Excess detergent can also weaken the floor finish and dull the shine. Failure to change the cleaning solution often enough is another common mistake. This results in the use of a solution that lays down more dirt than it picks up. Still another common problem is using too much water in rinsing. This practice can result in water or cleaning solution penetrating through cracks and joints, causing tiles to become loose and leading to their curling at the edges. In many instances, reliance on a neutral cleaner will permit *damp mopping* to achieve results that are virtually the same as those of wet mopping.

Certain safety concerns are associated with mopping. People have received serious facial and eye injuries from mops that have been left standing in buckets. Mops left in buckets should be leaned against a wall. When being carried, a bucket should be held in one hand and the mop handle in the other. In all cases, mop handles should be carried straight up and down.

Dry buffing. Dry buffing is most commonly accomplished with a single-disk floor machine. Use of the proper pad is essential. Before the machine is used, however, the floor should be wet-mopped or damp-mopped with a neutral cleaner to prevent the buffer from forcing dirt into the finish, and to prevent the machine from scattering dust and dirt which then settles on all surfaces, creating a possible health hazard.

Other floor care

Other floors may range from unfinished concrete to stained, painted, or varnished wood. The cleaning regimen developed should consider the type of usage likely, the nature of the surface, and the kind of wear it will receive, appearance objectives, and safety, among other factors. In the case of unfinished concrete floors that may experience spotting with oil, it may be necessary to use solvents on a periodic basis, provided all appropriate safety precautions are observed. Once the solvents are removed, additional cleaning may be necessary to prevent a slippery surface and to prevent situations where dirt or solvent residue is tracked onto other surfaces. In a similar manner, stairwell steps are often painted concrete. The surface needs to be kept clean, but care must be taken to select a detergent or other cleaning solution that will not dull the paint's finish, nor create a slipping hazard. In this respect, the nature of the paint also must be considered.

In most instances such as these, it is ill-advised to make assumptions or guess about the specific type of cleaning techniques required. Errors can be very costly. By contrast, a consultant or other qualified party needs to provide details and recommendations only once. Then as new products and materials become available, their applicability can be evaluated effectively in light of the knowledge already established.

Carpet care

Carpet care can be segregated into three types of activities: routine cleaning, shampooing, and spot cleaning.

Routine cleaning. Routine carpet cleaning is performed with a vacuum cleaner. Daily cleaning of large, high-traffic areas usually is done with a 30-inch or larger two-motor vacuum. In offices, elevators, and other smaller high-traffic areas, the machine of choice usually is an upright vacuum cleaner with a driven brush. Many also consider the upright the best for less frequent (such as weekly) cleaning of carpeted areas, because it lifts the carpeting's pile, loosening embedded dirt and grit. (Upright vacuum cleaner heads should be fitted with a padded cover to prevent damage to furniture, doors, and other wood surfaces.) A wand-type vacuum also is useful, especially for reaching areas that are not generally accessible to an upright, such as under furniture and around baseboards. The wand-type unit can also be of value in cleaning in areas that are heavily used during the day, as may a carpet litter vacuum. "Backpack" vacuums are being used extensively for corners and edges.

Shampooing.   Wet shampooing is usually performed for general carpet cleaning. Dry techniques often are used when fast turnaround times are essential. In either case, shampooing should not occur until after the carpet has been vacuumed with a driven brush vacuum cleaner to remove dry dirt and raise the pile. Various equipment is available for *wet shampooing*. When a single-disk floor machine is used, a team approach to cleaning is advisable. One worker operates the machine to apply shampoo to an area, a second worker passes through with a wet vacuum to pick up the foam. This approach helps prevent overwetting, which can lead to excessive drying times, carpet shrinkage, or mildew damage. Machines similar to a single-disk floor machine, designed solely for rug cleaning, do not clean the carpet pile as deeply, but they require only one operator rather than a team. Since such equipment helps prevent overwetting, it permits more frequent cleaning and, thus, more effective carpet care.

Equipment also is available to provide *steam cleaning*. Also called *water extraction cleaning,* this method does a better job of cleaning, often removing stains that otherwise would require spot cleaning. Because of the degree of wetness involved, water extraction cleaning should be used only on an intermittent basis, in connection with other methods. Depending on the amount of carpet that must be cleaned, it may be wiser to have water extraction cleaning performed on a subcontract basis. Note that it often is good practice to shampoo carpeting before extraction, to loosen the dirt. Then, using only water in the extractor, more detergent can be removed from carpet fibers and backing. Reliance on a carpet/floor dryer is highly recommended to speed drying time.

Dry shampooing is accomplished by covering the area with "dry shampoo," material such as fuller's earth or fine hardwood sawdust that has been impregnated with a volatile hydrocarbon. The material is then brushed into the carpet manually or with electrically driven brushes designed for the purpose. The solvent in the dry shampoo evaporates ("volatilizes") and, as it does so, it draws up soil from the carpet into the medium used. The medium is then removed from the carpet, typically with an upright vacuum with a motor-driven brush.

Mop-on and spray-on carpet cleaners also are available. These can consist of wetting agents with solvents and emulsifiers that are applied with a short-strand mop, using a brushing motion, or a sprayer. Bonnets are used to pick up solution and soil.

Spot cleaning.   Spot cleaning is applied to clean up stains before they have a chance to "set" and ruin the carpet's appearance. The key to effective spot cleaning, then, is good communication. As soon as the spot is noticed, housekeeping should be contacted.

Experienced custodial personnel say that, depending on the composition of the surface and the nature of the stain, it may be best to try water first. Often cold water is more effective than hot water because hot water can cause a stain to set. Of course, water alone has no cleaning ability, which is why it also is essential to have a spot cleaning kit on hand. These kits typically contain two bottles of cleaner, one for water-soluble soils and one for oil-soluble soils. Before either is used, it should be tested on a small area of carpet that is hidden from view, to ensure that it does not create a bigger problem than the one it is intended to eliminate. (Well-equipped custodial facilities usually have on hand specialized cleaners for removing blood, grape juice, red wine, urine, and other stain-inducing materials.)

Restroom cleaning

Restroom conditions all too often are less than satisfactory and, by some accounts, are responsible for 80 percent of the complaints received by management. Restroom cleaning should be performed at least on a daily basis, applying a germicidal detergent solution from a plastic spray bottle to help prevent contamination from one surface to another. All surfaces should be cleaned. This includes the inside of stall doors in particular. Frequently the stall is opened and everything is cleaned without the custodian actually being inside the stall. In such cases, the inside of the stall door—the only object scrutinized by those using the facility—can go untouched.

In those restrooms designed for the application, solution can be applied via a pressurized cleaner. Once it falls to the floor, the solution is simply squeegeed to the drain. The push plate of a litter container is another surface that often goes overlooked. When that occurs, those with litter to discard will simply throw it on the floor, not wishing to touch something that obviously is contaminated. The lips of toilet bowls and urinals are other surfaces that often go uncleaned because they are hidden from view. Because these areas often go uncleaned, bacteria and scale (from waterborne minerals) build up there. They should be cleaned on a regular basis and on an as-needed basis if regular cleaning is insufficient. Need can be determined by custodians who hold a small mirror in position to see the inside of the lip. An acid descaler applied with a bowl mop is sufficient to do the job. Some custodians get carried away with the cleaning power of acid descalers, however, and may use them too frequently. This can cause damage to other surfaces with which the acid may come into contact. A safety problem may be created as well. In some instances it may be best to have the acid used only by personnel trained in its application.

Periodic cleaning (such as monthly) is required of those restroom elements that are above eye level, such as light fixtures and piping.

Those responsible for cleaning usually are also responsible for assuring that adequate paper supplies are in place, namely, toilet tissue, seat covers, and hand towels. In addition, they should check to assure that soap dispensers are full and working properly, and that other devices also are in proper working order. Checklists can be helpful.

Room care

Room care generally involves the daily removal of litter and floor and carpet care. Cleaning under desks and other furnishings is particularly important. It also is important to clean "above" by removing dust from the tops of lamp shades, shelves, tall furniture, and similar areas that often go overlooked. Ceilings, diffusers, grills, and other room elements above the 6-foot level also go overlooked in many cases. They are relatively easy to clean through use of a tank-type or pack-type dry vacuum equipped with an extension wand. Such items should be included on a checklist to help assure that they are cleaned or at least reviewed by a supervisor. Likewise, the door frame needs to be looked at since it, too, often goes untouched. Typically, the door to a room is left open, so neither the person cleaning the room nor the one cleaning the corridor sees that side of the door frame where the hinges are located. One or the other (typically the person with room cleaning responsibility) should be specifically assigned to clean that area.

Wastebaskets usually are lined with a plastic liner, and these are removed rather than the wastebasket being emptied. Nonetheless, wastebaskets should be checked to ensure that plastic liners have not been punctured or ripped, permitting food or liquids to gather on the basket surface itself.

Walls in a room need to be checked closely. Daily "spotting" should be performed to remove dirt and smudges that gather, typically on or near light switches.

Note that custodial staff often needs the support and understanding of building management and room occupants. It is virtually impossible to provide effective floor or carpet care if countless items of furniture, boxes, and stacks of papers must be moved. Likewise, the tops of desks cannot be cleaned when papers of all types are in the way. (Custodial staff should not move papers about.) It should be understood by all that good floor or carpet care will be provided when there is no obstacle course in the way, and that desktops and other surfaces will be cleaned when papers are removed from them.

Custodial facilities care

The condition of custodial facilities and equipment can and often does indicate the attitude of the custodial staff. The space itself should be clean from bottom to top, side to side. Empty boxes and litter of any type should be out of sight. All tools with handles should be hung in a vertical position, and they should be in proper condition; for example, wet mop heads should look and smell clean. (When they are stored dirty and wet, bacteria multiply and cause a sour smell.) Likewise, the electric cords of vacuum cleaners and floor machines should be clean (so they don't drag dirt across floors, carpets, and furniture) and properly coiled. Cords should also be checked to ensure none is abraded or otherwise damaged, causing a safety hazard.

When the custodial facilities and everything inside them indicate that custodial personnel take pride in appearance, chances are the rest of the building receives a similar level of care and attention.

Custodial Equipment and Supplies

Whether custodial services will be performed in-house or by contract, property managers need to be familiar with the equipment and supplies used in custodial operations. By having this understanding, property managers can better appreciate their options; the pros and cons of using one method versus another or one type of material versus another.

Manual equipment

Effective selection of manual equipment can help assure maximum worker productivity. But workers first must understand proper use of the equipment, for example, how to avoid spreading dust when dry mopping or how to prevent splattering when wet mopping.

Novice property managers in particular can be stunned by the complexities associated with some of these operations, and the significant differences between the right and wrong way, with respect to the results obtained, or the amount of work required to obtain effective results. They also tend to be surprised by the amount of knowledge necessary to provide proper maintenance of certain items, or to know which particular piece of equipment is best for a given application (such as straight-bladed squeegee versus curved). In essence, even when it is "just" manual custodial equipment, those who provide training and supervision must really "know their stuff" in order to derive maximum productivity from workers, and maximum utility from the investment in equipment and supplies.

Brooms. Traditional brooms are manufactured from undyed cornstraw stock (hence the name straw broom or corn broom). At one time categorized by weight per dozen, brooms generally are used only in areas where dust will not be raised, or where they are more practical than pine brushes, dust mops, or vacuum cleaners. Large (40-pound) brooms are generally used to clean heavily soiled areas. Smaller brooms (32- to 24-pound) are used for regular cleaning of certain areas, such as outdoor stairs. They also may be used before vacuuming, to sweep carpeted areas near baseboards.

Toy brooms (light-duty brooms with a 24-inch handle) are typically used in conjunction with a dustpan to clean up litter in public areas, such as cigarette butts. *Angle brooms* are used for stairs and corners.

Brushes. Brushes can be generally categorized in terms of their composition and function. In terms of composition, consider the material from which the block is made (wood, plastic, or metal), the shape of the block, the filling material (plastic, animal bristle, vegetable bristle), and the length of the filling material. Typical brushes used by most custodians include the following.

Bowl brushes, also known as commode brushes and sanitary brushes.

Counter brushes, used to reach into corners or to sweep dirt or debris into dustpans.

Deck scrub brushes, used to scrub floors or other badly soiled, rough surfaces. The brush can be used with a handle or by hand.

Baseboard brushes, specially designed deck scrub brushes used to clean a baseboard and the adjacent floor area at the same time.

Hand scrub brushes, also known as "scrubs," are used to hand-clean equipment, fixtures, or small floor or other areas of medium coarseness.

Fountain brushes, which have hollow handles to dispense cleaning or rinsing solution, are often used to clean windows. By using extension handles, they can clean surfaces that are several stories above the operator.

A wide array of other brushes is used, each for a specific application, such as wall brushes, venetian blind brushes, radiator brushes, even bed spring brushes.

Proper brush maintenance calls for their cleaning when soiled, following guidance from the manufacturer in light of the brush composition. (Bowl brushes should be washed and disinfected daily.) Brushes with long handles should be hung vertically. Others should be either hung or otherwise stored to prevent damage to filling.

Push brushes. Also known as pushes or sweeps, push brushes are used for floor cleaning in selected areas. (Due to the dust they raise, they should not be used in administrative, food service, or similar spaces.) By selecting a brush with as long a block as practical for a given task, the task can be accomplished that much faster, and the brush will last longer. Longer life can also be obtained by rotating the handle in the block to prevent excessive wear and keep the brush clean and flexible. When heavily soiled, some fillings can be cleaned in neutral detergent and rinsed; they are then shaken (for straightening) and hung to dry.

Carts. Several types of carts normally are used in custodial operations. These include waste carts (janitorial barrels) to collect and transport waste (sometimes just a drum on a dolly), and utility carts (multifunctional carts that often include a litter bag and space for mops, buckets, and the like). Waste carts should be fitted with padded covers to eliminate the unsightly black line that can occur on a wall when the waste cart is pulled along.

Dust mops. When properly applied and maintained, a dust mop is the ideal tool for quickly and effectively removing loose soil from a smooth dry floor. Several types are available, the most common being the rectangular cotton dust mop, available in widths up to 5 feet and secured to a wood block or metal frame and handle. U-shaped frames or heads are also available to collect litter (in the enclosed area) while also removing dust. Large V-shaped mops are used for congested areas, as are swivel-type mops, which permit the user to change the position of the mop head by twisting the mop handle.

Cotton is not the only material from which mops are made, but many consider it the most cost-effective, since it will last long with proper care. Proper care includes daily vacuuming and treatment to enhance its dust-collecting ability, and laundering when soiling becomes noticeable.

Wet-mopping systems.   A wet-mopping system consists of a mop, buckets, a wringer, and a bucket transport. Buckets are available in various sizes and shapes and are made of different materials. Plastic buckets usually are preferred because of their low cost and resistance to corrosion. Also, they make little noise when in use.

Typical operations require two buckets; one for detergent and one for rinse water. Three-bucket systems are also available. (Systems using one less bucket are appropriate when a neutral cleaner is used since it eliminates the need for rinsing when normal floor maintenance is involved.) Buckets are mounted in a cart or hand truck designed for the purpose, and a wringer is placed on one of the buckets. For larger operations, a 30- to 60-gallon mopping tank is available, with two to three compartments and a built-in wringer. (Today's wringers do not wring mops; they squeeze them. Wringing shortens a mop's life.)

Mops are either permanently affixed to a handle or can be removed from a wooden or metal frame. Cotton mops can be used for many purposes and are easily cleaned. Rayon mops are lighter and more absorbent, but are not as effective in applying wax. Cellulose sponge mops are more absorbent and durable when used on smooth floors, but they are far more costly. Lightweight sponge mops with built-in wringers are useful for tasks such as stair cleaning and wall washing.

New mops should be soaked in warm water for at least 20 minutes before use to remove excess oils and entrapped air, thus to enhance absorbency. Mops should be rinsed whenever the water is changed, and they should be washed frequently. Loose mop strands should be cut off to prevent splattering. They should be hung strands down, in an area that permits air circulation and drying.

Squeegees.   Squeegees are used to move large quantities of water on a floor to a floor drain, a pick-up pan, or for removal by a wet vacuum. Curved-headed squeegees can move more water, but they cannot be used when pulled back. It generally is advisable to keep extra squeegee blades on hand because they are relatively fragile. Squeegees should be stored in a cool dry area, and should not be left outside to dry, since the sunlight will damage the rubber.

Window squeegees are used to clean windows or other smooth glass areas, such as mirrors.

Other manual equipment.   Some of the other manual equipment commonly used includes the following.

Safety signs and other equipment to warn people of wet floors (extremely important in preventing accidents and the claims and costs they can lead to)

Lambskin applicators to apply wax and seals

Detergent guns that dispense cleaning solutions through water or air pressure

Dustpans

Feather dusters and treated dusting cloths

Lambswool dusters with extension handles

Ladders, scaffolds, and other equipment for cleaning walls and other overhead areas

Proportioners for mixing proper quantities of detergents or chemicals

Gloves, aprons, hard hats, goggles, and other equipment for safety in working with certain equipment, or in certain areas, or with certain chemicals

Sprayers

Sponges

Scrapers

Rags (of terrycloth or Turkish towel material)

Padded vacuum covers

Padded barrel protectors

Power equipment

The usual justification for purchasing power equipment is the time savings it will provide. A better result can also be obtained, along with extended surface life.

Close analysis is essential in evaluating the effectiveness of a piece of equipment, or one model or brand over another. Insofar as the labor-savings potential is concerned, ask to see the device being used in a real situation by a typical member of the custodial staff, as at a nearby building where it is in use. The numbers that are used by the manufacturer or the manufacturer's representative typically are derived under ideal conditions.

It is important to know also about the amounts and types of chemicals or other materials used by the equipment, and the resulting cost. Inquire, too, about energy consumption and its cost. (The time of day when the equipment is used may have an impact.)

Who stands behind the equipment? the manufacturer? the distributor? both? How available are spare parts? Where are they shipped from? How easily and quickly can the product be repaired? How available is service? from whom? for how much? Does the device pose any special storage requirements? What about storage space and security there?

In essence, if you are going to get involved in the acquisition (purchase or leasing) of equipment, you should proceed only when armed with all the information you need to make a truly informed decision. Some of the most commonly used power equipment is described in the following.

Floor machines.   Single-disk floor machines account for approximately half of all funds spent on powered custodial equipment. Through the use of different pads or disks, as well as other attachments, the same machine can be used for scrubbing, buffing, sanding, and scarifying floors, as well as rug shampooing. For large hard-surfaced floors, however, high-speed buffers or burnishers generally are preferred.

The efficiency of a floor machine is proportional to the area of the brush or pad that comes into contact with the floor. As such, a 24-inch machine is about four times as effective as a 12-inch machine, and a 21-inch model is twice as effective as its 15-inch counterpart.

Among the most popular floor machines are the 15- and 16-inch models, often chosen due to their first-cost economy. A larger machine costs very little more, however, and the difference generally can be paid back quickly due to time savings. But other sizing factors need to be considered, including the total area to be maintained, the amount of congestion, portability (if the machine must be carried downstairs or moved between buildings), stability (larger machines are more stable but do not do as good a job with uneven floors), and weight per square inch (in light of the operations to be performed). Additional factors, not related to size, include horsepower, brush speed, noise level, adjustability of the handle, and ability to clean under furniture, among others.

Many types or brushes are available for machines, depending on the nature of the task. Note that brush diameter is measured across the middle of the pad, from bristle tip to bristle tip when the pad is under weight. Floor machines can use smaller pads than their capacity, but not larger ones. Various types of pads are used for different buffing operations.

The solution tank is a commonly used floor machine accessory, principally for scrubbing carpets. It can also be used to spread detergent prior to scrubbing, although some find that applying the detergent solution with a mop produces superior results. Grinding and sanding attachments also are available, as are vacuum attachments, used to remove the dust created in buffing.

Vacuum cleaners.   An extensive variety of vacuum cleaners is available. The most versatile is the *wet-dry vacuum* for suctioning solids and liquids. These typically are equipped with a round or square tank of 5- to 20-gallon capacity. Many housekeeping specialists prefer wet vacuuming to mopping, because it leaves a cleaner, drier surface.

Dry vacuums are used for dry cleaning only. These range from tank types to uprights, including those equipped with power rollers to raise a rug's pile. *Pack-type vacuums* are dry types that are worn on the back like a knapsack, or carried on a shoulder strap, for use in confined areas.

Scoop-type vacuums are wet-dry units that have a squeegee mounted in front of or behind the tank, causing the squeegee to pick up liquid as the operator pushes the tank forward.

Almost all vacuums are available with a variety of attachments, connected to the hose by a metal wand. (Extension wands are available for overhead cleaning.) Specialized attachments include those for cleaning venetian blinds, crevices (such as those between radiator fins), dust mops, upholstery, and carpets, as well as floors, walls, and other surfaces and devices. They can also be used for blowing and spraying.

Other power equipment.   Other power equipment in common use includes the following.

Self-contained extractors inject a hot water solution into the carpet and then vacuum it out. They do a better job than a single-disk floor machine. However, depending on the specific equipment being compared, a floor machine may be less likely to damage the carpet.

Dry foam generators lay down a lather from a liquid detergent solution and brush it into a carpet's pile. Some have a built-in vacuum.

Brightening devices are used to brighten the surface of carpets by using solvent or granular materials. These can be obtained as attachments to single-disk machines.

Automatic floor machines, also known as autoscrubbers, are self-propelled devices that dispense detergent onto a floor, scrub it with one or more brushes, and then vacuum the solution into a waste reservoir. Because there is not time for detergent to provide chemical cleaning action, more than one pass may be required for particularly soiled floors.

Steam cleaners comprise a steam generator, solution tank, hose, and nozzle to clean heavily soiled surfaces through a combination of chemical action, turbulence, heat, and force. Special safety precautions are necessary to protect the operator and surrounding areas.

Wall washers usually have two tanks, one for detergent solution, the other for rinse water. Air pressure forces liquid through a hose into a trowel that is covered by a porous cleaning pad.

Louver cleaners are used to clean lighting fixture louvers. Careful selection of the cleaning materials is essential to prevent damage to special coatings and other surfaces.

Can washers are used to wash garbage cans and other waste receptacles.

Chemicals

Although custodial operations depend on a wide array of chemicals, most are used somewhat infrequently and in small quantities. Six types of products dominate chemical purchases. These are general detergents, neutral cleaners, floor finish strippers, floor finishes, disinfectants, and hand cleaners. Selection of the right product for the job will help assure effective results. Improper selection can be costly.

General detergents. Detergents are formulated for specific applications, such as hand cleaners and floor strippers. While there is no such thing as a true all-purpose detergent, custodial work does require a general detergent for mopping floors and other general cleaning functions. To be effective, the detergent formulation should consider the hardness of the water with which it will be mixed. It usually is advised that the general detergent should have a pH of 7.0 to 9.5, so it does not create excessive foam (requiring a second rinsing or leaving a film), and should not contain any ammonia, solvents, abrasives, free alkali, free oils, or fats. Synthetic detergents (as opposed to those that contain soap) generally are preferred, because they do not leave a residue. Use-to-dilution ratios not exceeding 2 ounces of detergent per gallon of water are recommended.

Neutral cleaners. Neutral cleaners represent a significant advance over general detergents. Their composition is such that they clean as well as most general detergents, but do not require rinsing.

Floor-finish strippers. Experienced property managers strongly suggest that finish strippers be obtained from the same source that supplies the floor finish, because the stripper must be formulated to remove a specific substance. Use of the improper stripper can create chemical reactions that can ruin a floor.

Floor finishes. Many types of floor finishes are available. Thoughtful selection is essential to help ensure that the floor is protected from abrasive wear, looks good, and requires minimum labor to retain an attractive appearance.

Solvent or spirit waxes are used principally for wooden floors that would be damaged by water-based or similar products. *Water emulsion waxes* typify these latter products. Originally developed for use with composition tile, they consist of an emulsion of carnauba wax (a natural product scraped from the leaves of a South American palm tree) in water. After the material is applied, the water evaporates, leaving only the wax. Various substances are added to the carnauba (and other natural waxes used) to affect properties such as leveling, softness, slip resistance, and sheen.

Water emulsion waxes have several drawbacks, including their slipperiness, propensity for darkening, and the need for dry buffing in order to produce a sheen. For these reasons, water emulsion waxes have been replaced by *synthetic polymer finishes*, except in areas where sandy or gritty soils will result in scratching of the harder polymer surface.

As do water emulsion waxes, polymer finishes, too, have particles suspended in water. Metal-link polymers are among the newest, containing interlinked metallic ions that create a finish that resists removal by detergents.

Disinfectants.   As defined by the federal government, disinfection means killing 99,999 of 100,000 organisms under controlled conditions. Disinfection is necessary in all buildings, in some (such as hospitals) more so than others. In office, multifamily residential, and similar types of buildings, disinfection is appropriate in restrooms, food service and preparation areas, vending areas, and locker rooms. It is appropriate, also, for telephone ear pieces, mouthpieces, and handholds.

Marketing of disinfectants is controlled by the federal government, but only to the extent that products are shipped on an interstate basis. Depending on the manufacturer, then, it may be wisest to purchase only those products that are subject to federal oversight.

Synthetic phenols kill a wide range of organisms and are odorless. Quaternary ammonium chemicals, or "quats," are also used. They afford good odor control, low sensitivity, and high dilution ratios, and they are odorless, nontoxic, and nonstaining. Other, more specialized disinfectants also are available.

Hand cleaners.   Both soap (made from naturally fatty materials) and synthetic detergent are available in a variety of forms, ranging from solid (bar, powdered, and chipped) to liquid. Of them all, *bar soap* is among the least expensive, but it is not recommended because it would be a "community product," that is, a number of people would use it. For this reason the public restrooms of many office buildings rely on liquid dispensers. Liquid materials can also be used in lather dispensers. These have a "deluxe" quality about them, but they use only half as much soap as liquid dispensers, because a special valve mixes air into the soap to create the lather.

Special products are available for maintenance workers and others for heavy-duty hand cleaning. These consist of granular products as well as pastes and lotions for removing grease.

Other chemicals. The other chemicals typically used in custodial operations are many and varied. They include some of the following.

Carpet-cleaning chemicals include dry shampoos, foam-producing cleaners, spot cleaners (solvents and detergents), and surface brighteners.

Antistatic materials are sprayed on carpets without metallic fibers to reduce the static electricity that commonly occurs in winter, due to low humidity levels. Static can be particularly harmful to electronic equipment.

Abrasive cleaners are available as powders, pastes, or lotions. The lotion type should be the first choice, because they have the smallest particles and do the least damage. Over time, powders can take the plating off metals.

Deodorants generally are used to mask odors. Where possible, the cause of the odor should be identified and eliminated.

Descalers are acid-based liquids for removing mineral deposits, especially those under toilet bowls and urinal lips. To avoid causing damage, descalers should not be overused. They should be applied only by trained personnel wearing appropriate protective clothing and face shields.

Drain openers should not be used by custodial staffs, some experts recommend, because they can lead to rapid gas buildup in drain pipes, creating a blow-back situation that can cause serious injury. In any event, they can also corrode pipes, a particularly costly problem in older buildings.

Dust mop treatment causes dust particles to adhere more readily to mop (or other) surfaces.

Foam depressants are silicone-type chemicals used to reduce the amount of foam in detergents. Where foaming is a continuing problem, a different detergent formulation usually is called for.

Glass cleaners with isopropanol (to accelerate evaporation) are appropriate for cleaning small glass areas. For larger areas, window-cleaning detergents are called for. Note that ammonia-containing glass cleaners should not be used on plexiglas, Lexan, or similar materials, since ammonia can damage such surfaces.

Metal polish is used to maintain the finish of brass, bronze, and copper. Most polished metal surfaces are being designed out of new construction due to the high cost of maintaining them.

Sealers are permanent or semipermanent floor finishes that are categorized as *penetrating* (when they sink into the pores of the floor material) or *surface* (when they stay on top). *Water emulsion sealers* are similar to water emulsion polymer finishes, except that they contain more solids and thus last longer. *Solvent sealers* have better wear characteristics but are more difficult to remove. The most popular are phenolics, epoxies, and polyurethanes.

Seal strippers are used to remove sealers. Water emulsion sealers are removed with the same chemicals used to remove polymer floor finishes. Solvent sealers are removed with chemicals essentially similar to those in paint strippers.

Solvent cleaners are used to remove oily, greasy materials, or tar that cannot be removed by soaps alone or by synthetic detergents. Solvents such as kerosene, pine oil, or alcohol dissolve the material, then suspend it for emulsification by a synthetic detergent. Highly toxic solvents, such as carbon tetrachloride, and those that are flammable or explosive, should not be stored or used by the custodial department. Only persons trained in the use of such materials should apply them.

Paper goods and other materials

Custodial staff is usually responsible for ordering and maintaining proper supplies of the paper goods used in restrooms. These include toilet tissue, paper towels, and seat covers. In some instances certain types of paper goods are ordered from certain suppliers because only that supplier's goods fit the existing dispenser. In such instances, alternatives should be investigated, especially so because many such dispensers or their connecting devices can be fitted with adapters to make use of other goods possible.

Custodial staff is also responsible for the hand cleaners used in restrooms, and for plastic wastebasket and trash-can liners.

Developing and Pricing the Contract Cleaning Work Scope

The purpose of a work scope is to make crystal clear exactly what it is that needs to be done. Generally speaking, the fewest problems occur when the work scope is a highly detailed, prescriptive specification. For example, the specification might say, referring to an illustration:

> *Area 10, Carpet:* Portion A of carpet, shown by the dotted line, shall be vacuumed daily using an upright vacuum with power roller. (All upright heads shall have padded cover installed.) This same area shall be dry shampooed weekly using ABC Company Dry Shampoo, which shall be swept down and vacuumed.

By specifying what will be done where, the frequency involved, and the specific chemicals, methods, and equipment used, there is little room for interpretation, and little need for assumptions. How to get "there" from "here" is the focus of this section.

Perform a building audit

The purpose of the building audit is to obtain a graphic representation of every surface in the building that will require cleaning. This only needs to be done once, and then can be updated as changes are made. While unquestionably the work can be tedious and tiresome, it really is essential to help minimize the opportunity for misunderstanding, and also to help plan, schedule, and budget.

Drawings can be used to indicate the nature of the floor coverings and the locations of major pieces of furniture and partitions. Drawings should also be prepared to illustrate the ceilings and walls. The ceiling drawings would show the locations of any light fixtures, diffusers, or returns, as well as their composition. Wall illustrations would indicate the locations of any windows and doors, as well as of any significant pieces such as mirrors, framed or unframed paintings, and other ornamentation. By having this level of detail, it is possible to walk through the building, area by area, answering pertinent questions. For example, if there is a major painting on the wall, it might be asked, "When we wash the wall, do we take the painting down?" If it is a particularly valuable painting, it might be appropriate for it to be taken down for the custodial services company to avoid the liability exposure.

Just as floor surfaces would be indicated, so would wall surfaces. If it is a painted wall, the type of paint and color should be specified. If the wall is papered, the type of paper should be shown, indicating the range of operations that may be necessary.

The more detail that is provided, the better. There is, after all, a major difference between a light blue nylon carpet and a dark blue woolen one. Likewise, an actual inspection will reveal the conditions one can expect to find. If a given office is frequently cluttered with boxes on the floor and paper on the desk, specifications should so indicate. Either extra time will be allowed to remove the clutter, or it will be made known ahead of time that the clutter makes effective cleaning impossible on a routine basis.

Checklists and other materials that can be useful in preparing this task are available from the International Sanitary Supply Association (ISSA) and the Building Service Contractors Association International (BSCAI), as well as from consultants and contractors.

Determine the level of care required

The level of care required depends on a variety of factors. Obviously, in some buildings the highest quality possible is essential. In others, a dramatically different requirement may exist because of budgetary restrictions.

In all cases, it should be a goal to achieve that level of cleanliness that will help assure full life of whatever it is that is being cleaned. If carpets receive inadequate vacuuming, for example, they may become irreparably soiled and otherwise damaged. By the same token, if a given type of operation is performed too frequently, premature aging may occur.

By having a complete, illustrated building audit, it is possible to indicate exactly what operations are to be performed, where they are to be performed, how often, using what equipment and materials. Adjustments can be made later if it is found that the specification is insufficient or wasteful, or if budget limitations make cutbacks necessary.

Avoid work scopes that are vague or judgmental. For example, any specification that says, "Clean as necessary to help assure a good appearance," is wide open for interpretation. Understandably, it is faster and easier to prepare a specification in that manner, but at bidding it requires contractors to make assumptions, and implementing them can result in friction, as when the manager's definition of "good appearance" and the contractor's vary by a wide margin.

Determine overall needs

Overall needs generally go beyond cleaning alone. Supervision is necessary, as is inspection and reporting. Most contractors will have their preferred methods, and many in a given area will operate in similar manners, reflecting the preferences of property managers and owners in that area.

Most reputable contractors will provide a baseline degree of quality control below which they will not go. For them, every building they serve is an advertisement. Few wish to be associated with what could be interpreted as inadequate work, even if that is what the owner prefers.

Price the contract

Several methods are used to price a custodial management services contract. The goal should be using a method that is fair, reasonable, and comfortable for both parties, and which creates a reward for good performance. In business, the reward is profit, and for the contractor this is derived in three ways. First, there is the direct profit from the work being performed. Second, there is future profit to be derived from that work, assuming the project will continue because the work quality is good. Third, there is the profit to be made from work gained through referrals.

For the owner, profit is derived from better occupancy rates and less space turnover. Cleaner conditions also translate into more longevity for cleaned surfaces, and thus fewer replacement costs over the years. And for managers, the ability to keep owners happy with a minimum amount of oversight certainly can translate into profit.

The ideal situation is not going to result simply because a contract is priced properly, but it is almost impossible to achieve the ideal when the work is priced improperly. Contractors need incentives to try their best. When they are capable of doing well, and want to do well, providing a tangible reward can make it happen. On the other side of the coin, spending valuable time trying to "nickel and dime" a contractor to keep expense to a minimum will almost assuredly lead to a deteriorated relationship and lower-quality work.

Especially when it comes to custodial services, "You get what you pay for" is an apt expression. Naturally, no one should pay too much. But paying too little can be an equally serious error.

For the most part, the cost of the contract will depend on the time required for the work involved, the hourly rate paid, the equipment and materials used, and the contractor's overhead. An indication of time requirements is given in Tables 8.1 to 8.4. Naturally, actual time requirements will vary.

TABLE 8.1   Floor-Care Operations Time in Minutes per 1000 Square Feet

	Degree of obstruction			
Activity	None	Slight	Moderate	Heavy
Dust mop	7	9	11	13
Damp mop	14	19	24	28
Wet mop and rinse	28	38	48	56
Vacuum (floor) dry	15	19	24	30
Vacuum (floor) wet	30	38	48	60
Vacuum (carpet) dry	20	24	29	35
Sweep	10	13	16	20
Scrub (manual)	75	105	120	135
Scrub (16-inch single disk)	50	60	85	100
Scrub (19-inch single disk)	25	30	43	50
Hose and squeegee	20	24	29	35
Strip and rewax (2 coats)	200	225	260	305
Buff (16-inch single disk)	25	30	43	50
Buff (18-inch single disk)	15	20	25	30
Buff (20-inch high-speed, 1500 r/min)	5	7	10	14
Autoscrubber/vacuum (single pass)	22	25	—	—

TABLE 8.2   Time Required for Walls, Partitions, Doors, Windows, and Related Items

Activity	Seconds required
Walls and partitions	
Dust	2 per square foot
Damp clean	5 per square foot
Vacuum	5 per square foot
Wash	
Painted surface	10 per square foot
Tile	10 per square foot
Marble	5 per square foot
Clear glass	90 per square foot
Opaque glass	5 per square foot
Doors	
Dust	40
Damp clean	80
Spot clean	50
Wash both sides	150
Windows, wash	8 per square foot
Other	
Framed picture, dust	15
Window ledge, dust	2 per linear foot
Window ledge, damp clean	4 per linear foot
Venetian blind, dust	210
Venetian blind, damp clean	420

TABLE 8.3   Time Required for Restroom

Activity	Seconds required
Basin and soap dish, clean	120
Bradley basin (semicircular), clean	180
Bradley basin (circular), clean	300
Door, spot clean	50
Fixtures, destain	180
Mirror (large), clean	60
Mirror (average), clean	30
Napkin dispenser, clean	15
Napkin dispenser, refill	90
Receptacle, empty and wash	30
Receptacle (paper towel), clean	10
Receptacle (paper towel), empty liner and wash	20
Shelving, clean	10–15
Soap dispenser, clean	10
Soap dispenser, refill	60
Toilet and partition, clean	180
Towel (paper) dispenser, refill	90
Urinal, clean	120
Wainscot	4 per foot

TABLE 8.4 Time Required for Office and Other Cleaning Operations

Activity	Seconds required
General dusting	720 per 1000 square feet
Ashtray	
Dust	15
Damp clean	30
Bookcase (4 feet by 4 feet)	
Dust	40
Damp clean	80
Chair	
Dust	20–40
Damp clean	40–80
Wash	50–100
Coat tree, dust	15
Desk	
Dust	20–30
Damp clean	40–60
Wash	360
Clean and wax	600
Strip and rewax	900
Wash glass top	120
Desk tray	
Dust	10
Damp clean	20
Drop light, vacuum and wash	200
File cabinet	
Dust	25
Damp clean	50
Fluorescent luminaire, vacuum and wash	360
Sofa, dust	150
Table	
Dust	20–40
Wash	360
Clean and wax	600
Strip and rewax	900
Trash can, wash	240
Wastebasket	
Dust	15
Damp clean	30
Empty and wash	45

Types of contracts.   Several types of contracts are used, as follows.

Periodic rate/uncontrolled input.   The most common type of contract is called "periodic rate/uncontrolled input." It identifies precisely what has to be done, where it has to be done, and the conditions that must be established and maintained. The work scope would prescribe, for each identifiable area:

The nature of the work to be performed and its frequency

The method to be used in performing the work

The equipment to be used in performing the work

The nature of supervision to be used

The frequency and nature of inspections and reports

The contract provides that the company is paid a certain amount of money for its services at prescribed intervals (periodic rate). Input is uncontrolled in the sense that the customer pays for results, irrespective of the contractor's cost of producing those results.

Periodic rate/controlled input.   Some managers recommend that a periodic-rate/controlled-input contract is superior because it helps ensure that any significant new economies that emerge are shared. It is essentially the same as an uncontrolled-input contract, except that a certain number of worker hours are required. Should the number of worker-hours needed to do the work shrink, contract renegotiation is usually called for. In most cases, new equipment is the cause of time/labor savings, and the investment in the equipment increases overhead. Surely the contractor should be rewarded for a wise investment, and just as surely, any reward that seemingly comes at another's expense will ultimately have a negative effect. Contract renegotiation thus can be geared toward increasing the contractor's profit while reducing the owner's cost.

Cost plus percent profit.   A cost-plus-percent-profit contract gives the contractor a profit equivalent to a fixed percentage of cost. This is not generally recommended since it can encourage inadequate performance and low productivity, because profit increases when costs go up.

Cost plus fixed fee.   This is similar to cost plus percent profit, except that the profit percentage is replaced by a fixed fee. That seemingly minor change can create a world of difference, since the fee can be variable. If desired conditions can be maintained at less cost than anticipated, the fee can go up to create incentives and rewards. If desired conditions do not materialize, the fee can be reduced. Again, it must be recognized that obtaining quality work should be the principal goal. Almost always, that requires paying a fair and reasonable price.

Management fee. A management-fee contract is used when the contractor is employed to manage the owner's or manager's in-house custodial work force.

Other types of contracts. The other approaches available are only as limited as the imagination. In virtually all cases, however, effective contracts are clear and concise. They identify what is to be done, how, when, and where; they identify the costs; they contemplate the "what-ifs." Intelligent contractors understand that they are best off when they provide the quality and concern needed to retain a customer indefinitely. Owners and managers realize that they are best off when they have a contractor they can rely on fully to do a good job in order to merit the trust that is the cornerstone of any long-term relationship.

9

Insurance

Introduction

It is imperative to ensure that each property managed has the appropriate types of coverage and the appropriate amounts of each. It is equally imperative to understand that insurance is never foolproof. In some instances you may not have the coverage you thought you had, or—even when you do—the nature of the loss may be such as to not be covered. In a true worst-case scenario, you may have the coverage, but the insurer may be unable to pay, for example, because it has gone bankrupt. In other words, do not rely on insurance policies as your sole means of risk management.

Another important point to grasp is this: even when all insurance coverages are as appropriate as they possibly can be, even when every feasible insurable risk is insured, insurance still is a second-place finisher to effective risk management. Risk management is superior because it helps prevent incidents to begin with, and it permits a rapid response to those that do occur, to mitigate losses as fully and efficiently as possible. Consider the following scenario. A woman parks in the basement of your new mixed-use building, which includes 30 retail shops on the ground floor, 250,000 square feet of office space, and 80 condominium units, 52 of which still are for sale. After shopping in the building, the woman returns to her car. Her arms holding several packages, she fumbles for her keys and, as she does so, she hears a voice say, "All right lady. This is a gun." She feels what she assumes is the barrel of a gun being poked into her ribs, is forced into the car and, ultimately, is robbed and raped. In the investigation that ensues it is discovered that your security force had been operating two people short because of illnesses, and the supervisor of security, who was new to the position, had neglected to do anything about it. A number of other infractions are alleged by the woman's attorney.

As it so happens, insurance covers you for the financial losses you may suffer, after you satisfy the deductible. However, there are certain things that insurance cannot compensate you for. Among these, first and foremost, are the feelings of guilt you may encounter for having been negligent, or having allowed a possibly negligent situation to develop. Knowing that you did not do all you reasonably could have to have prevented an incident or, worse, knowing that you were careless and thereby allowed an incident to occur, can leave emotional scars.

Consider, too, the impact of negative publicity. Newspapers, radio, and television can ballyhoo such incidents to gigantic proportions. As a consequence, a building can quickly gain an image for being unsafe, creating a damaging impact on retail sales, sales of condominium units, and even leasing of office space. Although procedures can be implemented to offset the losses or potential losses, these procedures can be costly; even the best may be only partially effective. Also consider the time that will be spent defending the claim. Records will have to be researched; a variety of individuals will have to be interviewed; experts will have to be called in; and you and your staff will likely have to respond to interrogatories, depositions, and other forms of pretrial discovery. Typically, hundreds of hours are expended, demanding that other work you need to accomplish will have to get done during "nonworking" hours, creating a strain on personal relationships, undercutting the quality of the work produced, and otherwise creating difficulties. And, on a personal basis, it could mean that you gain a blot on your record and the "opportunity" to look for work elsewhere, just as it could also mean the loss of a client in the case of a fee management property management firm.

If this scenario sounds greatly exaggerated, you probably have not experienced it yourself or been close to those who have. It *does* happen. And while headlines may not always result, other difficulties do emerge, and insurance cannot possibly compensate for the damage. Nor is this a new observation. It is at least as old as the ancient dictum that "an ounce of prevention is worth a pound of cure."

Although Chapter 10 discusses risk management in greater detail, it cannot be denied that having proper insurance is also part of overall risk management. When the term risk management is used, however, most people think in terms of loss avoidance and mitigation. Insurance is that element of risk management that focuses on *risk transfer,* that is, the transference of risk of loss from one party to another. This concept is discussed more fully in the following section.

Risk Transfer in General

Insurance is not the only risk transfer method, but it is the most reliable and most commonly used. Understand, however, that most forms of coverage include at least some *self-insurance* in the form of a deductible. Since most losses are smaller ones, raising the deductible has more of an impact on premiums than lowering the limits. In other words, it would save more, in most cases, to raise a deductible from $10,000 to $15,000 than it would to lower the limit from $1.5 million to $1.3 million.

The other form of risk transfer is an indemnification, whereby another party is obliged to accept certain risks, typically as a cost of doing business, or as the cost of doing business *with you*. As discussed more fully in connection with contracts, indemnifications create inherent dangers. Stated briefly, they must coincide with public policy in order to be upheld in court. In other words, you cannot ask for more prevention than the public, via prior tort law decisions, has decided is appropriate. For example, in many states indemnifications requiring another party to pay the costs of your negligence may not be upheld. The indemnification must also be clearly written to ensure that almost anyone with a high-school education can understand exactly what is meant. Often indemnifications are not worded clearly, and this can result in a need for legal action to obtain enforcement, and the cost of that action may be almost as much as the amount you hope to recover. Recognize, too, that the party who accepts an indemnification may not have the wherewithal to implement it because, for example, the party has no money at the time the claim is made, or because the party is a corporation that dissolved itself soon after the work was complete.

It is reasonable to ask for appropriate indemnifications and, as part of overall risk management activities, it likewise is appropriate to assure (to the highest degree possible) that the indemnifying party will have the ability to honor the indemnification. To some extent, this can be done by reviewing not only the indemnifying party's financial condition, but also the party's insurance. In some cases, the building owner, the property management firm, their various officers, and so on, should become named insureds on the other party's policy, which is yet another form of risk transfer.

In no case should it be assumed that an indemnification provides the coverage you hope it will. In no case should you assume that another party is insured because the other party says it is. In no case should you assume that you and others have been named insureds on someone else's policy because that someone else said that it has occurred. As part of overall risk management with respect to risk transfer, *everything* should be verified and documented. Unquestionably, that meticulous an approach takes more time and effort than a more casual and relaxed approach, which explains why some firms are far more risk-prone than others. This is something that underwriters consider in setting their rates, as discussed in the following section.

Insurance Basics

It is worthwhile for property managers to understand how the insurance industry works in general, and some of the key considerations that apply to a number of different policies. Note that the discussion in this section is skewed principally to liability coverages.

The industry and its principals

The insurance industry comprises four principal parties: insureds, insurance agents, insurers, and reinsurers.

Insureds. Insureds are those to whom a policy's coverage is extended. It is important to know who that is, a feat that may be more difficult than you suppose. If a property is insured, does it mean that the owner is insured? Almost certainly it does, but who is the owner? Is it an individual? a holding company? a partnership? a corporation? Are all persons who are owners and partial owners covered? What about their heirs and assigns? If the building is managed by an independent property management firm, is that firm covered? Is it specifically named, or is it covered because it is an agent, and the law of agency applies? But what is the law of agency in your state? Does it apply to the firm and all property managers? Do the property managers have to be named? When was the last time you examined the policies? If there has been a change of some type, has that change been incorporated into the policy, as with respect to "named insureds?" Do not assume that you or any other party is an insured. *Know it for a fact.*

Insurance agents. Insurance agents sell insurance and obtain a commission from each sale. Some specialize in just one type of policy but, more commonly, they offer a variety of coverages from one or several insurers. Careful selection of an insurance agent is always advisable, because effective agents do far more than sell. With regard to most types of liability insurance, they should at least provide guidance in completing the application form, because many of the questions asked are subject to interpretation. Answers given affect the premium and in some cases determine whether or not coverage will be offered. Agents can also give advice on techniques firms can use to lower the cost of their coverage, and should be able to pass along information about new policies or policy provisions, as well as on loss prevention measures you can use. Insurance agents also are among the first people called when a claim is filed, or when a situation suggests that a claim probably will be filed. As such, they should be available to provide guidance when needed.

Insurers. Insurers are the companies that issue policies. They establish what their policies do and do not cover, limits and deductibles, and the premium that must be paid. They also handle any claims that are made. Those responsible for these functions are actuaries, underwriters, and claims managers.

Actuaries. Actuaries compute the odds that a given risk will materialize and the ultimate probable cost of damages. In doing so, they rely on the law of averages (probability theory) determined through analysis of historical data.

When an insurer refuses to provide coverage for a certain type of exposure, as has occurred in recent years, the decision usually results from guidance provided by actuaries, typically because they know the risks are huge, but they are unable to calculate them reliably. Refusing to cover a risk is a major step for insurers; it is a decision not to sell their product.

As you probably are aware, most insurers (as of January 1990) exclude pollution coverage from their liability policies. At one time insurers offered this coverage without significant restraint, until they were inundated with major claims resulting from long-term damage. At that time policies were modified to cover only those losses caused by a sudden release of pollutants. In one case, however, a court determined that sudden-release coverage applied to a long-term problem because the long-term problem clearly had to be caused by innumerable sudden discharges. That being the case, the court also ruled that each such sudden discharge had to be covered to the full limits of the policy. Given the court's attitude, and fearing (with good reason) that it would be emulated in other cases, the industry decided to terminate pollution coverage.

Underwriters. Underwriters evaluate each applicant to determine the extent to which various risks (identified by actuaries) are likely to affect it and, accordingly, what the firm's premium should be, assuming its application is accepted. In some cases, evaluations are based exclusively on a review of an applicant's written responses to application form questions. In others, written responses are used mostly to determine whether the application should be rejected or studied further. If further study is indicated, representatives of the insurer will actually visit the firm to conduct an in-depth underwriting review. While many properties and property managers have been hard hit by rapidly spiraling insurance costs, most are in a position to reduce these costs, as discussed in this chapter.

Claims managers. When everything is running smoothly for insureds, the only contact they may have with their insurers is an occasional bill or newsletter. The true test of an insurer occurs when a claim or preclaim situation emerges. In fact, does the insurer offer preclaim counseling? If so, by whom? What are the person's qualifications, capabilities, and attitudes? How quickly and effectively does the company respond to a preclaim situation? to an actual claim? Who are the lawyers that insurers recommend to their insureds? What are their reputations? Are they known as professional and knowledgeable, or something less? And what is their attitude? Is their principal concern "doing right" by the insured, or is it "doing right" by the insurer? By all means, speak with insureds who have actually had to go through a claim or preclaim experience with an insurer. To purchase insurance based solely on the premium could be a serious mistake. If an insurance agent is unwilling to identify appropriate people with whom to check, casual discussion at association meetings and other get-togethers should be of value.

Reinsurers. As their name implies, reinsurers insure insurers. The manner in which they operate differs from the insurers' in that they often purchase certain "layers" of risk. For purposes of illustration, assume an insurer has issued a policy with a $1 million limit and a $50,000 deductible. The insurer retains the $50,000 to $250,000 layer and then transfers the $250,000 to $500,000 layer to Reinsurer A and the $500,000 to $1 million layer to Reinsurer B. The amount that the insurer pays to the reinsurer is determined by underwriting factors similar to those used by the insurer.

Reinsurance helps bring stability to the insurance industry because it diffuses major losses. A comparatively small insurer that faced a $100 million loss on its own would possibly have to declare bankruptcy. In actuality, however, its losses would be limited only to the risks it decided to retain or was unable to have others accept.

Insurers determine how much risk they will retain and how much they will transfer to reinsurers based on a number of variables. The more that is transferred to reinsurers, however, the more the insurer's rates are determined by factors over which the insurer has little or no control. And the reinsurance market can be volatile, especially so since as many as half the firms worldwide are not long-term participants. They enter the market when investment prospects look good; they leave when other opportunities beckon. Those who are new to the industry tend to accept the "high-end" risks because, historically, these involve the layers that are the least likely to be penetrated, and thus require the least resources to accept. In recent years, however, penetration of the uppermost layers of liability policies has become far more common, forcing many of the newcomers to leave the industry or, in some cases, to go out of business.

The long-term reinsurers, many of which are insurance company subsidiaries, understand the market well and are prepared to accept some of the "bumps and bruises" that occur from time to time. However, when they are alone in the market, the amount of capital available is greatly reduced, thus reducing the amount of premium that can be written, that is, the capacity of the market. Capacity fluctuations have a direct bearing on the price you pay for coverage.

The cyclical nature of capacity

Capacity fluctuations affect liability insurance costs in accord with the basic laws of supply and demand. When capacity is so high that supply exceeds demand, premiums moderate and a buyer's market prevails. When demand exceeds supply, however, the situation is reversed. The cost of insurance rises and a seller's market is created. Historically, capacity rises and falls in cycles. In the late 1970s and early 1980s, insurers operated at the peak of a capacity cycle and liability insurance was relatively inexpensive. By the mid-1980s, insurers were operating in the trough of a capacity cycle and insurance rates were high. A review of the factors associated with this cycling provides excellent insight into the inner workings of the industry.

Generally speaking, insurers and reinsurers have two sources of income: underwriting income, derived from their insureds' premium payments, and income derived from investments such as stocks and bonds, buildings, mortgages, and loans.

When the investment market is strong, conventional investors generally try to obtain as much money as they can to increase their involvement, typically by borrowing money from banks or other lenders. Although investors incur an interest expense when borrowing funds, their calculations show that their investments should generate enough income to pay the interest and still provide a profit.

Insurance companies do not have to rely on lenders to obtain investment funding. They already have a ready source of income: cash from premium payments. Thus when the investment market is strong, they take steps to increase their underwriting income. They can do this by lowering their rates to attract insureds from other insurers, or by relaxing their underwriting standards to accept risks they might otherwise refuse. Insurers recognize that either practice will increase underwriting losses. But that is the price that has to be paid—tantamount to interest—in order to increase participation in the investment market. Their calculations show that despite increased underwriting losses, they will still enjoy healthy profits because of the income they can earn by investing the increased premium dollar cash flow.

It is important to note that insurers' underwriting losses are subject to certain accounting requirements imposed by regulatory agencies. When a claim is filed, the circumstances surrounding it must be closely analyzed to determine how much it will ultimately cost the insurer. Even though actual payout may not occur until 3 to 5 years (or more) after the claim is filed, the insurer must immediately set aside an appropriate amount in "loss reserves" to assure its ability to "make good" when the need arises. The amount set aside must approximate the full amount likely to be paid out. These loss reserves then are invested.

In the late 1970s and early 1980s, investment opportunities were particularly strong because there was such a high rate of inflation in the United States. Even relatively safe investments were providing double-digit returns. These high rates attracted numerous investors to the reinsurance market. By accepting risks that would not require payouts until 3, 4, or 5 years later, they derived immediate income to fund their investment ambitions. As a consequence, the insurance industry's capacity was increased; insurance rates and underwriting standards fell.

When the United States altered its monetary policies in the early 1980s, inflation was reduced dramatically and high-yielding safe investment opportunities all but disappeared. Reinsurers left the market in search of greener pastures, and capacity was drastically reduced. But that was not the only problem facing the insurance industry. Due to the low rates offered, insureds had been encouraged to increase their coverage, and low underwriting standards had made insurance available to those who previously could not obtain it. As a consequence, claims rose to record levels, fueled in large measure by society's growing litigiousness and the availability of so many "deep pockets." This situation caused insurers and state regulators to reexamine loss reserves, and many discovered an alarming situation. Due to inflation and other factors, they had seriously underestimated the cost of many losses. Since high-yielding investments were not available to help make up the difference, insurers had to transfer immediately vast amounts of money from capital to loss reserves. Since this diminished the money available for investment significantly, insurers had to look to underwriting income—rather that investment income—as their principal source of profit. This shift resulted in a precipitous rise in the cost of professional liability insurance as well as more selective underwriting standards.

Some observers claim that the rapid rise in liability insurance rates experienced in the mid to late 1980s indicates that liability insurers are mismanaged. In truth, however, they are simply reacting to competitive pressures with which all business entities must contend. An insurer that seeks to attain stability by not lowering its premiums and underwriting standards when others do will quickly find itself losing business.

Those who claim that insurance companies are mismanaged also contend that insurers should be subject to more regulation, such as that imposed on electric, gas, and other utilities. As it now stands, regulation is effected on a state-by-state basis, but the level of control is primarily product-based. State insurance regulators strive to assure that a company is legitimate and can make good on any policies it sells. By contrast, public utility commissions take a close look at everything a regulated utility does, and thus become far more involved in the review of management philosophy and decisions. Insurance companies could be controlled to that extent only through a federal apparatus and given the size, strength, and lobbying capabilities of the insurance industry, federal control is not likely to become a reality in the foreseeable future. In addition, federal control could not be easily exercised over reinsurers, because many are headquartered outside the United States. As a consequence, the liability insurance market will probably continue to operate in a largely unregulated manner, and in responding to economic trends, it is likely to remain somewhat volatile.

Occurrence coverage versus claims made, a world of difference

Some forms of liability insurance still can be obtained on an occurrence basis. For the most part, however, claims-made coverage is replacing occurrence. The difference between the two is significant, and property managers must be conversant with the differences and how they affect risk.

Occurrence-based. Occurrence-based coverage provides that the policy in force at the time of the event triggering a claim—the occurrence—affords protection from the claim, no matter when the claim is filed. For example, assume that Property A is covered by a commercial general liability (CGL) policy in 1980. During that year a person is assaulted and robbed in the building's underground garage. Five years later—in 1985—that person sues the owner of the building. The owner would be protected by the occurrence-based CGL policy in force during 1980, even though the owner has since changed carriers.

Claims-made. Claims-made coverage works in a much different way. It provides coverage only for claims filed against the insured while the policy is in force, subject to any prior-acts protective coverage or "tail" provisions.

Prior acts. In those areas where there are no prior-acts limitations, the policy in force at the time of the claim covers the claim no matter when the claim-causing event occurred. In the hypothetical case above, for example, the claims-made policy in force in 1985 would cover the owner of Property A for the assault that occurred in 1980, and the issuer of the occurrence-based policy would be in the position of providing excess coverage. In other words, if the plaintiff were awarded $150,000, and the owner's two policies (the old and the new) each had a $100,000 limit, the new claims-made policy would provide $100,000 (less any deductible), and the old occurrence-based policy would provide $50,000 (less any deductible). If the award had been $50,000, the claims-made policy would have covered it all.

It is growing more common for insurers to limit prior-acts coverage, in some cases to no prior acts whatsoever. In those instances where all prior policies have been occurrence-based, so severe a restriction may pose little risk, assuming there is no question about the nature of the prior coverage, that the prior coverage is adequate, and that the company that issued the policy is and will likely continue to be solvent. The extent and nature of potential claims-causing events must also be considered.

Generally speaking, most owners will benefit from having a reasonable amount of prior-acts coverage in most policies. The extent of prior-acts protection usually is negotiable. It must of course be recognized that gaps will be left in prior-acts protection unless the extent of this protection is extended each year.

Tail. Tail is another element to consider with claims-made policies. More formally known as a *supplemental reporting period option,* tail provides for a continuation of a claims-made policy's coverage after the policy has expired, for claims resulting from events that occurred while the policy was in force.

Typically, insurers offer a 5-year tail, and it would apply to any claims of which the insurer is notified *while the policy is in force,* and up to 60 days after the policy's termination. For example, assume an assault occurs 20 days after a claims-made policy has expired. The owner notifies the insurer and the owner then is protected by the expired policy for up to 4 years and 345 days. If for some reason a claim is not made during that time, then the protection is gone. Longer extended periods are available, including unlimited reporting periods, provided the incident involved occurred during the policy period. Knowledge of the statute of limitations that applies can be of value in determining an appropriate tail period.

Some policies include a tail provision at the time they are purchased. In other cases, an offer to purchase tail will be made by the insurer within 60 days after a policy expires, assuming it is not being renewed. Know what the insurer's tail provisions are before you buy a policy. Generally speaking, it will be wisest to purchase the tail at the same time you buy the policy (assuming it is available for purchase at that time), since costs may rise substantially by the time you get ready to make the purchase. Feasibly, conditions may be such that tail may not be offered.

Per incident and aggregate

Per incident and *aggregate* are commonly used terms that may not be fully understood. Assume, for example, that the policy in question has aggregate limits of $2 million, plus limits of $500,000 per incident, and a per-incident deductible of $25,000. Basically, this means that, no matter how many claims or losses an insured may suffer in a year, the most an insurer will pay on behalf of the insured during the policy period is $2 million, less whatever deductible may apply.

The deductible applies in each instance, and includes the cost of defense. The maximum the insurer will pay in any one instance is $500,000 less the deductible. What could happen is illustrated in Table 9.1, where it is assumed that the owner's policy pays a maximum of $500,000 per incident, has a $25,000 deductible, and a $2 million aggregate. Other features of the policy include the owner's ability to apply cost of defense to the deductible, and the insurer's ability to reduce the maximum amount to be paid by the amount it spends on defense. In the first claim, the defense spends $60,000 on legal fees and related costs, and the claim is settled for $500,000. The owner pays the full deductible amount—$25,000—toward the cost of defense. Then, after settlement is reached, the insurer expends its full per-incident exposure of $475,000 on the settlement and legal fees, leaving the owner to pay for the balance of the settlement, $60,000. In the second claim, the owner pays for the full cost of defense ($10,000) and $15,000 of the settlement. The insurer picks up the rest of the settlement, at

TABLE 9.1 Hypothetical Payment History; $500,000 Limit, $25,000 Deductible

Claim no.	Total cost of		Owner pays			Insurer pays	
	Defense	Settlement	Cost of defense	Balance of deductible	Settlement	Cost of defense	Settlement
1	60,000	500,000	25,000	0	60,000	35,000	440,000
2	10,000	50,000	10,000	15,000	0	0	35,000
3	35,000	100,000	25,000	0	0	10,000	100,000
4	75,000	750,000	25,000	0	350,000	50,000	400,000
Total	180,000	1,400,000	85,000	15,000	410,000	95,000	975,000

$35,000. At the end of the year, the owner will have paid $510,000, not including the cost of the policy itself, and the insurer will have paid $1,070,000.

In determining how best to structure your policies, consider what is typically spent on the types of claims you will most likely confront, to determine the most appropriate deductible and per-incident coverage. Then determine how frequently claims are likely to be filed in order to determine what the aggregate coverage should be. No one on staff should ever take the attitude of "so what, we're insured," because many types of insurance do not provide the extent of protection that may be assumed.

Note: Not all policies' coverage is reduced by the amount of defense. In some states, in fact, that aspect of coverage is illegal, since the cost of defense can quickly erode whatever amount is left to pay those who have been damaged. You should know the law in your state, just as you should know what your policy actually does and does not do. Likewise, examine any cost of defense options. In some cases, the insurer will contribute 80 percent of the insured's legal costs, so that most of the deductible typically is paid toward the settlement or award.

Pro-rata coverage

With respect to liability insurance, coverage generally is *pro rata*. In other words, if a building is worth, say, $10 million, you might consider insuring it for $5 million, under the theory that no more than $5 million worth of damage will occur at any time. However, if a $5 million loss does occur, the maximum that will be paid is $2.5 million because of the pro-rata feature. In essence, the percentage of full value you insure for is the percentage of full payment you will receive.

Package versus monoline

A commercial package policy is one policy that comprises at least two coverage parts, each such coverage part representing a discrete form of insurance, such as automobile. For the most part, the discrete elements are also available separately, as monoline policies. Although it takes only two coverage parts to form a package policy, many property managers prefer to combine a number of coverages, because it is far simpler to coordinate in that manner. Candidate elements of a commercial package policy (CPP) include commercial property, commercial general liability (CGL), crime, inland marine, boiler and machinery, and commercial auto, each of which is discussed in this chapter. As indicated, each policy, whether purchased as monoline or as part of a CPP, is subject to a variety of endorsements that can add or delete certain coverages.

Note that the various policies offered by different insurers tend to be similar to one another, following materials developed by the Insurance Services Office (ISO), an industry-sponsored group. Once a given policy is approved by a state's insurance commissioner, all insurers are free to offer it.

Admitted versus nonadmitted insurers

Most states have regulations that require insurers to participate in something that is tantamount to a guarantee fund. In other words, should an insurer experience financial difficulties, insureds in the state would be "made whole" (or as close to whole as possible) by the fund. Those firms that agree to participate in the fund are referred to as "admitted," and those that do not participate are referred to as "nonadmitted," or by similar terms. Generally speaking, states require nonadmitted insurers to notify those seeking information that coverage is not guaranteed. In other words, there is a possibility that the insurer would for some reason not cover a claim, and the insured has no recourse through the state. To the extent that admitted and nonadmitted insurers offer the same coverages, but the nonadmitted carrier charges less, it would have to be up to the insured to determine the risks of dealing with a nonadmitted carrier, and to judge whether the saving justifies the risks.

Types of Coverage

It is worthwhile to review and comment on several types of coverage commonly needed in the management of real property. The policies reviewed are those applying to commercial property (including coverages for building and personal property, building ordinances, commercial glass, builder's risk, and business income), boiler and machinery, flood, commercial general liability, business auto, garage, umbrella liability, commercial crime, inland marine, and directors' and officers' liability.

As complete as the list may sound, experienced property managers recognize it as far from all-inclusive. And as extensive as this discussion may be, those with experience realize that it does little more than provide highlights and warnings. As will be seen, insurance is not only complex; it also tends to be extremely precise in terms of what is and is not covered, who owes what duty to whom, and so on. A casual approach to the review of policies simply will not do. Whoever is in charge of insurance must know *precisely* what the various terms mean, and exactly what is covered and what is not. For example, you may assume that a boiler of some type is covered for all risks, only to discover that damages are not covered, because the explosion was caused by events inside the boiler, rather than outside the boiler.

It is the responsibility of property management to have adequate insurance. Achieving adequacy can be accomplished only by knowing what is and is not covered. Note, too, that coverages can change from year to year, due to subtle but important modifications made by insurers. Do not assume that the renewal of a policy means the continuation of identical coverage.

Commercial property coverage

Commercial property coverage applies principally to commercial firm protection and allied lines, including commercial glass. The typical policy contains seven basic elements.

1. A policy cover or jacket that may include a table of contents and/or an index, as per requirements in some states or the preference of the insurer.

2. Common Policy Declarations Form.

3. Commercial Property Declarations Form, which can be combined with a Common Policy Declarations Form.

4. Common Policy Conditions Form, which relates conditions common to all commercial lines of insurance.

5. Commercial Property Conditions Form, which relates to commercial property coverage parts.

6. Commercial Policy Coverage Forms, which describe what is and is not covered, and the conditions applying to each. These conditions often are referred to as loss conditions or additional conditions. Separate sections relate definitions and identify insurance limits, the deductible, and optional coverages. The specific type and number of forms available are subject to change from year to year, but the basics typically include building and personal property, glass, condominium association, condominium commercial unit owners, builder's risk, business income, legal liability, extra expense, leasehold interest, and mortgage holders' errors and omissions, several of which are discussed below.

7. Cause of Loss Forms identify the perils that are covered and the relevant exclusions.

Building and personal property coverage is the principal part of commercial property coverage. By endorsement, or as indicated in the declarations, it is used to cover the direct physical loss of buildings and contents and individual property categories, such as tenant improvements. Note that the coverage applies to completed buildings only, except that additions under construction may also be covered, if not covered otherwise.

Coverage. The covered property may be a building, your business personal property, the personal property of others, or any combination of the three. *Building* includes outdoor fixtures and property used to service the building, such as lawn mowers and snow plows.

Business personal property can also include mowers, plows, and so on, including owner-supplied furniture in tenant spaces. Definitions are not a concern when both elements (that is, building and business personal property) are part of the same coverage. Note that coverage on business personal property usually can be split into smaller units with the same or different limits for each. Likewise, specific coverage can be written for tenants' improvements and betterments.

Some property may be specifically excluded by the policy, but often such excluded property can be covered by endorsement; *additional property not covered* endorsements also are available. The property typically excluded includes, among many others, currency; deeds; evidence of debts; securities; aircraft; automobiles; cost of excavating, grading, filling, or backfilling; building or equipment foundations; lawns; outdoor radio or television antennas; retaining walls; and underground pipes, flues, and drains.

The specific *causes of loss* covered by a policy are stated in separate Causes of Loss Forms. The Basic Form covers losses due to fire; lightning; explosion; windstorm or hail; smoke; aircraft; vehicles; riot or civil commotion; vandalism; sprinkler leakage; sinkhole collapse; and volcanic action. A Broad Form includes the basics plus breakage of glass; falling objects; weight of snow, ice, or sleet; and building collapse (under certain conditions).

Special Form coverage also can be had to cover virtually any risk of direct physical loss (all perils), except those specified. Theft is included, unless it is specifically excluded by the insurer or because underwriting provisions are such that coverage cannot be applied. Also included is coverage for property in transit and water damage (including the cost of the repairs necessary to the system). Coverage also applies to repair damage caused by the melting of snow or ice on buildings ("ice dam").

The *Earthquake Form* may be used only in conjunction with the Basic, Broad, or Special Form. It provides coverage against earthquake and volcanic eruption, explosion, or effusion. The volcanic action peril covered by the other forms relates to above-ground effects of a volcano, such as lava flow, ash, and airborne shock waves.

Certain additional coverages that are automatic extend the insurance beyond direct physical damage. These include an allowance for debris removal as well as a fire department service charge. Another coverage, *preservation of property,* provides insurance of covered properties for a given number of days at locations other than the described premises. Coverage extensions available include additional amounts of insurance—excess coverage—over and above other coverages. For example, a *newly acquired or constructed property* extension provides up to a given amount (usually $250,000) of coverage over and above the limit selected for builder's risk coverage. (Note that $250,000 seldom is sufficient and can be increased.) Similar extensions apply to personal effects and property of others, valuable papers and records, property off premises, and outdoor property.

Building ordinance coverage can be an important attribute of property coverage, and usually is available via endorsement. Typically, it contains four parts, as follows.

1. *Increased cost of construction* coverage is particularly important for older buildings which do not comply with the current building code. In the event of their destruction, these buildings would have to be rebuilt according to code. However, the coverage provisions of conventional policies generally relate to the cost of damage or the replacement cost. Complying with new codes can result in substantially increased costs, which is precisely why increased cost of construction protection may be important.

2. *Contingent liability from operation of building codes* is valuable coverage with respect to building codes which require that, given certain circumstances, partially completed buildings must be demolished. For example, if a building is 35 percent damaged, insurance may provide 35 percent of value. However, if the building code states that the nature of the damage is such that the building must be torn down, this endorsement would cover the value of the undamaged portion.

3. *Demolition cost* coverage would pay the cost of demolition in the event a damaged structure must be razed.

4. *Time element building ordinance* coverage would cover the increased rents that would have been collected had it not been necessary to raze the undamaged portion of the building and rebuild, versus repairing the structure only.

Another important coverage relates to *loss of off-premises power or utility service,* valuable in those circumstances where loss of utility services can result in loss of rental or other income.

Limits and deductible. The policy's limits usually apply per occurrence, as opposed to being aggregate. The usual deductible is $250, but higher amounts can be obtained. The deductible applies on a per-occurrence basis, and an annual aggregate deductible is available by endorsement.

Loss conditions. Loss conditions are spelled out fairly well in standard forms. It is essential to understand these and to comply with their requirements. For example, when a loss involves a possible violation of law, the police must be called and a copy of the police report must be submitted.

Commercial glass coverage

Commercial glass coverage includes the cost of replacing plate glass, along with any lettering or ornamentation on the glass. (A complete description of lettering and ornamentation is required.) Also covered is the cost of removing debris. Covered causes include breakage as a result of virtually any event except fire and war, as well as accidental or malicious damage from acid or chemicals.

Optional coverage may be needed in the case of plate glass whose surface area exceeds 100 square feet. Note, too, that coverage is not applied to buildings that are vacant for more than 60 consecutive days, unless the coverage is "bought back" from the insurer for an additional premium. Also, if required by law, the policy will pay for the cost of replacing glass with safety glazing material when such was not installed to begin with.

Inland marine coverage—*not* glass insurance—is needed to insure stained glass, stained glass in leaded sections, memorial windows, art glass, mosaic art, rotogravure screens, half-tone screens, and lenses.

Builder's risk coverage

Builder's risk coverage applies typical building and personal property coverage to buildings under construction. Covered property includes foundations; fixtures; equipment; machinery used to service the building; the insured's construction supplies and materials when they are in, on, or within 100 feet of the premises; and temporary structures such as scaffolding, cribbing, and construction forms. Coverage may be extended to include building materials and supplies owned by others, provided they are in the insured's custody and control, are located in or on the covered building or within 100 feet of its premises, and are intended to become a permanent part of the building. Land is specifically excluded from coverage, since it is covered under "sinkhole collapse" of the basic commercial property policy. Also excluded (except when covered by a specific endorsement) is damage to plants, shrubs, leaves, and trees; radio and TV antennas, towers, or masts, as well as their lead-in wiring; and signs that are not attached to the building.

Builder's risk coverage can be written to cover the interests of the owner and/or the contractor, and should cover the full *completed* value of the building or other structure, including all permanent fixtures and decorations. Coverage should begin as soon as construction begins above the level of the lowest basement floor or, in the case of slab-on-grade construction, when construction starts.

Business income (interruption) coverage

Business income or business interruption insurance covers an insured for loss of income caused by a necessary suspension of business activities arising from a direct loss at the premises. Coverage provides net income plus continuing expenses (virtually the same as gross income less noncontinuing expenses), with net income being defined as pretax profit. Loss of rental value is included, as is extra expense coverage, that is, expenses incurred to minimize the interruption of business. Note, however, that the extra expense coverage does not apply to businesses for which the need to maintain operations is a principal concern. These businesses would include newspapers, law offices, bakeries, dairies, and others for which a separate endorsement is available. Coverage also applies for up to 30 days after business is resumed, to consider losses incurred while the business gears up for resuming normal activities.

Boiler and machinery coverage

Boiler and machinery coverage is designed to fill certain gaps in commercial property and commercial general liability (CGL) coverage. The commercial property coverage gap that is bridged is the latter's exclusion of damage to steam boilers, steam pipes, steam turbines, steam engines, and water-heating equipment when the cause of the damage is a condition or event *inside* the equipment. Furthermore, unlike CGL and property damage coverages, boiler and machinery coverage applies to the liability of the insured for property of others in the insured's care, custody, or control.

Equipment covered by boiler and machinery coverage for loss or damage resulting from accidents is defined in four object definition endorsements. These include, in general, the following.

1. *Pressure and Refrigeration Objects Endorsement.*   This covers boilers; electric steam generators; fired and unfired vessels; refrigerat-

ing and air-conditioning vessels and piping; small compressing and refrigerating units; and auxiliary piping.

2. *Mechanical Objects Endorsement.* The endorsement covers engines; pumps; deep-well pumps; compressors; fans and blowers; wheels and shafting; enclosed gear sets; and miscellaneous machines.

3. *Electrical Objects Endorsement.* Covered items include transformers; rotating electrical machines; induction feeder regulators; solid-state rectifier units; and miscellaneous electrical apparatus.

4. *Turbine Objects Endorsements.*

Three forms of coverage are available: conventional boiler and machinery coverage; small-business boiler and machinery coverage; and small-business boiler and machinery Broad Form coverage. Various endorsements also are available, including actual cash value; additional expediting expenses; boilers, fired vessels and electric steam generators; extended liability for property of others; and furnace explosion.

Flood insurance

Flood insurance is made available under the National Flood Insurance Act of 1968. The General Property Form applies to large residential buildings (including condominiums and cooperatives), as well as to nonresidential buildings and their contents. The Dwelling Form is used to cover family risks, including the personal property of condominium or cooperative unit owners. Note that unit owners can also obtain flood insurance to cover their interest in the structure when the structure is underinsured or uninsured.

As defined in a flood insurance policy, a flood is:

> A general and temporary condition of partial or complete inundation of normally dry land areas from (1) the overflow of inland or tidal waters, (2) the unusual and rapid accumulation or runoff of surface waters from any source, or (3) mudslides (mudflows) which are proximately caused by flood, as defined above, and are akin to a river of liquid and flowing mud on the surface of normally dry land areas, as when earth is carried by a current of water and deposited along the path of the current.

Flood insurance does not cover a wide array of listed perils, most or all of which can otherwise be insured. These include rain, snow, sleet, freezing, thawing, and flooding confined to the structure or its immediate vicinity due to causes such as water-line breakage, seepage, and hydrostatic pressure.

In the event of a loss, a flood insurance policy covers the actual cash value of the insured property at the time of the loss. Recovery may not exceed the cost of repairing or replacing the property within a reasonable period after the loss. Items covered in *building* coverage include, among others, the building itself; attached additions and extensions; permanent machinery and equipment; and the owner's personal property used to service or maintain the building, provided it is kept in an enclosed structure.

Contents coverage applies either to household items or to other-than-household items, *but not both.* Other-than-household contents can include merchandise and stock of all kinds; furniture, fixtures, equipment, and machinery owned by the insured; and improvements and betterments to the building when the insured is not the building owner. With respect to household items, certain sublimits apply to items such as fur and jewelry.

Flood insurance does not cover valuable papers of any kind, structures built over water, livestock or crops, trees or shrubs, aircraft, or motor vehicles, among numerous other exclusions. Also not covered are buildings whose cash value is located principally more that 49 percent below grade, certain elevated buildings, and structures that primarily are containers.

Flood insurance does cover certain expenses incurred to avoid further damages, including the cost of sandbags used to protect a building (when the building is covered), and the cost of removing and storing contents for up to 45 days (when contents are covered).

A loss deductible applies separately to each building loss and each contents loss. The basic deductible is $500, but deductibles as high as $5000 are available. (Higher deductibles can result in premium savings of as much as 35 percent.)

Generally speaking, flood insurance coverage can be issued no sooner than the fifth calendar day after the application date and payment, to prevent owners from purchasing it when a flood is imminent. However, coverage is available immediately at the time of transfer of a property when the new owner has applied for it previously, or when the new owner takes over an existing policy.

Commercial general liability

Formerly known as comprehensive general liability, commercial general liability (CGL) coverage extends to:

Premises/operations liability

Products/completed operations liability

Contractual liability

Personal and advertising injury (including wrongful eviction, wrongful entry, false arrest, and malicious prosecution)

Medical payments

Fire-damage legal liability

Broad Form property damage

Host liquor liability (covering the owner or lessor of a premises involved in the liquor business, who is not involved in the business)

Incidental medical malpractice

Nonowned watercraft

Limited worldwide liability

Additional persons insured

Extended bodily injury

Automatic coverage for newly acquired organizations

The intent of the new CGL is to provide truly comprehensive coverage, to help ensure that nothing is forgotten. Naturally, the insurer is permitted to eliminate certain aspects of coverage, including that for products/completed operations; personal and advertising injury; advertising injury only; medical payments; fire-damage legal liability; and for certain types of contracts (leaving only coverage for lease of premises, sidetrack and easement agreements, and other specific types identified).

Those insured by a CGL include the named insured; partners; spouses of individual proprietors; directors; executive officers; stockholders; members; real-estate managers; and certain of the insured's employees. Should the insured die, coverage is extended to the insured's legal representative and property custodian.

Organizations that are newly acquired or formed by the insured, which are owned by the insured or in which the insured holds a majority interest, are also covered automatically for up to 90 days. Note, however, that coverage is limited to events that occur after the organization becomes insured.

The general aggregate limit approach, adopted in 1986, represents a turnabout from prior policies which established significant per-occurrence limits instead. This makes it essential to have adequate aggregate limits in a policy, and to have effective umbrella liability coverage. In addition, in those instances where more than one property is involved, and all are covered by one policy, it is important to stipulate via endorsement that the aggregate limits selected apply on a *per-location* or *per-project* basis.

The new CGL is subject to a number of conditions. Among other things, these conditions require the insurer to continue the policy's coverage despite the insured's bankruptcy; to identify an insured's occurrence reporting requirements; to defend the insured even when it believes another insurer should, and then (as necessary) effect collection from the other insurer; to give 30 days written notice of nonrenewal; and the conditions direct the insurer to provide certain information to an insured upon the latter's request.

The limits of liability associated with the new CGL are unique. One aggregate limit applies only to products/completed operations claims; the other aggregate limit—called the general aggregate limit—applies to all other coverages combined. Beneath the two aggregate limits are limits applying on a per-occurrence basis, each with a fire-damage limit and a medical expense limit. A personal and advertising limit also is established.

Note that legal costs are deducted from the aggregate limits. This not only reduces the insurers' financial exposure, it encourages rapid and low-cost resolution of claims. (It is estimated that the costs of defending claims instituted before this change were approaching 50 percent of indemnity costs.)

Many of the new CGL policies are available on either a claims-made or an occurrence basis. When claims-made is offered, it usually provides 5 years of tail coverage for claims reported to the insurer within 60 days after the policy's termination date, provided the injury or damage occurred before the end of the policy period, but not prior to the policy's retroactive date. Once the basic tail period elapses, the insured may purchase supplemental tail coverage that lasts for an indefinite period, but for an amount no greater than the aggregate amount of that in the basic tail period. While the basic tail period is in effect, the policy does not apply if another policy is in force. During the supplemental tail period, the coverage applies on an excess basis, that is, if the limits of a primary policy are exhausted.

Note that a CGL insurer must notify the "first named insured" about any intention to cancel or not renew coverage, versus the earlier policy (1973 CGL) which implied that *all* named insureds would be notified. It is prudent for property managers to require, via endorsement to each policy, that the property manager be given at least 30 days' notice of cancellation or nonrenewal, and that the notice be sent by certified mail.

Business auto policy

A business auto policy usually comprises a self-contained policy as opposed to a coverage part that is combined with basic provisions to create a policy. A business auto policy (BAP) provides business with selected liability and physical damage coverages in the event of accidents during the policy period. The BAP now in wide use was established several years ago to replace combinations of coverage parts, such as comprehensive automobile liability, basic automobile liability, and nonfleet physical damage.

Persons insured by the policy include the named insureds and those whom the named insured has specifically authorized to use the vehicles. Note, however, that only the named insured is covered for vehicles used by authorized drivers, and which are not owned or hired by the insured (that is, only the named insured is protected by Employers Nonowned Liability protection). Likewise, the insured's BAP does not cover the vicarious liability of the owners of autos covered but not owned by the insured.

It is important to be familiar with the coverage extended to temporary substitute autos, as well as those that are rented when employees are on the road. Generally speaking, it is less expensive to obtain appropriate coverage for rental vehicles via a BAP (if not part of basic coverage) than it is to pay for insurance via a rental company.

The *liability insurance* protection of a BAP usually contains a single limit for bodily injury and property damage. If split limits are desired, they usually can be obtained via endorsement. *Specified perils* coverage combines fire, theft, and combined additional coverages into one package, but fire or fire and theft coverages are available by separate endorsement.

Comprehensive and collision coverages are the principal forms of a BAP's physical damage coverage. They can be obtained separately or, by endorsement, together as combined physical damage coverage. When applied to autos and light trucks, deductibles of $100 to $1000 are available, up to $2000 on heavy trucks; and up to $3000 on extra-heavy trucks.

Garage policy

Garage policies typically provide liability, garagekeepers, and physical damage coverages for garage operations and automobiles (owned and nonowned). The same policy is used by automobile dealers (franchised and nonfranchised) as well as nondealers, such as storage garages, public parking facilities, and repair shops. Given the relatively diverse special needs of dealers and nondealers, either an Automobile Dealers' Supplementary Schedule or a Nondealers' Supplementary Schedule is used.

Liability insurance provisions are generally the same as those associated with a basic auto policy, with insurance for bodily injury and property damage claims being combined under a single limit of liability, and split limits being available by endorsement. Definitions of who is and is not insured likewise are similar to the BAP's.

A number of exclusions and limitations appear in most policies. For example, coverage of watercraft is specifically excluded. Note, too, that a number of perils that are included can in many cases be deleted, because they do not apply, such as escalator coverage, coverage of tank trucks and trailers, and coverage of dramshop liability.

Garagekeeper insurance is important for covering vehicles in the insured's care, custody, or control. The coverage can be purchased as conventional legal liability coverage; as direct loss coverage (excess coverage over the customer's insurance); or without regard to liability, as direct coverage on a primary basis. All three provide a single package of protection against fire, explosion, vandalism, theft, civil commotion, and vandalism. Comprehensive coverage usually is offered as an option, along with collision coverage (subject to various deductibles).

Physical damage insurance addresses the ownership exposures of dealers and nondealers. It does not apply to physical damage of customers' cars.

Umbrella liability coverage

Umbrella liability insurance serves as excess or extended coverage for liability associated with underlying (primary) commercial general liability (CGL), automobile liability, and employers' liability (workers' compensation) insurance policies. To the extent that the umbrella policy provides an additional layer of coverage for the same exposures considered in an underlying policy, it provides excess coverage. In other words, once the limits of an underlying policy are exhausted, the umbrella would "kick in." To the extent that an exposure is not covered by an underlying policy, even if it is specifically excluded, the umbrella extends coverage to provide protection, although typically the insured has a significant retained limit, such as $10,000 or $25,000.

In most instances, an umbrella policy is subject to an aggregate limit applicable to all injury and damage except that arising from automobile-based exposures or those arising from completed operations or products. The cost of defense is included in the aggregate, and usually is included, too, in the aggregate applicable to completed operations or products. A per-incident limit also applies, but defense costs usually are not subject to it.

Umbrella policies have not been standardized and thus can vary considerably from one another. For this reason it is imperative to read and be fully familiar with the exclusions and limitations involved, as well as the definitions. In other words, an umbrella policy does not cover *all* exposures that underlying policies may not cover. Common areas of exclusion include asbestos; pollution of any kind; unfair discharge or discrimination; property of others in the care, custody, and control of the insured; aircraft and watercraft; and ERISA liability. These others may include punitive damages, even though they are insurable in a number of jurisdictions, either due to legislation which states specifically that punitive damages are insurable, or due to the absence of legislation which says that they are not insurable. Understanding the types of situations that remain uncovered is essential in structuring an effective risk management program, since lack of coverage may suggest that additional insurance may be wise (if available) or that special precautions should be taken to maximize an organization's ability to avoid the exposure.

As a general rule, umbrella insurers will examine the underlying policies closely, as well as the nature of the exposures involved and the applicant's past loss history.

Commercial crime coverage

As with most other CPP parts, commercial crime coverage consists of several elements, including Common Policy Declarations, Common Policy Conditions, Commercial Crime Declarations, Crime General Provisions Form (and/or a Safe Depository General Provisions Form, Crime Coverage Form), and any endorsements.

The insurance generally is available in the form of 10 different plans, each of which combines various forms of coverage. The following Commercial Crime Coverage Forms exist.

Form A/Employee Dishonesty. It reimburses an employer for the dishonest acts of covered employees.

Form B/Forgery or Alteration. It indemnifies the insured and banks where the insured has savings or checking accounts against loss stemming from forgery or the alteration of checks, promissory notes, and other specified instruments.

Form C/Theft, Disappearance, and Destruction. It covers the theft, disappearance, or destruction of money or securities inside the premises, inside a banking premises, or in the custody of a messenger.

Form D/Robbery and Safe Burglary. It covers property other than money and securities from robbery of a custodian or (optional) messenger, or from safe burglary.

Form E/Premises Burglary. It covers property other than money and securities from robbery of a watchperson or a burglary.

Form F/Computer Fraud. It covers money, securities, and other property.

Form G/Extortion. It covers money, securities, and other property.

Form H/Premises Theft and Robbery Outside the Premises. It covers property other than money and securities when it is inside the premises, and when it is outside in the custody of a messenger.

Form I/Losses of Safe Deposit Boxes. It covers securities lost by theft, disappearances, or destruction, and property other than money or securities lost due to vandalism, burglary, or robbery, when such property is in a safe deposit box inside a depository vault, or while the property is being removed from or deposited into the box inside the depository.

Form J/Securities Deposited with Others. It covers securities against theft, disappearance, or destruction while on deposit in a depository or in a custodian's premises, or while being transported by a custodian.

Form K/Liability for Guest's Property—Safe Deposit Box. It covers loss, destruction, or damage to any property of the insured's guest when the property is inside a safe deposit box in the premises.

Form L/Liability for Guest's Property—Premises. It covers a guest's property (other than specifically excluded items) while it is in the insured's possession in the insured's premises.

Form M/Safe Depository Liability. It covers loss, destruction, or damage to a customer's property while it is in the premises inside a vault, or inside a safe deposit box inside a vault, or while it is being deposited in or removed from either.

Form N/Safe Depository Direct Loss. It is basically the same as Form M, except that the latter's maximum payment, as several others', is limited to the insured's legal obligations, whereas Form N insures the property without regard to the insured's liability.

The composition of the various plans is indicated in Table 9.2. Their applicability is generally as follows.

Plan 1/Combination Crime—Separate Limits. This plan applies to any insured except one that is eligible for a financial institution blanket bond. Note, however, that some of those eligible for the financial institution blanket bond may also be eligible for this coverage; for example, small loan companies and personal finance companies.

Plan 2/Combination Crime—Single Limits. The plan also applies to any insured except those eligible for a financial institution blanket bond.

TABLE 9.2 **Composition of Commercial Crime Plans**

Plan no.	Title	Coverage forms													
		A	B	C	D	E	F	G	H	I	J	K	L	M	N
1.	Combination crime/separate limits option	×	×	×	×	×	×	×	×	×	×				
2.	Combination crime/single limits option	×	×	×	×										
3.	Storekeeper's Broad Form	×	×	×	×	×									
4.	Storekeeper's burglary and robbery				×	×									
5.	Office burglary and robbery					×			×						
6.	Guest's property/safe deposit box											×			
7.	Guest's property/premises												×		
8.	Safe depository													×*	×*
9.	Excess bank burglary and robbery					×									
10.	Bank excess securities				×										

*M and/or N.

Plan 3/Storekeeper's Broad Form.   This form would be used by any insured with a single premises employing no more than four people.

Plan 4/Storekeeper's Burglary and Robbery.   Plan 4 applies to any insured, but covers burglary and robbery only, with a $50 limit on money.

Plan 5/Office Burglary and Robbery.   This plan covers burglary or robbery of money, securities, or other property from an office.

Plan 6/Guest's Property—Safe Deposit Box.   This plan is used by those with lodging facilities.

Plan 7/Guest's Property—Premises.   This plan also is used by insureds with lodging facilities, but is somewhat broader in scope than Plan 6.

Plan 8/Safe Depository.   Plan 8 applies to insureds other than financial institutions.

Plan 9/Excess Bank Burglary and Robbery.   This plan applies to federal- or state-chartered banking or trust companies.

Plan 10/Bank Excess Securities.   This plan also applies to federal- or state-chartered banking or trust companies.

Commercial inland marine

Commercial inland marine insurance is used mostly, but not exclusively, by retailers. It involves 12 classes of coverage, all on an all-perils or all-risk basis.

Valuable papers and records coverage applies to the physical loss of valuable papers and records that are maintained according to the insurer's underwriting guidelines and protective safeguard requirements. Papers and records also are covered when they are in transit or in others' premises.

Signs coverage applies to neon, fluorescent, and mechanical signs, as well as others of that nature, as opposed to billboards or ordinary fixed signs. All covered signs must be scheduled, with a fixed limit being assigned to each.

Accounts receivable coverage is valuable for those with extensive accounts receivable, due to credit policies. Coverage applies to the cost of recreating records (provided they are stored properly) and actual losses resulting from the inability to restore receipts.

Mail coverage is used principally by bankers, insurance companies, securities dealers, and others who regularly use the mail to deliver valuable items.

Other coverages apply to camera and musical instruments dealers, jewelers, mobile agricultural and construction equipment dealers, physicians' and surgeons' equipment, theatrical properties, cameras and musical instruments used for commercial purposes (commercial articles coverage), films (for movie and audio or video tape producers), and floor plans (for sale merchandise that has been financed).

Directors' and officers' liability insurance

Most directors' and officers' (D&O) policies are written in two ways: to cover directors and officers directly, or to reimburse the corporations or other entities that pay for the directors' and officers' defense costs.

A wide array of policies is available, with varying types of coverages. In almost all cases, however, the coverage is provided for wrongful acts, such as breach of duty, neglect, error, omission, or misstatement, provided such wrongful act, or alleged wrongful act, was committed solely by virtue of the individual being an officer or director of the company. (Note that most policies permit more than officers and directors to be insured, including plant managers, division managers, personnel managers, and so on.)

A number of wrongful acts usually will be excluded. Typical of these are libel or slander, gaining personal profit or advantage to which the insured was not entitled, dishonesty, and losses covered by other insurance.

Under provisions requiring the insurer to reimburse the company which has reimbursed the directors or officers, the basic exclusion usually applies to losses that are otherwise insured.

Nonetheless, some insurers specifically exclude claims of bribes to government officials, wrongful discharge, discrimination, or antitrust violations.

Most of the policies issued to larger organizations have a self-insured retention requirement of $20,000 or so, as well as a participation requirement of 5 percent. Insureds are required to report any notice of potential claim, including those given orally, as soon as they learn of such. In case the policy is canceled by the insurer, the insured usually has some type of extended discovery option, such as an additional 12 months of protection for claims arising during that period which stem from occurrences made while the policy was in force. Typically, policies are issued on a 3-year basis, and the cost of the extension may be 25 percent of the 3-year premium.

Another form of coverage available is issued directly to a specific director, covering all the various exposures the individual may have as a director of different companies. The individual would pay for the coverage directly and, feasibly, would prepare charges back to the company served. In fact, the Internal Revenue Service reportedly has indicated that the insurance premiums paid by companies for D&O coverage are deductible as ordinary and necessary business expenses.

D&O coverage also is available for a variety of smaller entities, including small businesses, small financial institutions, and small organizations and associations.

Property managers in particular may be concerned about their exposures when serving on the board of an organization such as PMA or the Institute of Real Estate Management (IREM). While the national boards of these groups generally are covered, the chapters may not be. Realistically, the likelihood of such groups being hit with a suit is somewhat remote. Exposure increases when the organization has a code of ethics which is regularly enforced, or when it offers a certification of some kind, or can somehow deny a business advantage to some party. Very often, in such cases, the party who feels aggrieved will file a suit, claiming that the denial, suspension, or revocation of membership or certification was motivated by competitive instincts. Property managers should also be familiar with other coverages they or their employers may have. Some of these may also afford protection for service on business-related boards and committees. Note, however, that coverage may be affected by an individual's status in a group, that is, whether the individual is a member individually, or a representative of a firm that is a member.

Property managers should also be familiar with any state laws that apply with respect to the liability of those who serve on the boards of various types of groups, especially charitable organizations, as well as condominiums, cooperatives, and homeowner associations.

Selecting Insurance, Insurers, and Related Factors

How much insurance is enough for the various exposures confronting a property owner? How much coverage should be associated with each policy and with each coverage afforded by a policy? With which insurer should a firm deal? These and other questions are ultimately associated with risk management and, therefore, are covered in the following chapter.

Risk Management

Introduction

Risk is intrinsic to the human experience. We cannot avoid it and we cannot eliminate it. But we can manage it and thereby take a step toward reducing the likelihood that we will be victims and, if we are, toward reducing the severity of the consequences.

For property managers in particular, risk management is complex and can be costly. But the complexities and costs that can arise without effective risk management dwarf those associated with proper procedures.

As discussed in Chapter 9, insurance is essential to proper risk management. But having insurance in and of itself does not constitute risk management. A number of tasks must be accomplished first, beginning with identification of *all* the risks. Once that task is performed, property managers must identify the steps available to reduce those risks, the practicality of these steps, and their cost. Alternatives will present themselves in many cases and should be examined closely. Which is the more effective, all things considered? Often that is not an easy decision to make, because so many interrelationships are involved. For example, closing a swimming pool can eliminate a major risk exposure, but it can also result in lower occupancy rates and more turnover. By contrast, keeping the pool can result in a major insurance bill. But by installing more signage, and by taking other steps to enhance safety, such as removal of a diving board, safety can be improved and risks reduced. In turn, this should result in a savings on insurance premiums the value of which can help offset, maybe even more than offset, the cost of improving safety.

Generally speaking, many techniques are available, and often they can be funded by increasing a policy's deductible and using the premium savings to invest in safety improvements that more than compensate for the risk created by opting for a higher deductible.

The need to become ever more involved in risk management stems in large part from our civil justice system. It is continually imposing more responsibility on owners to make their facilities safer for tenants, residents, employees, visitors, and others. Some say that our national litigiousness has gone too far, and that we have become lawsuit-happy. It is difficult to deny these allegations, and it is somewhat encouraging to see the pendulum swinging, even if slightly, in the opposite direction. In truth, however, it also is refreshing to see how lawsuits and the threat of suits are resulting in a greater concern about pollution and other such problems of the past, which remain with us today, and which—had they not been attended to—most certainly would pose a far greater problem in the future than that which ultimately will exist.

In any event, the fact remains that owners are expected to abide by higher standards than in the past, and they risk serious penalties, in one form or another, if they do not. It is the property manager's responsibility to help owners comply, and this is done best through effective management of risks. In the long term, the initial time and money invested should pay significant dividends.

Conduct a Risk Audit

Risk management begins with a thorough and comprehensive risk audit. This means a comprehensive review of everything capable of being reviewed, from human resources management policies through security procedures, contracting methods, and so on. The goal is to determine what you have in place, the risks or exposures that are created or are left untouched, and the alternatives available for reducing risk. Some of the areas to consider are indicated in this chapter. Recognize that this discussion is highly general to create somewhat of a broadbrush overview.

Human resources

Insofar as risk management is concerned, human resources management, or HRM, applies in particular to preemployment screening. This is not to say that effective management of individuals is not important; it is. In reality, however, such functions generally are up to the various functional managers, such as the director of security. In smaller operations, of course, that could be one person; a chief cook and bottle washer, in essence. Of particular concern to property managers and owners is a claim of *negligent hiring*. Typically it arises after an incident of some type caused by the negligence of an employee who, reasonable research would have shown, should not have been

permitted to perform a specific function. For example, you hire someone to perform miscellaneous activities at a property, including occasional driving to perform errands of one kind or another. While on one
of these errands, the individual causes a severe automobile accident.
The attorney for the injured party performs some research and learns
that the employee has been involved in a number of prior accidents,
and has had the driver's license revoked twice before. Thus, the claim
against you charges that you were negligent by hiring this person to
drive or, alternatively, you were negligent in assigning the person to
drive. "But the person lied on the employment application," you respond. That's not good enough. If you asked the question to begin
with, as you should, it indicates you contemplated that the person
would be driving. Given the foreseeable problems that could result,
you should have known that relying totally on a person's response is
not adequate. After all, it is common practice to exaggerate on
résumés and employment applications. And it is not reasonable to expect a person to answer a question honestly when doing so almost certainly will result in the employment opportunity evaporating.

Supposing you had not asked about the driving record on the application or during the interview process? In that case, you should never
have given the individual the responsibility to drive on your behalf—
no matter whose car it is—until you checked out the person's record.

Bear in mind that the courts generally are sympathetic toward
those who suffer injury, and they seek to make the injured whole, that
is, to compensate them for their losses. This has resulted in new definitions of responsibility, in terms not only of what an employer is responsible for doing but also in terms, of who is responsible. When the
responsible party has no deep pockets, an effort often will be made to
somehow implicate some other party who is in a position to pay.

Who is doing what in your operation? What are the foreseeable hazards involved? Have you done everything you reasonably can to help
ensure that everyone who is doing anything that has any type of danger associated with it is somehow qualified to do it and otherwise is
insured? By taking such steps, you help minimize the likelihood of
something going wrong, and if something does go wrong, you can help
ensure that you are covered by insurance or—at the very least—you
can present a reasonable defense, indicating that you were not negligent; that sometimes, no matter how careful someone may be, something can happen. In going through this procedure, consider what
some of the dangers may be.

First and foremost, you have to consider the personal safety of people in the building. If you have your own security force, has the background of each individual been scrutinized carefully? Can others in
the building really rely on these people, or does their presence create

a false sense of security, because they are not qualified to do what their positions and uniforms suggest they are qualified for?

What about other persons who are in your employ? Anyone of them who may have access to a tenant's or resident's space for whatever reason certainly should somehow be cleared insofar as background is concerned. No one expects you to do the impossible in this respect, of course, but some type of reasonable inquiry is needed. It would not look too good for you if it were found that Mrs. Jones, who has long had a serious drug problem, was found guilty of theft, or if Mr. Smith, who has a record of sexual assault, is found guilty of raping a resident in her apartment.

Did you know that young Billy Doe suffered from vertigo before you sent him up the ladder to paint? While it may have been reasonable to expect him to tell you that, maybe he was in fear of losing his job. You should have asked, it may be argued. And that might just be enough to result in an award to young Billy, because otherwise his workers' compensation benefits will not be sufficient.

What about drug addiction? You must realize that people who are addicted will often steal to support their habits, and will sometimes commit acts of violence. What are you doing about the situation? Are you screening prospective employees? Are you testing those who get involved in accidents? Are you testing those whose behavior strongly suggests that a drug problem may exist? Testing can be done in a reliable manner. In fact, tremendous sums of money can be saved, *and* your risks can be significantly reduced. Consider, for example, the case of the Warner Corporation, one of the nation's largest mechanical repair companies, headquartered in Washington, D.C. Under the direction of company CEO Tom Warner, the organization began drug testing new hires and those involved in accidents in 1985. By 1990, the company was spending about $12,000 per year on testing. At the same time it was saving almost $400,000 per year, due principally to greatly reduced workers' compensation and auto insurance premiums, thanks to far fewer accidents.

Does everyone on your staff who handles chemicals of any kind, including those used in janitorial operations, understand how to handle them safely, as well as the hazards associated with them? Do you train people in safe handling? Do you have the equipment needed for safe handling, including equipment such as fans to provide ventilation where and when appropriate?

What about the people on your staff who handle money? Have their backgrounds been thoroughly checked? Is the chief financial officer aware of the indications of problems, such as people who never take a vacation or whose spending habits seem more lavish than their incomes would suggest? Are you or whoever else oversees the chief financial officer aware of warning signs? Are the people involved appropriately bonded?

What it all boils down to, then, is that you should have on hand, for *every* position in your organization, a job description, which indicates exactly what tasks are being performed in each position, and exactly what type of experience a person needs to perform these appropriately, along with the types of licenses, permits, certifications, or other credentials. In every case where a credential of some type is needed, you must make a reasonable investigation to help ensure that the person actually has it. And where training may be needed, you must verify through testing and observation that the person already has it, or you should provide it yourself and, through testing and observation, ensure that the lesson was taken. Also be aware of physical factors. If a position may require climbing a ladder, is the person subject to vertigo or other physical problems that could result in an accident? Is a person physically capable of driving? Does the person have any allergies to any of the chemicals that may be used in the operations? If a person works in an office where smoking is allowed, is the person subject to asthma or other problems? In fact, can the person tolerate smoky conditions?

It is not necessarily easy to do this checking. However, after you go through it once, you should be able to establish checklists of various types that will facilitate your work in the future. As a consequence you should be able to avoid some of the many problems that befall those who do not have the time to do things right and, as a result, suffer the consequences.

Note this important point: once you perform these tasks properly, document your activities. Each person should have a personnel file. In each file you could include a job description, notes from prehiring interviews, forms or memos indicating that the individual's background has been appropriately checked (including for immigration law compliance), other documentation of completed training, and so on. Sometimes, despite the best of your efforts, problems will occur, and it will be your word against someone else's. Without documentation, you can be in a defenseless situation. Remember the time-tested business adage, "If it's not in writing, it didn't happen."

Policies. A number of liabilities exist with respect to the basic rights of employees and former employees. One of these is sexual harassment. This can take the form of someone demanding sexual favors in order to grant a raise or promotion, or of sexual innuendos or other similar activities. Naturally, no one can expect an employer to read other people's minds. However, an employer can be expected to let it be known that sexual harassment will not be tolerated, and that specific means and methods are available to help resolve any such problems that arise. Should you become aware of a problem, you absolutely cannot ignore it and hope it will go away. It won't.

Likewise it is important to take appropriate action with respect to minority and gender rights. You want to assure, to the maximum extent possible, that there is no discrimination based on race, sex, or other factors, such as nation of origin. Any and all decisions in these respects, and also as they relate to questions asked during interviews, must be job-related. If a position requires someone capable of routinely lifting 50-pound bags of materials, do not assume that only a man can do it. If two people are being considered for a position, document why one got it and the other didn't, especially when the two differ in terms of sex, race, religion, skin color, or other factors.

It may also be worthwhile to establish a written policy of involvement, whereby all employees—ideally all residents and tenants, too—are encouraged to report any and all situations that may be problematic in any way, shape, or form, such as people who look suspicious, light bulbs that are burned out, or tripping or slipping situations. In a similar manner, if you are aware of various conditions that could give rise to problems, but which are not readily capable of being modified, you should give adequate notice. For example, if the situation is such that it may be commonplace to hear profanity or even dirty jokes, you may wish to include in an employment application a paragraph such as the following.

> In the position you are seeking to fill, it is likely that you will hear profanity uttered by others, as well as some "dirty jokes." While management discourages such utterances, we cannot eliminate them. Accordingly, we must ask, can you easily tolerate profanity in conversations about you, and can you easily tolerate jokes?
> ____ Yes ____ No

The extent to which such a question on an employment form may hold up in court, should it come to that, is unknown. However, juries of one's peers tend to be reasonable. Clearly, such a notice creates a fair and reasonable warning. And if an individual says, yes, I can tolerate these things, and later sues on grounds that they cannot be tolerated, it is doubtful that reasonable people will be overly sympathetic to the plaintiff. Note, however, that having someone's signature on a piece of paper does not give management the right to ignore bad situations.

Another policy you may wish to adopt relates to references. A number of employers have been sued, successfully, for indicating false causes for dismissal, which have made it difficult for an individual to obtain work elsewhere. Some employers counter this potential by having a policy which requires those relaying information about former employees to indicate no more than a person's Social Security number, date of employment, and date of separation. Another approach that could be worthwhile is to write a letter to each person whose employment is terminated to act as a letter of referral, which lays down exactly why the person was dismissed and/or which identifies other attributes that are typically matters of concern, such as, Would you hire this person again? In that way, each such letter could be checked by an attorney before it is issued, and anyone asking for a reference could be told to obtain a copy of the letter from the individual.

Generally speaking, you also will do well to have an employee policy handbook. Your handbook should be reviewed carefully before being finalized, however, to ensure that it complies with applicable laws and regulations. In reviewing the suggested contents of a policy manual, recognize that each subject should be written to answer the questions Who, What, Why, When, and Where, as applicable. The Why is generally the most important, and frequently the one most often overlooked. Typical contents might include the following.

1. *Notice of intent.* In some instances it has been successfully alleged by former employees that they were unjustly dismissed because the cause for their dismissal was not covered in the policy manual. It is thus essential to assure the firm has as free a hand as possible, and that the policy manual does not create precisely the type of problems it is designed to prevent. Wording such as Notice 10.1 may be advisable.

2. *Introduction.* This section should briefly describe the purpose of the manual. Usually, its purpose is to acquaint all personnel with policies of the firm, and to help assure their consistent, uniform application.

3. *History of the firm.* All employees should have some familiarity with the background of a firm, at least so that they feel a part of a continuing tradition. This section could also include a discussion of the firm's philosophy.

4. *Organization and services.* This section can discuss the man-

---

Notice

This policy manual has been prepared to present information about most policies in force at the time the manual was prepared. It is expressly understood that, absent specific employment contracts to the contrary, continuing employment of any individual is a matter of mutual consent. Any employee may leave at any time, for any reason the party initiating the decision believes appropriate at the time. The company reserves the right to change policy at any time, and will make a reasonable effort to notify all employees of any such change as soon as possible after it has been adopted.

Notice 10.1

ner in which the firm is organized and the various services provided. Charts that show responsibilities and reporting relationships can be helpful.

5. *Discrimination.* It is prudent to make clear that the company does not discriminate based on race, religion, country of natural origin, sex, or age, and that it is against company policy for any employee to do so.

6. *Sexual harassment.* This section should explain what sexual harassment is and that it is cause for immediate dismissal.

7. *Confidentiality.* Certain documents, such as personnel records and client lists, should be regarded as confidential and not for voluntary disclosure to any other party except with the express permission of the firm. The manual should identify what the confidential documents are. This can be of value should an employee seek to benefit by using that confidential information at another firm.

8. *Personal assistance.* The company should consider having some type of program in effect to help employees who run into a problem, such as dependency on drugs or alcohol. Assistance should be available on a confidential basis.

9. *Drug and alcohol testing.* If a company has programs of drug and/or alcohol testing, reasons for it should be made clear. Testing should be carried out on a nondiscriminatory basis. It may also be necessary to have employees sign special waivers of one type or another.

10. *Workday, workweek, and pay period.* Explain when the workday begins and ends, the number of days in a workweek, and the pay period. As necessary, provide separate discussion for salaried employees versus those who receive an hourly wage. Does the firm prefer employees to eat lunch outside the office? Does it not care? This information should be expressed.

11. *Apparel and appearance.* Some firms prefer to indicate the type of clothing that people should wear, depending on their work for the firm. Others indicate what is not acceptable, and some just don't care. Attitudes should be stated.

12. *Use of company phone.* The policy usually is to minimize personal calls, both outgoing and incoming.

13. *Use of other company equipment.* Policies affecting employee use of other company equipment should be made clear. This would include computers, copying machines, and so on, as well as automobiles.

14. *Leave.* Identify how the company's leave policies operate, what they encompass, which leave is paid and which unpaid, and so on. This section should discuss vacations, holidays, sick leave, personal leave,

leave for jury duty and military reserve service, extended leave (as for pregnancy or illness), and so on. Policies should also be developed as to employees' accumulation of vacation and other paid time off from one year to the next. Some firms require employees to take their vacations or simply lose the benefit.

15. *Insurance programs.*   Explain what is offered, where more information can be obtained about the programs, what the various sharing formulas are (for example, 100 percent employee coverage but no contribution for family coverage), and so on.

16. *Retirement programs.*   These are handled much as insurance programs. In most instances, manuals provide a summary of the benefits, with more comprehensive discussion being available from another source, such as the director of personnel or the CEO.

17. *Education benefits and programs.*   Explain the company's attitude toward continuing education and the types of additional education individuals should obtain. Indicate how one goes about learning more about educational programs available, whether or not time off is given to attend them, who pays, and the extent to which certain types of educational attainment—such as earning a license—are met with increased responsibilities, more pay, and so on. If programs are conducted on an in-house basis, indicate whether attendance is voluntary or mandatory.

18. *Raises and promotions.*   This section should indicate the frequency of salary reviews, identify the persons who conduct them, and discuss key factors considered in granting salary increases. The same should apply to promotions as well as lateral mobility. Almost all employees want to know what they have to do to get ahead. A professional organization makes that known, and follows through on its promises.

19. *Bonuses.*   If the firm gives bonuses, employees should be told how they are calculated. It generally is wise to indicate that a bonus is not automatic, nor can one be guaranteed from year to year, when—in fact—one cannot be guaranteed.

20. *Moonlighting.*   A company usually cannot forbid all moonlighting, but it may be able to forbid moonlighting that would expose the company to liability. This latter result could occur if employees do on a moonlighting basis the type of work they perform for the company, and it could somehow be construed that the ability to moonlight is a company benefit, thus making the company liable for any negligent acts of moonlighting employees.

21. *Disciplinary action.*   Most firms want the right to dismiss anyone at any time, for no stated cause. To do this without legal reper-

cussion, it generally is necessary to make that policy known, both in an initial advisory notice and in a disciplinary action section. This does not obviate the need to spell out the specific types of actions that could result in immediate dismissal for cause, such as lying to one's superior or too many unexcused absences. It may also be appropriate to have policies relative to a "monitoring period" that would be tantamount to a probationary period, as well as suspension.

22. *Termination procedures.* This section would indicate who owes what to whom in the event of termination, in terms of factors such as unused vacation time or outstanding educational loans. It usually is wise to perform exit interviews with employees who are leaving, to learn how the company may be able to improve itself.

A number of other matters should also be discussed, and it may be appropriate to prepare separate manuals for different categories of employees, such as salaried versus hourly. In all such cases, however, some type of legal review may be appropriate in view of the growing amount of litigation between employers and employees or former employees. In that respect, it is commonly advised that employees should sign a receipt when they are given a copy of the policy manual, and that—2 weeks later—they should be required to sign a statement indicating they have read the manual, understand its implications, and agree to abide by it.

Contractors

Many of the risks associated with your own personnel can also arise from contractors. As such, you should demand of contractors at least the level of scrutiny that you demand from your own employees. If contractor personnel will have access to tenanted areas, for example, what kind of supervision will be provided? What types of background checks are used? What about drugs?

Most contracts you enter into should have indemnification provisions, indicating that any liabilities created by contractors should be borne by contractors, at least to the extent that they are responsible for them. While most contractors will agree to such provisions, not all who do so actually have the ability to meet them. You must assure yourself that contractors can live up to what they agree to. For this reason you need to know about their financial stability and their insurance. Nor can you freely take a contractor's word that the company is properly insured. You need to obtain a certificate of insurance from the insuring company, and you should satisfy yourself that the insurer is reputable and is itself in a strong financial position. You should also require the insurer to notify you in the event that the contractor's insurance coverage is canceled or not going to be renewed. Whenever possible, the property owner, property manager, and other appropriate parties should also be made insureds on a contractor's policies where appropriate.

By all means, check with other parties before retaining a contractor. This is done not only for risk-reduction purposes, but also to help ensure that the firm is capable of doing what it says it can. Of course, document what you learn.

Tenants and residents

Note that liability and other problems can flow to you from residents and tenants. As such, you want to ensure that whatever you do to manage risk is emulated to a reasonable extent by tenants and residents, since their failure in that respect could come to roost on your doorstep. As an example, if you manage shopping centers or malls, are all tenants complying with rules and regulations relating to the proper disposal of hazardous materials? Is the drycleaner following requirements? What about the hardware store? If you must comply with recycling laws, are tenants going along, as by separating their trash?

In multifamily residential areas, are tenants observing safety precautions? For example, are they making sure doors they open are locked behind them, or are they propping them open for convenience sake but, in so doing, permitting a security breach?

Consider, too, in the case of commercial buildings, the insurance policies which tenants are required to maintain by virtue of their leases. Are you ensuring that they are being maintained? Are you and other appropriate parties named insureds? How do your policies fit in?

And what about your leases? Do they reflect current conditions? Do they clearly explain who must do what and who is responsible for what? If they do not, then modifications are called for. If they cannot be made now, they should be made in the future. However, consider the interim exposure. What can you do about it?

Security

How much security is enough? Is it necessary for every commercial building, for example, to be surrounded by protection at the perimeter, closed-circuit television cameras (CCTV), high lighting levels, or access-controlled entrances and egresses? The answer to that question is, it depends.

Several key variables are of major concern. First, what is required by law? In most areas, different types of codes will exist to require certain safeguards. These may apply to the types of doors that must be used or the types of locks. It may relate to bars on ground-floor unit windows. Possibly it applies to lighting in certain areas. What is required in your area? If you do not know, then by all means find out.

In many areas, requirements will apply differently to different buildings, depending on a building's age. For example, it may be required to provide a certain type of front door on all buildings constructed after a given date. Accordingly, while it may not be mandatory to abide by a regulation that does not apply, it may be wise to, especially if upgrading can mean a legitimate reduction in liability exposure, that is, reduced risk.

Another variable to consider is area developments. If most properties with similar functions are doing things a certain way, is yours in step? Are you ahead or behind? If you are behind, you could be creating a liability exposure for yourself because, it could be alleged, you are not demonstrating the ordinary reasonable care being demonstrated by others in a similar position. It does not matter that you are complying with regulations. Remember that regulations, codes, and standards establish what is least acceptable. If it can be shown that most people in a position similar to your own are operating above that baseline, you could be facing problems. And do realize that while your actions may be taken to prevent liability exposures, you actually are also doing your best to prevent the types of incidents that result in liability problems, along with attendant difficulties that are impossible to insure.

Still another factor to weigh is the state of your security. Generally speaking, if you do something to enhance security, you must maintain it, since you give people reason to rely on it. If a door that is kept locked is pried open, it should be repaired quickly. If it cannot be repaired quickly for some reason, put everyone in the building on notice, in writing, that a problem exists. Explain what it is, what you are doing about it, and steps they can take in the interim.

Lighting.   Your outdoor lighting should be a key concern. Effective lighting can be the single most cost-effective security element, because good lighting can make it difficult for a person to hide. Consider where people could be walking at night. Are walkways well illuminated? What about parking areas and building entrances? If despite existing lighting there still are places for people to hide near those areas where people may frequently be moving, then more lighting may be called for, or some physical modifications.

Note that lighting must be checked from time to time, because the lighting you have for safety and security changes over time. Light output diminishes as lamps (light bulbs and tubes) age, and as dust and dirt build up on the surfaces of lamps and reflective coatings inside luminaires (fixtures). Likewise, trees and shrubs grow and can obscure lighting that originally was intended to reach certain areas.

An investment in good lighting can pay wonderful dividends, because lighting that is installed outside—when it is well designed—can provide far more than security. In the case of retail stores, for example, effective lighting can help attract shoppers. At night it can enhance the curb appeal of multifamily residential developments.

More specific information about lighting is provided in Appendix B, which includes excerpts from *Lighting for Safety and Security,* published by the National Lighting Bureau with the assistance of the Property Management Association. The National Lighting Bureau has a number of well-written, well-illustrated guides that are designed for use by nontechnical people who must make important decisions about lighting. A free National Lighting Bureau publications directory can be obtained by contacting the National Lighting Bureau (2102 L Street, N.W., Suite 300, Washington, D.C. 20037).

Other security installations. Security installations used outdoors are many and varied. They range from a fence at the perimeter of the property, or elsewhere, to CCTV, motion detectors, and other devices. Anything installed should perform effectively. If breakdowns cannot be detected remotely, physical inspection is required. An example of remote detection would be a centralized security system that is monitored in a building or at some other central location, through which an alarm would sound to indicate that a detector is not functioning, or which would indicate that a CCTV camera is not working because no picture is seen or it is faulty.

If physical inspection is performed, it should be performed routinely, according to two criteria. First, inspection should be done regularly, such as once a week. If such inspections are made, they should be made both at night and during the day. At night one would be able to determine the effectiveness of lighting, where underbrush may have to be cut back, and so on; during the day one could inspect perimeter security, including fences, windows, and doors. It should be matter of policy to have checklists for inspections, and to require that these be completed during rounds and submitted to appropriate individuals. In that way, you can help assure that the work is being done properly, and that you have documentation of that fact.

In the second instance, inspections should be performed after any unusual event, such as a severe windstorm, major rainfall, or heavy snowfall. Situations such as these can cause problems of all types, including creation of slipping or tripping hazards and obscuring of lighting or breakage.

Do your inspections reveal that you have everything you need? For example, what are you doing about security in parking areas? If the parking area is open to people who may be up to no good, what are you doing to detect them? Is there CCTV installed in basements or outdoor parking areas? If so, are the CCTV screens being monitored on an on-going basis? Do you have adequate lighting? Have you informed people about what they should do to avoid assault and injury? In other words, you should conduct a comprehensive tour of your facility, inside and out, to determine where the security problems may be, and what you can do about them. In fact, will a security installation handle the problem? Would lighting be helpful? Something more than lighting? Is it necessary to have security personnel on patrol? If so, should a system be in place requiring the security guard to check in at regular intervals?

Security personnel. As already noted, it is essential to help assure that security personnel are adequately equipped for that work, not only in terms of their experience and training, but also in terms of their backgrounds. Note, too, that in the case of shopping centers and other commercial buildings, security personnel often act as sources of information, responding to the questions of people. They thus should be able to respond effectively, to help enhance the image of the facility and of management.

Security policy and procedures. You need to ensure that effective security policies are in place, and that set procedures are used to help assure that these policies are fulfilled. One of the most important of these policies relates to keys or, stated generically, access control. If management has the ability to enter any tenanted area, commercial or residential, then some form of adequate key control is necessary. People should be required to sign in and out for keys. In appropriate cases, keys should not be given out, but instead an individual should be accompanied to a space and accompanied on the return. Remember, no one is asking you to create a fortress or to assume full liability should anything unfortunate occur. However, you are required to act in a reasonable manner by abiding by law and adhering to the standard of care by which most other reasonable people in your position abide. And remember, too, that security is a major concern, something you should not be making evaluations of or decisions about except with expert assistance.

For those property managers involved with multifamily housing, drugs are a particular concern. Unless action is taken quickly, a property can go downhill at a blindingly fast pace, resulting in loss of residents, loss of revenue, and loss of property value. In addition, suits against owners of drug-infested housing are now on the upswing, brought by neighbors who charge that allowing a property to serve as a drug market creates a nuisance. PMA members have been at the

forefront of activities developed to combat drugs in housing. Appendix
D illustrates three case histories, which point out how—and why—
vigorous action is needed to combat the problem.

Physical review

At the same time as you perform a physical check for security, inside
and outside a building, consider a general physical review. What
about walkways between a parking area and the building? Are there
naturally occurring obstacles that could cause a tripping or slipping
accident? Are stair treads treated with an antislip ingredient or covered in an antislip material? Is there adequate lighting in stairwells,
both for security purposes and for safety? Have oil leaks been covered
over in parking lots, indoors and outside? What about mechanical
equipment? Is it being properly operated and maintained? Are janitorial closets being kept clean?

In fact, you may find it worthwhile to conduct a physical inspection
of everything at least once a year, or once a quarter, or even once a
month. If a checklist is developed, it does not take much time or effort
to do an effective job. Note that, in many instances, timing could be
such that the work begins at the time of day when that which should
be seen during daylight hours is seen, while that which should be seen
at night is checked subsequently.

Report

The final step of an audit should be a report, which identifies what the
shortcomings are and what the potential liability exposures and other
risks may be as a result.

Examine Paperwork

Once you have reviewed a risk audit report, the next step is to examine the "paperwork."

Insurance policies

Key among the paperwork to look at are existing insurance policies.
Generally the following rule-of-thumb review procedure has been recommended.

1. *List all policies.* All policies should be carefully listed. Indicate
the property involved, the type of policy, what is covered and what is
excluded from coverage, date of expiration, and such other information you deem important; such as occurrence versus claims made.

2. *Check values.* For the risks involved, what is the insurance limit and what is the exposure? In other words, if you suffer a total loss, will the policy provide adequate compensation?

3. *Check insureds.* Who are the named insureds? Is everyone covered who should be? Very often this kind of analysis is performed soon after ownership is transferred. Are the appropriate parties listed as owners? What about partnerships and joint ventures, especially when a policy covers more than one property? Has the insurance company been properly notified if a transfer has occurred?

4. *Evaluate property.* Check the declarations. Is the property covered the same one that is described? In some cases alterations will have occurred and they have not been reported to the insurer, due to oversight or for whatever other reason. Be sure that everything that exists and has to be covered is shown.

5. *Consider usage.* Has usage remained the same? In some cases changes in tenancies will modify usages, and that could mean voided insurance coverage. For example, is light manufacturing now occurring in a space that formerly was used for warehousing, or vice versa?

6. *Evaluate endorsements.* What gaps are created or closed by endorsements? What else could you possibly cover by endorsements? Consider coverages that should be provided by tenants/residents and/ or contractors. Do policies reflect what you are doing in that respect?

7. *Evaluate extent of coverage.* Is everything included that should be included? For example, if the owner has installed new fixtures inside somewhere, or otherwise upgraded or added, have increased values been considered in the policy?

8. *Check risks.* In some cases, certain significant exposures may not be covered in one or several policies. One of these might be water damage, which is always troublesome. And if water damage is covered, is it covered fully? What about damages caused by a flood? Have new tenancies created new risks? Have you covered the risks? Has the tenant?

Leases and contracts

Examine all commercial leases. Some of the following features should exist in leases.

1. *Owner as named insured.* All leases should indicate that "the owner" should be a named insured of the various types of policies required of the tenant. Note that you might want to refer to "the owner"

or "the owner and property manager" in generic terms. In that way, should ownership or management change, the lease should indicate exactly what types of policies are involved, the minimum limit for each, and the maximum deductible.

2. *Obtain minimum guaranteed coverage amount.* Tenants who have more than one location will often insure all locations with one policy, with the result that an aggregate limit applies to all locations. As a result, due to a mishap at some other location, coverage for yours may be eliminated during the policy period. To guard against this exposure, your lease could require the tenant to obtain a policy endorsement that provides for a minimum amount of guaranteed coverage for your location.

3. *Make tenant's coverage primary.* Require the tenant, through endorsement or other means, to assure that, in the event of exposure, the tenant's policy is primary and the owner's is excess coverage. Very often this will save the owner far more than it costs any given tenant.

4. *Obtain waiver of subrogation.* A subrogation clause in the tenant's policy means that the tenant's insurer can step into the tenant's shoes in order to effect collection. For example, a delivery person trips because the person fails to see a small stair in the tenant's space. The delivery person's attorney claims the stair was a safety hazard, and the tenant's insurer settles. However, the insurer has the tenant sign a subrogation agreement, permitting the tenant's insurer to seek reimbursement for the settlement payment from you or your insurer. Through a waiver of subrogation clause, the insurer would not be able to seek such reimbursement. The tenant will probably have to pay extra for the clause, but it can be had. Do note, however, that if the owner is named insured on all appropriate policies, a waiver of subrogation may be unnecessary, since an insurer usually cannot seek reimbursement for payment from a named insured.

5. *Require approval of insurer.* The lease should indicate that you wish to approve the insurer. Generally speaking, you want to ensure that the insurer is admitted so that, in the event of a bankruptcy, the state's guarantee fund will pay for at least part of the exposure. In addition, you may want to require an insurer of a given size.

6. *Require notice.* The owner and/or property manager generally should be given 30 days written notice, by certified mail, of any policy agreement, as well as cancellation or nonrenewal.

7. *Require proof.* The lease should require the tenant to furnish a certificate of insurance indicating that all requirements have been complied with by the insurer.

8. *Reserve the right to modify insurance requirements.* Your lease should permit the owner to require a tenant to increase insurance coverage and/or limits for cause, for example, because the number of employees has increased or because of policy changes. You generally would want to agree to be reasonable, and not make the demand too often. For example, in the case of a 10-year lease, you would not be permitted to order a change more often than once every 2.5 years.

9. *Reserve the right to pay the premium.* Insert in your lease a clause that permits you to pay the premium on a tenant's insurance policy to prevent its being canceled, and to collect the amount from the tenant as additional rent. Furthermore permit yourself to obtain a replacement policy, also at the tenant's expense.

Consider, too, all agreements with contractors of different types. Are they fulfilling their requirements, including those related to coverage? Consider also the leases themselves and the contracts with contractors. Are they written as well as they could be? Are appropriate indemnifications in place? And, if indemnifications are there, will they be upheld in court? Does the tenant/resident or the contractor have the ability to make good? Remember, words are all right as far as they go, but they may not stand you in good stead when what they promise has to be actuated.

In evaluating the paperwork, consider what happens when two things relate to one another; such as if two parties have coverage for basically the same thing, under what series of events does Policy A cover and when does Policy B apply? For example, both an owner and a property manager will have commercial general liability policies in most instances. It is now common in most areas for the property manager's policy to serve as excess coverage over the owner's. Is that your case? What about the relationship between your, the owner's, and the tenant's CGL policies? If you do not know the answer to these questions, you should learn them, because otherwise you cannot manage risk.

Evaluate Options

An analysis of your risk audit report and paperwork should identify a variety of loopholes. Some of the typical options you will have to manage risk include the following:

Obtain insurance coverage.

Increase insurance limits.

Require tenants/residents to obtain and/or increase coverage, and to name the owner and property manager as named insureds.

Require contractors to obtain and/or increase coverage, and to name the owner and property manager as named insureds.

Add endorsements to insurance policies of your own, and/or the owner's, and/or the tenants'/residents', and/or the contractors.

Modify an existing condition or procedure through repair, replacement, addition, or elimination.

In some cases you may discover that you will be able to reduce the risk or increase the insurance coverage. If it comes down to a question of one but not the other, you almost always will be better served by reducing risks, given that insurance does not cover certain major losses (of time, bad publicity, and so on), and that, by reducing risk, you may be able to obtain savings in insurance premiums that help offset the cost.

Consider, too, techniques for freeing up more funds by lowering the cost of insurance.

Lowering insurance costs

Insurance costs can be lowered in several ways. First and foremost, almost any insurance policy you have can be reduced in cost when the severity of the covered risk is lessened. This applies certainly in the case of CGL. But it also can apply in the case of workers' compensation/employers' liability coverage, automobile policies, and others. It is necessary to call the enhancements you have made to the attention of insurers, of course, but you might be surprised at how significant some reductions can be.

You can also transfer risk to policies of others, such as residents/tenants and contractors. Be sure to call highly effective procedures to the attention of your insurers. In this respect, note the potential of using endorsements to help assure that your policy for the same exposure would serve as excess limit over the other party's insurance. This can be done through endorsement of the other party's policy, which makes it clear that that policy will be primary.

Another procedure for reducing insurance costs is to raise the deductible. Although this approach may result in more exposure, you may be able to lower that exposure through different financial techniques, which is something to be discussed with a financial consultant. For example, if you use the premium savings derived from a higher deductible to buy a variable life insurance policy, you might be able to accumulate in 3 to 4 years an amount of money (in the form of cash value) that more than covers the additional deductible. In the event you need to pay a deductible, you could borrow from your policy to do so. Most of the interest paid back on the loan goes to your policy account, but accumulates tax-free until withdrawal. However, the interest paid is tax-deductible. (Note that tax laws change, so the applicability of this approach needs close review.)

Another possibility is to establish a special retirement account for a principal of a firm, or for the property's owner, into which one would contribute, over and above everything else contributed, the amount of money saved by raising the deductible. Ordinarily such deposits would be taxable to the owner or other party involved. However, if the account is kept available to the company to pay any claims, or to otherwise be subject to creditors' claims, then it might be possible to defer the owner's or other party's tax payments until the money is actually withdrawn. In this instance, of course, the account would be subject to claims by those seeking compensation that otherwise would flow from insurance. Again guidance from a financial professional is essential before initiating any such program.

Yet another procedure for lowering the cost of insurance, which either of the two strategies mentioned or those like them could accomplish, would be to totally self-insure certain exposures, such as plate glass. Before taking such steps, it is essential to consider how much actually will be saved and what the exposure may be.

It is also possible to lower your insurance costs by working with one or more agents who will aggressively seek competitive bids. If you are really a good risk, insurers should be anxious to have your business, especially when the potential of multiple properties is indicated. Note, however, that not all insurance companies have equal financial strength. All are rated by the Alfred M. Best Company in *Best's Insurance Reports* on two bases. A letter is used to indicate a company's overall financial strength, profitability, and effectiveness in paying claims. The letters range from C (fair) to A+ (excellent). Numbers are used to indicate the firm's financial size, from 1 to 15, with 15 being tops in terms of the insurer's actual size and funds available to pay claims. Insurers that have lower ratings generally charge less, but there is more risk in dealing with them. Remember, an insurance company does not earn its stripes in terms of how much it charges for policies. It shows its value when it's time to provide service. Do your best to select companies that will be there when needed. *Note:* Take this same approach with residents/tenants and contractors upon whose insurance you will rely. Contracts and leases should probably indicate that the insurer used should have an A. M. Best rating of A/7 or A+/7 or higher, and should otherwise be satisfactory to the owner.

You may want to consider having all or certain groups of policies with the same insurer. Not only may it help assure a lower rate, but it can also make "appropriate action" easier to obtain in some cases. Consider the example of a building owner whose building refrigerant units broke down due to faulty compressors. The problem was covered by the boiler and machinery policy in effect. The insurer had the choice of replacing the compressors at a cost of $8000 each, or of rebuilding them on site at a cost of $7200 each. Although the latter option would have saved $800 per unit, it also would have resulted in areas of the building having to be shut down. Such a shutdown would have forced activation of the business interruption insurance, and would have created uninsurable relationship problems with tenants. The adjuster really did not care about business interruption or related problems. His only concern was saving $800 per unit, until he learned that his company also issued the business interruption policy. A quick check with his superiors confirmed exactly what the property manager had said, namely, that it would be cheaper to install new compressors, all things considered.

In all cases, when lowering insurance costs through one means or another, be sure to recognize how risks may be increased and to consider additional steps you can take to reduce the severity of those risks without undue expenses.

Obtain Assistance

Risk management is not the type of activity you should attempt to pursue on your own. While you most definitely want to be involved in fact-finding, you should have others to rely upon. Whether or not one individual or firm can provide everything you need is an open question, but that may be the case.

Start with peers who have had experience in this area, as well as with insurance agents. Whom do they recommend? Chances are an experienced agency can offer effective assistance in reviewing policies and what you need, and may also be able to recommend others for additional reviews, such as a security consultant who can review physical conditions, policies, and procedures and a mechanical engineer to review central station equipment and operations. Whoever reviews your insurance policies can probably review your contract and lease insurance requirements, and recommend changes.

Do not try to stumble through this process on your own. There is far too much at stake. Rely on others who are qualified, and be sure to advance your own knowledge in the field. A number of books are available, and trade publications of all types usually provide a continuing series of valuable articles. Do not put it off. Some of the biggest losses experienced by property managers and owners were not only easily avoidable, but they should have been avoided because the people involved knew better. There is no reason to ask them, "If you had to do it all over again, would you have done it differently?" because you know the answer is, Yes. Learn from their errors, so you do not have to learn from your own.

Advertising and Promotion

Introduction

Advertising is a promotional tool; a technique applied to gain attention for something or someone; a product or service; a company; even a philosophy. The audience whose attention is sought may be as small as one person, or as large as everybody. It may be undefined ("the general public") or far more narrowly circumscribed ("males aged 35 to 45 with an annual income of $75,000 or more").

For any type of long-term campaign to be effective, all appropriate forms of promotion should be considered to help assure the development of a balanced approach that is effective *and* cost-effective. Relying on advertising alone is seldom appropriate. Any number of options is available for application in addition to advertising, to supplement it or, in some instances, to supplant it. These alternatives could include magazine or newspaper articles, being featured on local television and radio, holding an open house, and so on.

In developing any type of promotional effort, the first step is identifying the goal. Exactly what is it that promotion is supposed to do? In the case of a new apartment community, it would *not* be the goal of promotion to effect a rent-up. Instead, the goal would be getting people there so they can see the facilities for themselves. Likewise, when an ad is placed to hire someone, the goal is encouraging qualified people to apply.

Although this general point—start by identifying your goal—seems extremely basic, people overlook it. They begin with the assumption that advertising sells and go from there. In fact, it is usually the aim of promotion to create a situation; it is people who do the selling. Misconstruing the situation can lead to problems.

In order to articulate your needs, several basic questions should be answered: Whom are we trying to attract? What methods are available for us to reach these people? Of those methods, which are most cost-effective? How can we best use available media to obtain attraction? These and other concerns are addressed in this chapter. If you have not considered them before, you should do so now. To the extent that other promotional means may be suggested, you might want to obtain information from other sources. Consider, for example, a magazine article that talks about your property management firm, extolling it for the application of modern management techniques and the old-fashioned desire to please clients, in large part by pleasing its own employees and those who rent space in client-owned properties. Such an article would have credibility because it does not appear in paid space and would be authored by a third party who, presumably, wrote in an objective fashion. The article would also have longevity, since reprints could be used for several years. Flexibility would be yet another attribute of such an article because it could be presented with other materials for purposes of reaching new personnel and clients. It could also help turn your firm's reputation into an asset at the leasing office, and thus establish another asset with respect to your client-attraction abilities.

Advertising does not have as much credibility as do certain other forms of promotion because anyone can buy space or time. And because people use advertising to say good things about themselves or their products, even children know that ads tend to accentuate the positive and wholly overlook the negative.

Advertising also has relatively little longevity, unless there is something extremely remarkable—and memorable—about it. For that reason it is a short-term promotional means. It becomes long-term only through continuing reinforcement, that is, by repeating the same or complementary messages over and over again.

To a very real extent, advertising is an overutilized promotional technique. Many other, far more effective techniques exist, but few are as simple as advertising. Which is exactly why people rely on it so much. True: the most successful firms use advertising. But they also rely on a host of other techniques, starting with the "hottest" forms of communication: those involving "eyeball-to-eyeball" contact.

Don't sell advertising short, of course. When it comes to renting or selling residential or commercial space, attracting new employees, or otherwise trying to get a message through to a vast number of people, advertising is essential. It can be enhanced substantially by other techniques, but—no matter how you look at it—advertising is a must. It can be very costly, however, so a concerted effort must be made to derive maximum "bang for the buck."

This chapter relates some of the key points you should be aware of to help strengthen your knowledge and decision-making abilities. In advertising, as with so many other activities associated with property management, your best results probably will come from reliance on outside sources who are professionals in their own fields. If results are to be maximized, however, you cannot abdicate your responsibilities; you must provide effective direction and oversight. By doing so, you cannot only help assure that you get "there" from "here," but also that you have a pleasant trip.

Identifying Your Targets

The target or audience for your advertising is all people who want what you have to offer and have the ability to pay for it. Some may be looking high and low for what you have. In that case, it may only be necessary to insert a notice in the classified advertising section of a local newspaper. Others may not even be consciously aware that they are interested in what you have. In that case it might be necessary for "the message" to reach them through several media, and be effective enough to pique their interest or curiosity. "It can't hurt just to take a look" is often the phrase that initiates the journey toward a major transaction.

When what you have is in short supply and great demand, a classified ad may be all the promotion required. If something less than such an ideal situation exists, however, the basic precepts of target identification should be exercised in order to identify the most appropriate message, methods, and media.

Residential space

When residential space is being offered, rental requirements are a basic consideration in target audience identification. If a low- or moderate-income unit is available, promotion may not be necessary to attract prospects. A public or private referral source will probably have a waiting list of people who are qualified and anxious to move in. That situation may not exist in the case of a small, inexpensive unit not designed with public assistance residents in mind. This could even take the form of a room in a private home that might be let to someone new to the area and waiting to find a job and get settled; someone who is just starting out in a new position but not yet settled; or a person in the process of separating from a spouse. The point? By identifying who might be interested in a given type of space, you can focus much better on the most cost-effective medium.

If you are looking to attract college students, it might make more sense to spend $100 on ads in a college-published newspaper as opposed to a smaller ad in a major daily, if only because the college paper ad immediately says (by virtue of its context), "Students are welcome." The same might apply to a house made available for rent, where the rent would be paid by several students on a shared basis. And if the college paper is not seen as a reasonable alternative to the major daily, then at least it is perceived as an effective supplement. And naturally, if the college or university has an office of housing assistance, as many do, it might be wise to let personnel there know the house is available. Local hospitals may also have a housing assistance office that finds space for visiting physicians, student nurses, or others, and much the same may apply to other types of institutions, including corporations.

If the available space is somewhat "high-ticket," and it is not desired or permissible to allow several "roomies," a different approach is required. For a single unit, it makes sense to insert a classified ad in a newspaper and/or an apartments-available guide or service. Those looking for such a space would seek out such resources to find one, and the rent quoted would automatically screen out those who cannot afford to pay. For whatever reason, however, a classified ad may not be desired, or it may not be sufficient given aggressive competition that may be vying for the same prospect. In that case, the basic question must be asked: "Who would be in a position to want this type of space and be able to pay for it?" Is it suited more for a single adult than a married couple or other adult pair? Is it suited more for those with young children or without?

When a rental community is new and a large number of units must be rented, display advertising will usually be placed in local newspapers as well as in apartments-available guides. It would also be appropriate to prepare a brochure and even to rely on radio advertising. Direct mail may be another adjunct used. In all of these situations, the advertisement will communicate not only by what it says, but also by the way it says it. The most effective ads are those that communicate most effectively to the target audience, that is, the most likely renters.

In most instances, the developer of a rental community will design the project with certain target groups in mind, relying on architectural styles and amenities geared to these groups' perceived tastes and preferences. Advertising should likewise cater to the target groups' tastes and preferences.

In the case of an existing rental community, "Who might be interested?" probably can be answered best by identifying who currently lives there, that is, how many single adults, how many adult pairs, how many families with children, the ages of the heads of the household, their income, and so on. Do not overlook existing tenants as sources of potential renters. Some who now have a one-bedroom apartment may want a larger one; others might want to downsize. Some may have a friend or relative who might consider a unit, may know of a coworker who needs a unit, and on so.

Commercial space

Commercial space implies different things to different people. For some it means office or retail space, to others it means nonresidential, including office, retail, warehouse, and so on. The broader "nonresidential" definition is applied here.

When commercial space is available, it may be sufficient to use the local classifieds. Usually it isn't sufficient, however, making additional promotional steps necessary. A wide range of effective adjuncts is available, especially when an urban area is involved. Additional print media might include a local business-oriented newspaper or magazine, or the newsletter of a group whose members might be interested, such as, that of a local consulting engineers' or architects' association or a local physicians' or dentists' society. If organizations such as these do not accept advertising in their newsletters, perhaps they sell their newsletter mailing lists for purposes of direct mail. Alternatively, if you frequently have such space available, it might be worthwhile to become an associate member of such a group (if possible). That way you will be among the first to know when a member needs additional or new quarters.

Especially when commercial space is involved, word-of-mouth advertising can be extremely effective. If association membership is used for networking purposes, as suggested here, word-of-mouth advertising can be achieved with relative ease. As an example:

J. D.:   Mr. Smith? This is John Doe with MNO Property Management. I was at the Consulting Engineers' Association meeting last night and Bill Jones suggested I give you a call. He said you're starting your own firm and need some space.

M. S.:   I already found it. But I tell you, Joe Green does need some, and he'd really appreciate hearing from you. His number is....

More than basic networking may be required, but it does not take an advanced degree to apply additional steps. For example, if you read that a local firm has just won some type of large contract, it would be logical to conclude that the firm may need additional people to perform the work, and additional space. This could mean conversion of existing space (and possibly the need for warehouse space) or simple addition of space, which could mean either another 5000 square feet, or a whole new office that comprises 50,000 square feet, as opposed to the 35,000 now available.

When the available commercial space is in a new building, consider whom the developer had in mind. It also is appropriate to consider who the existing tenants are and who possibly could benefit from being in the same building. Alternatively, it might be appropriate to consider the area. Who would save money by being able to call on a number of nearby clients, or who would be in a position to gain significantly by having so many prospects within walking distance? If your business involves selling a service to trade associations, for example, you would respond more to an ad or flyer that states, "within walking distance of 250 trade association offices," as opposed to one that says "convenient downtown location." By knowing who your targets are, you can custom-design an ad which addresses their particular needs and desires. In addition, you can often place such an ad in a low-cost medium, such as a newsletter, or be able to use a highly selective yet low-cost mailing list.

It is a time-honored business axiom that, to be successful, you must "hunt where the ducks are." To determine where, it first is necessary to find out who the ducks are. Undoubtedly, many of them can be reached through classified advertising in conventional media. The most successful "hunters" are more likely to use unconventional media and, at times, unconventional ammunition. They can do this without taking any significant chance when they have taken the time to develop a profile on their ducks and who they might be.

Other

In some cases you may not be trying to sell anything at all; you may be advertising to hire a resident manager, porter, or someone else needed on staff. The same basics apply: hunt where the ducks are. This may mean a classified ad or it may mean a number of tactics in addition to that, particularly those associated with word-of-mouth advertising. Always think in terms of whom you are trying to reach and the communications channels available to reach them. When no one channel in particular will guarantee results, several must be applied.

Identifying Available Media

Available media are not at all limited to those that have classified sections. Especially when demand is weak, or supply is plentiful, relying on more media is necessary in order to reach more prospects. This elevates costs, of course, so you must be selective. Selectivity yields the best results only when the full array of availabilities is considered.

The following is an annotated list of media that may be available to you. You should be able to locate many through the *Yellow Pages* or the PR departments of organizations such as the local Chamber of Commerce, Board of Trade, or Rotary Club. The local United Way office may also be a source of leads because most of their offices compile a comprehensive media directory each year.

1. *Daily newspaper.* The classified section will be read by those looking for something specific. The more headings under which you can list what you have, the more likely it is you will find a prospect. When headings differentiate between furnished and unfurnished apartments, it may be advisable to list an unfurnished unit under both headings since furniture can easily be rented to suit a prospect's needs. The same approach can be used for small office space.

Most daily newspapers have standard sections in each issue or special sections on certain days, such as a real estate section on Friday, Saturday, or Sunday. When a group of apartments is available, or substantial commercial space, placing a display ad in a real estate section makes sense. That does not necessarily mean that it makes more sense than an alternative, however, particularly when a restrictive budget is in effect and you can do one or the other, but not both. In such cases it may not be best to advertise commercial space in a real estate section, because prospects may more likely be reading the business section. Recognize that most daily newspapers are fairly large and relatively few people will read them word for word, page for page. Your best bet is placing your ad in that section which your prospects are most likely to read. If the budget is large enough, it may permit more than one ad, for example, the same ad in two sections, different ads in the same section, or different ads in different sections, designed to appeal to different interests or different benefits associated with what you have available.

Work closely with whomever you rely on for assistance, as well as a newspaper's advertising representatives. In some instances a special section, such as a once-a-week real estate section, will have far more "shelf life" than a regular daily section. Ad reps should be able to provide data in that regard.

2. *Weekly newspaper.* Weekly newspapers vary significantly in terms of their content. Some are community-oriented, have their own reportorial staff, and are highly regarded for local news. Others may be little more than advertising sheets, complete with coupons of all types, that may not be reaching your market. Conversely, some "ad rags" may be reaching your market, but your competitors may not use them for the purposes you wish to.

Method of delivery can be an important issue with respect to weeklies. Those that are mailed are more likely to be read. In apartment buildings, for example, papers may be piled on a table or may otherwise be delivered in bulk. Maintenance people may simply pick these up and throw them away.

3. *Specialized newspapers.* Many areas are served by one or more specialized newspapers. These could include a weekly (or more frequent) business paper or one covering a more specialized area of interest. Those that cover business are obvious candidates for ads that relate to commercial space or services available from your property management firm. But do not overlook such publications as potential media for advertising certain types of residential space, such as a midtown penthouse ideal for the chief executive who wants to walk to work.

4. *Classified guides.* Classified guides are specialized publications designed specifically to make certain types of availabilities known. These are epitomized by the *Apartment Shoppers Guide* publications that are published in many cities. The frequency with which these publications are issued may make them impractical for advertising just one apartment. Nonetheless, some firms find it practical to advertise single units because, if they become rented, chances are similar apartments will be available.

5. *Yellow Pages.* "Regular" *Yellow Pages* advertising can be defined as that which is pursued by or on behalf of the local telephone company. This advertising should be institutional in nature, that is, it should advertise a service of some type, such as property management, apartment or condominium management, apartment buildings, and so forth. This type of advertising tends to be expensive, because so many people—prospects and nonprospects—are being reached. The *Yellow Pages* can be effective, of course, but not necessarily for what you offer. You may be entitled to a small free line listing and that may suffice, unless you want additional listings under additional categories. In many areas, more than one *Yellow Pages* book is available. Some may be published by competing telephone companies; others may be published by independent entrepreneurs. In determining how much advertising to do in these publications, ask, "To what extent will people use the *Yellow Pages* (or this particular set of *Yellow Pages*) to find services such as I offer? To what extent will they rely solely on *Yellow Pages* and not seek other sources of referral? To what extent will the size of my ad make a difference?"

6. *Local magazines (general).* Major cities are usually served by at least one magazine that provides an overview of area goings-on. In some cases these can be excellent media, particularly when the goal is establishing a building as a prestige location, be it residential or com-

mercial. For some businesses and executives, attaining a certain image is important. Being located at the "in" building helps assure that image is realized or at least supported. Advertising can in large measure establish image, especially when the audience being reached comprises those who are about the city and developments within it. Readers of these magazines also tend to be among the most affluent and influential members of the community.

Some city-oriented magazines are circulated free of charge to all persons who reside within certain areas defined by their ZIP codes. Typically, all or most all of the areas selected are "upscale," creating effective demographics for advertisers who sell upscale merchandise such as furs, jewelry, and expensive cars. Some prospective advertisers ignore these publications solely because they are "freebies." That can be a mistake; network television is a freebie, too.

7. *Local magazines (specialized)*. Larger urban areas can often support a local business-oriented publication. Some may be published weekly, others every other week, once a month, once a quarter, or once every 6 months. Some may be annual and thus intended more for long-term reference. Frequency may be a factor. Depending on how they are used, an advertisement placed in a monthly may or may not receive as much readership as one placed in a weekly that has the identical distribution list. If the decision comes down to one or the other, the one with more frequency may be better. It will permit you to reach a person more than once over the period of one month, or to reach the person at least once. (Most people do not look at every page. As such, your ad may be seen only once out of every three or four times it appears.) Of course, the monthly might be read more closely because there is more of a chance for doing so; it stays current longer. In these cases it can be impossible to know which choice is the right one, assuming a choice must be made. The best guidance usually is derived by speaking with a sample of people who read the competing publications. What are their reactions, based on their own reading habits?

Specialized local magazines may also include those that are intended for property managers or, more likely, all those involved in real estate. These may be effective media for ads promoting your firm's services, assuming they are read by owners or those in a position to advise owners. By the same token, using such a publication to establish a solid image for your firm might be effective if your firm is on a growth cycle, and you are looking to attract personnel.

8. *Tip-ins*. Tip-ins are typified by the subscription cards that are inserted in magazines (and then proceed to fall out when the publication is read). Reliance on tip-ins can be of value when the tip-in is a somewhat large piece and the overall cost is less than that of advertising in the selected media.

9. *National magazines (local editions).* When an image must be established or a major project is being announced or has significant space available, the local edition of a major national publication might make an excellent advertising medium. The local edition is basically the same as any other edition, except that it has a number of pages reserved for local advertisers. This lends a great deal of prestige to an advertisement or ad campaign, since it takes on the luster gained from an affiliation with a "biggie," such as *Time, Newsweek,* or *Business Week.* The ability of such ads to actually sell—in addition to build image—cannot be discounted.

Some organizations in a given city will purchase, say, 100 pages of local advertising each year, and obtain a significant volume discount. They then resell the space to local advertisers for less than what the latter would have to pay the magazine, but more than what the broker paid.

10. *Newsletters.* Especially in urban areas, any number of local associations exist and many have newsletters. These can comprise some of the most effective advertising media because of the "purity" of their readership (for example, all area doctors or all area lawyers) and the relatively low cost of having a large ad that will likely be read (or at least noticed) by all readers. Although many of these newsletters exist, it often is difficult to learn about them because the groups that publish them are volunteer-run and do not have a permanent office or staff. The best way to identify them is by contacting people who probably belong to a given group. Do not overlook groups in which you may be active, such as the Chamber of Commerce, Board of Trade, or Rotary.

11. *Association directories.* The annual membership directories of associations in which you are an associate member, or in which associate membership would be appropriate were it available, might be excellent media. Very often such space is available at low cost. A preferred location, such as the outside back cover, may be the most beneficial.

12. *Mailing lists.* Mailing lists are used for direct-mail efforts, of course, and associations are likely to be the best source of these for a given type of market. Some organizations will give you a mailing list (or set of labels) free of charge when you take out an ad. Some may also have a large "prospect" mailing list that can be made available. Organizations that do not publish a newsletter still may have a mailing list, if only for purposes of issuing meeting notices and annual dues statements. Mailing lists can also be obtained for mail-outs to given ZIP code areas or, on a national or regional basis, to contact specific types of individuals or organizations.

13. *Flyers and direct-mail items.*   It is not unusual for some firms to use direct mail in announcing space available or a building for sale or lease. Although such mailings are costly, it may only take a relatively few sign-ups to make the effort worthwhile. (Response rates of 2 to 3 percent are considered good.) The pieces that often are used for purposes of direct mail can also be used as handouts at the project itself, or at other places or events where distribution would be appropriate. In some cases it also makes sense to prepare flyers that are not intended for direct mail. This could apply even on the individual unit rental. For example, an inexpensive flyer can be made using a typewriter and Polaroid photo, describing a house or even an apartment unit. The flyer could be placed on a bulletin board, could be given to appropriate officials for their distribution, and so on.

14. *Hitchhikers.*   Hitchhiking is a new approach that is similar to relying on a tip-in. It is applied by putting two publications in one clear plastic bag. As an example, a national tennis magazine often is delivered in a plastic bag which contains the mail-order catalog of a company offering tennis apparel, racquets, footwear, and so on. As such, hitchhiking is principally a technique to lower the cost of direct mail.

15. *Radio.*   Radio is often a highly cost-effective advertising medium since given stations or given programs tend to have very narrowly defined audiences. Once you know who your target audiences are, it should not be too difficult to pick out radio stations that will reach them. Note that some stations may carry specialized programming, such as a business newsweekly or even a business call-in type. Depending on the nature of the audience, this might be the kind of program that could be sponsored on an ongoing basis to establish an image and name recognition for your firm (as a source of service or employment, or both), or it could be used from time to time to describe specific property available for lease or for an executive's (or other type of listener's) residential use.

Most radio stations, as most other advertising media, will be able to provide extensive data on who listens and when they listen, their economic status, age, and so on. Some marketing reports will focus on the number of listeners who may need precisely what you have to offer.

16. *Television.*   Television used to be suited to mass media only, but this has changed due to the advent of cable. Because many stations can now get by with the lesser revenues resulting from fewer viewers, there is far more diversity and specialization. In some areas, a general station geared to the local community may be suited as a medium to advertise residential units. A local business program may be well-suited for advertising commercial space or property management services.

17. *Public service notices.*   Companies do not buy commercials on public service educational television and radio channels. However, firms that contribute do get mentioned and usually the announcer will also note the firm's slogan, for example, "Film Classics is supported in part by a grant from MNO Property Management, Anytown's leading source for downtown office space." These stations have taken on somewhat more of a commercial bent because they must compete with commercial stations. If you would not consider supporting such stations for purely public-spirited/image reasons, the wisdom of making a contribution (or additional contribution) can be evaluated much as any other "media buy" would be.

18. *Billboard.*   Billboard advertising can be effective. The number of persons driving by can be significant, and the message can be forcefully etched in their minds when it is noticeable for some reason. When your message may be seen at least once per day by 50,000 or more commuters, an appropriate message may be one indicating that your firm should be contacted whenever an apartment and/or commercial space is needed. Such advertising, as many other types, is seen not only by the intended audience—prospective renters—but also by the owners who have space for rent. As a result, high-visibility advertising can also attract owners who welcome aggressive leasing tactics on their behalf.

19. *Transportation advertising.*   If billboard advertising is appropriate, it may also be worthwhile to pursue transportation advertising, such as ads on the tops or backs of taxicabs, ads outside and inside buses, or ads inside commuter rail cars and at stations.

20. *Other.*   The list of "other" media for advertising is almost limitless. It includes matchbooks, the backs of park benches, parking meters, bathroom stall door ad panels, bowling alley score pads, and more.

Most media should be able to provide general details about their audience. Of key importance are the demographic breakdowns, that is, data relating to the age and gender of the audience, income levels, and so on. Those media that deliver the types of people you have identified as your targets should be the best at "bringing home the bacon." But that does not mean that the media which can do it are best for your purposes.

Eliminate the undesirable.   Minimize the amount of "wheel-spinning" necessary by eliminating out of hand any media that are inappropriate to what is being advertised. For example, if you are looking to hire an experienced porter, you know that a major television campaign is not warranted. The same applies to advertising 1000 square feet of office space. But don't be overly hasty. If you have 100,000 square feet (or more) of office space to lease in one or more buildings, television advertising may not be out of the question, especially if the area has business-oriented programming. You do know, of course, that using in-bus transit ads to make office space availability known is inappropriate, but in-station advertising may be wise given the readership of a mass transit rail system, such as Washington, D.C.'s Metro.

Also eliminate media that are completely out of the picture because the image created by the medium is not compatible with the image created by what is being advertised. Be circumspect, however. There may be much more to a medium than meets the eye.

Identify cost per prospect. The first step toward analyzing media is to establish how many of your prospects the medium can provide. For example, assume you have identified your principal prospects as married couples aged 30 to 54, whose annual family income is $40,000 to $60,000. Local television station WPMA can deliver 10,000 who fit into that category during its 6:00 P.M. news broadcast. Its total audience during that time slot is 50,000. The cost of a 30-second spot is $2500. WPMA says its rates are the best, since it will only cost ($2500 ÷ 50,000 viewers =) $0.05 per viewer. But you are not interested in all viewers; just the 10,000 who are prospects. As such, the cost *per prospect* is ($2500 ÷ 10,000 prospects =) $0.25 per prospect, a significant difference.

Whenever a mass market medium is used, the cost per prospect is significantly higher than the cost per reader, viewer, or listener. To make as accurate a calculation as possible, use the most precise data available. This is best illustrated by virtue of the demographics which most television stations can provide with respect to the viewership of each program, and who the viewers are likely to be during "shoulder" periods, that is, the time between programs. As an example, consider programming on Channel 3. Program A is followed by Program B; both have a fairly solid viewership and the audiences are similar. Accordingly, it can be assumed that many people will leave their sets tuned to Channel 3 and thus will see the closing of Program A, then "shoulder materials"—including ads—followed by the opening of Program B. If there is a major change in viewership, however; if a switch is likely to be made between Channels 3 and 4, the shoulder material might not get viewed. This is one of the reasons why major advertisers often buy all major channels at the same time, so that even the worst "channel hoppers" will see the ad, if not on 3, then on 4, 5, or 6. Property managers seldom have an occasion to advertise to such an extent, except when they are leasing or selling units in a substantial project of some type.

Radio stations also provide data on specific programs, but usually to the extent that the programs they produce correspond to standard time periods, such as, 6:00 A.M. to 10:00 A.M., usually referred to as "morning drive time." Stations may or may not furnish data on time periods with less listenership. Note, however, that demographic data may relate more to average daily listenership than actual listenership of a program. In other words, while television lets you know the make-up of any given program's audience, radio may let you know the make-up (in percentages) of the average audience, and then give you a sample-based projection on the number of persons listening at any given time.

In the case of major daily newspapers, overall circulation tends to say very little about the readership of the section in which your ad appears, or the specific page in that section. In some cases you are permitted to specify the section in which you want your ad to run, either at an extra cost or at space rates that apply solely to that section. In the latter case, an extra cost might be necessary to secure a specific position within the section.

Classified advertising in a major daily often works well because people who are looking for a residential unit to rent or a job will often check the classifieds. In some cases a classified ad will encourage those seeking it to refer to a display ad elsewhere in the paper, for example, "See display ad in Friday's Real Estate Section."

Budgeting

Merely placing an advertisement in a medium does not necessarily mean that a prospect will be reached. In the case of radio, for example, prospects must have their radios on and tuned to the channel on which you are advertising at the time you are advertising. They also must hear your ad, and—somehow—the ad must register. Whenever a major effort is ongoing, the vagaries of "hit or miss" are counteracted, usually by extensive advertising in each medium and widespread coverage of media. It's costly, to be sure, but it works, especially when the same prospects may be reached by ads in newspapers and magazines they read and on billboards they see on the way to work.

Characterizing advertising needs

A property manager's advertising needs generally can be broken down into four distinct types:

1. Unanticipated need
2. Occasional need on a regular basis

3. Designated-period promotional push

4. Long-term

Unanticipated need advertising usually relates to the job that needs filling or a rare apartment vacancy. Classified advertising is mostly used.

Occasional needs occurring on a regular basis are most commonly experienced by larger property management firms. They are the ones who need to hire about 50 porters and five or more resident managers each year. They may also have a number of apartments available on a regular basis. The "catch" is that they do not know exactly when these needs will be experienced. Nonetheless, because they will arise, it will usually pay for these firms to apply techniques similar to those suggested for long-term advertising. These approaches, such as display advertising, can then be augmented with classified ads, if necessary.

A defined-period promotional push is associated with the effort needed to fill up a recently constructed or newly refurbished building with a great deal of space available. In such campaigns, several media will be penetrated heavily for three or four weeks, sometimes more, and then the advertising is tapered. Particularly when larger buildings are involved, it usually is inadvisable to curtail all advertising because vacancies will almost inevitably occur. As such, once the "push" is over, it is appropriate to convert to advertising designed to accommodate the occasional need that arises on a regular basis. This approach can also generate a waiting list so that, when a vacancy does occur, those who have expressed interest will be the first ones contacted.

A long-term advertising effort is an institutional campaign. This is often mounted to help assure your company's name and image are placed in front of prospects on an ongoing basis. In that way, when a time comes that a certain service or product is needed, or bids or proposals are desired, your company will be considered.

Selecting media

No matter what type of effort is involved, a budget usually is applied. In some cases the budget is established based on historical or assumed needs. In others, as when a promotional push is planned, the budget may be developed based on proposed campaign costs, that is, instead of creating an allowance of $100,000 for promotion, assuming it will be adequate, one first sits down with an advertising consultant to map out the full campaign and create a budget based on the costs involved.

In selecting media, one has to consider what must be done to reach prospects. For example, a 3-inch square display ad in a 150-page

monthly magazine is not likely to be seen by all readers. If that is all
the budget allows, therefore, one must determine whether it might not
be more appropriate to use the money to obtain more space or time in
some other medium that is less costly. Similarly, you must evaluate
the wisdom of using one full page in a given medium or two half-
pages, under the assumption that the use of two half-page ads creates
more likelihood of at least one being seen. Color may also be an issue.
If the ad campaign is for space available, and it is priced to reach the
"high end" of the market, full-color print ads may be appropriate.

If in evaluating the available media the conclusion is, we have to be
in color if we use this medium, and if the cost is significant, it may be
better not to use the medium and buy more space in another. If the
medium is essential, then the budget has to be created for it. In most
cases, however, it is not necessary to use full color in order to create a
"high-brow" image. It is in all cases essential to determine what must
be done in order to derive maximum "bang for the buck" given the medium used. When a short-term campaign is involved, it almost always
is better to have a 10-spot "flight" on one radio station than one spot
on 10 stations. As such, the one station must be selected carefully. The
same applies to other media when the budget is tight.

As a general rule, use a medium in a manner that will help assure
that the usage pays off. It almost always is more effective to have one
high-impact ad in one medium than one less effective ad in three media. In the case of general print media (as opposed to classified guides
or other specialty items), the larger the medium, the less likely it is
that your ad will be seen, except to the extent that you can assure
placement in that space most likely to be seen by those you most want
to reach.

Establishing costs

Once you have identified which media will be used and to what extent,
overall costs must be established, that is, the cost of space and the cost
of production.

There are no appropriate rules of thumb when it comes to the cost of
producing display advertising and television or radio advertising. An
ad does not have to be costly to be effective. The quality of your promotional consultant is vital. In all too many cases, a given approach
will be suggested because the promotional consultant likes it and
wants to implement it because of his or her own feelings toward it.
Will it work? That is the principal issue. An effective ad pays for itself.

Note that production costs can include many things, depending on
exactly what it is you are producing. In the case of a radio spot, which

is read live on the air, there are no production costs beyond those charged by the agency for its time and talent. When a prepared spot is used, however, actors and narrators must be paid, studio time is employed, and so on. Much the same prevails when television spots are developed, except these can be far more costly, since many more people must be used and it often is necessary to go "on location." Print ads require typesetting and often need artwork and photography. Direct mail needs creative time, art development, type, printing, postage, mailing, and mailing lists.

Identify what your costs are likely to be. Do not be optimistic about deals or special approaches that may save money. Be pessimistic. If things work out well, you will be pleasantly surprised.

A Few tricks of the trade

A number of tricks of the trade can sometimes be applied to eliminate certain unnecessary expenses when you deal directly with a medium or with an agency.

Negotiating rates. Some media will negotiate rates; most will not. Those that do not can often provide sweeteners. These can take the form of additional time or space being provided at no cost, or—in the case of print media—an extra color being provided at no charge. In all cases, of course, bear in mind the old adage, "there's no such thing as a free lunch."

How do you determine a medium's position with respect to rate negotiation or sweeteners? Ask. If you are already a substantial advertiser, or are in a position to become one, a salesperson or publisher would be foolish not to work with you, provided there is competition. In areas that are served by just one major medium, however, or just one applicable medium, competition is reduced or nonexistent, and that creates a seller's market.

When you are dealing directly with a print medium that gives "recognized agencies" a commission, it may be possible to obtain consideration whose value is close to the commission that would have been paid. This consideration could be in the form of creative assistance, an additional color, whatever. Explain your logic to the sales representative; you will get—or should get—a reasonable response. When dealing directly with a broadcast medium, you should be able to get a few extra spots.

Most broadcast media are almost always in a position to throw in a few freebies. Typically, these will be aired in the wee morning hours, in time slots that otherwise might be given away to a charitable group of some type. You never can tell who may be listening, however, so the additional time should always be welcome. And you will be surprised—pleasantly—at how often some fairly good spots can be obtained.

If you make it extremely clear to a representative in a competitive market that some type of consideration will be very much appreciated, and is almost necessary, chances are something will be forthcoming. Don't forget that this something might be in the form of delayed payment.

As a general rule, when you deal directly, ask for concessions and, when dealing through an agency, instruct the latter to obtain concessions.

Junior page.   When advertising in a print medium, it is more effective to use a full-page ad because it is more noticeable. You can achieve almost all the impact of a full-page without buying one by purchasing what is called a "junior page." This amounts to an ad that is one-column narrower than a full page. When a full page is three columns wide, then a junior page would be two-thirds of a page. That may be too small. When a page is four columns wide, a three-column-wide junior page may work well. When a newspaper is involved, an ad that is one column narrower and a few inches shorter than a full page usually can achieve much the same impact as a full page.

Trucking.   A double-truck ad is one that involves two full pages side by side. Also known as a spread, such an ad is hard to miss, helping to assure that its message gets across. Part of the message often is an unspoken one, which says something about an organization which advertises in such a grand manner. Several tricks are valuable to maintain that image while conserving a few dollars. One is to create the effect of a full-color double-truck without paying for it by using a black and white portion of the ad on one page and full color on the other. Some advertisers achieve this by putting the headline (and possibly some copy) on the left-hand portion and then the full-color photo on the right.

Color and placement.   An ad that is not noticed is totally wasted, of course. This is why full-page or junior-full advertising often is recommended. Although larger ads cost more, smaller ads can be more expensive on a cents-per-reader basis, since fewer people notice them. Depending on the publication's rates, it may be advisable to use at least a splash of color in an ad, that is, one color in addition to black. When possible, have the ad appear on a right-hand page, preferably in the upper right quadrant.

Contract buys. Newspapers and some other media will work with you on a contract basis, with your rate depending on the amount of space you commit to. The difference in rates can be significant. Obviously, you would like to obtain the lowest rate you can. Just as obviously, you cannot obtain a rate you do not qualify for. However, it often is possible to justify a lower rate simply by assuming you will advertise more than you currently plan to. At the end of the contract period—typically a year—this will result in your having to pay the difference between, say, 9000 lines at \$0.10 (the 25,000-line rate) versus 9000 lines at \$0.30 (the 7500-to-10,000-line rate). This approach can ease cash flow and permits you the use of money that otherwise would not be available to you.

Remnant sales. You have undoubtedly picked up a magazine, newsletter, or some other print medium and noticed one or more public service ads, with the space being contributed by the medium's publisher. Publishers may donate space for a number of reasons. Some are personally or corporately committed to the cause being advertised. Some do it as part of an overall industry support effort. Some contribute to enhance their own image, to help ensure that the reading public perceives them as "public-spirited." In most cases, however, one cause tends to override all others: they couldn't sell the space. Thus you will also see some newspapers advertising use of their classified sections and television stations advertising their own shows.

Some media, rather than giving away space, will attempt to sell it through what is called "remnant sales." This means that an advertiser or advertising agency representative will be contacted at the last minute and told that an additional amount of space or time can be had on a remnant basis, far below normal rates. This does not work for classified ads, of course, but it can be of value for other types. In order to take advantage of remnant sales, you must have an ad (or a variety of ads) ready to go. The medium must also be advised of your interest, something usually done by speaking with the representative with whom you deal. Do note that some media prefer to give space away to charitable causes or advertise themselves rather than sell at reduced rates. If this is the policy of a medium with which you are dealing, you will be so informed.

Standby ads. Standby ads are similar to remnant sale ads. When standby is used, the publisher states, in essence, "I will have control over when the ad will run." This approach is typically used for newspapers, major dailies in particular. They can often guarantee that the ad will run sometime during a given week or longer period, but not which day. The rate difference can be significant, and savings will be genuine as long as the ad is not time-sensitive.

Preparing Classifieds

When a seller's market exists, a classified ad serves as a notice that you have available something a great many people are looking for. The situation is typified by the long lines of people who apply for just two or three job openings in an area where there is high unemployment. In such cases, there is no need to glamorize a position. It's enough to state in very terse terms the skills you need.

When a buyer's market exists, a classified ad must be worded cleverly in order to be as attractive—have as much pulling or attracting power—as possible. In fact, this rule applies in almost any situation, except when a seller's market prevails. And when it does, chances are even a classified ad will not be necessary.

What makes a good classified ad? That depends on what is being advertised and to whom. When it is something other than low- or middle-income residential space, chances are it will be worthwhile to spend a few extra dollars to provide highlights, and to avoid overreliance on abbreviations. Consider:

> SSpg/$900/mo. 2BR, den; LR, DR, 2Ba. AC. 587-6543.

versus

> Silver Spring, MD. Spacious 2-bedroom with separate den, eat-in kitchen (all modern appliances), separate living room and dining room. Two full baths in contemporary building. Established neighborhood convenient to Metro. Just $900 per month. Call 587-6543 for details. This is a rare opportunity.

The second version is obviously much more costly. But if it brings in five prospects while the other brings in just one or none at all, the first one is the more expensive of the two, because it did not work.

It can be said that some property managers prefer the first approach in almost all cases because they are not skilled enough to write an effective ad. This is nothing to be ashamed of. While we all may share a common language, some of us are far better writers than others. Not recognizing that, and not obtaining writing skills when they are needed, is something to be ashamed of. Always use the right tool to get the job done.

Evaluating Results

In cases where you use several media, it usually will be appropriate to evaluate the effectiveness of each, so you can make more effective selections in the future. In other cases it doesn't make any difference. If it doesn't make any difference, do not burden people with the procedures necessary to obtain the information. In other words, if you always place the same classified ad in the same two media, and will likely do so in the future, there is no point in attempting to determine if Medium A outpulls Medium B. By contrast, if you will use one but not the other, or if you will advertise more in one than another depending on results, evaluation is appropriate.

A variety of techniques can be used to obtain the information you need. In general, they can be categorized as passive or active. Passive techniques are those that do not require a prospect to do anything but respond. Active techniques are generally preferred, in part because they involve you (or your representative or agent) directly with the prospect.

Passive techniques

It is a common passive technique to somehow key the advertisement, so that you automatically know to which ad the people are responding. For example, an ad in Medium A might encourage people to call Mr. Green for more information, while the same ad in Medium B directs them to call Mr. Blue. This approach also has the benefit of alerting those handling the phones that the call coming in to the person in question—in this case, Mr. Doe—is "about the job," since they are asking for Green or Blue rather than Doe. Of course, this approach does not tell you whether or not job seekers (or other callers) got the information directly from the ad, or indirectly from others who showed them the ad. Also, this approach is not effective when more comprehensive efforts are under way. In some instances, these more substantial campaigns may be amenable to a coupon approach where prospects are encouraged to bring in a coupon and receive a gift of some type. The coupon, of course, is marked to indicate which medium it appeared in. The same approach, when used on radio or television, encourages prospects to mention the announcer's name to receive something free. Even when such tactics are appropriate, or are marginally appropriate, you have to determine how it may affect image, the kind of people it might attract (versus the type you want to attract), and so on.

Active techniques

The most effective active technique usually is the direct question, posed in an eyeball-to-eyeball manner. When someone responds to your classified ad seeking a resident manager, for example, "where did you hear about the job?" is a perfectly reasonable question. You've probably been asked it yourself, and you have answered, knowing why the information was sought.

In the case of a project whose advertising will be ended once a complete sellout or rent-up is achieved, do inquire, if only because you may be involved with similar campaigns in the future. Where does the traffic come from? From one ad in one medium, from several ads in the same medium, or a combination? Prospects can be asked to complete a brief questionnaire. Preferably, you should complete the questionnaire for the person, asking the questions aloud. Begin with, "Mr. Smith, we're trying to determine which advertising works best for us. Could I take about 25 seconds and ask you a few questions?" It's a reasonable request, and—by tracking results—you should be able to identify your best advertising value, that is, which medium or combination of media attracts the most prospects per dollar spent. Remember, too, that a prospect is someone who can afford what you have for sale. A medium that brings in a good number of people who are not qualified to buy what you are offering is counterproductive. Alternatively, your advertising may not be effective enough.

Sources of Assistance

Assistance can be obtained from a number of sources. You generally will want to rely on that source or combination of sources that can meet all your usual needs—large and small—quickly, effectively, and for a reasonable fee. In selecting a source, or sources, it first is appropriate to establish exactly what it is you need and want.

Establishing your needs

For many firms, advertising and promotional needs are essentially limited to the placement of classified ads, to make the occasional vacancy known, or to find a porter or other project employee. If needs are really confined to this, and if people respond quickly to ads, there may be no point in relying on outside sources. In fact, many firms conduct themselves just that way and are completely satisfied. Or so they think.

Any property management firm that wants to get ahead must make itself and its services known. It's one thing for opportunity to knock; it's something else again to make sure opportunity has been invited and knows how to find the door.

Many property management firms will benefit from having an active, concerned promoter on their team to develop ideas that may be of value. This does not mean that the firm has to establish a massive promotional budget, because it does not necessarily cost a fortune to take a good idea forward. Many of the best ideas emphasize imagination much more than cost. Of course, it will be necessary to pay an "idea man," assuming you can find someone who is a self-starter and is willing to meet with you on a regular basis.

Are you too small to rely on a large promotional firm? Not necessarily. If you consider all the money you spend each year on all types of advertising, news releases, direct-mail pieces, printing, and other types of graphics, chances are the sum is relatively large. But is it large enough? And if you are stretching things in order to be somewhat attractive to someone you have to pay to serve you, are you really entering into the right type of relationship? Consider the alternatives available in light of your actual needs.

Free-lancers and moonlighters

Free-lancers and moonlighters will often be used by even some of the largest agencies in town to meet certain specialty needs. Free-lance writers are readily available. You will see their ads in the classified section of newspapers, *Yellow Pages,* and so on. Some have formed referral companies or associations.

You can find free-lancers also by going to obvious sources. Newspapers, magazines, and other print media in an area can be contacted. Speak with an editor or writer to ask if they know of a free-lance writer for a particular need—article, brochure, direct-mail piece, and so on. You could contact a college's or university's journalism or English department to make a similar request.

Need a graphic artist? Again, consult classifieds, *Yellow Pages,* or a college's or university's art department, as well as a graphics department of a publication. Many printers can also provide graphics help. The growing use of desktop publishing equipment makes it relatively simple to derive fairly good graphics at a modest cost. Many free-lancers know others active in different areas. Writers may know artists, artists will know photographers, and so on.

A good free-lancer may be able to serve as a source of ideas. It may be a college professor of journalism or public relations, or someone with just a general business background; perhaps someone who has retired, but still likes to "keep a hand in." Such individuals are ideally suited to help in even some of the basic areas, such as preparing "snappy" classifieds to advertise space or seek employees, or to prepare a "Dear Resident" letter or even something more. However, when it comes to a major campaign of some type, where comprehensive, coordinated services will be needed to fulfill tight schedules and deadlines, relying on free-lancers simply will not do.

Advertising agency

An advertising agency can be as small as one person who relies on outsiders, such as the free-lancers and moonlighters mentioned. Even so, such an individual could provide more benefit than a free-lancer, because he or she could serve as the coordinator, the collector and dispenser of ideas, the person who handles assignments and scheduling, and so on. If yours would be a relatively small account, a "one-man band" may be all you need. On the other hand, it may be ineffectual if the individual has several clients and is attempting to satisfy all. While such a person's intents may be laudatory, there are just so many hours in a day. An unforeseen illness or accident could destroy implementation of a carefully planned event.

Advertising agencies that employ at least several people are relatively commonplace. They are capable of identifying appropriate media and preparing schedules, conceiving the overall promotional approach, and implementing all or some of it, from production through placement, follow-up, and billing. Many such firms will rely at least partially on certain outside sources, however, because there seldom is a point to carrying all needs on staff. Doing so results in a larger than necessary overhead burden and limits the firm creatively. As an example, different types of photography frequently are needed. One does not send a strong studio photographer to take care of newsphoto needs; some studio photographers are not equipped to handle architectural photography. As such, to keep one photographer on staff does not make sense in many instances. It often is best to keep a number on call, so the person best suited to the nature of the task can be relied on to minimize cost and maximize quality.

Not all agencies are equally strong in all areas. Some may be particularly adept at direct mail, while others are more known for their television work than print promotions. Some are known for their work in real estate campaigns; others may be new to that area, but eminently capable nonetheless.

While most advertising agencies are highly adept in their "strong suits" (for example, broadcast rather than print), some are notoriously weak in others. They can grow weaker still the two additional services are included for which many claim competence—marketing and public relations. In fact, some who claim competence in these areas really have little understanding of what they involve and do not provide effective services at all. While public relations activities in particular can have strong beneficial results, they may not be pursued because an ad agency does not know how or because it can make more money from advertising.

Public relations firm

Many public relations firms are not public relations firms at all. Instead, they are lobbying organizations that employ a large number of "outs" to press the flesh of the "ins," for example, the former Secretary of Widgets (during the prior administration) who knows the current Secretary of Widgets, whose principal area of concern coincides with the field where a client has significant interests. The activity involved takes place on the national level, in Washington, D.C., and is mirrored on a smaller scale in every state capital and in most city halls as well. If you need political influence, therefore, public relations/lobbying will be of benefit. But that type of power does not necessarily help when it comes to leasing commercial space to a private sector entity, letting a two bedroom-plus-den, or locating a new building engineer.

A public relations firm that will help you relate to your public is not easily found, believe it or not. Many are set up to handle industries and associations rather than specific companies. This is not to say they do not exist; they do. But you should be careful in selecting one for your needs, assuming one will fill the bill.

Services provided by public relations firms typically will include the development and issuance of news releases, the development of magazine and newspaper articles, and stimulation of concepts and ideas that will attract positive media attention. Many of these firms employ just a few people; others provide a much larger personnel complement. Size is not a particularly important issue, however, unless you intend to rely on the firm for advertising and other services as well.

In the case of a major campaign of some type, you may be well-served by relying on a public relations firm and an advertising agency, provided the two communications groups are able and willing to communicate professionally with one another.

The truth about contacts. Selecting one firm over another because it supposedly has "contacts" in the media can be a mistake, since contacts usually don't help all that much. Consider this scenario: You have a somewhat interesting project. A prospective provider of promotional services tells you, "I can get that story into the *Anytown Sunday Blah* because I know the real estate editor." In truth, you can get in touch with the editor just as the promoter can (who supposedly knows him). Just pick up the phone and call. You almost assuredly will be called back. If the story is good, the editor will want to use it. If the story is not that good, the editor won't want to use it. You do not need a contact to sell a good story. Smart editors are not going to risk their jobs, or their medium's audience (and ad revenue) by publishing or airing a mediocre (or worse) story.

The key is to develop a good story. This means that you have to find something interesting or unique about your firm or project so that it makes interesting reading. Remember, newspapers (as other media) are in business to turn a profit. They make money from ad revenue and, to a much lesser degree, subscriptions or newsstand sales. People read or listen because they are interested. A contact generally will be of value only when several good stories are vying for available space. In other words, by having a contact, you may get your story used ahead of another, whereas, without the contact, the situation may have been reversed. The real help the promoter can give is in figuring out the "angle," that is, identifying something about the story that will make good reading. The ability to do that is far more valuable than contacts.

Selecting a Firm or an Individual

Many of the issues associated with selecting a business communications firm are the same or similar to those associated with selecting consultants, discussed in Chapter 12. However, the differences are significant enough to warrant separate consideration here.

Size factors

When you are important to your communications consultant, chances are you will obtain the attention and quality of service you want. Importance often is established in terms of size. In other words, if yours is a relatively small account, you would not want to deal with a "megafirm" because you might become lost. As such, you should want to deal with a firm that is "just the right size," that is, large enough to take care of your principal needs, but not so large that your account is virtually meaningless. But beware of rules of thumb and generalities.

Realize that an ad agency or public relations firm—any service organization, for that matter—is only as effective as the persons assigned to your account. An eager and bright account executive in a larger firm may find your needs particularly challenging or otherwise refreshing, and provide continually effective services. By contrast, the head of a smaller agency may be incapable of giving you what you want not because of size, but because of competence or attitude.

The issue of commissions and markups

A consultant should serve as a client's trusted advisor. A fee is paid for this service. When the relationship is such that the consultant can earn money from it by doing something other than providing service to the client, it may be difficult to provide the unfettered guidance that should be the hallmark of such relationships. Consider including in your discussions, negotiations, and agreements a distinct provision which requires the consultant to waive commissions and markups.

Commissions.   Many media grant a 15 percent commission to a recognized agency. (A recognized agency is an individual or organization to which a medium extends credit.) Regrettably, the advice of promotional consultants may be influenced by commissions. They may advise the use of the medium that pays a larger commission by virtue of the commissionable percentage or higher rates, or they may advise more advertising than necessary.

Not only can commissions create interference, they can also create some ridiculous situations. If a person spends 10 hours preparing "just right" copy for space or time slots that cost $1000, the commission is $150. If just half the time is spent on a "so-so" ad that costs $50,000 to print or air, the commission is $7500.

Work with an agency to establish an effective relationship that disregards commissions. Know who will be working on your account and their hourly rates. You should insist on receiving an itemized bill each month, showing who worked on what and what the cost is. Any commissions received by the agency should be turned back to the client—you—as a credit to the account.

Saving money is not the object.   If a firm is used to receiving a certain level of remuneration for its services, it is not about to do equally good work for less money. You want your consultant to be satisfied. You also want the relationship to be free of outside influences. Make it clear that you are willing to pay the "going rate"; you just want it calculated in a more professional manner. You do not want a doctor prescribing Medicine A over Medicine B because A's manufacturer provides a kickback and B's does not. For the same reason, you do not want an advertising consultant recommending one medium over another, or more "medicine" than needed because of media kickbacks.

If an agency is absolutely adamant about not taking the suggested approach, find out why. If you do not like the explanation, chances are you can find a firm that will work with you on the basis you prefer.

Markups. Whether or not your agency works on a commissionable basis, it will bill separately for any outside expenses that may be needed. These will include a number of in-house expenses, too, depending on the extent of staff; for example, whether or not it employs graphic artists.

Many agencies (as many property management firms) will mark up any out-of-pocket expenses incurred on the client's behalf. Be certain to determine what rate—if any—is used before signing a contract and, whenever possible, negotiate these away.

As an example, consider the company that marks up everything by 15 percent, except that which comes with a 15 percent commission already. Why? Basically, the firm is selling the talent of its personnel on an hourly basis. If you are willing to pay expenses incurred on your behalf directly to the source, or to pay the agency before it pays, so it does not have to use its own money, there is no justifiable reason for a percentage markup. Is it used to cover bookkeeping time? In most instances, the cost of that time already is computed in overhead. If it is not, however, then certainly the company does not pay its bookkeeper based on the amount of money handled. As such, you should only have to pay for the few minutes it may take to handle the data associated with your account.

Few agencies will pay a medium until the client pays. However, they often will be required to pay if the client defaults. You, therefore, may wish to establish a relationship whereby, in exchange for no add-ons (or commissions), you agree to pay within a certain number of days and, if you do not, that you will pay an additional amount.

Identify your needs

The first step in selecting a source of assistance is to identify your needs, including those related to commissions and markups. Write your needs down. The act of doing so gives you an opportunity to evaluate what you are really looking for. You may consider that your needs are limited only to assistance in placing classifieds. But is that really accurate? Are you getting the results you want? If not, wouldn't you also like the consultant to help in better wording and in identifying alternate or additional media for your consideration? What about corporate growth? Are you satisfied with it? Do you want additional accounts? If so, what can you do to get them? Will advertising help? Chances are it will. Chances also are that advertising alone will not be enough. If that's the case, are you willing to spend the time required to use alternative techniques? If not, then growth may be impossible. If so, then you may need marketing and public relations assistance. Perhaps you would benefit from a day's time with a top-flight promoter to help you flesh out ideas or, better yet, to identify goals and then help in the development of a concept to make those goals more attainable.

If you do not take the time to write down everything you need and want, it's most doubtful that you will ever get everything you need. And recognize, too, that it may be impossible to get everything from one firm. A professionally oriented firm will be the first to let you know that, namely, that it can help you in some areas, and in others it can recommend another firm for your consideration.

Identify and contact candidate firms

A number of options are available to you with respect to finding what you need. You could use the *Yellow Pages*; consult with colleagues and peers; contact the offices of trade associations in which you are active; contact newspapers to see whom they suggest; and so on. Do also bear in mind that you can locate free-lancers and moonlighters—if their services will be adequate for your needs—through contacts identified in this chapter.

Once you have identified candidate firms—consider individuals to be firms of one—send each a memo indicating what your needs are, and what your selection criteria might be. As shown in Notice 11.1, you do not have to be elaborate.

Evaluate responses

Prepare a list indicating the firms to which you have sent the invitation to respond. Keep track of when each responds. A firm that waits to the very last minute when it comes to attracting new business will perhaps wait even longer than that when it comes to fulfilling deadlines. Also take a close look at what any cover letter may indicate. A firm whose cover letter contains typographical errors or misspellings obviously cannot be characterized as an organization that pays close attention to details. If a communications consultant cannot communicate effectively on its own behalf, it can hardly be expected to communicate well on your behalf!

Evaluate respondents

Evaluate the respondents by examining what they have sent. Do you like the style? Are they providing samples prepared on a budget far

---

MEMORANDUM

To: ABC Advertising

From: MNO Property Management

Re: Annual Needs

Our company places approximately $25,000 worth of classified advertising each year. We also are anxious to increase our clientele and, toward that end, plan to develop some institutional advertising, coordinated with other forms of promotion, image upgrading, and so on. We are seeking a firm that is looking to grow with us; that can meet our needs through in-house resources and outside staff; that is imaginative, clever and detail-oriented; that will regard us as a good account and provide the level of attention we crave.

If you are interested in our account, we would most appreciate hearing from you. Please send us information about your firm and its key personnel. Also identify at least three current clients and provide samples of work you have done for them or others.

If you have any questions, please call:

John M. Nop
555-1212

Responses must be received by November 8.

Notice 11.1   Memo soliciting interest of advertising agencies.

larger than yours? An effective response will indicate what the firm has done for organizations such as yours, or at least firms in the same economic category vis-à-vis advertising.

Of major importance: speak with current clients. Are they pleased with the firm in general? What about the individuals assigned to their account? Are they anxious to please? quick to respond? Are billings correct? Is the quality of work good? Does it bring in results? Is the firm adept in all its undertakings? Has it scored well in public relations (if desired) as well as advertising? These and other questions should be asked.

Once you complete your general review and discussions with clients, you should be able to identify three firms you consider most qualified. Meet with representatives of each, preferably at their places of business, so you can get a better "feel" for them as organizations.

Interview candidates

In setting up an interview with a firm, make it clear to those with whom you speak that you want to meet the people who will actually handle your account. All too often you will meet with the most convincing individuals, such as the "top brass" of a firm, and then will never see them again. While it is acceptable for them to meet with you, by all means talk about your needs with those who will be fulfilling them. A firm is only as good as the people assigned to your account.

In conducting the interview, consider it similar to one you would use when hiring someone. As such, let the agency representatives do most of the talking. Naturally, you will have a few key questions you want answered, and by all means take notes about the answers. Some of your questions might include the following:

Who will be assigned to my account and what will their responsibilities be?

What are their backgrounds and experience? May I examine samples of their recent work?

Who are some of the clients they serve in a capacity similar to mine?

What is your charging structure? What are the hourly rates? May I see sample bills? Are hours worked and tasks pursued identified?

Are commissions credited to my account? Are markups eliminated if payment is made by me before you pay?

How do you perceive me going about accomplishing my goals? What types of promotions should be used? How much should I budget?

Who are my key audiences/publics? What type of image should I attempt to establish?

What do you think some of my or the firm's weaknesses are? How do we try to overcome them?

What types of routine work do you have others do? What do you do totally or partially in-house?

Do you have other clients in my line? If so, how will you avoid a conflict of interest? If not, how do you derive the experience? If you have experience from the past, with whom? Why was the relationship terminated?

What is your policy with respect to competitors? If a larger competitor of mine comes along, will you drop me?

None of these questions is posed for purposes of idle curiosity. Some relate to issues you want to know about directly, such as the experience of those who will work your account. Others relate to the character of the firm you are dealing with. A firm that will handle competitors in a somewhat small market perhaps does not have a well-developed sense of ethics. A firm that would drop a long-standing client in favor of a larger competitive one is not very loyal. Of course, a firm that says it wouldn't do such a thing may not have too much business savvy. Again, the interpretation of answers is your business. You are the one who has to feel comfortable.

Do not fail to interview the three principal candidates. True, you can shortcut this step. As you no doubt are aware, however, most shortcuts lead to problems. Recognize that your stock in trade is your reputation; your reputation is your image; the firm you select is being entrusted with your image and reputation. If you take that lightly, chances are you do not have the reputation of being an astute organization because any organization that truly is "in the know" recognizes how important it is to select a communications consultant with care.

Select your consultant

After interviewing all three firms, consider contacting any additional individuals you deem appropriate. As an example, you should probably speak with those who deal with the same account representatives you will be working with. You may also wish to inquire of any of the media you intend to use about the reputation of the firm.

Once you feel comfortable that each of the three firms has been reasonably straight about its work and reputation, rank them in preferential order. If for any reason you learn something that displeases you about any, then do not consider it.

Formalize the relationship

In order to formalize the relationship with the top-ranked firm, you would notify it that, in fact, it is considered tops. Then meet with the firm to go over precisely what it will be doing for you within a defined period of time. For example, if it will be developing a media campaign to make your firm better known to prospective clients, you would probably want to receive the following:

Identification of the various media and, for each, information about rates, readership, costs per prospect, and image impact

Suggestions for an overall theme and the benefits and drawbacks of each

Messages to be conveyed and extent of promotion

Suggested graphics; final graphics

You will want to know what the firm's policies are with respect to commissions and so on, and about how much you should expect to pay for space (once the program is developed), artwork, creative time, and so on. In essence, you do not want any surprises, nor do you want confusion or disappointments.

The firm should be willing to identify the schedule it will be working with, its charges, estimates for the project—even if it is only ongoing activities—and so on, all of which can become part of the formal contractual agreement.

Once all these aspects of the relationship are committed to writing, and you agree with them, the contract can be signed and the relationship can begin.

Chapter 12

Dealing with Consultants

Introduction

The business world is filled with consultants, or so it seems, but very few genuine experts. As we use the term consultant in this book, what we really are talking about is an expert, someone who knows the subject inside and out.

Those who profess expertise but do not really have it to some extent have an upper hand, because the property manager is not really in a position to spot guidance deficiencies until it is too late. How many were "stung" by the crop of energy conservation consultants that appeared on the scene after the OPEC nations' petroleum embargo in the early 1970s is anybody's guess. More recently, environmental consultants are coming to the fore. Not only do the charlatans walk away with money they do not deserve, they impose tremendous expense and inconvenience as a cause of their faulty guidance, and the time they cause to be wasted can result in relatively small problems becoming seriously large ones. The point? When dealing with consultants, remember that you do not buy a consultant's services. What you buy is the consultant's reputation. As such, *check it out!* Consultants are vital, and the good ones can save you amounts of money that go far beyond their fees.

Determine the Kind of Consultant You Need

After a while, many property managers gain in-depth knowledge of a number of issues, and can readily qualify as experts themselves. But the very best of them all understand where their own knowledge begins to get weak, and where they need help. In fact, it always has been a hallmark of a professional that the individual will not give advice about issues in which the professional is not expert.

Know when you need an expert, and when you do, determine what kind to get. Money should not be that major an issue, because, in the overall scheme of things, the fee paid to a consultant typically amounts to little if anything at all. This occurs because the consultant is part of a process. For example, if you need to have a problem-prone parking lot repaved, the true cost is the cost of the consultant and the cost of the repaving, less the cost of what you would have paid for the repaving without the consultant. And it may be worthwhile to look at the numbers over a 5-year period, too, since methods suggested by the consultant may be able to lower long-term costs greatly, even though the initial expense is higher.

In many instances, an individual or a firm will be available to provide highly specialized expertise, for example, structural or other consulting engineers who provide roofing consultation or geotechnical or other consulting engineers who can provide guidance on paving. The advantage of dealing with these types of consultants is their widespread knowledge. For example, a specialist in roofing should be fully aware of all the options available, and be able to suggest which is best all things considered. In that way you can obtain truly expert guidance presented for your benefit only. By contrast, a roofing consultant with a limited background can only provide guidance with respect to the systems the individual knows well, whereby a better system may receive no mention at all. Someone who works for a contractor will recommend only the types of systems installed by that contractor, and a manufacturer's representative will only recommend the manufacturer's product. If in a given case the limitations of some of these latter situations are not limitations, then these clearly could be the best people to deal with. For example, if you are committed to using products made by ABC, then an ABC manufacturer's representative, backed by an application engineer at the factory, may be the best alternative. But if you are not committed to that product, then you may need someone who can tell you which is best. That someone might be a reputable contractor, if that contractor is familiar with the kind of system you have and are required to stay with. In essence, as a first step, consider the type of consultant you need in general.

In some cases, you will be unable to locate the kind of consultant you would prefer. For example, there may be no coatings consultants in your area. In that case, you may have to lower your sights somewhat or take another look. Chances are your area is served by a highly professional painting contractor, and one of the most experienced workers, maybe even a top company executive, might be willing to enter into a special contract with you, solely to provide guidance, with it being clearly understood that the guidance would apply whether or not the firm does the work.

If you are convinced that you need a consultant whose expertise you cannot obtain locally, then it probably will be worthwhile to bring in a consultant from out of town, especially when the guidance used will result in considerable expense, or potential expense as through risk exposure and its mitigation.

Note, however, that an out-of-town consultant should be aware of local conditions. Someone who has practiced a number of years in a dry climate may give recommendations that are not suited for a humid area.

Consider, too, whether or not you need someone who is a registered professional, or if someone else will do. In roofing matters, dealing with a professional engineer often is recommended, because plans and specifications may have to be prepared, and very often you would benefit from field observation of the contractor's work to help ensure that plans and specifications (or at least applicable codes and standards, or basic precepts of good workmanship) are adhered to. A professional engineer with experience in paving design might be best suited for dealing with pavement, but certainly a highly experienced contractor or former contractor who can install what might be needed could be just as qualified, and perhaps even more so.

In most areas, the degree of complexity involved will help suggest the degree of competence you need. A person without a professional registration may actually be far more knowledgeable and better suited for the work than a professional registered counterpart because of individual differences. Thus, it might be unwise to make generalizations about whom you need (in terms of registration or certification) until you examine the qualifications of the individual involved and, in particular, the records of client satisfaction.

Locating Consultants

Consultants can be located in a number of ways. The *Yellow Pages* are one source, but for many property managers they almost never are the first choice. Instead, the first calls are made to peers in order to determine whom they have used in similar circumstances, and what their results have been. Those that are highest rated are likely to do the best work, and they are the ones most likely to have exactly the kind of experience you need. Note, however, that consultation often is a personal activity. One person acts as the project manager and is backed by a team. But it's the project manager who makes everything happen, and some are far better than others. For that reason, some firms have mixed reputations: deal with Al and everything runs well; deal with Bob and nothing runs at all. As such, when obtaining recommendations about firms, be sure to ask with whom the peer dealt at the firm. When a number of names are offered, it usually indicates that the firm is exceptionally well managed, and you will get good results no matter with whom you deal.

It is possible that your peers will be unable to suggest anyone or anyone worthwhile. In that case the *Yellow Pages* may be of help, but it is unlikely. The expertise sought may just not be available in your area, or not offered, at least not in the commercial sense. As an example of "alternative consultants," consider the arrangement described with respect to retaining a contractor as a consultant, provided you believe that the contractor has the capability of acting in that mode. Some do, and some don't. Also consider local colleges and universities. Large state facilities often have specialists on staff, teaching and pursuing research in a variety of ways. A call to a university's public information officer can often work wonders in this regard, and chances are you will be called back in a day or so with exactly the information you need.

If the college or university is unable to help directly, the people there might be able to steer you to others. The same applies to contractors. Likewise a call to a manufacturer may lead you to a consultant.

In your search for reliable consultants, do not overlook those who would probably run into them on a somewhat frequent basis. For example, fire department personnel are probably in a position to identify some topflight fire safety consultants. Police can probably tell you about security companies with whom they have dealt. Engineering laboratories might have experience with a number of roofing and paving consultants and possibly with some coating consultants, too. And so the list goes on, bearing in mind that some property managers also may have what it takes.

Another possibility, when a rare expert is involved, is the trade association or professional society comprising such individuals. The *Encyclopedia of Associations* can be of great value in this regard, especially given its topical index. Another possibility are trade periodicals. A call to an author can often yield information about articles that have been written or individuals to contact. The *Directory of Periodicals* identifies almost every publication that exists.

Determining the Overall Procurement Approach

Early on in the process it is necessary to determine the method you will use to retain a consultant, assuming that you are not merely using a manufacturer's representative or some other "free" source.

Two approaches are available. One you probably are familiar with. It is bidding. Typically, you identify the consultants you consider qualified, or you know of irrespective of qualifications, and ask all to submit information about themselves and a bid for their services. The problem with this approach in general is the variation in bids, stemming directly from the different scopes of work, scopes of service, work scopes, or work specifications (all those terms mean basically the same thing) each proposes, and the different personnel each will assign. If in putting together a biddable work scope for a contractor, you say that you need guidance in terms of swimming-pool management, for example, one contractor's bid may assume a comprehensive inspection of your facilities and related maintenance records, whereas another may be talking in terms of having a computer print out the SOP (standard operating procedure) bid specification. Invariably, in such loose procurements, those who are likely to do the most thorough work are those penalized the most, since their bids seldom are in the same ballpark as the others' bids. Those who bid the lowest often are those proposing the skimpiest work scopes. They may later require a work-scope change order so that the work they do is the same as the work of those whose bids were noncompetitive. The catch: the ultimate fee sometimes paid to the "low ballers" is higher than what it would have cost had you hired the thorough consultants whose proposal was not considered.

One way around this is to develop your own work specifications and ask each consultant to bid on it. This approach is fine, assuming that all the consultants would do the work in the same way, which is very doubtful. Of course, the question remains, where would the bid specification come from? Who would prepare it?

In fact some of the most qualified consultants of all will not even consider responding to a bid request, because they do not have the time to get into a talent auction. They do good work, they charge a reasonable fee, and they're busy all the time.

The alternative to bidding is commonly termed QBS, for qualifications-based selection. By using this approach, you identify potential consultants and ask each to submit information. These qualifications statements are reviewed in depth, and clients are called to gain their insights about experience. Then, based on the claimed experience of each, and based on what the clients have to say, you rank the prospects and arrange for interviews. You visit the offices of each and, based on what they have to say about your work, how they would approach it, whom they would assign, and so on, you identify who you believe is best qualified, who is second best, and so on.

Once that is done, you open discussions with the most qualified firm. These discussions center on what your objectives are. By posing problem questions, the consultant should be able to learn more about your objectives and what you are capable of doing on your own. Then the consultant can determine which services will be of most benefit to you, and you then enter into a discussion of why these services will be of value, how much they cost, the alternatives to them, the risks of not performing this or that, and so on.

Once discussions are done, you will have created a comprehensive scope of services that should meet all your needs. The consultant then is in a position to define how much it will cost to implement that scope, in terms of fees and expenses.

If you have some experience, you will know whether or not the fee is reasonable. However, if you have not had extensive experience, then you should want to expand the questions you ask prospective consultants' clients in the prior step. Exactly what did the consultant do for you? you should ask. And how much was charged? You can also ask peers about what to expect in terms of fees, to help ensure you are not being gouged. Realistically, however, it is doubtful that you will get overcharged, for two important reasons.

First, if the estimate is as good as your research suggests, an overcharge is unlikely, because no firm can take advantage of its clients and hope to earn a solid reputation.

Second, most consultants who are engaged via QBS realize that the quality of their performance—not the fee—is the key element in determining whether or not a long-term relationship will be established with the client. As a consequence, they are more than likely planning to charge a reasonable fee, knowing that the client, treated well, may just become a client for life, and a referral source for life.

Why not simply prequalify firms and allow only the top three to bid? Again, the work-scope issue intervenes. The mutual work-scope discussion between the consultant and the client helps assure an intimate understanding of one another, and a combined focus on doing the work well. By contrast, without a perfect work scope, each bidding consultant is likely to focus on developing a work scope each can live with, albeit somewhat skimpy, in order to submit the low fee the client assumedly is looking for. Do not encourage consultants to submit low fees. They can do so, but it will be at the expense of the quality of the work they do. Maybe they will not analyze alternatives as closely. Maybe the plans and specifications they develop will not be as detailed as they could be. Perhaps they will rely on conservative design that is inexpensive to procure but costly to implement. In fact, any number of methods can be applied to minimize consultants' expense and increase profits, all under the assumption that doing quality work won't pay off, since the next project will also be available only if the fee is low enough. Through mutual work-scope development, which is unique to QBS, you can be best assured of specifying the work you need done, and you can be reasonably assured that you are not overpaying. After all, who else but the firm most qualified to do the work is most qualified to help determine what that work should consist of?

Evaluating Qualifications in Light of Needs

Assuming you do opt for QBS, you will implement its precepts. A key concern relates to the capabilities of those individuals involved. Although you may not need a full spectrum of services at this time, you might need them in the future. If that is the case, you may want to look for someone who can provide more than you need at this time, because you want to build a relationship and might need more services later, for the same or for some other building.

Typical services which consultants provide include the following:

1. Routine inspections, reports, and recommendations for action
2. Comprehensive inspection, including visual inspection, observation of employees, taking of samples, laboratory analysis of samples, and report
3. Development of plans and specifications for reconstruction, demolition, reinstruction, and so on
4. Procurement of whatever government permits may be necessary
5. Development of bidding documents
6. Contractor prequalification
7. Observation of construction or even full construction management
8. Preparation of inspection forms and operating instructions, training of employees, follow-up training of employees and monitoring of their work, and reports

Thus, while a college professor may be able to provide some guidance, the individual may not be able to provide a continuance of service under a single responsibility. Do you need that? Might you need it in the future? These are the kinds of issues you must consider. Generally speaking, you will be best served by a consultant who will serve well over the long term; someone who gets to know and understand your approach to matters and your objectives; someone who can work with you well, through a bond of trust.

When you have determined the services you are looking for, you proceed through the additional steps of QBS: interviews, work-scope development, and so on. Once the work scope is developed and the fee is presented, you have the option of modifying the work scope as to a lower fee. Is that wise, all things considered? Chances are it is not. If the consultant is really a good one, the work scope should be "right on." Therefore if you must lower the fee, be careful. The consultant should be able to help by explaining the risks associated with each change. If for some reason you are unable to negotiate a satisfactory fee, then by all means close discussions with the consultant deemed most qualified and open them with the consultant who is ranked next best. If the same results occur, however, adjust your expectations and increase the budget.

Developing the Contract

Once you identify an acceptable scope of services and fees, you can also develop a schedule. At that point you will be ready to enter into a contract with the consultant. The contract will in many respects be similar to one you entered into with a contractor, although it will also differ. Model terms and conditions between a client and a consultant are presented in the model contract at the end of this chapter. Some of the issues of particular concern include the following.

Work scope and fee

Spell out exactly what consultants are supposed to do. Each phase of work should be accompanied by a fee projection indicating, for example, how much time each category of person will be spending on each phase, and the unit fees involved, either including overhead and profit, or with overhead and profit applied through a multiplier. If a lump-sum agreement has been worked out, the hourly breakdowns may be unnecessary. Whenever a lump sum is used, however, it often is wise, depending on the nature of the work, to establish a contingency reserve in contemplation of unanticipated conditions. On the other hand, if an hourly rate schedule is agreed to, the contract should have a "cost not to exceed" clause, which specifies that the consultant will inform you of conditions which indicate that the original estimate may be exceeded. Such a clause should further stipulate that a failure to notify you of a potential overrun may result in the consultant not being paid for the additional work.

The work scope should also detail exactly what it is consultants are responsible for. For example, if they are to observe construction, they will not have stop-work authority, but will be responsible for providing reports of what they observe. Such reports are to be rendered, for example, within 5 days of completion of construction or on a weekly basis. The goal of this detailing is to ensure that you and the consultant have 100 percent communication and to avoid, "gee, I thought you meant..."

Timely performance

Timely performance usually is desired, but it should be spelled out clearly rather than using a vague general term such as "time is of the essence." Indicate the date by which certain tasks should be completed and permit allowance for conditions beyond the consultant's control, such as inclement weather, which makes it impossible to conduct an inspection or perform other weather-dependent work.

Proven techniques and materials

Although innovation is always welcome, few owners want their properties to be guinea pigs. Accordingly, you may wish to insert into the contract a clause which limits the consultant's design or other recommendations to proven techniques and materials. In any event, it is appropriate for property managers or owners to satisfy themselves that a given approach is likely to work because it has worked elsewhere. Therefore the consultant (and/or contractor) could be required to identify similar area projects where given recommended techniques or materials have been applied. Property managers should speak with management personnel of each such project to assess their satisfaction. The time spent is well worthwhile.

Certification

Do not ask a registered professional engineer or architect to "certify" that construction has been completed according to plans and specifications, assuming that construction monitoring—not construction management—is involved. A certification is tantamount to a warranty or guarantee, and thus could transfer liability for improper workmanship from the contractor to the design professional. If this occurs, any professional liability coverage that the design professional may have is likely to be voided for the project. It could be difficult to collect either from the consultant or from the contractor. It is best for the consultant merely to "state" or "declare" (instead of "certify") that, in the consultant's professional opinion, construction has been accomplished according to plans and specifications, based on observations, but that—in any event—each party involved on the project is obliged to fulfill contractual responsibilities.

Indemnification

The consultant should be willing to indemnify, hold harmless, and defend the owner and the owner's agents for and from any claims or losses resulting from the consultant's negligent professional acts, errors, or omissions, in proportion to the degree to which the consultant's professional acts, errors, or omissions result in such claims or losses. When a registered professional engineer is involved, stronger wording in some cases cannot be covered by professional liability insurance, making the stronger wording self-defeating.

It is true that some consultants will accept much stronger wording without a "peep." It could be an indication that the consultant is uninsured and, as such, has no insurance policy that can be voided. Alternatively, it could mean that the contractor simply is unaware of important business issues. In that case you have to ask yourself whether this is the consultant you really want to deal with, since those that are sloppy about business matters may be sloppy about technical issues, too. Note, also, that some consultants simply may have nothing to lose, and thus will agree to the strongest wording you can think of.

Generally speaking, experienced property managers advise, do not rely on an indemnification for any significant protection. If you need protection, obtain insurance. And, perhaps most important of all, rely on a competent consultant. In that way, the likelihood of having to enforce an indemnification or to seek relief from insurance becomes small.

Exculpatory clauses

Some consultants may seek to insert clauses in a contract in order to reduce their risk exposure. One of these is called "limitation of liability," whereby the consultant's aggregate liability to the owner, contractors, and subcontractors is limited to a flat sum (typically $50,000) or the fee, whichever is higher. This creates a liability exposure to the owner, who would underwrite all losses above the liability limit. Some owners are willing to accept these limitations; others prefer to negotiate a higher limit, with the consultant usually increasing the fee by a modest amount to consider increased risk. The maximum limit which most consultants will accept is equal to their professional liability insurance coverage. It is unreasonable to ask a consultant to accept unlimited liability, if only because this presupposes financial resources which do not exist.

Another clause often applied when an existing roof, pavement, or other structure is involved requires the owner to indemnify the consultant from errors or omissions of the previous or original designers. This is a reasonable clause and should be accepted. However, the consultant should be required to notify the owner or the owner's agent promptly after a prior design error or omission is detected.

Still another clause requires the owner to indemnify a consultant for hidden conditions (latent defects) that are discoverable only after an existing structure, or a portion of it, is removed. This clause, too, should be accepted, again, provided the consultant is required to notify the owner or the owner's agent immediately after a hidden condition is discovered.

Note that the three clauses discussed here comprise just a few of many. Whenever a contract is offered, read it carefully. If you are unsure of a meaning, either seek legal assistance or have the consultant explain it to you in writing and in plain English. Have the explanation incorporated into the contract: "It is mutually agreed by the signatories hereto that the previous clause shall be interpreted to mean that..."

Dispute resolution

Some consultants will indicate in their contracts how disputes will be resolved, often through binding arbitration. If this is not acceptable, offer a modification. Always attempt to create an alternative to litigation, so the money involved can go principally to those to whom it is due, rather than to attorneys. Some property managers prefer a method whereby each party to a two-party dispute selects a "conflict resolver," and the two conflict resolvers select a third, and these three together effect a resolution that is binding.

Others give high marks to an approach developed by ASFE/The Association of Engineering Firms Practicing in the Geosciences, the construction industry's most advanced organization with respect to alternative dispute resolution (ADR). Called Med/Arb 2, it permits the client and the consultant to identify dispute resolvers "up front." Generally speaking, two are needed: a mediator and an arbitrator. Should a dispute arise, the client and the consultant have 7 days to resolve it. Should their attempt be unsuccessful, the previously selected mediator can be called in. If mediation is almost completely successful, the disputants can call upon the mediator to become arbitrator and settle the few outstanding (and typically minor) issues. If that approach is not tenable, then—after 30 days—the parties move on to binding arbitration. Design Professionals Insurance Companies, a major insurer of architects and consulting engineers, report that mediation is proving to be the most successful ADR technique of all. Med/Arb 2 is described in Appendix A.

Client/Consultant Model Contract

This model contract is offered for review purposes only. Reliance on any contract has a number of legal ramifications. No contract should be prepared or signed without the guidance of qualified legal counsel. This model presupposes that the owner or the property management firm, referred to as CLIENT, and the engineering, communications, or other firm, referred to as CONSULTANT, have developed a schedule of deliverables, indicating what will be delivered when, and a fee schedule, indicating who gets paid how much. Both of these documents are referenced in the following model.

1. *Work specification*
   a. CLIENT and CONSULTANT have reached an agreement as to the work to be performed and the schedule indicating when deliverables shall be completed by CONSULTANT. This work specification is appended to this AGREEMENT as Attachment A, and is through attachment made a part of this AGREEMENT.
2. *Fee schedule*
   a. CONSULTANT's prevailing fee schedule has been presented to and agreed to by CLIENT and is appended to this AGREEMENT as Attachment B, and is through attachment made a part of this AGREEMENT. CONSULTANT agrees to notify CLIENT of any change to such fee schedule no later than [thirty (30)] calendar days before such change goes into effect.
3. *Billing and payment*
   a. CLIENT recognizes that time is of the essence with respect to payment of CONSULTANT's invoices, and that timely payment is a material part of the consideration of this AGREEMENT. CLIENT shall pay CONSULTANT for services performed in U.S. funds drawn upon U.S. banks and in accordance with the rate and charges set forth herein. Invoices will be submitted by CONSULTANT from time to time, but no more frequently than every [four (4)] weeks, and shall be due and payable within [thirty (30)] calendar days of invoice date. If CLIENT objects to all or any portion of an invoice, CLIENT shall so notify CONSULTANT within [fourteen (14)] calendar days of the invoice date, identify the cause of disagreement, and pay when due that portion of the invoice, if any, not in dispute.
   CLIENT shall pay an additional charge of [one-and-one-half percent (1.5%)] (or the maximum percentage allowed by law, whichever is lower) of the invoiced amount per month for any payment received by CONSULTANT more than [thirty (30)] calendar days from the date of the invoice, excepting any portion of the invoice amount in dispute and resolved in favor of CLIENT. Payment thereafter shall first be applied to accrued interest and then to the principal unpaid amount.

Payment of invoices is in no case subject to unilateral discounting or setoffs by CLIENT.

Application of the percentage rate indicated above as a consequence of CLIENT's late payment does not constitute any willingness on CONSULTANT's part to finance CLIENT's operation, and no such willingness should be inferred. If CLIENT fails to pay undisputed invoiced amounts within [thirty (30)] calendar days of the date of the invoice, CONSULTANT may at any time, without waiving any other claim against CLIENT and without thereby incurring any liability to CLIENT, suspend this AGREEMENT (as provided for in Section Four, Suspension) or terminate this AGREEMENT (as provided for in Section Five, Termination).

4. *Suspension*

   a. Upon [fourteen (14)] calendar days' written notice to CONSULTANT, CLIENT may suspend CONSULTANT's work. If payment of CONSULTANT's invoices is not maintained on a [thirty (30)] calendar day current basis by CLIENT, CONSULTANT may by [fourteen (14)] calendar days' written notice to CLIENT suspend further work until payment is restored to a current basis. Suspension for any reason exceeding [forty-five (45)] calendar days shall, at CONSULTANT's option, make this AGREEMENT subject to renegotiation or termination, as provided for elsewhere in this AGREEMENT. Any suspension shall extend the time schedule for performance in a manner that is satisfactory to both CLIENT and CONSULTANT, and CONSULTANT shall be compensated for services performed and charges incurred prior to the suspension date, plus suspension charges. Suspension charges may include, but shall not be limited to, services and costs associated with putting documents in order, rescheduling and reassigning personnel and/or equipment, and issuing necessary or customary notices to appropriate agencies. Compensation to CONSULTANT shall be based upon CONSULTANT's prevailing fee schedule and expense reimbursement policy.

5. *Termination*

   a. CLIENT or CONSULTANT may terminate this AGREEMENT for reasons identified elsewhere in this AGREEMENT, or for other reasons which may arise. In the event such termination becomes necessary, the party effecting termination shall so notify the other party, and termination will become effective [fourteen (14)] calendar days after receipt of the termination notice. Irrespective of which party shall effect termination or the cause therefor, CLIENT shall within [thirty (30)] calendar days of termination remunerate CONSULTANT for service rendered and costs incurred, in accordance with CONSULTANT's prevailing fee schedule and expense reimbursement policy. Services shall include those rendered up to the time of termination, as well as those associated with termination itself, such as modifying schedules or reassigning personnel. Costs shall include those incurred up to the time of termination as well as those associated with termination.

6. *Standard of care*

   a. CONSULTANT warrants that CONSULTANT's experience, knowledge, and character qualify CONSULTANT for the particular duties in connection with the services CONSULTANT agrees to perform through this AGREEMENT. CONSULTANT shall strive to perform these services in accordance with professional standards.

7. *Insurance*

   a. CONSULTANT shall secure, pay the premiums for, and keep in force until the expiration of this AGREEMENT adequate insurance as provided below. Such insurance is to specifically include liability assumed by CONSULTANT under this AGREEMENT.

   (1) Workers' compensation insurance as required by local and/or state jurisdiction(s).

   (2) Umbrella general liability insurance with a limit of not less than [five million dollars ($5,000,000)].

   (3) If automotive equipment is used in the operation, automobile bodily injury insurance with limits of not less than [two hundred fifty thousand dollars ($250,000)] for each person and [five hundred thousand dollars ($500,000)] for each accident, and property damage liability insurance, with limits of not less than [one hundred thousands dollars ($100,000)] for each accident, and medical pay coverage of [ten thousand dollars ($10,000)] regardless of fault.

   b. All policies for liability protection, bodily injury, or property damage shall include [name of owner] and [name of property management firm] as additional insureds as respects operations under this contract.

   [Owner's name]   [Property management company's name]

   [Owner's address] [Property management company's address]

   c. A certificate of insurance for workers' compensation and public liability together with a properly executed endorsement for cancellation notice shall be furnished as stipulated in the preceding paragraph. The certificate shall be delivered to CLIENT. The insurance companies providing the above coverage shall be satisfactory to CLIENT.

d. Notice of any policy change shall be furnished to CLIENT within [seventy-two (72)] hours of such changes being made.

8. *Confidentiality*

a. CONSULTANT agrees to keep confidential and to not disclose to any person or entity without CLIENT's prior written consent all data and information of whatever kind generated by CONSULTANT or furnished to CONSULTANT by CLIENT in the course of CONSULTANT's performance hereunder; provided, however, that this provision shall not apply to data which are in the public domain or which were acquired by CONSULTANT independently from third parties not under any obligation to CLIENT to keep said data and information confidential.

9. *Indemnification*

a. CONSULTANT agrees to hold harmless and indemnify CLIENT from and against liability arising out of CONSULTANT's negligent performance of the work.

10. *Curing a breach*

a. In the event either party believes that the other has committed a material breach of this AGREEMENT, the party maintaining such a belief shall issue a termination notice to the other, identifying the facts as perceived, and both parties shall bargain in good faith to cure the causes for termination as stated in the termination notice. If such a cure can be effected prior to the date by which termination otherwise would be effective, both parties shall commit their understanding to writing, and termination shall not become effective. If in curing an actual or alleged breach either party shall waive any rights otherwise inuring to that party by virtue of this AGREEMENT, such waiver shall not be construed to in any way affect future application of the provision involved or any other provision.

11. *Governing law*

a. Unless otherwise provided in an addendum, the law of the state of [_____] will govern the validity of this AGREEMENT, its interpretation and performance, and remedies for contract breach or any other claims related to this AGREEMENT.

12. *Dispute resolution*

a. In the event of a disagreement about the withholding of payment, the assessment of damages, or any other matter arising out of this AGREEMENT, CONSULTANT and CLIENT shall each appoint one person and these two shall select a third person who shall act as chairperson, and these three persons shall resolve the disagreement and the resolution shall be binding on both parties.

13. *Recovery of dispute resolution costs*

   a. In the event that legal action is brought by either party against the other, the prevailing party shall be reimbursed by the other for the prevailing party's legal costs, in addition to whatever other judgments or settlement sums, if any, may be due. Such legal costs shall include, but not be limited to, reasonable attorney's fees, court costs, expert witness fees, and other documented expenses.

14. *Notices*

   a. Any notice given hereunder shall be deemed served when hand-delivered in writing to an officer or other duly appointed representative of the party to whom the notice is directed, or if sent by registered or certified mail to the business address identified in Section [_____] of this AGREEMENT.

15. *Project representatives*

   a. CLIENT shall furnish representatives who shall make decisions on CLIENT's behalf when requested to do so by CONSULTANT. The following designated CLIENT representatives shall be available on an on-call basis as required by CONSULTANT, and shall be called in the order listed herein. In the event the first listed representative cannot be contacted, the one listed second shall be called, and so on, until contact is made.

Contact's name	Contact's telephone
	(W) _____
_____	(H) _____
	(W) _____
_____	(H) _____

16. *Titles*

   a. The titles used in this AGREEMENT are for general reference only and are not part of the AGREEMENT. Parties to this AGREEMENT are advised to read each provision and rely on the guidance of legal counsel as necessary to help assure a complete understanding of all provisions and the obligations imposed through acceptance.

17. *Severability*

   a. CLIENT and CONSULTANT have entered into this AGREEMENT of their own free will, to communicate to one another mutual understandings and responsibilities. Any element of this AGREEMENT later held to violate a law or regulation shall be deemed void, and all remaining provisions shall continue in force. However, CLIENT and CONSULTANT will in good faith attempt to replace an invalid or unenforceable provision with one that is valid and enforceable, and which comes as close as possible to expressing the intent of the original provision.

18. *Integration*

   a. This AGREEMENT comprises a final and complete repository of understandings between CLIENT and CONSULTANT. It supercedes all prior or contemporaneous communications, representations, or agreements, whether oral or written, relating to the subject matter of this AGREEMENT. Each party has advised the other to read this document thoroughly before accepting it, to help ensure that it accurately conveys meanings and intents. Acceptance of this AGREEMENT as provided for below signifies that each party has read the document thoroughly and has had any questions or concerns completely explained by independent counsel and is satisfied. CLIENT and CONSULTANT agree that modifications to this AGREEMENT shall not be binding unless made in writing and signed by an authorized representative of each party.

19. *Survival*

   a. All obligations arising prior to the termination of this AGREEMENT and all provisions of this AGREEMENT allocating responsibility or liability between CLIENT and CONSULTANT shall survive the completion of the services hereunder and the termination of this AGREEMENT.

20. *Acceptance*

   a. The signatories below represent that they are duly authorized to represent the entities for whom they accept this AGREEMENT; that they have read this AGREEMENT and understand it in full; that they are fully prepared to abide by all elements of this AGREEMENT; and that to all these understandings they indicate their consent by their signatures below:

Accepted for client   Accepted for consultant

Date   Date

Witness   Witness

Chapter 13

Dealing with Contractors

Introduction

Many property managers can cite stories of how they have been stung by contractors over the years. Many contractors can tell stories about how they have been stung by property managers. In fact, so many such stories exist, it sometimes seems that entering into a contractual relationship is almost like entering into a boxing ring. That should not be the case.

The purpose of a contract is to set forth what the work entails, and to identify the terms and conditions parties of the contract agree to. It is penny-wise and pound-foolish to use a contract as though it were a trap. All you should seek is what you are willing to pay for, and for the most part, to derive maximum economy, you should seek and be willing to pay for maximum quality.

Selecting the Approach

How will you retain a contractor? by bidding? There are alternatives, and you should be aware of them. These alternatives are most valuable when what you seek may vary from contractor to contractor. In other words, bidding is particularly appropriate when you know exactly what you want, and all bidders will deliver the same thing, such as a new Chevrolet with specified options. However, where there is room for interpretation or judgment, bidding may not be the best, because the product will vary.

Negotiation

A negotiated contract often is developed with one contractor. Typically, the contractor involved is a firm headed by someone you know or have dealt with for many years, and whose judgment you can trust. Nonetheless, a negotiated contract presupposes you know what a reasonable price is. If you do not, then you need to rely on someone else with experience.

Whenever design and construction or reconstruction are involved, participation of the contractor can be a valuable benefit. It permits the contractor to evaluate design during its development, and to identify any potential errors or omissions, ambiguities or inconsistencies. Ideally, this occurs when the contractor is responsible for both design and construction (turnkey or design/build), but this approach can create problems. Key among the problems is the fact that the architect or engineer involved owes a principal duty to the client or employer, namely, the contractor.

When you determine that a negotiated approach may be most worthwhile, and when your own experience or the ability to rely on a consultant give you important oversight capability, selection of the contractor becomes a key issue. The approach suggested is virtually the same as that used for retaining consultants. Invite all eligible firms to submit expressions of interest and statements of qualifications. Speak with others for whom the contractors have worked. A company selects that firm which is best, all things considered.

Bidding

Bidding is appropriate only when you can be reasonably certain that all contractors will produce the same results, or when you at least have specifications so complete that the contractor's work product can be easily evaluated. Unfortunately, this can sometimes be easier said than done. No matter what the occupation or profession, some individuals and firms seem determined to increase their profits by doing something that's just not right, such as using inferior products or omitting steps in a process because they can be hidden.

Do not open the bidding to one and all. Prequalify bidders by asking all to submit statements of qualification and by asking each to identify their five most recent projects. You may also ask them to identify work in progress, for example, something being painted or paved, or a property where ongoing services are being provided (swimming-pool management or custodial management, for example). Speak with the property managers involved. How satisfied are they? What quality of work is being provided? Is the contractor quick to follow up on complaints? Once you are satisfied that a contractor is reputable, then—and only then—allow the firm to participate in the bidding.

Preparations for the Bidding Process

Developing the work specification

Development of the work specification is essential. The more detailed it is, the less room there is for misunderstanding, and the more likely it is that the contractors will be bidding on the same specifications, permitting an apples-to-apples comparison.

The simplest method of handling this work is to rely on a consultant who can develop comprehensive bid specifications, prequalify contractors, oversee the bidding, and monitor construction.

In some cases, property managers rely on contractors to also serve as their consultants. Most contractors can provide a work specification, as well as the inspection and analysis on which the work specification is based. Because the contractors realize that the specification they develop is likely to be used in soliciting bids from themselves and from their competition, each is likely to develop the specification in a manner which tends to favor that contractor's own particular way of doing things, the products preferred, and so on. This is natural; contractors who did it any other way would not stay in business too long. However, this does not prevent you from asking each interested contractor to suggest alternatives and to price each one. Each such alternative should be fully explained to indicate why it is better, or at least as good as whatever is included in the specification.

Obviously, it would be a waste of time to deal with several contractors during the inspection and specification development stage. Select one contractor—the best, most reputable, and most experienced you know of—to provide assistance. If you do not already have a relationship with such a contractor, use procedures suggested for selecting a consultant to identify the most reputable, experienced contractor you can.

Note that performance specifications can be obtained from a number of additional sources, including appropriate associations and peers. Books also contain such specifications. But be advised that a generally applicable performance specification is not likely to fit your needs precisely, and thus can create more problems than it is worth. Use such models exactly as they are intended; as models for the development of a specification that reflects *exactly* the conditions you are dealing with, and the service you want.

Prebid review

As part of the process, you should require each prospective bidder to review the property involved. A bidder who does not come to the property is usually going to base the bid on assumptions, and this can lead to problems. Indicate what a contractor needs to do in order to gain access to the property so that the contractor can perform the inspection. You may want one person to have authority on site to report who, in fact, did visit the property. Simultaneously, you can conduct (or have conducted) a tour of the property (or permanent elements of it) at a certain time, starting from a certain place.

Prebid conference

Particularly when construction is involved, when questions may exist, or when the work is somewhat complex, it may be wise to conduct a prebid conference. At this time, you or your consultant can answer any questions that arise, typically technical questions. These questions need answers, of course, and they should be somehow inserted into contract documents. In some cases it is best to conduct a prebid tour of the facilities at a given time and, immediately following, hold the prebid conference.

Prepare bidding documents

The bidding documents typically consist of an unsigned contract, sometimes accompanied by plans and specifications, as when construction is involved, or at least by drawings to indicate the areas of work. Again, the goal is not to "snooker" the other party. Instead, the purpose is full communication, so that there are no nasty surprises later on.

Some people like to believe that written contracts are unnecessary; a handshake will do. In fact, a handshake *will* do to create a contract. The problem is, it's not a good contract, since everything is based on trust and one another's recollections of what was said. As long as problems do not develop, everything is fine. However, problems can lead to disputes, especially when third parties are involved, and that can lead to serious troubles.

In some cases, the work is needed on a regular basis, but the projects tend to be small. It would be a tremendous "pain" to create a new contract for each engagement. In such cases, an annual "open-ended" contract would be suitable. In fact, such contracts can be entered into with a number of contractors, including those who offer the same services, so that a phone call is all that is needed to activate the agreement for a specific project.

In all cases, have an attorney review any contract before you sign it or, when it is one you develop or issue, before you issue it. This does not mean that the attorney should turn it into "legalese." However, you do want some assurance that the contract does not have any significant legal loopholes or shortcomings.

Beware of model contracts that have been developed by associations on behalf of their members. Typically, such contracts are biased in favor of the contractor. For the same reason, beware of contracts prepared by the contractor. The reasons are, or certainly should be, understandable. In fact, they are so understandable that the law presupposes that the party that develops the contract will bias it in favor of that party. For that reason, when a question of contract interpretation arises, courts will almost invariably decide *against* the party that drafted the agreement.

Owner or Property Manager/Contractor
Model Contract

Elements of a model contract are given in this section. Most of the provisions are sometimes referred to as "boiler plate," because they are used so frequently for a variety of contractor needs. *Never use a boiler plate* without first performing a close review to assure adequacy, given the need to effect changes over time and to consider the specific nature of each project. Note, also, that some of the provisions may be mutually exclusive, or may not be consistent with the work specification. *Review your specifications closely for consistency.* Do your best to eliminate any inconsistencies, ambiguities, errors, and omissions. Your goal, and the contractor's, should be an effective agreement that leaves nothing to assumptions. Assumptions often are the root cause of disputes. Disputes benefit no one except those retained to resolve them.

Note that in this model certain numbers, such as those to indicate amounts of insurance coverage, are shown parenthetically. These are highly variable; the preferences of property owners, property management firms, and others, as well as prevailing market conditions, should be reviewed with particular care.

You should not expect any source of assistance—other than an attorney—to provide help with anything except the prescriptive work specification. *Under no circumstances should an agreement be issued or signed until after an attorney has reviewed it in full.*

The following discussion reviews some of the provisions included in the model.

General

General information essentially serves to describe the general circumstances involved. The clause used in the model is as follows.

---

1. *General*
   a. Work is to be done at [location] [for systems and equipment] [in areas] designated on attached drawing(s). The building involved is owned by [name of owner] and is managed by [name of company]. [Name of property manager]—the PROPERTY MANAGER—will serve as the approving agent for the AGREEMENT. Work shall include all labor, materials, equipment, and supplies necessary to perform the work required in a condition suitable to PROPERTY MANAGER and CONTRACTOR during that period beginning [date] and ending [date].

It is recommended strongly that, whenever applicable, drawings be included to indicate exactly where the work is to be performed. Even though you and the person with whom you discuss the contract may have a crystal-clear understanding of what is needed, where and when, you probably will not be on hand to oversee the work, and the persons representing the contractor will probably be in the same position. In other words, you want to do your best to "idiot-proof" the agreement, so there can be no doubt as to what it is that has been agreed to.

The work

"The work" comprises the work specification, which can either be included in the contract or, as is more common, added as an appendix to the agreement, becoming part of it in that manner.

Two types of work specifications can be applied. One is a performance specification, where the contract identifies the results desired. This approach is not generally recommended, because it leaves too much up to the contractor. This is not to say that the contractor will attempt to cheat. It simply means that the contractor may in all good faith do something or use something that the property manager was not anticipating and objects to. By providing a highly definitive work specification, which identifies exactly what will be done *and* the results to be obtained, little is left to the imagination.

The contractor should be advised (in writing) to submit alternatives and to identify options and the prices for them. In addition, depending on the nature of the work, it can be wise to require the contractor to identify rates for personnel, equipment, and material that may be required to complete the work after changed conditions are discovered. Appropriate wording for these conditions might include the following.

---

2. *The work*

    a. The work to be provided is detailed in the work specification appended hereto, and made a part of this AGREEMENT. CONTRACTOR represents that CONTRACTOR is expert in the type of work being requested, and has applied this expertise in review of the work specification. CONTRACTOR further represents that the work specification is complete in every detail for the type of results which are desired, and—if not—that CONTRACTOR has identified any errors, omissions, inconsistencies, or ambiguities it has discovered. In addition, CONTRACTOR shall identify any alternative approaches of which CONTRACTOR is aware, as well as optional activities and, for each, the benefits to be derived, additional costs, and such other factors of which PROPERTY MANAGER should be aware in order to make an effective decision. To the extent that additional work not now foreseen is necessary, it shall be performed only with PROPERTY MANAGER's approval, at the rates indicated below:

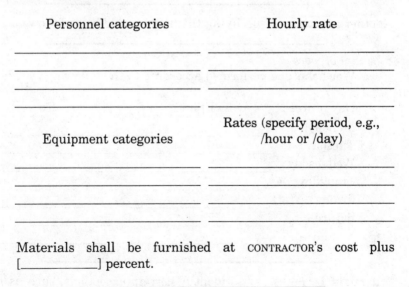

Personnel categories   Hourly rate

Equipment categories   Rates (specify period, e.g., /hour or /day)

Materials shall be furnished at CONTRACTOR's cost plus [_____] percent.

Note: Whenever safety aspects are involved, or dislocations of some sort, it would be appropriate to either specify performance aspects of the work, or require the contractor to submit a plan for review. In other words, if barricades are needed in a parking lot, what about the parking situation? You do not want to get into the situation of having to say, "This approach isn't acceptable because it will inconvenience shoppers too much," only to hear, "Well, we can do it another way, but we hadn't contemplated that and it's a lot more expensive." Especially when safety issues are involved, do *not* tell the contractor what to do. The contractor should be fully in charge of the means, methods, and sequences of the work and all safety aspects. If you specify who is to take care of safety issues, you—not the contractor—could be liable in the event of any problems.

Hours of work

Hours of work should specify the days of the week during which the work can be performed, and the times of day. This information can be included in the work specification, or in the general terms and conditions, as follows.

---

3. *Hours of work*
    a. Work shall be performed [Monday through Friday] from [9:00 A.M. to 4:30 P.M.], and [Saturday] from [10:00 A.M. to 3:00 P.M.].

Another approach to specifying the hours would be as follows.

---

3. *Hours of work*
    a. Work shall be performed according to the following schedule:

Day of week	From	To
Monday		
Tuesday		
Wednesday		
Thursday		
Friday		
Saturday		
Sunday		

It might be necessary to identify certain exceptions, such as holidays, and it may be appropriate, too, to indicate whether all work or some work may not begin before the start time. For example, it may be permissible for a paving contractor to come in early to set up barricades and then hold back on the noisier work until later.

Personnel standards

Generally speaking, the property manager needs the flexibility to have a contractor's worker thrown off the job if the individual is not satisfactory for any reason. A typical reason might be foolishness on the job, or behavior that indicates the worker is intoxicated. Appearance may also be a factor, especially in those cases where image is important. Particularly when workers have access to office or residential spaces, it may be appropriate, for example, to require the contractor to have a drug-testing program in effect, or to screen the backgrounds of employees. Such activity reduces the chances of something going wrong in those respects, and should a negative outcome ensue nonetheless, the provision indicates the owner's or property manager's reasonable efforts to prevent it.

Commonly used language for personnel standards is as follows.

---

4. *Personnel standards*
    a. All work shall be performed by personnel who shall be properly trained and otherwise qualified to perform assigned tasks.
    b. All personnel shall be neat and shall conduct their work in a professional manner with minimal disturbance to the contracting party. If any of CONTRACTOR's personnel are not satisfactory to OWNER or PROPERTY MANAGER, CONTRACTOR shall replace such personnel with those who are satisfactory.
    c. CONTRACTOR shall use all reasonable care, consistent with CONTRACTOR's rights to manage and control the operation, not to employ any persons or use any labor, or use or have any equipment or permit any condition to exist, which shall or may cause or be conducive to any labor complaints, troubles, disputes, or controversies at OWNER's place of business, or which interfere or are likely to interfere with the operation of the business.
    d. CONTRACTOR shall immediately give such notice to PROPERTY MANAGER, to be followed by written progress reports as shall be reasonably necessary to advise PROPERTY MANAGER of any and all impending or existing labor complaints, trouble, disputes, or controversies and the progress thereof that CONTRACTOR believes may interfere with the operation of the business. CONTRACTOR shall exert a best effort to resolve any such complaint, trouble, dispute, or controversy.
    e. CONTRACTOR shall oversee and obey (and compel CONTRACTOR's officers, employees, guests, invitees, and those doing business with CONTRACTOR to observe and obey) the rules and regulations of OWNER and such further reasonable rules and regulations which may from time to time during the effective period of this

AGREEMENT be promulgated by OWNER for reasons of safety, health, preservation of property, or maintenance of a good and orderly appearance of the area.

Supervision, observation, and inspection

Particularly when somewhat complex work is involved, such as that based upon plans and specifications prepared by a design professional, construction monitoring is called for. Monitoring involves a representative of the owner or property manager watching the contractor, to determine whether or not plans and specifications are being adhered to. The following language often is used.

5. *Supervision, observation, and inspection*
   a. CONTRACTOR shall furnish qualified supervision to oversee all operations.
   b. OWNER or PROPERTY MANAGER shall have the right at all times to examine or have examined the supplies, materials, and equipment used by CONTRACTOR and to observe the operations of CONTRACTOR, CONTRACTOR's agents, servants, and employees, and to do any act or thing which OWNER may be obligated or have the right to do under this AGREEMENT.
   c. CONTRACTOR agrees to give PROPERTY MANAGER a minimum of [forty-eight (48)] hours' notice of the inspection of CONTRACTOR's supervisor, so OWNER or PROPERTY MANAGER may be present.

Equipment

It should be up to the contractor to determine what type of equipment is needed, and to help ensure that it can perform as needed. If the property manager is in the position of evaluating the equipment, then the property manager may have to bear a penalty if the equipment does not function as it should. As such, the contract should be clear that, in the event of any equipment problems, the contractor would have to correct them at the contractor's expense.

6. *Equipment*
   a. CONTRACTOR shall furnish all equipment necessary to perform the work in accordance with the work specification and whatever governmental and other codes and standards may apply. CONTRACTOR warrants that all equipment will be of such type as

to cause no hazard or danger reasonably foreseeable. CONTRACTOR agrees to be solely responsible for the adequacy of all equipment.

Materials and supplies

In certain operations, the accuracy of materials and supplies is essential. Contractors may propose "or equals" when various brand-name products are specified. The problem with "or equals" is that they seldom are truly equal, and the deficiencies involved may not be discovered for months or even years after the operation is complete. This is one of the reasons why monitoring of the contractor's work can be important (especially when contractors are selected on the basis of low bid), and why it is prudent to require bidders to identify any alternatives, as follows.

---

7. *Materials and supplies*
   a. CONTRACTOR shall employ only those materials and supplies identified in the work specification. CONTRACTOR shall not deviate from specifications unless OWNER or PROPERTY MANAGER first is apprised of the proposed alternate, and approves such alternate after having examined it. If testing or any other type of analysis is required to verify acceptability, CONTRACTOR shall bear the cost of such analysis.

Licenses and permits

The contractor should be responsible for whatever licenses the contractor must have, and should also be responsible for obtaining permits. The permitting process itself can be a problem in some areas and, for that reason, the contractor might ask or otherwise seek to have the owner or property manager obtain the permit. In some cases, it may be suggested that work requiring a permit be performed without one. Such suggestions always should be rejected out of hand. Consider the following language, and be sure that a mechanism is in place to ensure that licenses and permits are provided as required.

---

8. *Licenses and permits*
   a. CONTRACTOR confirms that CONTRACTOR has all necessary licenses and standard operating permits to perform the work herein de-

scribed, such licenses and permits consisting at least, but not necessarily entirely, of the following:

[insert listing]

As confirmation thereof, CONTRACTOR shall submit copies of said licenses and permits and such others as may apply with this bid.

b. CONTRACTOR warrants that all permits required to comply with paragraph c, following, will be obtained in a timely manner, and that copies of same will be provided to OWNER or PROPERTY MANAGER or duly authorized on-site management representative before operations requiring such permits are commenced.

c. CONTRACTOR expressly warrants that CONTRACTOR shall be responsible for abiding by all applicable codes, regulations, standards, etc., which may be required by all applicable local, state, and federal jurisdictions and their respective agencies, offices, bureaus, and other administrative/regulatory entities.

It should be recognized that the contractor usually is not required to abide by various elements of the building code when the work has been designed by a party other than the contractor, and the contractor is simply following the plans and specifications prepared by others.

Insurance

Insurance is an essential element of risk management. It is not enough to simply require the contractor to be insured. It also is essential to verify the coverage. The contractor should be required to submit certificates of coverage, and the adequacy of those certificates should probably be evaluated, too, especially when particularly risky work is involved, such as when pesticides are being used.

How much coverage is sufficient? Your own insurance agent should be able to give you some suggestions. Also consider common limits that prevail in the industry, something that can be determined by speaking with contractors and peers.

Note: As important as insurance is, it typically has a number of loopholes. Even when it does not, however, having to seek protection through insurance indicates that something significant has gone wrong on the project, and, undoubtedly, a number of people will have been inconvenienced, aggravated, and otherwise perturbed. In short, do not rely on insurance as a substitute for quality control. High-quality performance of the work is among the most significant loss preventives of all.

9. *Insurance*
   a. CONTRACTOR shall secure, pay the premiums for, and keep in force until the expiration of this AGREEMENT adequate insurance as provided below. Such insurance is to specifically include liability assumed by CONTRACTOR under this AGREEMENT.
      (1) Appropriate bodily injury insurance, with limits of not less than [one million dollars ($1,000,000)] for each person and [one million dollars ($1,000,000)] for each accident.
      (2) Workers' compensation insurance as required by local and/or state jurisdiction(s).
      (3) Property damage liability insurance with a limit of not less than [one million dollars ($1,000,000)] for each accident.
      (4) Umbrella general liability insurance with a limit of not less than [five million dollars ($5,000,000)].
      (5) If automotive equipment is used in the operation, automobile bodily injury insurance with limits of not less than [two hundred fifty thousand dollars ($250,000)] for each person and [five hundred thousand dollars ($500,000)] for each accident, and property damage liability insurance, with limits of not less than [one hundred thousand dollars ($100,000)] for each accident, and medical pay coverage of [ten thousand dollars ($10,000)] regardless of fault.
   b. All policies for liability protection, bodily injury, or property damage shall include [name of owner] and [name of property management firm] as additional insureds as respects operations under this contract.

      [Owner's name]   [Property management company's name]

      [Owner's address] [Property management company's address]

   c. A certificate of insurance for workers' compensation and public liability together with a properly executed endorsement for cancellation notice shall be furnished as stipulated in the preceding paragraph. The certificate shall be delivered to PROPERTY MANAGER. The insurance companies providing the above coverage shall be satisfactory to OWNER and PROPERTY MANAGER.
   d. Notice of any policy change shall be furnished to PROPERTY MANAGER within [seventy-two (72)] hours of such change being made.

Indemnification

For an indemnification to be worthwhile, it must be reasonable. The reasonableness of an indemnification generally is determined by tort law in the state where the contract will be enforced. In some cases, a contractor may be held liable only to the extent that the contractor's negligence resulted in a claim. In others, the contractor can be liable for more than a fair share, depending on the wording used. Generally speaking, whenever a contractor could be required to pay for the negligence of others, the wording of the indemnification must make such liability absolutely clear. Again, any type of "sneaky" wording used generally will be interpreted against the party that drafted it, making it self-defeating.

---

10. *Indemnification*

   a. To the maximum extent permitted by law, CONTRACTOR agrees to indemnify, hold harmless, and defend OWNER, PROPERTY MANAGER, and property management firm, their officers, employees, agents, heirs, and assigns, from and against any and all claims or damages arising from CONTRACTOR's performance of this AGREEMENT, as well as acts committed during the course of this AGREEMENT by any of CONTRACTOR's officers, employees, guests, invitees, and those doing business with CONTRACTOR.

Performance bond or retainage

Most government agencies insist on a performance bond and are willing to pay the relatively high price involved. Most of those in the private sector prefer not to pay the cost of a performance bond. As an alternative, some rely on a retainage agreement; others rely on neither. A typical retainage provision would read as follows.

---

11. *Retainage*

   a. OWNER shall retain [ten percent (10%)] of each payment requested by CONTRACTOR to help assure sufficient available monies for fully satisfactory completion of the work. All retainage, less any amounts expended therefrom in accordance with [paragraph _____] shall be provided to CONTRACTOR within [thirty (30)] days of final inspection and approval by PROPERTY MANAGER.

Generally speaking, a retainage provision is inappropriate for ongoing services, such as pest control, custodial management, or water treatment. In those cases, it usually is sufficient to include a payment-withholding clause in payment provisions, such that the owner or property manager can withhold payment for any services whose adequacy is in dispute.

Guarantee

Various types of guarantees can be applied, as described in preceding chapters. The following is a general type of guarantee relating to services. More specificity usually is appropriate.

---

12. *Guarantee*
    a. CONTRACTOR warrants that CONTRACTOR is fully competent and equipped to perform the work required in a professional manner, fully consistent with OWNER's objectives, the standard of care generally prevailing for such work, and all applicable standards. Accordingly, should a problem with such work occur during the course of this AGREEMENT or within [sixty (60)] calendar days after its expiration, and should it be shown that the cause of such problem is faulty work or CONTRACTOR-provided materials, CONTRACTOR shall repair such problem fully at CONTRACTOR's own expense.

Board involvement

In the case of condominium communities, cooperatives, and homeowner associations, the contractor may have to make a presentation to the board of directors, or, in some instances, members of the board or of the community may participate in some of the work. This is most common in the case of grounds care, but is not limited to that. A clause advising the contractor is appropriate, and the following may be worthwhile.

---

13. *Board involvement*
    a. CONTRACTOR agrees to attend at least one meeting of the [condominium's] [cooperative's] [homeowner association's] board of directors to discuss, plan, and coordinate the services to be provided by CONTRACTOR.

Duration of contract

The duration of the contract should be spelled out specifically. The reference given in general information (paragraph 1) normally is not specific enough. The following might do.

14. *Duration of contract*
    a. This CONTRACT will go into effect at [_____A.M. or P.M.]
       on [day of the week, month, date, year], and shall conclude im-
       mediately after [_____A.M. or P.M.], on [day of the week,
       month, date, year].

Contract extension

Particularly when the services provided are ongoing, such as water
treatment or custodial management, an automatic contract extension
provision can be worthwhile.

15. *Contract extension*
    a. This AGREEMENT shall automatically be extended after its expi-
       ration for a period of [one month] [one year] providing no in-
       crease in charges is involved. CONTRACTOR shall give [sixty (60)]
       days' prior notice to PROPERTY MANAGER in the event that the
       AGREEMENT is to be automatically extended, or if any increased
       charges will be required. Such written notice shall be given to
       PROPERTY MANAGER at: [name of property management firm,
       address].

Contract termination

Either party should have the right to terminate the agreement, provided the other party has adequate notice, permitting effective planning. A typical termination clause reads as follows.

16. *Contract termination*
    a. Either party shall have the right to terminate this AGREEMENT
       without penalty of any kind provided [ninety (90)] days' writ-
       ten notice is given. If CONTRACTOR wishes to effect such termi-
       nation, CONTRACTOR shall do so by contacting PROPERTY MANAGER
       at: [name of property management firm, address].
           If PROPERTY MANAGER wishes to effect such termination, PROP-
       ERTY MANAGER shall do so by contacting CONTRACTOR at: [name of
       contractor's firm, address], attention: [_____].

Payment

A variety of payment provisions can be used. In the case of specific services, such as that for asphalt paving, payment may be made in thirds, with one-third being provided upon signing of the contract, another one-third when the work is halfway done, and one-third at the conclusion. Retainage provisions may also apply, and should be coordinated. In the case of ongoing services, such as water treatment, monthly payments may be required.

It is important to have a good understanding about payment. If the property manager intends to drag out payment, and use the contractor as a source of a loan, the property manager has to expect to pay for this additional service, since the contractor will have to pay for a loan, or will lose use of money that otherwise should be in the contractor's bank account. In short, fair is fair. Establish reasonable provisions and abide by them.

Commonly used payment provisions are as follows. Note that subparagraph c should be coordinated with whatever retainage provisions are included.

---

17. *Payment*
    a. Payment will be made in [number] [equal] payments. CONTRACTOR will send bill to PROPERTY MANAGER at: [name of property management firm, address]. Such bill will be sent on the [first, fifteenth, last, etc.] day of the month of service and shall be paid, subject to retainage provisions, within [thirty (30)] days, subject to restrictions in subparagraphs b and c, below.
    b. CONTRACTOR shall pay all applicable taxes, including sales tax on materials supplied.
    c. CONTRACTOR agrees that OWNER or PROPERTY MANAGER may withhold payment to CONTRACTOR when OWNER's property is damaged or destroyed by poor performance or defective equipment or materials used by CONTRACTOR, or for unsatisfactory performance under this AGREEMENT. CONTRACTOR also agrees that CONTRACTOR shall be liable to OWNER for actual damages for replacement or repair of property, materials, or services caused by this damage or destruction of OWNER's property, or for unsatisfactory performance.

Additional provisions may be appropriate, depending on the nature of the services being obtained. For example, it is not uncommon for contracts for pool management to include the following provisions.

---

    d. CONTRACTOR shall furnish as an addendum to CONTRACTOR's submission a list of unit rates indicating the cost of operating and maintaining the pool on days additional to those enumerated in the work specification, as well as for providing additional categories of personnel for any given day.

    e. In the event that the pool must be closed to perform repairs or for any cause other than action or inaction on the part of CONTRACTOR, CONTRACTOR shall refund to OWNER the sum of [_____] dollars for each consecutive day of closing beyond the [third].

    f. In the event CONTRACTOR is required to pay personnel more than anticipated as a consequence of a change in the minimum wage law, or if CONTRACTOR is otherwise obligated to assume more overhead or expense as a consequence of circumstances CONTRACTOR was powerless to control and could not have reasonably predicted, this AGREEMENT shall be adjusted to recognize CONTRACTOR's additional costs, which were unforeseeable at the time this AGREEMENT was entered into.

Financing

As an inducement to attract customers, some contractors provide financing for a project. If one or more contractors offer this, or if it is an important consideration, the following language may be applicable.

---

18. *Financing*

    a. CONTRACTOR agrees to finance the cost of this project, provided that an amount equivalent to [thirty percent (30%)] of the contract price is paid to CONTRACTOR within [thirty (30)] days of project completion. The balance due shall be paid in [six (6)] consecutive monthly installments, each comprising [eleven and two-thirds percent (11.67%)] of the full price of the work performed less the down payment, plus interest of [thirteen percent (13%)], such payments to commence within [sixty (60)] days of project completion. As an example, assuming a contract and total project cost of [_____] dollars, the schedule should be:

	Date	Amount
Project completion	March 31, 19__	$_____
Down payment	April 30, 19__	$_____
1st monthly payment	May 31, 19__	$_____
2nd monthly payment	June 30, 19__	$_____
3rd monthly payment	July 31, 19__	$_____
4th monthly payment	Aug. 31, 19__	$_____
5th monthly payment	Sept. 30, 19__.	$_____
Final payment	Oct. 31, 19__	$_____

Change orders

Change orders can be covered by a separate paragraph. It is important that all change orders be approved *in writing*. Change orders are a principal source of conflicts, many of which could be avoided through better communication. Usually it is effective to permit change orders to be signed and transmitted via facsimile. In that way, as soon as the contractor's representative discovers the need for a change order, the individual can call the property manager to discuss the matter, then issue a written change order by fax to the property manager, who then signs the faxed change order and faxes it back to the contractor's representative in the field.

19. *Change orders*
   a. All change orders shall be described in writing, and each must be approved by the signature of [owner's consultant] [property manager]. Requests for change-order payments based on additional work not approved by the [owner's consultant] [property manager] shall not be honored. OWNER will honor change orders that are sent by facsimile to [owner's consultant] [property manager], signed by [owner's consultant] [property manager], and returned to CONTRACTOR by facsimile.

Delays

More often than not, timely completion of the work is an important consideration. To create an inducement for timely completion, many contracts include a provision for delay damages. In the clause that follows, provision is made to account for delays that the contractor experiences as a consequence of the owner's actions or inactions, as well as delays that are occasioned by acts of God. This approach is considered fair. One-sided contracts that require the contractor to bear all cost of delays are not uncommon. Generally speaking, however, they can be costly, since astute contractors must include in the contract price the cost of such contingencies should they materialize.

---

20. *Delay damages*
    a. CONTRACTOR warrants that CONTRACTOR has the personnel, equipment, materials, and supplies necessary to begin this work within [＿＿＿＿＿] days after this contract shall be placed into effect. CONTRACTOR shall submit to PROPERTY MANAGER in writing, by no later than [＿＿＿＿＿] days prior to commencing work, CONTRACTOR's intended schedule for work performance and attendant requirements for owner/management assistance. The actual cost of any delays caused by OWNER shall be paid by OWNER within [three (3)] days of CONTRACTOR's presentation of written verification of each such cost. As to delays caused by CONTRACTOR, CONTRACTOR shall pay [＿＿＿＿＿] dollars per day for each day completion is delayed beyond the date identified above, [except that the completion date shall be extended by two days for each one day lost due to circumstances beyond contractor's control, to account for scheduling difficulties which contractor will likely experience as a result of unanticipated delays.] In the event such unanticipated delays shall be caused by circumstances over which OWNER also has no control, e.g., inclement weather, OWNER shall pay to contractor [fifty percent (50%)] of CONTRACTOR's actual unanticipated additional costs for materials.

Plan and project review

If a plan and project review clause is not included as part of the overall language used in the work specification (paragraph 2), it should be set out separately, as indicated below. The purpose for this is to put the contractor on notice that "low balling" or "buying in" will not be acceptable. Some contractors use this unfortunate tactic by identifying possible errors or omissions in the contract documents, and bidding low to win the contract, then imposing costly change orders later. Contractors with a reputation for that kind of activity should not be invited to bid.

21. *Plan and project review*

    a. CONTRACTOR warrants that CONTRACTOR is expert and fully experienced in all aspects of the work involved, has personally inspected all areas where work is to be performed, and has personally reviewed work specifications. Based on this expertise, experience, and review, CONTRACTOR affirms that, to the best of CONTRACTOR's knowledge, work specifications are complete in every detail and shall, when executed, provide results which OWNER seeks, except as may be noted by CONTRACTOR in CONTRACTOR's submission.

Curing a breach

It is not uncommon for one party to accuse the other of breaching certain provisions of the contract. It is worthwhile therefore to establish provisions for curing the breach, since completing the work usually is in the best interest of all parties. The following language may be of value.

22. *Curing a breach*

    a. In the event either party believes that the other has committed a material breach of this AGREEMENT, the party maintaining such a belief shall issue a termination notice to the other, identifying the facts as perceived, and both parties shall bargain in good faith to cure the causes for termination as stated in the termination notice. If such a cure can be effected prior to the date by which termination otherwise would be effective, both parties shall commit their understanding to writing, and termination shall not become effective. If in curing an actual or alleged breach either party shall waive any rights otherwise inuring to the party by virtue of this AGREEMENT, such waiver shall not be construed to in any way affect future application of the provision involved or any other provision.

Dispute resolution

As already noted, failure to identify a dispute resolution mechanism can result in litigation becoming the only option. Alternative dispute resolution (ADR) can provide much more effective results, since it typically can be put into effect immediately, and can lead to a satisfactory resolution, often without creating the ill will commonly associated with litigation. The Med/Arb 2 approach discussed earlier and explained fully in Appendix A is considered highly effective and is referenced in the provision below.

---

23. *Dispute resolution*
    a. Any disputes arising out of this AGREEMENT shall be resolved according to procedures developed for [Med/Arb 2, appended to and made a part of this AGREEMENT. The individual selected to mediate such disputes is _____ . The individual selected to arbitrate disputes which cannot be resolved by mediator is _____ .]

Techniques for apportioning the cost of dispute resolution also should be indicated. When an ADR method is employed, it is common to require the neutral (namely, the mediator or the arbitrator) to indicate who pays how much. A technique that is sometimes used when litigation is involved is indicated below. It requires the losing party to pay for the winner's cost of defense. This provision is not enforceable in all states.

---

24. *Recovery of dispute resolution costs*
    a. In the event that legal action is brought by either party against the other, the prevailing party shall be reimbursed by the other for the prevailing party's legal costs, in addition to whatever other judgments or settlement sums, if any, may be due. Such legal costs shall include, but not be limited to, reasonable attorney's fees, court costs, expert witness fees, and other documented expenses.

Another approach is the following.

---

24. *Recovery of dispute resolution costs*
    a. The costs of dispute resolution shall be apportioned by the neutral.

Integration

Integration is a term applied to a provision that makes it clear that the contract contains all understandings. Any oral agreements entered into before the contract was developed or discussed, or during the contract closing, do *not* apply, unless both parties want them to. A typical integration clause is as follows.

25. *Integration*

    a. This AGREEMENT comprises a final and complete repository of understandings between OWNER and CONTRACTOR. It supercedes all prior or contemporaneous communications, representations, or agreements, whether oral or written, relating to the subject matter of this AGREEMENT. Each party has advised the other to read this document thoroughly before accepting it, to help ensure that it accurately conveys meanings and intents. Acceptance of this AGREEMENT as provided for below signifies that each party has read the document thoroughly and has had any questions or concerns completely explained by independent counsel and is satisfied. OWNER and CONTRACTOR agree that modifications to this AGREEMENT shall not be binding unless made in writing and signed by an authorized representative of each party.

Project representatives

It is important for the owner to indicate who the project representatives are and how they can be contacted should the need arise. Consider the following clause.

26. *Project representatives*

    a. OWNER shall furnish representatives who shall make decisions on OWNER's behalf when requested to do so by CONTRACTOR. The following designated OWNER representatives shall be available on an on-call basis as required by CONTRACTOR, and shall be called in the order listed herein. In the event the first listed representative cannot be contacted, the one listed second shall be called, and so on, until contact is made.

Contact's name		Contact's telephone
_____	(W)	_____
	(H)	_____
_____	(W)	_____
	(H)	_____

Titles and severability

A provision on titles is somewhat common to help ensure that titles that are misleading are not grounds for a formal claim. Severability means that the voiding of one clause does not void the entire agreement. Two provisions covering these issues are as follows.

27. *Titles*

   a. The titles used in this AGREEMENT are for general reference only and are not part of the AGREEMENT. Parties to this AGREEMENT are advised to read each provision and rely on the guidance of legal counsel as necessary to help assure a complete understanding of all provisions and the obligations imposed through acceptance.

28. *Severability*

   a. OWNER and CONTRACTOR have entered into this AGREEMENT of their own free will, to communicate to one another mutual understandings and responsibilities. Any element of this AGREEMENT later held to violate a law or regulation shall be deemed void, and all remaining provisions shall continue in force. However, OWNER and CONTRACTOR will in good faith attempt to replace an invalid or unenforceable provision with one that is valid and enforceable, and which comes as close as possible to expressing the intent of the original provision.

Notices

A provision should be included to indicate the formal mechanism by which notices related to the contract should be given by one party to the other.

29. *Notices*

   a. Any notice given hereunder shall be deemed served when hand-delivered in writing to an officer or other duly appointed representative of the party to whom the notice is directed, or if sent by registered or certified mail to the business address identified in Section [_____] of this AGREEMENT.

Survival

A survival provision makes it clear that clauses relating to liability and related issues survive completion of the work. In fact, the contract actually stays in effect, at least in part, until the statute of limitations expires, unless other situations prevail. For example, in some states the contractor's obligations are over once the owner accepts the contractor's work.

30. *Survival*

    a. All obligations arising prior to the termination of this AGREE-
MENT and all provisions of this AGREEMENT allocating responsibility or liability between OWNER and CONTRACTOR shall survive
the completion of the services hereunder and the termination
of this AGREEMENT.

Interpretation

The manner in which a contract will be interpreted can depend on
prior court rulings, just as survival issues can depend on the laws or
prior decisions of individual states. More often than not, this is where
states laws apply. In other cases, however, differences can arise, especially when the owner is headquartered in one state, the contractor in
another, and the project is located in a third. In all cases, therefore, it
can be wise to include the following clause.

31. *Governing law*

    a. Unless otherwise provided in an addendum, the law of the
state of [_____] will govern the validity of this AGREE-
MENT, its interpretation and performance, and remedies for
contract breach or any other claims related to this AGREEMENT.

Acceptance

In submitting a bid or proposal, the contractor would sign the acceptance line. It would be up to the owner to sign an acceptance with the
offer that is accepted. A typical acceptance clause might read as follows.

32. *Acceptance*

    a. The signatories below represent that they are duly authorized
to represent the entities for whom they accept this AGREEMENT;
that they have read this AGREEMENT and understand it in full;
that they are fully prepared to abide by all elements of this
AGREEMENT; and that to all these understandings they indicate
their consent by their signatures below:

_____   _____
Accepted for owner   Accepted for contractor

Date _____   Date _____

Witness _____   Witness _____

Bid and prebid information

Bid and prebid information can be included with other terms and provisions, or it can be part of a general notice. Typical clauses follow.

33. *Prebid inspection*
    a. All bidders are [encouraged] [required] to visit all work sites prior to the prebid conference. [An inspection will be held on [day of week, month, date, year], commencing at [_____A.M. or P.M.], and leaving from the front lobby.] [Bidders can visit at any time prior to the prebid conference, from [_____A.M. or P.M.] to [_____A.M. or P.M.], [Monday through Saturday], by presenting a copy of this material to the building manager and providing other appropriate forms of identification.]
34. *Prebid conference*
    a. All bidders are encouraged to attend the prebid conference. This conference will be held as follows:

    Date: _____

    Time: _____

    Location: _____

    b. If you intend to attend the prebid conference, please complete the attached card and return to:

    Name: _____

    Adress: _____

35. *Delivery of bids*
    a. All bids shall be received in duplicate at the PROPERTY MANAGERS office.

    Name of property management firm: _____

Address: _____

Attention: _____

To be considered responsible, bid must be received no later than [time] on [day of week, month, day of month, year].

Med/Arb 2 Contract Provision

The following contract provision for Med/Arb 2 was provided courtesy of ASFE/The Association of Engineering Firms Practicing in the Geosciences. It is included, together with material about some 25 other types of alternative dispute resolution (ADR), in ASFE's landmark work *ADR: Alternative Dispute Resolution for the Construction Industry.**

Med/Arb 2

1.0. *Coverage*

    1.1. The parties agree to submit all claims, disputes, or controversies arising out of, or in relation to, the interpretation, application, or enforcement of this agreement, including dispute resolution procedures, to sequential mandatory discussion, mediation, and arbitration for resolution of all disputes before, and as a condition precedent, to self-help, arbitration, judicial action, or other remedies. This mandatory procedure will resolve each dispute within one hundred (100) calendar days. Any deadline falling on a federal holiday or weekend will be the next working day. Breach of this disputes process shall constitute a material breach of contract for which the aggrieved party may recover all costs, including attorney's fees, interest, and other expenses necessary to resolve the dispute through litigation.

        The obligation to discuss and then mediate and arbitrate covers all disputes arising from every aspect of the project

---

*Available from ASFE, 8811 Colesville Road, Suite G106, Silver Spring, Md. 20910.

to be built by the owner, including, but not limited to, design, engineering, bonding indemnification, labor, material, and services, and the acts or omissions of any related party for whom a party to this agreement may stand responsible.

The owner and all other parties to this agreement accept responsibility for: their agents; design professionals; architects; engineers; construction managers; sureties; indemnifiers; insurers; contractors (i.e., any person or organization that has an agreement to perform all or a portion of the project); subcontractors (i.e., any person or organization that has an agreement to perform a portion of the project); and materialmen (i.e., any person or organization that supplies materials or equipment for the project, but does not perform labor at the site).

1.2. As a condition for participation in the project and their agreements to perform labor or provide materials or services, the owner and all other parties to this agreement assume responsibility for binding their design professionals, architects, engineers, construction managers, contractors, subcontractors, and materialmen whose portion of the work or materials supplied amounts to $5000 or more, and all insurers and sureties to these mandatory discussion, mediation, and arbitration procedures. The parties specifically acknowledge in writing their acquiescence to this procedure by the express incorporation of mandatory discussion, mediation, and arbitration into each of their respective agreements concerning the project.

2.0. *Selection of a mediator*

2.1. Prior to the contract award for the design work, an independent mediator free of conflict of interest and financial bias shall be selected by mutual agreement of the owner, the prime design professional, the construction manager (if involved in the design phase), and any other parties, including the contractor or known potential contractors involved at the inception of the project. The parties shall share the independent mediator's fee and expense in accordance with paragraph 4.10. Later parties to a dispute may adopt the existing mediator or select a mediator in accordance with paragraph 2.2 of this contract clause.

2.2. In the event of failure to select a mediator under this process, when a party enters the project after selection of the original mediator, or in any instance when the selected mediator is unable or unwilling to serve and a replacement cannot be agreed upon by the parties, a mediator shall be chosen by the primary mediator if one exists. An impartial group such as [_____] shall appoint a mediator if the other methods leave a vacancy.

3.0. *Mandatory discussion*

    3.1. The parties agree to request, in writing, informal discussions directly between principals of each party, with authority to settle all disputes, of any dispute under this agreement immediately after a dispute arises. Discussions must be resolved within seven days by written agreement, or an impasse shall have occurred. All written notices must be evidenced by a document confirming receipt (certified mail or its equivalent) by the opposing party.

4.0. Mandatory mediation procedure

    4.1. By agreement, when a party refuses informal discussion, or after an impasse in discussions, any party, by written request to the mediator, shall initiate mandatory mediation of any dispute. The party initiating mandatory mediation shall furnish a copy of its written request to all interested parties. A party requesting mandatory mediation shall furnish copies of this request to all actually or potentially affected parties by registered mail or such other medium by which the receiving party acknowledges receipt in writing. The request must contain sufficient facts to notify the opposing party of the nature of the dispute. At the discretion of the mediator, failure to make such request may act as a waiver of claim. A request for mandatory mediation shall take precedence over and toll all other notice requirements for remedies concerning the same dispute, so that a party seeking mandatory mediation shall not be prejudiced by this request.

    4.2. The parties agree that the authority of the mediator shall extend to all disputes arising on or after the date of the parties' contract concerning the project.

    4.3. All documents, discussions, and other data developed during mediation shall remain confidential and not be disclosed by a mediator to any party not a party to the mediation.

    4.4. On application of any party, or in the mediator's own discretion, the mediator may involve any other party to this agreement, in privity of contract, by giving advance written notice of mandatory mediation proceedings to such other party.

    4.5. All parties specifically acknowledge that the mediator, in the mediator's own discretion or upon the application of any party included by the mediator, may meet individually with any party while excluding other parties as determined within the discretion of the mediator.

4.6. The parties may offer such evidence to the mediator as they desire and shall produce such additional evidence or testimony as the mediator may deem necessary. The mediator shall be the judge of admissibility of the evidence offered. Conformity to legal rules of evidence shall not be necessary. The mediator shall endeavor to facilitate the presentation of evidence in a manner that is fair to all parties in order to arrive at an expeditious resolution.

4.7. All parties agree to expedite all hearings and produce all relevant documents. The recommendation of the mediator shall be rendered as soon as possible after receipt of notice of dispute but always within thirty calendar days of the inception of informal discussions. Mandatory mediation shall be conducted in accord with the following schedule, intended as firm deadlines rather than goals, unless waived in writing by all affected parties. Within one week of request for mandatory mediation, the parties shall furnish all records of any form, on a confidential basis, to the mediator with a copy to the opposing party. The mediator shall confer, or meet with, all parties to hear arguments, take evidence, suggest a basis for settlement, and take other action to resolve the dispute. Within thirty days of the original request for informal discussion, the mediator shall make final settlement recommendations. This schedule shall be a maximum period for mediation of disputes. The parties agree to seek earlier resolution whenever possible.

4.8. All mediation hereunder shall be conducted in the City of [_____] pursuant to the laws of [_____].

4.9. Under special circumstances, the mediator may, at the mediator's discretion, consult specialists in engineering, construction, law, or accounting as a consultant to assist the mediator in arriving at a recommendation.

4.10. The owner shall pay the mediator's initial engagement fee, if any. Thereafter, mediator fee will be apportioned in accordance with the mediator's judgment among the parties to the dispute. The costs of recording and transcribing the testimony, the fees of any consultant(s) to the mediator, and such other costs incurred shall be apportioned equally, or as determined by the mediator, among all parties; except that the mediator may relieve any party of any obligations as to costs if the mediator determines that the opposing party's position was frivolous or the party was unnecessarily joined in the proceeding. In that case, such fees and costs shall be apportioned among the remaining parties to the proceedings.

4.11. A mediator may award interest (at a rate of [＿＿＿＿＿] percent), attorney's fees, accounting fees, consultant fees, and other appropriate relief to the aggrieved party when the opposing party's position appears frivolous.

4.12. A mediator may require a payment bond, letter of credit, or escrow of assets to assure compliance with any settlement reached through mandatory mediation.

5.0. *Mediator's decision*

5.1. After failure of mediation to resolve a dispute, in full or at all, any disputant shall have the right to request the mediator to unilaterally decide all unresolved issues. The mediator and all other parties enjoined in the process shall then have three calendar days in which to accept or refuse this request. Acceptance must be unanimous.

5.2. Parties shall be bound by rules set forth hereinabove, for Mandatory Mediation, except the mediator shall render a decision which shall be as binding upon the parties as those entered into of their own accord. The timetable given below shall apply.

6.0. *Binding arbitration*

6.1. After failure to mediate a dispute, or failure of mediation to resolve a dispute, an aggrieved party shall request binding arbitration immediately upon refusal of a party to enter mediation or upon completion of mediation without settlement of a dispute. The request for arbitration shall be in writing, specifying the nature of the dispute, addressed to the following arbitrator, with copies to all interested parties by a means intended to result in written confirmation of receipt. The primary arbitrator shall be [＿＿＿＿＿]. He or she shall be a person other than the mediator described above. Any failure to agree upon an arbitrator shall result in appointment of an arbitrator, or panel of arbitrators, by [＿＿＿＿＿] within 20 days of a request for arbitration.

6.2. In those instances when the resolution of a dispute may be expedited by a panel of three arbitrators and all of the parties to the dispute so agree, they may appoint such a panel. When the parties have agreed to a panel but cannot come to an agreement as to the individual arbitrators, the arbitrator shall revert to the originally appointed arbitrator; or failing that, by the process set forth in this clause. No one, particularly a surety, indemnitor, or insurer, shall be bound to any of these proceedings absent written proof of its receipt of specific notice to join these dispute resolution proceedings ten days prior to the inception of any mediation hereunder.

6.3. On application of any party, or in the arbitrator's own discretion, the arbitrator may involve any other party to this agreement, in privity of contract, by giving advance written notice of arbitration proceedings to such other party. No party shall be bound to any decision of the arbitrator without an opportunity to participate in the arbitration.

6.4. The parties shall offer such evidence to the arbitrator as they desire and shall produce such additional evidence or testimony as the arbitrator may deem necessary. The arbitrator shall be the judge of admissibility of the evidence offered. Conformity to legal rules of evidence shall not be necessary. The arbitrator shall endeavor to facilitate the presentation of evidence in a manner that is fair to all parties in order to arrive at an expeditious resolution. The arbitrator may require production of any evidence necessary to resolve a dispute.

6.5. All arbitration hereunder shall be conducted in the City of [_____].

6.6. An arbitrator may award interest, attorney's fees, accounting fees, consultant fees, and other appropriate relief to the aggrieved party when the opposition party's position appears frivolous.

6.7. All arbitrations shall be free of any bias, conflict of interest, or other prejudicial taint. Arbitrators shall not undertake any discussion of the dispute with one party without the presence of all interested parties or their agents, unless those parties fail or refuse to be present after due notification by the arbitrator(s).

6.8. The parties all share equally the arbitrator's fee plus any out-of-pocket expenses of the arbitrator.

6.9. The parties shall furnish all relevant information, documents, and arguments to the arbitrator within seven days of the request for arbitration. Unless agreed by all parties to a dispute, the arbitrator shall issue a binding decision within 100 days of the initiation of informal discussions.

7.0. *Time schedule*

    7.1. This clause seeks to hasten the solution of the dispute as soon as possible after a factual dispute arises. Therefore the following time schedule must control unless altered by mutual agreement.

Day 1	The aggrieved party notifies the party with whom the aggrieved party has the contract.
Days 1–7	Mandatory discussions must take place.
Day 1	Mediator is notified.
Day 8	If mandatory discussions fail, the mediation phase is initiated.
Day 30	If mediation fails to resolve all issues, the desire of disputants to have the mediator decide outstanding issues on their behalf shall be made known during Days 30 to 33, and if the mediator shall decide outstanding issues, the mediator shall formulate this decision and present the report sometime during days 34 to 50. Alternatively, if there is insufficient desire to have the mediator so decide, the binding arbitration phase may be entered during this period.
Days 50–80	Binding arbitration takes place if activated.
Days 80–100	Report of the arbitrator(s) is presented within this period.

    7.2. Please note that the schedule indicates the latest day a phase may start. The days shown are calendar days, except as stipulated in Section 1.1.

8.0. *Exclusions*

    8.1. This procedure shall not apply to disputes arising out of death or personal injury.

The following information about lighting for safety and security is taken from *Lighting for Safety and Security,* published by the National Lighting Bureau, with the assistance of the Property Management Association. These excerpts have been reprinted with the express permission of the National Lighting Bureau, and the author is grateful for the Bureau's aid.

Introduction

This guide has been prepared to give nontechnical readers important information about lighting and its ability to enhance human security and safety. Although some of the discussion relates to indoor lighting, most of it focuses on outdoor lighting, because outdoor lighting is the most effective and least expensive form of security. Unlike security personnel, closed-circuit television, sensors, detectors, and other security systems and devices, electric illumination is highly visible. Just a single light can in some cases be seen miles away. Up close, a few strategically located fixtures can be enough to discourage would-be vandals, thieves, or muggers. These.are the kinds of people who need darkness. Lighting denies it to them. Facade lighting can make it impossible to avoid detection near windows and doors. Parking-lot lighting can make auto break-ins unwise.

Effective security lighting is a deterrent. It creates a threat to those who would threaten others and their property. What is security lighting? Does it use special lamps or fixtures? special poles? No. It is lighting that uses conventional equipment and materials to achieve a given effect: security. But security is seldom the only effect. Outdoor lighting can also have an impact on safety, appearances, the extent to which a given facility or area can be readily identified, and other factors. These other effects occur whether or not they are intended. If they are not intended, the results will probably be negative. On the other hand, when all the various effects are considered in design, chances are they can be accomplished well to derive far more value from outdoor lighting.

The functions of outdoor lighting

Outdoor lighting provides *security* at night by denying burglars, vandals, muggers, and other perpetrators the shroud of darkness they need to pursue their goals. *Safety* is something else effective outdoor lighting can deliver, and not just in the sense that an area can be rid of muggers or that people can see others far enough ahead to take evasive actions when merited. Safety also means being able to see steps in a path leading from a parking lot to a building. It can mean walkway illumination such that puddles left by a rain storm can be avoided, along with fallen slippery leaves and branches. Safety can also be improved when drivers are better able to see pedestrians or other vehicles while backing a car out of a parking space. A lighting system can be designed to provide security and safety at the same time.

Identification is another function of effective outdoor lighting, because it can cause a building or other structure to stand out. Facade lighting can be used to do this by illuminating windows, doorways, and other potential entrances. This makes it far easier to see someone attempting an unlawful entry, thus establishing both a preventative and a means for catching someone in the act, or at least providing for effective identification. Facade lighting can result in tell-tale shadows being cast when someone who should not be on the grounds walks between the luminaries—lighting fixtures—and the facade of the illuminated building. Identification is also enhanced by lighting that creates different color effects, to differentiate one building from another, to indicate different pathways or walkways, or to help eliminate the confusion or disorientation that can occur after the sun goes down. All outdoor security lighting provides some identification at night. How much it provides and how well, depends on how effectively the function is considered in design.

Environment integration is an outdoor lighting effect that connotes lighting's ability to act as a unifying force, typically among separate buildings that do not appear to work together during the day. For example, many college campuses are showcases for the work of many architects active in different periods. In some cases the variety can create disharmony during the day. At night, when a common system of lighting is applied, all can be brought together into an instantly recognizable whole. The sense of security people derive from such lighting is no accident. In fact, security may be the primary purpose of lighting that also integrates an environment.

Beautification is a particularly pronounced effect of outdoor lighting. Effective designers can use electric illumination, much as artists use paint, to highlight selected portions of man-made and natural elements and thereby create appearances impossible to achieve during the day. It is for this reason that many who have been to our nation's capital report that it is far more elegant at night.

Attraction also is a function of effective outdoor lighting, often coming as a by-product of other effects. In the case of a motel, for example, lighting can help attract a potential patron by communicating that the facility is secure, and by making the establishment visible, identifiable, and pleasant to look at. For similar reasons, lighting can boost retail sales by attracting shoppers to safe, secure, and inviting shops and centers at night.

Recreation is yet another aspect of outdoor lighting, permitting the use of areas that would otherwise go unused at night. At an apartment complex, for example, lighting can permit people to use large grassy areas, be it for games such as volleyball, badminton, or croquet, or just for informal get-togethers. The same light that opens up the area also helps make that area and others more secure.

As valuable as the many effects of lighting are, many remain unattained because people forget that more than security and safety is involved. Don't make the same mistake. The same lighting necessary to provide security and safety can be used to provide identification, environment integration, beautification, attraction, and even recreation. The value derived from these additional benefits can be substantial, many times greater than whatever additional cost—if any—is invested to achieve them.

Bottom-Line Benefits

Economic analysis is as valid for evaluating security lighting alternatives as it is for evaluating any other investment. The key to making an effective analysis is considering all the major factors. Too often decisions are based on energy considerations alone. This can be a serious mistake, especially so since that which consumes the least amount of energy may be incapable of achieving the purpose for which it was installed.

Lighting is not installed to consume energy. It is installed to fulfill security, safety, identification, attraction, and other needs. Each of these has a value connected with it, at least to the extent that one can prevent a costly loss. The best lighting system is the one that creates the most value.

The following discussion of lighting's many bottom-line benefits is comprehensive. Identify those which apply to your situation. Select a lighting system that can help you fulfill all your objectives, not just those associated with light.

Fewer security-related problems

Effective security lighting can help prevent a number of security-related problems by displacing the activity that gives rise to these problems. After all, why should those who want to perform an idle act of vandalism do so in a well-illuminated area, where they may be detected and identified, as opposed to an area hidden in darkness? The direct problems that can be avoided include vandalism: spray painting of walls, breaking of windows, destruction of shrubs, knocking over containers of different types, and otherwise making an embarrassing mess. Repairs can be aggravating, time-consuming, and costly. Many owners would rather not report the minor damage to an insurer for fear of higher premiums or policy cancellation. The ugliness must be cleaned quickly in those circumstances, where it could otherwise affect business or create a negative image, possibly one which says, "this area is dangerous."

As those with experience will relate, vandalism may be the least serious problem. Others include break-ins and assaults. Assaults may lead to legal action in some cases, a problem discussed below. Break-ins can lead to significant losses when the material taken is irreplaceable or uninsured, or when it consists of data stored in a computer. The value of such losses can be huge. A number of security problems and services can be used to prevent them. These include security patrols, sensors of all types, and closed-circuit TV (CCTV), among others. Of them all, however, only lighting can be seen from a distance to create a significant deterrent effect. This is not to say that you should rely on lighting alone. But it does point out the danger of *underrelying* on lighting. Electric illumination is among the least costly of all security measures and is also the most effective.

Maintenance of image

Facilities that are well illuminated not only look good, they will often gain a deserved reputation for being safe and secure. High levels of illumination are for many people synonymous with safety and security. But think about the downside. Whenever security breaks down—when someone is assaulted in a parking lot or on a walkway between a parking lot and a building—there always is a potential for damaging publicity. While lighting cannot under any circumstances guarantee security for an area, more lighting almost always is better insofar as security is concerned. To the extent that effective lighting can make any unfortunate nighttime occurrence less likely, one has that much more assurance that a facility's image will not be tarnished.

Avoidance of legal problems

Sometimes an unfortunate incident goes virtually unnoticed by the news media until an injured party institutes a law suit whose size seems to be newsworthy. No matter that a $25 million claim may be settled for $1000. The claim can make headlines while the settlement goes unnoticed. The real legal problems are not those associated with the negative publicity, however; those are image problems. The legal problems are those associated with cost. Insurance almost never covers all the costs. A deductible usually must be satisfied and, until it is, one has to pay attorneys, expert witnesses, and private investigators. There is also the matter of time lost to review files, answer interrogatories, participate in depositions, and confer with attorneys. In fact, having to deal with a claim that stems from an assault or accident of some kind can easily create an unreimbursable cost of $25,000 or more, not including the financial impact of the negative publicity that might result. To the extent that effective security lighting can make such claims unlikely, it can save tremendous amounts of money. And to the extent that an owner can demonstrate concern through investing in effective security lighting, it makes claims that much easier to defend. The real problems can arise when it is argued that an owner was negligent for failure to provide more or better lighting, or to maintain the existing system well.

Reduced security costs

Many facilities employ a variety of security measures. On college campuses, for example, it is common to use lighting, CCTV, and security patrols. By increasing reliance on any one of these, it often is possible to reduce reliance on others. Effective measures that are comparatively low in cost are those that merit emphasis. In security, the most expensive tool is personnel and the least expensive is usually lighting. Documented cases show how reliance on more and better lighting can permit less reliance on security forces to create significant savings. Lighting can do this, without compromising safety, because of its deterrent aspects and because it permits security personnel to see faster and more accurately. In many cases lighting can attract more people to illuminated areas, something else which in and of itself can enhance security.

More use from existing areas

Particularly in the case of campus-type layouts, such as those of colleges, universities, and multifamily residential communities, lighting can be used to make areas usable at night. For example, security lighting concerns may suggest that lighting should be installed in a certain area to provide 0.5 footcandles of illumination. If more lighting is installed, however, that area could be used at night to enhance lighting's recreation-inducing effects. Any such advantage can be of great value, particularly in areas where there is strong competition. Besides, with effective lighting controls it is possible to provide the additional light only when it can be used, that is, it would be reduced after midnight and could be kept relatively low when weather is unpleasant.

Curbside appeal

The sight of people enjoying a facility's grounds at night usually can enhance the facility's curbside appeal. Curbside appeal also is improved by lighting that makes a building look better or that attains environment integration while at the same time creating a sense of safety and security. Increasing curbside appeal can create other benefits, too, such as more shopping for retail facilities or more rentals for apartment communities.

More retail sales

As more people work during the day, more shopping is being done at night, and because America's population is aging, more shoppers are older citizens. While security is a concern to all, it is of particular importance to older people because they are the ones who are least able to run or to defend themselves. Effective lighting creates a sense of security, which in itself is an important consideration to shoppers. It also provides safety, attraction, and identification. Precisely because of these benefits, as National Lighting Bureau case histories point out, better security lighting can attract more shoppers and thus contribute directly to more retail sales and profits.

Also consider those establishments which display their wares out of doors, as is the case with an automobile sales center. Effective security lighting can and should also serve as effective display lighting to add sparkle to the vehicles on the grounds. Particularly for those facilities located on somewhat busy roads, the security lighting system alone may be able to initiate sales to passers-by who are able to get a quick glimpse of the car of their dreams.

In some cases the beautification aspect of security lighting also can result in more sales. This can be the case when an apartment community is offering units. Beautiful outdoor lighting enhances the appearance and provides obvious safety, something that many people are looking for. The fact that this lighting also supports later hours for the leasing office helps mesh sales activities with many prospect's lifestyles. In essence, as more people begin to rely on the nighttime to take care of personal business, effective lighting can help determine where that personal business will be conducted.

Higher occupancy rates and less turnover

While better outdoor lighting will not necessarily increase occupancy rates or reduce turnover, it can be a significant factor in preventing problems in these key areas. Stated simply, effective lighting can help assure that people do not leave multifamily residential or commercial complexes because of lack of effective security lighting. To the extent that security lighting achieves other goals—beautification, environment integration, and so on—it can help maintain the highly positive attitudes needed to maintain high occupancy rates.

Beautification

As already noted, many if not most buildings and other structures can appear more handsome at night because lighting can be used to select what will and will not be seen and how the visible portions will be perceived. Beauty is not limited to buildings or other structures, of course. Lighting can be integrated with grounds to create special effects on flowers, shrubs, and trees. As beautiful as lighting can be, it can also enhance security. It can be used, too, for identification and attraction to increase sales or occupancy. In essence, something that is more beautiful is almost always more valuable. The cost of attaining beauty with light often is a tiny fraction of the value that light can create.

Enhanced building value

Shopping centers that do more business usually have higher occupancy rates, derive higher rents, and are more valuable and more easily sold. Apartment buildings that enjoy higher occupancy rates and experience less turnover also are more valuable and more salable. Office buildings that are well known as prestigious addresses often have higher occupancy rates and more value than otherwise. Effective outdoor lighting systems can be important factors that contribute to greater value. The value added through better lighting can easily be 10, 20, 100, or more times the cost of the new or improved lighting.

Insurance advantages

Most building owners are familiar with the myriad insurance problems that have gripped the United States since the mid-1980s. Insurance has been difficult to obtain at times, very costly, and, more often than not, less comprehensive in coverage.

Effective security lighting helps minimize risks associated with accidents and assaults, reducing the likelihood that insurance will have to be called upon to satisfy a claim. Furthermore, by pointing out to an agent or underwriter the effectiveness of lighting, and one's investment in it, it may be possible to obtain coverage when some others cannot, or to obtain coverage at more favorable rates. As most risk management professionals will say, however, risk avoidance would be a far more effective option than insurance were either—but not both—available.

Improved morale

Particularly in those instances where a building is located in something other than a "totally safe neighborhood," or when there have been problems in a parking lot or around a structure, the installation of security lighting—or enhancement of what already exists—can improve employee morale. In essence, effective security lighting can stand as an obvious statement of management's commitment to the safety and well-being of employees.

Note, too, that more than employee morale is involved. In cases cited in a federal study, installation of effective security lighting in inner city areas resulted in more police reports and apprehensions. It was said that one cause of this was better visibility; criminal activities could be seen better and perpetrators could be described more accurately. It was also noted that the installation of lighting was taken by some residents as a demonstration of "city hall's" concern, thus encouraging them to reciprocate by reporting what they had seen.

Increased production

As the United States economy becomes steadily more service-based, working late at the office has become part of many persons' normal routines. Continually more of these persons are women. As equal as they may be in a work setting, outdoors at night they can become victims of attackers who are larger and stronger. For many, inadequate lighting in a parking lot, indoors or outside, can mean a somewhat fearful conclusion to a long day's work. For some it can encourage leaving the office earlier than otherwise or it might mean less productivity as the day wears on, due to mounting apprehension. Just as installation of new security lighting or enhancement of an existing system can improve morale, so can it reduce anxiety and thus support later working hours and a relaxation of some of the stress that might otherwise prevail. As an example of the impact involved, consider a situation where the improvement consists of installing eight 400-watt high-pressure sodium (HPS) fixtures that are operated an average of 42 hours each week. If the installation encouraged just one $20,000-per-year employee to put in an average of 15 extra minutes each day, the annual value derived from that extra work would exceed the annual cost of energy consumed to operate the lighting, assuming an average cost of $0.08 per kilowatt-hour.

More profitability

When profit-making organizations invest in effective security lighting, they do so to cut actual or prospective losses. Thus, while the lighting may be an expense, it can help reduce the lost profits, which can result when safety is somehow breached. When a comprehensive analysis is performed, however, so that all of lighting's effects are considered and steps are taken to derive more benefit from each, a different scenario emerges. Of course, there is nothing wrong with lighting that helps assure profitability by preventing losses. Consider, however, that the same lighting system can do so much more by maintaining or enhancing image, improving curbside appeal, increasing building value, and so on. It should be noted, too, that these other benefits are very real and can be obtained with relative ease, provided they are sought.

In the case of public or other not-for-profit entities, profit is not the appropriate word, at least not in the business sense. However, in the sense that profit means benefit, the same basic concepts apply. In essence, one can realize tremendous benefit from security lighting. But even more significant benefit can be derived when the lighting installed for security is also used to achieve the many other bottom-line benefits lighting can provide.

Designing an Effective Lighting System

Achieving quality

Achieving quality in a security lighting system depends on far more than a skillful lighting design. When security and safety are involved, other concerns also must be addressed. The interrelationships between these concerns must be reviewed carefully to help ensure that overall objectives are realized. This concept applies to new construction as well as existing structures. In either case, the investment in new lighting, as well as overall safety and security efforts, will last a long while; often a decade, two decades, or more.

Identify those who should be involved

In order to identify the functions lighting should perform, it is essential to identify those whose guidance should be sought. The needs will vary depending on the nature of the facility in question. In most instances, however, needs can be divided between internal and external personnel.

Internal personnel include those who have or are responsible for safety and security issues, or who may be affected by them. In larger organizations, this may mean department heads. Overlook no one, because safety and security concerns affect virtually all staff and all persons who go into or out of a building, especially when it is near or after normal closing hours.

In the case of an office building, for example, those involved with human resources management should be contacted because safety and security affect morale. They may also affect one's willingness to put in overtime hours either before or after the close of the regular business day. Depending on circumstances, a building's leasing agent should be queried, because safety and security issues affect leasability of space and its cost.

If the building involved offers food service, the person who directs food service activities might be contacted. Is lighting needed to illuminate dumpsters which may otherwise attract unwelcome visitors, including those of the four-legged variety?

The director of building and grounds should be queried about suggestions of needs. A review of records could reveal that some areas are more prone to problems than others, be it in the form of vehicular accidents, slips and trips, or vandalism, for example.

The more people who are contacted, the better, if only because they will be given the opportunity to influence an extremely important element of their environment.

The outside personnel who may be relied upon include those who will provide guidance over the long term. These might include design professionals such as an illuminating engineer, landscape architect, or electrical engineer. It may also be appropriate to rely on a security specialist or those who specialize in certain areas of security, such as closed-circuit television (CCTV), remote sensors, actuators and controls, and integrated systems for either local (on-site) or remote monitoring. Bear in mind that fire safety needs usually must be addressed as well, and that at times fire safety requirements and security recommendations may be at odds. For example, it might be best to keep a given door locked for security purposes and unlocked or operable for fire safety purposes. Given today's array of equipment and the available control and monitoring strategies, it is possible to achieve reasonable solutions that satisfy different needs. The critical issue: you must know what these needs are. This leads to another area of concern, that is, the need to identify and understand all applicable codes and standards. Some of these may affect the degree to which security and fire safety systems may be integrated, they might limit the height of lighting poles, or they may prescribe certain minima. Do not assume that a specific need has been satisfied simply because a code requirement has been met. Codes and standards define what is least acceptable. The minimum may not be enough to meet your needs.

In all cases the overall team should include the property or facilities manager. These people tend to be highly effective generalists with respect to real property. As such, they can identify a variety of issues which others may overlook, and frequently can identify valuable sources of assistance. Recognize, too, that guidance and other assistance may be available from lighting manufacturers, insurers and their agents, your local electrical utility, the local police and fire departments, as well as associations that cater to the needs and interests of the profession, product, or service involved, or the building type—multifamily residential, commercial, retail, and so on.

Establish locations

Where in and around a facility do safety and security needs arise? Many of these already have been discussed: parking areas, accessways between a parking area and the building, at points of normal (doors) and abnormal (windows) ingress/egress, and indoors: hallways, stairways, and so on.

The next step usually is to determine what the overall protection philosophy will be. Guidance in this area of concern is available from a number of sources, including some of the *Electrical Design Library* publications produced by the National Electric Contractors Association. Is there to be perimeter protection? If so, in what form? Will the facility rely on a fence? If so, what kind? how tall? Will it work instead of or in addition to CCTV? If so, what kind of lighting will be needed? Would it be appropriate to use "invisible" light, that is, infrared? In some cases this may be preferable to normal lighting. In other instances the decision may come down to cost factors. Recognize, however, that the use of infrared may require reliance on a different type of camera, one that is more expensive. Maintenance issues also may arise.

The type of access controls used is also an important issue. A wide variety is available, including those that respond to different sounds as opposed to motion or physical disturbance.

To the extent that any given option necessitates reliance on some other option, all the interrelationships should be made known to help assure effective decision-making. A multidisciplinary approach is particularly important in this respect because of the variety of options. As an example, in designing stairways with safety issues in mind, it is

appropriate to use a tread and riser whose colors contrast, to help create greater visibility and thus reduce the potential for a slipping or
tripping hazard. In such cases, 3 footcandles or so of light might be
sufficient. However, if security is also a concern, it would be wise to
provide 30 footcandles of light because security needs are so different
from safety needs.

With lighting, as with other tools, merely having it is not enough.
The right type of light needs to be used, along with the right amount
in the proper location.

Attend to other issues

A number of issues need to be considered once locations are known.
One of these relates to separate wiring. Due in particular to the needs
of fire safety, it usually is wise to have all exit lighting on separate
circuits so that it will remain on despite a power failure. This type of
wiring is often required by code, and the code may also dictate the use
of an emergency standby power system which would operate these
lights.

Another concern might be systematic interrelationships. For example, the occupancy sensors used to detect the presence of intruders after hours might also be wired to cause all lighting in an affected area
to turn on when activated, in addition to sounding a local or remote
alarm. Alternatively, the occupancy sensors used in some areas to activate and deactivate lighting during the day could be used for security purposes at night.

The list of potential issues is huge, given all the different types of
facilities there are. By relying on a multidisciplinary team, most of
those germane to your facility can be identified.

Identify what else lighting could do

Once a general approach to safety and security lighting has been identified, along with whatever options may exist, it would be wise to so-
licit and consider comments about other objectives the lighting can
achieve. This is particularly the case outdoors, of course, and many issues often are involved. The premium required to achieve those other
objectives—beautification, environment integration, attraction, and
so on—is often relatively small. At this time, however, budget is not
an issue. Encourage people, from internal personnel to the consultants
being used, to develop a wish list.

Evaluate the options

How worthwhile will it be to make the additional investment that better lighting may require? If any type of prior analysis has been con-

ducted, such as that to establish function, the answer should be immediately evident: minimize assumptions by obtaining competent guidance. In most instances, however, you will discover that just a little lighting can go a long way, principally because the value of lighting's service is so disproportional to the small premium paid to install, operate, and maintain the better lighting needed to obtain these values.

For example, if better-quality lighting will lead to circumstances which together result in an office building's value being increased by one-tenth of one percent, the value generated may be $25,000. But one-tenth of one percent often is unrealistically low, as when lighting contributes to factors such as enhanced curbside appeal, longer tenancies, less turnover, and more profitability.

Bear in mind, too, that just as more lighting can often lead to more safety, so can more lighting in some cases pay for itself by substituting for some other option. For example, maintaining higher lighting levels may permit reliance on fewer or lower-cost CCTV cameras, or fewer security guards because central-station monitoring becomes more effective. Also recognize lighting's deterrent benefits, since it is the most conspicuous form of security.

Understand procurement

In evaluating the cost-effectiveness of lighting, consider the various lighting procurement options. While direct purchase is the most common option, it is not the only one. Outdoor lighting, in particular, may be leasable, thus reducing capital outlay requirements. Lease arrangements may be available from electrical contractors, the local electrical utility, or other sources, including companies that will lease almost anything.

Third-party providers may also be able to help, especially in those cases where a new system is replacing an old one. In these instances some providers obtain payment by sharing the dollar value of energy savings. As a consequence, the facility owner can obtain the new lighting without any investment. In cases where leasing the entire system is not practical, leasing at least part of it may by worthwhile, because it frees up capital that then can be used to enhance the system.

Recognize, too, that some local utilities may have programs available because they want to encourage more use of nighttime lighting. This permits them to sell more electricity at night, thus making more efficient use of generating equipment that would otherwise be idle. (Daytime power requirements in most areas of the nation are far more substantial than nighttime.)

What's available in your area? All the options should be identified and discussed.

Select the most cost-effective alternatives

The most cost-effective alternative seldom is the one that consumes the least amount of energy. Rather, it is the one that produces the most benefits. As such, to establish cost-effectiveness, it is important to identify the types of benefits that different types of lighting can provide, the extent to which a given approach can deliver a benefit, and the values involved. In the case of a shopping center, for example, lighting can provide so many benefits there is no point in skimping anywhere. This does not mean that lighting should be wasted. But it does mean that it should be used unsparingly, accompanied by energy-efficient design.

Which approach is best? Very often this will be determined by the numbers. One of the most widely used approaches calls for the calculation of *simple payback*. This is determined as:

$$\text{Simple payback (years)} = \frac{\text{initial cost}}{\text{annual savings}}$$

This approach would be used to compare a more expensive system to a less expensive one, or to consider the financial wisdom of adding a given option to a system.

As an example, assume System A costs $25,000 to install and will cost $5000 per year to operate and maintain. System B costs $28,000 to install and will cost $5500 per year to operate and maintain, *but* should increase retail sales enough to generate an additional $1500 per year in profits. As such, System B's installed cost (premium) is ($28,000 − $25,000 =) $3000. Accordingly, the payback for investing the additional money in System B would be:

$$\frac{\$3000}{\$1000/\text{yr}} = 3.0 \text{ years}$$

Similarly, if a given control system added to the system costs of $2500, but will shave the utility bill by $900 per year, the simple payback would be ($2500 ÷ $900/yr =) 2.8 years.

Another method of evaluating the payback period relies on its reciprocal, *simple return on investment* (SROI):

$$\text{SROI (\%/year)} = \frac{\text{annual savings}}{\text{initial cost}}$$

or

$$\text{SROI (\%/year)} = \frac{1}{\text{simple payback (years)}}$$

Accordingly, a system that costs $3000 more than another system, and which will generate an annual benefit of $1000, will have an SROI of ($1000/yr ÷ $3000 =) 33.3%/year.

Another method sometimes used to compare alternative investments involves *present value analysis*. This approach holds that 1 dollar received 1 year from now is not as valuable as 1 dollar received today, because today's dollar can be invested without risk to generate a given rate of return. If it is assumed that this rate of return is 10 percent, 1 dollar received today would be worth ($1 × 1.1 =) $1.10 in 1 year, or $0.10 more than 1 dollar received 1 year from now; 1 dollar received today would be worth ($1 × 1.1 × 1.1 =) $0.21 more than 1 dollar received 2 years from now.

To determine today's value (the present value) of 1 dollar received 1 year in the future, the above approach is reversed, to derive ($1 ÷ 1.1 =) $0.909; 1 dollar received 2 years from now would have a present value of ($1 ÷ 1.1 ÷ 1.1 =) $0.826.

Present value analysis can be particularly beneficial when somewhat complex factors must be evaluated. For example, assume you must decide between Option A and Option B, where Option A costs $4000 to install, saves $1500 annually, but will have to be replaced in 5 years. By contrast Option B costs $5000 to install, saves $1000 annually, but will last 10 years. Which is the better investment?

If one were to apply simple payback, which does not consider the time value of money, the total 10-year investment for Option A would be ($4000 × 2 =) $8000, creating a simple payback of ($8000 ÷ $1500/ yr =) 5.33 years. Option B would appear to be superior, with a simple payback of ($5000 ÷ $1000/yr =) 5.0 years.

When present value analysis is applied, a different picture emerges. The present value of Option A's $1500 annual energy savings over the next 10 years is $9217. The present value of the $4000 that will have to be invested 5 years hence is $2484. As a result, the net present value of Option A over the next 10 years is ($9217 − $2484 =) $6733. As such, Option A presents a savings-to-investment ratio (SIR) of ($6733 ÷ $4000 =) 1.68.

The present value of Option B's $1000 annual energy savings over the next 10 years is $6145, resulting in an SIR of ($6145 ÷ $5000 =) 1.23. Thus, although investing in either option would be better than simply "banking" the investment money at 10 percent, Option A is by far the better of the two.

Engineering economics texts provide far more detailed explanations of present value analysis, as well as tables and charts of factors to apply assuming different basic rates of return. Assistance in making these and other calculations is available from many of the sources cited in the next section.

Obtain guidance

Particularly when it comes to design guidance, it seldom is wise to select an individual or firm based on low bids. Bidding generally encourages someone to do something the least expensive way possible. As a consequence, the need to make a profit can become more important than the need to satisfy a client. When everyone is bidding to fulfill the same plan, such that each bidder's results would be about the same and could readily be evaluated by a common yardstick, bidding makes sense. But when design is involved, the client is relying on professional judgment. No two providers would produce identical results. Given the importance of design input, and given its long-term value, it is generally advised that clients select on the basis of competence, such as the designer's experience with similar projects or the satisfaction of other clients.

A growing number of people are recommending that contractors also be selected on a negotiated basis, because this process can affect the quality of their work. It permits them to become involved earlier, so they can provide guidance or comments during design. They also may be more aware of certain issues than others, such as the availability of certain products in the local area, similar systems that have been used, and whom to contact for details. In addition, whenever contractors or other businesses are retained on a negotiated basis, those involved recognize—or certainly should recognize—that their retention for the next project will depend on how well they perform this time, not how low they bid next time.

Once again, the watchword is quality. It is not achieved by accident, nor is it achieved by encouraging cheapened performance or materials. It costs more, and it just about always provides more.

Sources of Assistance

Lighting is important. System design makes the difference between achieving and not achieving goals. Some sources of assistance are indicated in this section. When it comes to obtaining design input, select individuals and organizations with care. A great deal is at stake. Be sure to determine the names of others whom a given source has served and contact those clients to assess their satisfaction. Consider visiting their facilities to see their systems in action.

National Lighting Bureau

The NLB has worked for many years to inform lighting system decision-makers about the benefits of effective lighting and the various options available to derive these benefits at minimal expense. The Bureau has many publications available, including *Getting the Most from Your Lighting Dollar,* a widely distributed primer on electric illumination, as well as guides relating to curing VDT viewing problems, conducting a lighting system audit, and lighting management as it applies to retail facilities, industrial operations, and modernization projects. An illustrated directory of Bureau publications is available free of charge. (National Lighting Bureau, 2101 L Street, N.W., Suite 300, Washington, D.C. 20037.)

Illuminating Engineering Society of North America

IESNA is an international membership organization with chapters (sections) throughout the United States. Many of its members are independent illuminating engineers. Other are affiliated with utilities, manufacturers, and other organizations. IESNA publishes the *IESNA Lighting Handbook,* a two-volume set that most lighting professionals consider the "bible" of the industry. IESNA also publishes some less technical materials which can be of substantial help. (Illuminating Engineering Society of North America, 345 East 47th Street, New York, N.Y. 10017.)

National Electrical Contractors Association

NECA is the national association of electrical contractors, with chapters throughout the United States. In addition to installing lighting systems, many electrical contractors have complete design departments. Some also are active in the area of equipment leasing and contract maintenance. To locate a NECA-member contractor, contact the NECA chapter closest to you or write the national office for a chapter directory. (National Electrical Contractors Association, 7315 Wisconsin Avenue, Bethesda, Md. 20814.)

National Association of Electrical Distributors

NAED is a national association of electrical distributors, those who stock and sell lighting system components, among other electrical apparatus. NAED sponsors comprehensive lighting seminars and is otherwise active in increasing its members' knowledge of lighting. Many electrical distributors can provide effective guidance on options available and their costs. (National Association of Electrical Distributors, 28 Cross Street, Norwalk, Conn. 06851.)

International Association of Lighting Management Companies

NALMCO is an international association of lighting maintenance contractors. In addition to providing contract lighting maintenance (such as scheduled lamp replacement and luminaire cleaning), many NALMCO members also perform reballasting and luminaire modernization, among other services. NALMCO conducts seminars and other training for its members and offers two certification programs, for Certified Lighting Management Contractors and for Certified Lighting Management Consultants. (International Association of Lighting Management Companies, 379 Princeton-Highstown Road, Cranberry, N.J. 08521.)

Manufacturers

Manufacturers can provide catalogs and other materials which provide information on their products. They also have a number of guides available, which provide some general information on lighting, specific types of components, and so on. In addition, manufacturers' sales representatives and application engineers can provide valuable assistance in the design and specification process. Most use sophisticated computer programs for these purposes. Some have computer programs which also provide data about life-cycle costs.

Others

Other sources of assistance include local electric utilities. Many have energy conservation or energy management departments, some staffed by specialists in lighting. The degree of assistance they can provide varies from utility to utility. Note also that some utilities offer incentive programs which can result in substantial cost savings. Speak with your local electrical utility representative to determine what help is available.

A state energy office may also be of value. Some have incentive programs they can make available. Most have publications that can be of assistance.

Especially in major metropolitan areas there will likely be chapters of national groups which can be of help, at least by providing referrals to their members. Many of these are listed in the local telephone company's *Yellow Pages* under the heading associated with membership, such as "engineers, consulting," "engineers, illuminating," or "contractors, electrical." Many also will be listed under "associations."

C

PMA Case Histories of Drugs in Housing

The following case histories were developed by the Property Management Association, based on presentations made at several of its seminars.

Case History 1

The problem

Extensive, long-term drug trafficking in an Adams Morgan apartment building.

Background

The 16-unit apartment was purchased in mid-1978. By the time the property went to settlement in mid-1979, it had become the home of a major drug dealing operation. One week after closing, the *Washington Post* named the property one of the largest retail drug outlets in Northwest D.C.

The property

When the new management team first visited the property, it was in a shambles. The door to one first-floor unit had been beaten with sledgehammers during a drug raid. The dealers took advantage of the damage by drilling out a 1½-inch hole through which money could be exchanged for drugs. Inside, drop slots had been built to hide the drugs in the event of a raid. The dealers also installed a buzzer connecting the main apartment to a secondary one, and had established an escape route out a window and through an interior courtyard. Business was brisk. Customers arrived at all hours of the day. Cars had easy access to the property by using the U-shaped alley that surrounded it.

When the new management team took over, it discovered that occupants of the worst first-floor apartments were not on the lease. The management then set out to remove the dealers from the property and transform it into a safe and peaceful community.

Confrontation

During the first week of operation, management changed all the locks and, on the door to the particularly troublesome first-floor unit, hung a sign reading "Business is Closed." Management seized the dealer's belongings from the apartment while protected by police, who waited for the dealer in three squad cars in the street. When the dealer approached the building, the police confronted him. "Are these your things?," they asked. "Do you want to identify yourself?" The dealer took his possessions and left without identifying himself. He did not return to the property.

Street sales

Although the dealers who had conducted business on the first floor were no longer in residence, their business was so significant they chose not to leave the neighborhood. Instead, they set up shop at the two entrances to the alley, creating the first "open-air drug market" in the Adams Morgan section of the city. It didn't take long for "turf" issues to surface, and then for violence to occur. According to the property manager, "I saw the first body fall. It was one o'clock in the afternoon, opposite an elementary school. I was on my way to lunch. Suddenly, gunfire. The wail of sirens. The kids had their heads out the window, and they kept them there until the hearse ultimately took the body to the morgue. That was just the first. In the 8 months that followed, into early 1983, five more people died. Violent, senseless deaths."

At the point where "only" four people had been killed, residents of the building began to panic. A small preschool had been set up in the basement of that building. Parents felt their children were in genuine danger. "We're being held hostage," they told management. "You have to help somehow."

Public demonstrations

Knowing something needed to be done, management began to discuss strategy with the police and various other groups. They decided to rely on public demonstrations. Residents joined with people from community organizations and churches to march in protest around the community. The goal was to gain public support and show the dealers that the people were determined to fight for the safety of their homes. The marches continued for 4 months, sometimes daily, sometimes weekly, sometimes hourly. The lobby of the building was turned into an office from which to organize the demonstrations. A remote telephone was installed and someone was there on an 18-hour-per-day basis reporting any suspicious activity to the police.

Since the property was no longer a secure place to buy drugs, business began to slow down. Ultimately, the street dealers left the neighborhood. Ironically, business of the dealers legally in residence thrived because their competition had been eliminated.

Litigation

Since management now knew who within the building was dealing, it instituted litigation to have the dealers evicted. The process was long and expensive. One of the managers was sued for libel for publicly naming one of the dealers. Yet, despite the expense and the tragedies that occurred, management continued with litigation. As a result, the property was quiet for several years.

The second wave

By 1987, crack cocaine had infiltrated the neighborhood. Several residents became addicted and then began to sell crack to support their habit. Management alerted Social Services in hopes that, with help available, residents would opt out of the drug life-style. If they chose not to, management began the eviction process.

Lessons learned

When a drug trafficking problem is first reported, one must turn to the present management staff for answers and information. The reasons for the depreciation of the property need to be uncovered to decide on appropriate action, such as training, staff changes, or evictions.

Management also found that if the principal dealers are forced off the property, entire operations will dissolve. It takes a certain amount of leadership to run a drug business. When the leaders are no longer there, the business will ultimately fail.

Creating a cooperative atmosphere in which people feel safe to express themselves is a key element in the turnaround of a property. When residents can communicate with staff, the staff is better able to target ways in which to alleviate the problems.

Management also pointed out that although an eviction is difficult to carry out, it can be a catalyst for a resident to start seeking help.

Case History 2

The problem

A suburban apartment community rapidly depreciating in value because of drug traffic.

Background

The 38-year-old 669-unit apartment community consists of 72 buildings connected by outside archways. The property manager believed that the site management personnel were doing their job effectively. This notion was dispelled in November 1987, when the property manager visited the property. The friendly waves the manager thought he was receiving from residents were actually drug dealer hand signals. The number of fingers they raised—one, two, or three—indicated how many rocks of crack cocaine they had to sell.

At the time only 12 units were empty. As the drug traffic increased, the vacancy rate followed suit; within 2 months, 100 units were empty. Residents would come into the office and say, "There is drug dealing above me and drug dealing below me. I'm moving out today." And they would. Then, compounding the problem, the dealers would move in, taking the vacant unit as their own. Ultimately, over one million dollars of income was lost.

Steps taken

When increased vacancies became a major problem, an inexpensive radio was installed in each vacant unit. By keeping the radio on, the management hoped to give the impression the unit was occupied and thus deter unauthorized entrance. When this did not work, alternatives were considered.

Sealing empty units. One of the first effective steps was to seal the doors of vacant units to prevent them from being forced open, and to seal the windows of ground floor units. Since taking such action is against fire code requirements, assistance was sought from the local fire marshal. Within a short time, the fire marshal gave management permission to weld shut the steel casement windows of ground floor units and install double-sided dead-bolt door locks on all doors. As such, even if the dealers were somehow able to break in, they could not open the door. The double-sided lock was not taken off until the day the new resident was to move in.

Police involvement. In conjunction with the police department, a program was created to pinpoint who was dealing and the units they were using. "No Trespassing" signs were posted, making it illegal for unauthorized people to come onto the property. Several off-duty police officers were hired to patrol in uniform. When unauthorized people (mostly buyers) entered the boundaries of the property, the officers gave each a letter. The letter stated, in essence, "Please take notice that you are prohibited from remaining upon, entering upon, or crossing over the land or premises. Violation of this notice may subject you to arrest and prosecution for trespassing." The police officer would record a person's name and address and then send that person a copy of the same letter, mailing it certified receipt requested. Once the receipt was returned, an individual who was stopped for the second time could be legally arrested. No arrests took place, indicating that the procedure discouraged buyers. It also gave the property manager a running record of who had been there. Through this process managers learned that the property had become a drug purchasing headquarters, even though only a few residents were involved in the drug business.

Locking the doors. The front doors to each building were locked and kept locked. This was not a fail-safe measure for keeping people out because they broke the locks. However, when a given lock was repeatedly broken, management received immediate "notice" of dealers' locations. The police were then told which entrances to watch most closely.

Registering cars. All cars belonging to residents were registered. If an unregistered car was found on the lot, it was towed.

Blocking the archways. The buildings are interconnected by approximately 15 outdoor archways. At night, dealers would run through the archways in order to move drugs from building to building. Six-foot barricades were installed, but people crawled through the 18-inch space at the top. Management responded by having scroll work added to the top of each barricade to eliminate the extra space. The barricades were then welded closed.

Fencing change. Making themselves comfortable, dealers used to sit on the split-rail fencing to await customers. The fencing was replaced by two-by-twelve flatboard fencing—known as pig-pen fencing—which looked fine, but was not suitable as a perch.

Solving multiple-entrance problems. After permission was obtained, Jersey walls were erected to close off two of the property's three entrances. It was difficult to apprehend people in cars, however, because vehicles could circle within the property. Accordingly, management installed wooden barricades to create dead-end streets across the back of the property. When these were destroyed by cars driving through them, concrete, cylindrical barricades were installed. Thereafter, cars were forced to leave the property by the same gate they entered.

Results

The police department and local politicians requested meetings with the residents to discuss the status of their community. At first nobody came, but as management evidenced its commitment, resident involvement grew. Today, families reside in what has become a quiet property with a low vacancy rate. To keep it that way, police officers have remained on the property and they continue to report any activity that may indicate that dealers are returning.

Lessons learned

When drug traffic first became a problem, the tenants didn't seem to care. But they were not apathetic; they were frightened and afraid to get involved. When management became aggressive, the residents followed suit. Management must be willing to put in time, energy, and money in order to get results.

If site personnel do not alert a property manager to developments at the property, they are not doing their job effectively, so retraining or reassignments are needed. If site personnel are not responsive, no amount of work or money will be able to turn the property around. Trained, responsible, trustworthy, and committed staff are essential on site.

Case History 3

The problem

Drug dealing tenants were using their subsidized housing community as a place to conduct business. The dealers actually comprised a large percentage of the occupants.

Background

The property manager thought the site management personnel were reliable and effective. A visit to the complex proved otherwise. The property manager realized an intimidated staff had not reported a drug problem at the project. The complex was inundated with dealers; as the manager drove into the parking lot, more than 45 men approached the manager's car trying to sell bags of crack. When the manager refused, the men kept lowering their prices. Unfortunately, the drug was plentiful.

Steps taken

Revamping the staff. The resident manager never told the property manager that dealers had penetrated the complex and continued to "work" there. Thus, the first step was to fire the resident manager. He was replaced with someone who was dedicated to resolving the problem. Other staff members were replaced with people who were willing to work hard and would not be intimidated by the situation.

Strictly enforcing the lease. Strict-enforcement-of-the-lease notices were issued to all tenants. The notices stated that those who did not comply with the rules would be taken to court. Drug dealers are very hostile to the controlled environment of a courthouse. Many felt threatened by the warning and evacuated, leaving bad debts and damaged units behind. Most importantly, however, they were gone.

Erecting a fence. Situated on a private-street cul-de-sac, there was only one entrance to the property. A fence was built at the entrance and protected by a guard and a guard dog. The uniformed man, complete with a dog at his side, deterred loiterers and unexpected guests from approaching the site.

Identifying the guilty. The guard's purpose was to require all guests to "sign in." This rule was replaced with one that better served management's needs: tenants had to sign in their own guests. This mandatory step doubled as an ideal tracking mechanism, since the dealers were those tenants with all the visitors.

Police involvement. Once the dealers were identified, a list of names was presented to the police. Undercover investigation led to arrests, and arrests led to evictions.

Registering cars. Residents were issued stickers for their cars. Cars without stickers were towed. The drug business works on a consignment basis. The distribution network suffered when cars containing "goods" were towed.

Results

Notices enforcing the leases were very effective, even if they had to be sent out two or three times. Drug-dealing tenants realized that if they continued dealing, they would lose their houses. The problem was eradicated, and today the complex remains drug-free.

Lessons learned

Drug trafficking had escalated to a ridiculous level by the time the property manager was even aware of the problem. Site management was a catalyst to the problem—an intimidated staff allowed the activity to occur. An aggressive staff is a must in keeping properties drug-free.

Police are a perfect alliance, although this step can take months to achieve. It's important to work up the chain of command and to continue to request police assistance. Persistence pays.

Time and money must be committed in order to resolve drug trafficking problems. Properties are economic investments and should be treated as such. If time and money are spent, chances increase that control of the site will be regained.

Index